Along The Way

A Life Journey Rooted in Faith and Love

Bernadette A. Moyer

Cover Art from original painting by

Bernard M. O'Connell Sr.

ALONG THE WAY

Copyright 2015 by Bernadette A. Moyer

All rights reserved.

This book may not be duplicated in any way without the express consent of the author, except in the form of brief excerpts or quotations for the purpose of review. Making copies of this book, or any portion of it, for any purpose other than your own, is a violation of the United States copyright laws.

ISBN Library of Congress Catalog Card Number

978-0-9666183-2-7

1st printing 2015

Along The Way

How many people will we meet along the way? How many experiences will be having along the way?

We hear the old phrase, **"one door closes and another door opens."** Many times we must close out one endeavor so that we are afforded the opportunity of engaging in another. Simply put we must give up something to be in a position to accept something new.

I watched a woman fight back tears today and I heard her say, "I am doing my best to accept this." Her Pastor was reassigned to another parish and will be leaving. I immediately could feel for her. Just four years earlier it was me who was fighting back the tears. That same Priest was leaving his assignment with me to move on to the parish that this woman attends. She has grown fond of him.

Today I watched him in action; he was different from how I remembered him. He was more mature, more embracing and much more open. He wouldn't have changed if not for moving about and going in a new direction. He closed one door and opened another; soon he will close his current door as he takes on a whole new challenge.

The same can be said for me, these past four years I have opened doors and I have closed doors. I have experienced much "along the way."

One of my favorite quotes is, *"You will always miss 100 percent of the shots that you do not take."* Wayne Gretzky

Every life has a beginning and middle and an ending and in the final analysis our life will be about all that we encountered along the way. Letting go used to be so hard for me, like the classic Italian Momma I wanted to hang on and hang on tightly with much love and passion. And yet today there is very little that I am interested in hanging on to.

We hang on at the expense of NOT letting go and therefore we are closed off when what we truly need to do is be open and receptive to what is next. Life is a living and a moving thing; it is about the journey and not the destination.

People choose the path in their lives and often fall into either a victor or a victim. We claim our role by the choices we make along the way. Each choice has its own consequences and each choice opens up something often at the closing of something else.

And my new favorite quote about change is **"May the bridges I burn light the way!"** Dylan McKay

"20 years from now you will be disappointed by the things you didn't do than by the one's you did. So throw off the bowlines. Sail away from the safe harbor. Catch the trade winds in your sails. Explore. Dream. Discover." Mark Twain

Here is to heading out and getting about and all that we experience "along the way."

A Fish Will Never Be a Really Great Rabbit

Don't even try and be a fish if you were born to be a rabbit! How often do we become frustrated when we try things that just don't fit our skill set? Or when we are tasked with a job that someone else deems is right for us? The best way to lose someone is to ask them to be something or someone that they just aren't.

In a world full of judgments and people that want to define others, or control them or twist them into what serves them it can be difficult to live an authentic life. I love young people because they are fresh and open and trying. I've learned that the best way to work with them is to let them go. As a mentor you can guide and support but the truly good ones already know their own strengths, gifts and talents.

We are all born with natural talents and abilities. Our God-given talents. We are meant to share them and to soar with them.

When we are true to ourselves life is easy. Our talent is what sets us aside from everyone else; it is our natural aptitude and skill. We have that touch that knack and flair when it comes naturally to us.

Romans 12:3-14 "For I say, through the grace given to me, to everyone who is among you, not to think of himself more highly than he ought to think, but to think soberly, as God has dealt to each one a measure of faith. For as we have members in one body, but all the members do not have the same function, so we, being many, are one body in Christ, and individually members of one another.

Having then gifts differing according to the grace that is given to us, let us use them: if prophecy, let us prophesy in proportion to our faith; or ministry, let us use it in our ministering; he who teaches in teaching, he who exhorts, in exhortation; he who gives, with liberality; he who leads, with diligence; he who shows mercy, with cheerfulness."

The only way to be truly happy is to be true to ourselves. We weren't meant to be like others, we were designed to be individuals. A fish can never live a happy and a whole life if he is trying to live as a rabbit. And a rabbit was never meant to live life like a fish. Don't even try it!

Be true to yourself that is what God made you to do and when our inner voice matches our outer life we are completely aligned for success and our own unique magic. You know who you are better and more fully than anyone else and any outside influence. Trust in you!

A Cross to Bear

Did you ever have someone in your life that all you ever wanted was the best for them? And yet in spite of it, and no matter what you did to help them, they just continue down a destructive path? It could be a friend, a family member, a colleague and you did everything humanly possible to help them and yet the outcome was always the same.

Their determination to hurt others, to fail and never come close to their God given potential outweighed anything that anyone else could do to help them. They just wouldn't do what was necessary to turn their life around. At some point, all you can do is pray for them, let them go and save yourself.

One of the largest growing groups in our society today, is family estrangement. There are numerous adult children that literally walk out the door on their families, and they never again return to their family of origin. For the parents that loved and supported their kids, it can be devastating and yet so many of the kids think little or nothing of it.

Earlier I read a heart wrenching post from a mother who stated at one point she had thoughts of suicide, she couldn't imagine moving forward in her life without her children. I could feel her pain. I know what it feels like to invest so heavily in another human being.

So many parents take it in and on themselves, they blame themselves. It took years for me, to step back and take a clinical look at my own family relationships and the generations and generations of estrangement. One could deduct it was learned family behaviors.

When I was younger, I knew a guy who was estranged from his mother, his father died before we ever met. In that relationship, I stood by him, it had to be his mother. It wasn't until after he died and time away allowed me to look at him. He was an alcoholic and always playing the victim. His behaviors seem to have lived on in his children. The alcohol abuse and the estrangement, have carried forward into the next generation, so is it in the gene pool, genetics? His children were mere infants when he left their life and yet so much of his behaviors are now present in his adult children.

A colleague was talking about his adult daughter that he put through college and graduate school. He was heavily invested in his daughter and paying her way to help ensure her future success. Imagine the sense of betrayal when he learns a year after the fact that his daughter has married? Not only didn't he know of the marriage but he wasn't invited to be there. How does he just get over this and continue in a loving relationship with his daughter, when he feels such betrayal?

We all have people in our lives that we love so easily, others that we tolerate and some that almost make it impossible to embrace them. Ann's daughter left home as a teenager, shortly after abandoning her family she has a baby. The baby is several months old before her family learns of his birth. More than a decade later, it's not Ann's daughter but the baby's father who reaches out to Ann to apologize for keeping her from her grandchild. He is sorry and now that he is a father for the second time, he fully appreciates the magnitude of his teen behaviors. Ann's daughter, decades later is still locked in her teenaged anger.

Jim has a wife and three daughters, he is friended by many in his religious community where he is an active working member in his church. Jim also has a history of being unfaithful to his wife and abuses alcohol. He was well supported for decades by his family, his friends and his church community. One day Jim went too far, the hurt that he bestowed upon his wife and friends made it impossible for them to keep Jim in their life. As a group, they decided it was finally time to let Jim go and to save themselves. It wasn't an easy decision but for them, it was a necessary one.

Everyone has some kind of cross to bear in life, it could be a disability, or an inner brokenness or relationships that don't go the way that we had hoped and planned. We all experience some kind of hurt and loss in life. Every cross that we bear, allows us to grow and to go deeper. Each experience adds to our life, when someone lets us down, we have the choice to learn forgiveness or to live in anger, we have the choice to focus on what we lost or we can concentrate on all that we have.

Letting go only feels like losing if we stop moving forward. Loving acts attract love, just as hate attracts more hatred. We choose if someone else's behavior defines us or not. We get to choose what we will do with every lesson learned. Will be become bitter and blame others, or will we pick ourselves up and move forward with the desire to fill our lives up with goodness and gratitude.

One of my favorite Lou Holtz quotes is, *"The secret to a long and happy marriage is a short memory."* Any time that we are in a long term relationship with our spouses, our family our children there is going to be times when we are disappointed and feel let down. It is our choice if we focus on that disappointment or make the choice to remember all that is good.

In my life, I have forgiven everyone, everything, and I didn't do it for them, and I did it for myself. Whatever they did to me, real or perceived, I didn't want to carry that cross and so I let it go. I don't want to be defined by those hurts and in some cases by those people. Lou Holtz, *"You'll never get ahead of anyone as long as you try to get even with him."* Letting go is what you do for yourself.

My favorite religious sent me a prayer card inside of an early Christmas card, it arrived just yesterday, **A Prayer for Mothers** and it reads; "*O God our Creator, pour forth Your blessings on those with whom You have shared the gift of creation. Hear our powerful pleas for the women who loved us into being.*

Intercede for all mothers this day, so that they may learn to draw their children to You. Teach them how to remain close to their children, even their sons and daughters who have gone astray. Bless our mothers with good health, long life and reward the eternal life in Your Divine Presence. Amen."

We all have a cross to bear, what we decide to do with that cross is what makes all the difference in the quality of our life and in the happiness and peace in our lives. Today I am thinking about so many that are hurting from my support group, from my friends and my family. With Christmas in my head and in my heart all I can say is try and take the lessons learned and leave the rest behind. There is so much love and goodness all around us, but first you have to let go and then you have to be willing to see it!

A Child is Born

A child is born and a mother learns that her heart has no boundaries. The love for that child is boundless and infinite beyond measure. For a mother a child begins in anticipation long before they arrive into this world. She carries that baby and cares for herself and the unborn child as she waits in much anticipation.

Most mothers only learn their hearts true capacity after they birth their first child. It is the purest love. A love that gives without expectation and a love that nurtures in thought and in deed long before a child is born.

Although I have mothered and raised three children, I have only given birth to one child. She was wanted long before her arrival. I always wanted a baby and yes I wanted a girl. She was much more beautiful than I could ever have imagined. Above all she was healthy at over eight pounds. Her hazel eyes came from her father but her determination and fierce spirit was all me.

She was an easy baby that seldom cried and smiled most of the time. She was more than any vision that I could have ever imagined her to be. She was a true blessing and a gift from God above. As long as I live I will never forget that first Christmas as we dressed her in a Santa Suit and sat her under the Christmas tree. She was the gift of Christmas 1980!

And less than three years later, I would have vivid recall of that Christmas too. Her dad died earlier that year. We went to my grandmother's house and joined my mother and my siblings there. I brought all her gifts as we drove through some rough winter weather. I was a waitress back then and had just finished working a long Christmas Eve family party. My pockets were full of cash but my heart was so sad. My sadness wasn't for me but for a child that wouldn't have a father.

When I met up with my mother and placed all her gifts under the tree I remember asking my mom, "Do I have enough gifts for her?" But what I really meant was how I could possibly give her anything that would take the place of never knowing her father or ever having any relationship with him.

I went into overdrive and worked like crazy. If I couldn't give her a dad at least I could work hard to give her a good life. A good education was paramount. Everyone that knew us knew that she was my whole world. I idealized her. To me, she was perfect, I only saw what I wanted to see and what I wanted to see was all good, all the time.

A child is born and we learn about love and about giving. We learn to open our hearts in ways that we could never conceive of and that the child is connected to not just our hearts but our souls. Each child comes to us as God delivers them. No one can conceive that this infant will tread on our hearts like we never anticipated and that when they are doing well our heart sings and when they are not doing well our grief is immeasurable.

No one knows what lies ahead in life; I am convinced that if most of us knew beforehand we wouldn't budge. Just as a heart is filled with love and anticipation that same heart can be destroyed by broken dreams and broken promises. Not everything works out the way that we imagine. Some things work out better and others perhaps not so much.

I have a card that I carry with me from my own mother. She wrote it after she graduated from Notre Dame College. I made all the food for her graduation party. The note reads, "You are a daughter to be proud of" and regardless of what transpired after that, I know that I am and that I was, "a daughter to be proud of."

Real love is when you want the best for someone whether they are in your life or not. It isn't about you; it is about them, that child that was born unto us remains just that.

"And I pray that you will have the power to understand the greatness of Christ's love ---how wide and how long and how high and how deep that love is ... Then you can be filled with the fullness of God." Ephesians 3:18 the fact that a child has been conceived means that God himself has spoken. Each child is a gift a gift from the Lord above.

A Child is Born

Lyrics by Barbara Streisand

A child is born

We've suddenly stepped through

A thousand dolls

A child is born

Her chin is like mine

But her eyes are yours

How perfectly formed are her fingers

We'll hold her close

Then let her go

How sweet to find

A part of ourselves

We knew nothing of

A child is born

A child that is born of our love

A Daughter's Love

Every Mother knows it isn't the gifts given but rather the words spoken and the written words that warm a mother's heart.

A College Entrance Essay in a Daughter's Own Words

"In being my mother, father, teacher, and best friend, my mother has made the greatest impact upon my life. At the age of twenty-three my mother was widowed and left to rear me on her own. Having all the worries of rearing a child my mother now had to act as both mother and father. My mother made a commitment that I would never be lacking or held back by the fact that I had only one living parent. It is normal for a mother to be protective of her child, especially her first born; my mother felt that she had to compensate for the death of my father. Her feeling was that early in life I had "one strike against me" and that she was going to push me hard to succeed. First working in a restaurant at night while I was sleeping to spend her days with

me and later changing professions to be a Realtor for the flexible hours, she did everything possible so that I not feel inferior. From taking me to the library and instilling a deep love of reading, to baking blueberry muffins for breakfast her actions always proved to me that I was as loved and accepted as the other children with both parents. I had the loving acceptance of a mother and disciplinarian of a father figure. While at times I broke out against the restraints, I always knew that my mother still loved me, and I have come to realize that the rules really were in my best interest.

The driving force behind all of my accomplishments has always been my mother, and when I have failed she has always been there to help me back up on my feet. At times I have balked at the high expectations she has for me, as any teenager would, but in the last few years I have come to realize that she wants me to be successful in life, and she is preparing me for what someone in the real world who will not be as caring. I will always remember how my mother tutored me in elementary school math when my grades were low; flashcards, writing, re-writing and saying the multiplication tables repeatedly swept me from the bottom of my class, to being the first person to raise her hand with the correct answer. No matter how difficult the task my mother is always there to teach me to persevere in spite of the obstacle.

Having one person in life who you know you can continuously count on is a great feeling. My mother has always been my chief confidante. I know that in times of trouble she is there to help and in times of happiness she is the first person with whom I want to share my news with. My mother has always been concerned with whether or not I was comfortable walking through the mall holding hands with her or being seen by my friends giving her a hug, not once have I ever had to be embarrassed by the fact that I love my mother. After going on a date or getting a new job my mother is the first person with whom I wish to speak, and is always the first person to give congratulations.

The loss of my father did not destroy any hopes my mother had for me but heightened them, and she gave me a sense of family even though largely it has been my mother and me. The multitude of roles she played in my life has the most significance out of any relationships I have had, and because of her influence, I am what I am today."

Note: The above essay was used with 5-separate college applications and this "daughter" was accepted into all of them, one of them, offered her a fully funded four year college scholarship.

Another Daughter's Handwritten Journal Entry

"My mom is amazing! She is like superwoman. My mother does sooooo much for me and my twin brother. My mother is a strong woman; she is always helpful and puts others before herself. My mom spoils me. She is always upbeat and active for her age. Out of my five best friends my mother is one of them."

A Joyful Heart

There is nothing more beautiful than a joy-filled heart. It is our choice to choose joy, love and peace. They are by far the most attractive accessories.

We worry about what we look like, are we attractive? Do we have the right handbag or the perfect shoes; is that our color lip gloss? But ... we look our best and we feel our best when we are wearing a joyful heart.

What we should concern ourselves with is how our heart look and feel does, are we creating love and joy. Our hearts are meant to be filled with love and joy. Choose a joyful heart and choose true beauty every single time.

"Joy is what happens to us when we allow ourselves to recognize how good things really are." Marianne Williamson

Ours is a joyful heart ...

A Lazy Sunday

Today is that kind of a day; a lazy Sunday. There are pork chops and sauerkraut in the slow cooker, the fireplace is burning wood and Happy and Chipper have been close by my side for much of the day. We didn't have any obligations today and it feels wonderful! Normally our days are full of activities and our "to do" list and a variety of work related projects. For me it is mostly writing projects and wedding officiant projects and home decorating and improvement projects.

My husband is on a wellness kick and working out regularly at the gym, he walks the dogs and tends to many home improvement projects too. Some days we accomplish so much but today we made an effort to enjoy that classic "lazy Sunday." We make no apologies for our lack of doing today. Most days we are on the run moving from here to there, always something to do and somewhere to go.

It feels great ...

My favorite line that I heard from a retired professional is "So what have you been up too?" The response was "As little as possible." Love that!

"Sunday clears away the rust of the whole week." Joseph Addison

How often do we fill our days and our schedules with meetings and activities and "things we must do and accomplish" and how wonderful to have a day and a time where the less you do the better you feel. Resting, reading, writing, hanging out with the dogs, talking with my husband, making and eating food ... it all sounds so heavenly and it is all right here and right now on this lazy Sunday!

Enjoying my Sunday and I hope you are too …

A Call to Ministry

The Lord works in mysterious ways! When I was "called" to minister, it was because I wanted to unite loving couples in marriage. I love being married and have been with my husband for more than two decades now.

After a seven year stretch working for my Archdiocese of Baltimore, I learned many things and met many wonderful people doing really great works. I also met some of the most ungodly and unchristian I ever knew or could have ever imagined existed. It started to make sense to me why so many left the Catholic Church and organized religion. Over and over I heard comments like "all they want is money" or "I just don't feel welcome there or connected there, we aren't embraced."

For me personally I have never believed that there is just one road to Heaven or that God has blessed just one faith as the supreme faith. Quite frankly any religious group that believes they are "supreme" "the only way" "the chosen ones" makes me really nervous and helps me to understand why there are religious wars. Wars that kill people in the name of "God" just doesn't seem right to me.

When a dear friend said, "the people sitting in the pews will never witness what you did, or there wouldn't be anyone sitting in those pews." I knew that I was done. I had seen and I had witnessed far too much. Other friends have tried to keep me connected by saying, "they are just people, and they are not God."

I don't want to knock anyone that has faith or doesn't have faith. I believe it is a personal relationship with God that matters most. It isn't my place to judge how people practice their faith or even those that declare they have no faith in God.

A few years ago, I would never have believed that I would decide to become and Interfaith Minister. I just wouldn't have felt good enough, but after seeing so many others with far less heart and soul and with the call to serve, I knew that ministry was right for me. I am older, more mature, been through much. It was God that stayed with me when many others let me down.

For years I have unofficially assisted with bereavement coaching. First it was for widows and widowers because I had been widowed and understood first-hand the grief process. Later it would be losing a daughter to estrangement. Now I help many other mothers with their experiences of loss through estrangement. Having a real life point of reference gives me insight and knowledge. Helping others allows me to take what I know and what I learned and share it.

The greatest part of my ministry has been in officiating weddings. To celebrate a couple coming together and wanting to become married it the best job ever. I hate even calling it a "job" it is a calling and a vocation. I know what marriage is and what a gift it can be when we are married to the right person, being able to marry couples in love is an all-out honor.

I have a passion for living a God-centered life and a prayer full life. I believe that people that are turned off by traditional church are because of the behaviors of other people and not God. We are not here to judge or to criticize we are here to learn and to love.

My ministry will always be about promoting love and acceptance, accepting all people, even those that don't fall into a particular mold or definition. To me, God created all of us not just the self-appointed "chosen" ones.

Two years ago I read the Bible from cover to cover. I had much theology in my life and many classes throughout the years but this time it was in my time. My Bible is beautiful too. It isn't black, white or any traditional colors. It is green and pink leather with a green background and pink flowers. It is like me, full of life and of color and not so traditional on the outside but very God centered inside.

The people that know me best say, "You are so accepting" and yes I am. I know what it feels like to be at the top of your game and I know what it feels like to be in the depths of despair. Life is rich that way. Most people are doing the best they can with what they have and what they know at any given time in their life. The people that I have a hard time with are the ones who openly set out to hurt and to destroy others, as much as I know that is a reflection of themselves and their own self-loathing I hope and pray that they use that same energy to heal and to better themselves.

It takes but moments to destroy what it takes years to build. I pray more and more each day and I pray for all the people. Let us make the choice to build rather than to destroy. It is always a choice.

A Parent Dies

Whether it is a family member, a friend or a member of your community who dies, you can help.

A policeman dies in the line of duty leaving behind five young children and his wife. A mother of three is murdered. A father dies suddenly of a heart attack, too young. A plane crash, an automobile accident, a suicide, or an illness can all result in the loss of a parent. Unexpected loss of a parent that comes far too soon can be very difficult to understand and to accept. Death is the one given we have in life and yet we refuse to talk about it. We think we are respecting the family's privacy by not bringing it up. Yet in one way we are only further alienating those who are already suffering. It is not uncommon for surviving spouses and their children to feel different, alone and isolated. These feelings may be natural and at a time when they may be at their greatest need for human comfort.

How often our heart strings are tugged when we hear of the death of a young parent? A parent who dies and leaves behind a spouse and children. We want to help, yet we do not know exactly what to do and say. So nothing is said or done, for fear of saying the wrong thing. We witness their grief while feeling helpless.

When a spouse and a parent die it has long and lasting effects on the family. The foundation the family is built upon is under major reconstruction. Expected or not the death and loss can be overwhelming. Initially most people will have their extended family support and that of close family friends. But before long everyone will return to their normal schedules while the family is left to grieve.

If you want to help in a personal way, here are a few tips:

What Do They Need

Understand that your family member, neighbor or friend may need many things. They may need time alone. They may need time to cry and talk about their loss. Listen well and allow them to speak. They may need to tell the same stories over and over again. I remember telling stories about my husband and his death many times. I knew that I was getting better and had purged much of the pain when one day I was tired of listening to my own stories.

Help With the Kids

It might be helpful to a surviving spouse if you extend invitations to his/her children to join your family for dinner or to see a movie. A parent who loses a spouse and has children may very well be operating with less energy.

Make Food

Consider leaving a casserole at the door step with a simple note that reads, "From Our Hearts" and your name. Sometimes picking up a few groceries or a cake or pie and taking it over to their house can mean so much to a surviving mom or dad that has no interest in cooking or eating at this time and yet has other mouths to feed.

What to Say

It is better to say things like, "I am very sorry" or "I cannot imagine your grief" rather than say "I know how you feel." We all react to grief and loss differently and we really do not know how another feels in a time of grief.

Be Patient

Do not tell a grieving adult or child to "get over it" or "you should be over it by now." Each person grieves in their own way. Many times because of parental responsibilities and a job, the surviving parent goes into "overdrive." They rise to the occasion, seemingly handling everything like a pro, only to have a delayed reaction six months or a year or two later. In my experience and with all the grief work I have done with surviving spouses many do not "bottom out" until about eighteen months to two years later. This is when many really feel the loss and have a greater awareness of the void in their life and have fully accepted the death. This is also when most people think that they are "over it."

Write Notes

Personal notes and cards can mean so much and are non-threatening. Writing about a happy or positive memory about the deceased person does so much to show and say "I valued him/her as well." It also says "They touched my life." The personal letters I received and the sharing of stories of my husband warmed my heart and made me appreciate that he mattered to others too.

Don't Forget Them

Many times during the weeks and months after the loss our efforts are more appreciated and needed the most. Largely because there is usually an abundance of support in the first few days and weeks, but it often withers as people move on and forget. In the early days and weeks the family is shocked or has yet to feel the full impact of their loss. Showing care and concern later can be so helpful and make a big difference.

Therapy Comes in Many Forms

Encourage counseling, inspirational books and movies and support groups. Others have suffered similar losses, they made it through and so will the survivors. Relating to others who have been there makes us feel less alone and better understood. Faith and religion help. Use phrases like "This group I have heard about is for widows and helped my friend Pat, how you feel about support groups?" Gift an inspirational book or a journal. Writing about their feelings can be helpful. Children may benefit from support groups and journals or sketch books too and help them with their thoughts and feelings.

The Holidays Arrive

Holidays can be the most difficult times as are anniversary dates. These are times when we may think about our loved ones the most. Acknowledge this. It is also a time when we reminisce about past holidays. Many times family and friends may decide not to mention the deceased as they fear it will be upsetting. Better to acknowledge the loss and communicate; "If you want to talk we are here for you" or in a quiet moment, "How are you doing today?" Never force the conversation, but do open the door to it. When we say nothing it is as if we are saying "Let's pretend everything is fine." We are afraid to say the wrong things and by saying nothing it may be interpreted that the deceased person is forgotten.

Children and Grief

Many times children, especially teenagers will try and shrug off their feelings of grief. They might even feel the need to put their own feelings aside in an attempt to help their surviving parent. They may feel the need to be strong and bury their own grief.

My Experience and Take Away

My daughter was just two when her father died. She was a smiling, happy child and as she grew an excellent student. It wasn't until high school when one of her close friends died, that she understood death. That death opened up her buried grief and the loss of her own father. It happens that when small children lose a parent to have their grief show itself and affect them much later in life.

Plants, flowers, books, pins, inspirational items all say "I am here and I care." One of the things that comforted me in my grief were books on death and dying, books that I could read and reach out for comfort in the dark hours of the night when I felt so very alone and needed comfort the most. My faith in God and my belief in Angels in many ways gave me comfort and saved me.

The single best thing we can do is listen and allow our grieving friend or family member the opportunity to talk and to cry. Often a well-timed hug can make a world of difference.

I am here today, to tell you that it is not easy and we will experience a wide range of emotions after we lose a loved one to death. I was blessed with the desire to connect with others who had already gone through this and their strength and support made it easier for me. Crying is so cleansing and when the tears stop and they will it is just like the rain, and so often the sun will shine again and even brighter!

Bernadette A. Moyer was widowed at age 23 and at age 32 met and later married a widower when his wife died leaving him to raise pre-mature infant twins. She raised three children, each of whom lost a natural parent. Her oldest daughter will be 35 this year and her adopted twins just turned 23.

She is the author of numerous inspirational articles and her book **Angel Stacey/Daddy in Heaven** is available at amazon.com. Her website is www.bernadetteamoyer.com and you can find her on Facebook at www.facebook.com/bernadetteamoyer or can write to her at bmoyer37@aol.com

A Rose Garden in Memory of My Mother

"Non che la rosa sensa la spina" translation *"there is no rose without thorns"*

When my father died in December of 2009 honoring his memory was an easy decision since he requested donations to the public library where he was a regular patron. I loved books, I am a writer, and it was what he wanted and so off went that $1,000 donation. My husband and I were happy to do it.

Two years later when my grandmother passed at the young old age of 101 her request was easily honored as well. I was working for the Archdiocese of Baltimore and she was a Catholic in good standing during her entire life. Her request was the local Catholic school in Lansford Pennsylvania. Again my husband and I were both happy that we were in a position to make that donation.

But what do you do for your own mother who decided 23 years before her passing to delete you from her life? It is coming up on that 1st year anniversary and I couldn't see myself writing a check for a donation to one of the places mentioned in her obituary. An obituary that didn't include me as her second born daughter.

I had to think long and hard about what was appropriate and felt right for me. Perhaps it was yet another example of my rebellious nature as even in her death I wasn't going to give in to her "wishes." The same "wishes" that would keep us apart for 23 years and the same "wishes" that would publicly deny that I was her daughter.

Several months after her passing I went to the cemetery where she was buried, by chance it was a cold and rainy day. As soon as I stepped out of the car, I could feel the tears streaming down my cheeks. The words came without any thought or prompting, I said, ***"I am here, you win, I came to see you."*** Even as I write this I am overcome with grief and the tears begin again.

I am a mother and I have had my share of "stuff" with my daughters and yet I can't imagine estrangement ever being my choice or denial ever coming from my side of the relationship. That just isn't me or how my heart works. Yet it was the choice my mother made and one that I have lived with.

Finally it came to me I will plant a rose garden and dedicate it to the memory of my mother. When I pass by or am working in it I will pray for her soul. Roses are beautiful and come in all colors and varieties. They are also thorny just like my relationship with my mother.

For my mother Inez, who left us on April 7, 2011 a real life living rose garden and the song Rose Garden, in your memory …

~ Rose Garden ~ lyrics by Joe South, recorded by Lynn Anderson

I beg your pardon, I never promised you a rose garden. Along with the sunshine, there's got to be a little rain sometimes. When you take, you got to give, so live and let live, or let go. I beg your pardon, I never promised you a rose garden.

I could sing you a tune or promise you the moon, but if that's what it takes to hold you. I'd just as soon let you go, but there's one thing I want you to know. You better look before you leap, still waters run deep. And there won't always be someone there to pull you out, and you know what I am talking about. So smile for a while and let's be jolly: Love shouldn't be so melancholy. Come along and share the good times while we can.

I beg your pardon, I never promised you a rose garden. Along with the sunshine, there's got to be a little rain sometimes.

But … there will be a Rose Garden for us, a real live living rose garden and it will be filled with life and with color and will be fragrant and beautiful just the way I would have wanted our relationship to be …

A Time for Reinvesting In Ourselves

It is becoming clear to me that our 50's will be a time of reinvesting in ourselves. For years we were living in the "sandwich" years between supporting ailing parents and raising our children. With two high demand careers, very little in the past ten years was about investing in ourselves. We spent our time and our energy on parents and on our children and we were happy to do it.

Between my husband and myself there is just one remaining parent and he is being well taken care of in an assisted living center. For so many years my husband was running him to the doctors, to the pharmacy and the food store. He literally was his father's lifeline to the outside world until severe dementia made it impossible for us to continue to support him. He needed 24-hour care. It was a hard decision but a necessary one.

Our three kids have all been raised and no longer need us to support them. It took some getting used to when you have supported children physically, emotionally and financially for decades. But like everything in life there is a beginning, middle and an ending. There is a light at the end of the tunnel.

We are still young and investment worthy as both my husband and I are gearing up for what is ahead for us. At this moment in time we have both turned to education and wellness as to where we are putting our energy and support. Brian is in City College securing a Maryland State license that will allow him to further his career. I am taking an updated business class.

For our health many of the procedures we have put off are being addressed. I am committed to securing a new smile! Lots of hours at the dentist office, no doubt!

At this time we are eating healthier and more organic fresh foods. We see the value in laughing more and pacing ourselves as we get through our work weeks and our off time. There is a new balance in our lives of both production and fun. We no longer have to put ailing parents and our children ahead of our own needs. No one told us that this would be the "all about us years." My husband loves having me all to himself.

Years ago I read that men never really "get their nicest or come into their own until their 50's" for us this seems to ring true. Going out with my husband is like going on a really great date. This past Wednesday he treated us to an Orioles baseball game. He secured really great seats on the first base line looking directly into the dugout. We sat just a few feet from all the professional ballplayers. He held my hand as we walked through the city streets. And he walked to bring me bottled water and was really tuned into whatever I needed or wanted to enjoy the experience.

There is something so sweet and so nice about being appreciated by a man you have loved and lived with for 20 years. He expresses his gratitude for all the many sacrifices I made, and those that I wanted to make in helping him to raise his twin children. We survived and even thrived in spite of many challenges throughout all these years together.

What we have right now is yet another opportunity to reinvest in ourselves and in our marriage. It is a great feeling to be afforded this opportunity and at this time in our lives. This is a period of time that we never talked about or one that I never even thought about but now that we are here, I am thrilled. I hope that all our friends and family members also get this same special time in their life. All I can say is isn't being in our 50's great? We are worth it. We have worked hard and now it really is all about us.

These are the reinvestment years and what greater cause for making an investment than in our own health and happiness!

A Very Happy Mother's Day

This past Mother's Day was a very happy day for me. It took weeks before I finally put my Mother's Day card away that my son gave to me. It was so touching because he talked about being an adult and his adult view of my mothering. Our tradition each year is that he takes me out to lunch or brunch and we see a movie. He takes off of work to celebrate with me. It means a lot to him. And it means so much to me too.

But this year I was blown away by the gifts of effort from both my son and from my husband. My son created a personal video that he shot for me by taking many photos off my Facebook page and adding music and his own text. It literally made me cry. And the one word that he used to describe me just made me so happy, the word was "wise" and who wouldn't want to be known for their wisdom? He said he was up late the night before creating it and for me it was a complete and unexpected surprise but so truly wonderful.

I am a huge fan of gifts of effort. My husband surprised me by adding two new rose bushes to the garden. He not only purchased them but spent well over an hour weeding the area where they were to be planted and then put them in the ground surrounded by new mulch. Every day when I pass that side of our home I am reminded of his labor of love. I appreciate it so much and love the outcome.

Last year I remember a special exchange when two of the interns that I engaged showed up unexpectedly in my office with a beautiful bouquet of flowers and a very large Mother's Day card too. I never saw it coming but was completely delighted. They both have mothers of their own that they hold in high regard and yet they thought of me too. A year later I still remember their thoughtfulness.

Mother's Day this year was a very happy day for me and almost a month later I am still basking in the love and the appreciation that I received and for the most part it was because the gifts were rooted in genuine efforts and heartfelt actions.

A Wedding Anniversary

I have always admired couples who get married and stay married. The couples who survive and stay together and can boast about 30, 40 or 50 or more years together as a married couple.

I have vivid recall of our wedding day and our entire honeymoon. We brought together two half families to create one whole family. I had an eleven year old daughter and Brian had newborn infant twins, a son and a daughter when we first got together. On our wedding day my daughter was 16 and the twins were just 5 years old.

We were so hopeful and so thankful to have found one another. We believed that God had blessed us and brought us together. There was so much that Brian and I had in common. We were both born in 1959 to large Catholic families and Italian mothers. There was a natural attraction for us.

I remember our first wedding celebration and I remember one a few years back in 2009 but there are many that I can't quite place in our history together. For me it was love at first sight. We became friends first and we took our time in getting to know each other. I remember our first kiss and our first time when we moved from friends to more than that.

Through the years it hasn't always been easy. We struggled as parents with our children. If we were guilty of anything we most probably overindulged them and never really held them accountable. Our hearts were always in the right place. We wanted them to have everything and deep down inside we knew they already didn't since all three kids had lost a natural parent to death.

For the marriage our big mistake was in not putting it first, our kids had immediate needs and so often the marriage got what was left over after our energy went toward work and then the children. Today and this year for the first time, we are empty nesters. You would think we would be swinging from the chandeliers with no kids in the house. Instead we are at another platform, unlike our wedding day when we had a game plan and we had purpose and together we were on a mission to raise our children.

Once again we have to find our footing and how to proceed now that the kids are gone. Everything has changed. Dinners aren't as big and as bountiful, the dishwasher and the laundry don't need to be run every single day. Grocery shopping is a different kind of challenge since we don't eat as much food or what kids eat. The house is quieter and several rooms are seldom used or even entered at all.

It's so easy to know what is next when you are raising children and climbing the career ladder. Once the kids are grown and you are at the top rung in your career things change. For the first time in my adult life I am living totally as an adult sans kids. It is all so new for me.

I haven't taken as good a care of myself as I should have in putting myself last, now that changes as I reinvest in myself for the next leg of this journey called life. My husband is a man that I will always love since he has played such a huge role in my life for almost half of my adult life. I may not always understand him or what make him tick, and I bet he would say the same about me.

Some people will never know what we have already experienced in these 20 years together as husband and wife. I have learned so much and I have learned so much about myself.

There is nothing like being with someone for this period of time to become fully aware of whom **you** really are. An intimate relationship can and will pull at you in ways that you could never have imagined. You will see each other in the best light and on the darkest days. Some days you will bring out the best in your partner and other days the absolute worst in them.

It is hard not to respect couples who weather the storms and the marriage ends in "until death do we part." Tomorrow we celebrate our wedding anniversary and we have no way of knowing what will unfold for us during this next year. What I do know is that I am smart enough to know, just like our beginning, our middle and our ending; it is all in God's hands ...

A Memory

What makes a memory? And what allows us to remember some things and to forget others?

On February 23, 1998 I planted a cactus at our second home in Lewes, Delaware. Why on earth would I remember that date? When I have planted many things throughout the years? That cactus is doing really well and has grown more than 6 feet during these past 15 years.

So why do I remember that date? Because I was planting that cactus when my then 17 year old daughter called to tell me that one of her closest classmates had committed suicide. This was the same date but 15 years earlier my daughter's father died.

I never held it against that cactus but recently have looked at it and wondered if by chance maybe I should get rid of it. After all every time I see it, I think of Abby and her untimely death.

Whenever I dial around the television and catch a glimpse of the reruns of **The Gilmore Girls** I fondly remember our daughter Briana and all the years we watched back to back episodes together. It was our time and the guys just left us alone. Most often we watched them in my bed and cuddled up together. They are fond memories for sure.

I have this same experience when I catch the TV series **Wings,** since my husband and I used to watch them every night after getting the twins ready for bed when they were just infants.

What makes a memory is it a good time or a bad time, a time to remember. One of the fun things for me is when old friends gather and start the conversation with, "remember when?" and the stories are abundant and just flow.

Over the Memorial weekend we celebrated at the beach with our same neighbors for more than a decade. When they moved in they were sans kids and now have two young sons running around on their bikes and scooters. Their kids are doing the same things our kids used to do. Our kids spent many summers at the beach and the community pool starting with the baby pool and all the way to becoming divers at the deep end. Now they are grown adults doing what young people do.

We have so many memories of so many fun-filled summers. I can't think of one bad memory as hard as I try. We often started summer vacation on the very last day of school with the SUV packed. Our tradition was listening to the classic song "Schools

Out" by Alice Cooper and singing it loudly as we drove to the ocean to start our summer vacation. We lived for our summers at the beach.

Every July 4th holiday and for many years we shopped at the Old Navy store for the All American Flag tee-shirt for all four of us. It was yet another small tradition and now serves as a fond memory.

You always remember weddings, funerals and baby births and Christenings. You also remember where you were when 9/11 happened and at my age when President Kennedy was shot and killed. Some things we never forget.

Our memories are the mental photo albums of significant events in our life often accompanied with a strong emotion. As we age our memories become like warm blankets that keep the chill off of us as we age. My husband and I share a long history filled with more than two decades of memories. We have history and isn't that what a memory is, our history.

Here is to making memories and keeping memories close to our hearts. Often a fond memory can take the sting out of an otherwise unpleasant experience. In our family we have so many wonderful memories and it is fun just pulling out the old memory bank and remembering them.

Happy Memories …

A Year of Discernment

What led up to my year of discernment?

In August of 2009, I got off a plane from Ft. Lauderdale, Florida with my husband Brian. We had just enjoyed our wedding anniversary celebration. We were revisiting where we had married on the beach in Ft. Lauderdale. That year 2012, we celebrated 20 years together.

Brian and I were feeling refreshed and so happy! It seemed that life was running smoothly for the last decade. That same day my newest book, *Halfway Home, The First 50 Years* was released and I already had several book signing and media events lined up. All book proceeds were being donated to my place of employment where I served as the Director of Development. The proceeds would benefit youth and young adults. In 1998, I lost a child and would spend the next 12 years of my career raising money for children's causes.

Our happy stretch was soon interrupted as I received a phone call informing me that my father wanted to gather all 8 of his children. He was dying. August 3rd 2009, I learned of his ill health and by December 9th of that year he was dead. It was a roller coaster with many mixed emotions.

In August of 2010, my supervisor, a Catholic Priest that I worked very closely with was reassigned and in the Priest shortage they were not replacing him. I was promoted to a position that I never asked for and became the Chief Operating Officer. I cried at his formal celebration party.

Then one of our twins abruptly decided to move out of our home where we all lived for more than 18 years. Six months after that and in April of 2011 both my mother and my grandmother died within a week of each other. There were numerous losses, all of them in a very short amount of time. I kept busy though. I wrote my autobiography as I continued to serve simultaneously as both Director of Development and Chief Operating Officer.

Inside though, the wheels were coming off. Losing both my parents caused me to take a good hard look at my life. Was I living the life that God intended for me to live? How many years did I have ahead of me? Was this it for me? I had inner turmoil and I knew that I was no longer feeling challenged but just going through the motions.

Our last child who was still at home had enlisted in the Navy and my 32 years of raising my children was about to come to an end. My autobiography was just about to be released when it caused a big stir as I wrote the truth about the many ways sexual abuse, alcoholism, deaths and estrangement had impacted my life. My book had a large amount of pre-sales and it seemed like it was going to do well.

July of 2011 my father-in-law was diagnosed with severe dementia and my husband was declared his guardian. He now lives in an assisted living center.

My promotion made me feel empty inside and in August of 2011 I abruptly resigned from my job where I had been successful for more than 6 years. My book that was days away from publication was killed in production as a result of threats of lawsuits from family members. They had not been in my life for decades but apparently stalk me and my work on the internet.

At work, I was "the last man standing" from the old guard. The Superintendent of Schools, The Director of Youth Ministry and my Priest Director were all gone. The one person who replaced them was someone I found to be extremely deceitful as he was originally hired as a "consultant" and got the back story as he was supposed to help elevate these departments. What he did was to get the drop on everyone and "lay off" the ones he didn't like or want to work with. I tried to like him but everyone I introduced him to made comments about his "arrogance" and his "ignorance." The writing was on the wall. It wasn't planned but it was the perfect storm as I left my career behind. I didn't know what was ahead but I did know that what I was doing was definitely in the past.

During the year I took off, I examined everything. I pulled inward and took a good hard look at myself and my life. What if anything did I want to change? At just over 50 years old I knew that I wasn't finished working. I had devoted 32 years of my life to raising children in my home. The question was what work could I see myself doing? What was next for me? Did I have another dream? I continued to write.

My husband became more than a rock for me. He was so loving, kind and protective. I had raised two of his children with him when their mother died. They were just newborn infants, a son and a daughter. He knew all the sacrifices I made in having the job that allowed me to be the flexible one since his job was much more rigid. As teenagers, I took the kids to work with me. They were trained to serve as lifeguards and kitchen aids. During their last years at home I spent the most time with them both at home and in a workplace setting. He knew I was grieving the loss of both my parents and of having come to the conclusion on raising children.

He gave me the freedom to explore many options. We looked at numerous business proposals and even made an offer to purchase a bed & breakfast. I received my certificate of ordination, so that I could marry couples and legally officiate wedding ceremonies. I finished my novel which is currently in the hands of a well-respected New York publishing house. I wrote and blogged almost daily. I cooked and cleared out our home. I re-connected with family members and high school classmates. I planted a bigger garden. Instead of going out to many lunches and breakfasts, I cooked and invited friends to visit me at home. I spent hours training our two young Bichons.

During my discernment year I looked at my friendships and took better care of the ones that mattered and let two long term friendships go. Neither one was healthy. I didn't shed a tear over either one of these relationships and I was surprised by this. It should have felt more like a loss and instead it felt good to let them go.

Friends that weren't as close seemed to gravitate to me and they came from very strong, sound and successful backgrounds. They are supportive, healthy and uplifting relationships that continue to help me to grow. God continues to bring the right people into my life at the right time. I trust Him now even more than I ever did before.

This past year I had very little anxiety as I knew I was in God's hands. My husband continues to be a dream and he smiles more these days than he ever did. Part of it comes from knowing we have raised our children and his success on the job. In his words, "It's our time now."

We updated our wills, made necessary changes in life insurance and auto insurance and we reassessed our entire lives together. The year is about to end and we have so much to be thankful for. In the end, we didn't make a residence move but instead reinvested in our existing property.

I made trips to Fort Meyers and Sarasota Florida, to Lancaster and Erie, Pennsylvania, Upstate New York and New York City, Virginia, Atlantic City, New Jersey and a few trips to Nashville,

Tennessee and Chicago, Illinois. I had the opportunity to spend a month over the winter and another month over the summer at the beach.

This week I was granted a job interview, I thought it went really well. I am interested and I hope they are too. I just started seriously looking and I am excited about the future. I know that the right thing will come at the right time. We leave for vacation in a few days. I will have my husband all to myself and we have plans to meet up with several friends while at the beach.

Many people supported me this year, some read my blogs, some came to see me and some call and communicate via social networking. I have received numerous cards, flowers, fruit baskets, gifts and hand written letters from priests, nuns, teachers, professors and my friends. As someone who has always been a big "giver" it was so nice to be on the receiving end of so many good people.

"It is through the struggle that we find enlightenment. " I struggled these past few years with many losses and today I feel brand new and ready to go again. I can't believe that what started out as so uncertain has once again brought me back to a safe and soft landing in God's grace.

Whatever is ahead, I already know that I will be successful at it. If past performance is an indicator of the future, I am certain of it. I don't know how much time I have left here on earth, there is nothing like your parents death to drive that fact home. But I know one thing for certain, life is for the living, live it!

My year of discernment came about so unexpectedly and yet today I couldn't be happier nor could I be more appreciative of all the many blessings that God had afforded me. Life is good!

Accepting and Respecting

Relationships end, people leave, people die and life goes on whether we like it or not. What relationship would we hang on so dearly for? Would we hang onto a boyfriend, a girlfriend, a parent or a child who has let us know they don't want us in their life?

When someone decides to leave our life and to walk away from us, they have that right and they can make that choice. We don't have to agree with them but we must learn to accept their decision and to respect their decision.

In my dating relationships, I was most often the person who didn't want it. It wasn't for me, it didn't mean that they were a bad person it just meant it didn't feel right to me. I never set out to hurt anyone by rejecting them. I can only think of one relationship where the guy left me and I got hurt. In the end, he was right; it wasn't the right relationship for either one of us. I know that we both learned so much from one another and I know that I am a better wife today because of that relationship.

I spent years being really angry with my mother; she couldn't and wouldn't see things my way. All that anger was a waste of time and of energy. There was nothing I could have said or could have done differently that would have changed our outcome. I learned to accept it.

The hardest relationship to lose was my daughter back in 1998. Having a child leave your life seems like the most unnatural act. Parents are supposed to die off first in the natural order of life. Estrangement is the death of a parent-child relationship. It is a painful loss and an unnatural one. For most parents it is really hard to accept and some have difficulty respecting it too.

During these last 15 years of my estrangement with my daughter, I have talked with many parents going through their own estrangement. In all those years and probably a hundred parents I only heard of a single reconciliation that stuck. After a severe car accident and near death experience of the daughter who chose the estrangement that lasted 7 years, it was her mother she called for support and care. Mother came and the relationship renewed itself.

More often I have heard about attempts that lasted for a dinner, a holiday or an event and it inevitable lead back to the estrangement. I think about it as "the first cut is the deepest." Someone who is capable of deleting you from their life, giving you days, weeks, months and years of the silent treatment can and will do It over and over again.

I initially had a hard time with my mother and with my sisters that followed her example, for years I thought, "I am her daughter, doesn't she love me at all?" I never had those kinds of thoughts with my sisters because even as little kids they weren't supportive or there for me. There really wasn't any love and therefore any love lost. My mother set the tone and the example as to how I should be treated and they easily followed it. After the grieving period and after the anger over my mother, I accepted it. At some point I just knew there was nothing there for me and I stopped pinning for that which was never going to be.

As a mother who absolutely loved and adored their daughter, this would be the loss that almost killed my heart and my soul. For many years she was my reason for living. She was my inspiration for securing a bigger and a better life. I wanted more for her than I ever even wanted for myself.

Losing that relationship was the hardest to recover from, my grief and pain was to where my skin hurt and I literally couldn't breathe. There was a period of time when I just wanted to die.

By the time she left I had already survived in a highly dysfunctional home, been widowed and left to raise a toddler, had another significant relationship end when he cheated on me and left me for another woman. Then sexual abuse would impact my family in a huge way where I felt I had no choice but to finally walk away from all of my family. They were never going to hear it, believe it and protect any children accordingly.

So when the light of my life left, I was like that's it, I am done. I have literally had enough.

It was during this time that I sought help, developed a deeper faith in God and learned to receive and appreciate the love and loyalty of my husband Brian. Without the grace of God and the love of Brian I would never have made it.

The process and the years that were filled with tears, heart break, disappointment, anger and finally acceptance finally brought me to a place of peace. I no longer hope and dream for that which will never be and it took almost 15 years to get to this place of acceptance and of respecting her decision.

You can't make anyone love you nor can you make anyone want to be included in your life. Most parents can't accept it or respect it and that leads to an open blistering wound that can't heal if we are waiting and expecting another outcome. Kids that can turn away from their parent with no regret or remorse have no interest in loving their parents. Hard as this is to accept, I have found it to be true.

If one party decides a relationship has no value and is unhealthy, you can pretty much guarantee that it isn't healthy on either side. Both parties contribute to the success as both sides contribute to the demise.

Parents have this notion that they want to achieve unconditional love for their children and silently believing that their children will return the favor and unconditionally love them too.

We need to think about that? What person whether a child or not can do anything to you and you will just keep on loving them? Could they lie about you? Take and take from you? Threaten you? Sue you? Can our children have license to any and all behaviors and we will just keep on loving them?

As parents we may want to but we are also just human, after time, loss, void, silence, anger, blame and nothing positive, why would any person go back for more of the same? Often what we want and what we are seeking is how we want it to be and it is not how it really is.

Accepting and respecting that not everyone is going to love us and some of those people may be our family members and our own children. Where it may be hard to understand how this can happen, accepting and respecting it is the greatest act of love and of grace.

Loving someone else enough to let them go and loving ourselves enough to let them go is a process that can take years to achieve, years of mixed emotions and up and down days. Rejection is part of life and has many lessons that accompany it. How we handle rejection says a lot about us. The only way to arrive at peace is to first accept it and then respect it.

Letting go is the ultimate act of love and grace ... everyone has their own time frame in doing so and for some it will be harder than others. I wanted things to be different, they won't be, and finally I accept it and I respect it.

What made it easier was in knowing the lost relationships weren't healthy for me. And that God knows best ... and that everything happens for a reason.

Accomplished ...

Every once in a while I get hung up on a word where I can't stop processing it and thinking about it and all its meanings. My new word is *accomplished,* a colleague recently referred to me as "accomplished" and for days now it has stuck with me.

How do we define "accomplished" does it change and grow as we do? I've always believed that to truly become accomplished you have to love what you do and have the discipline to practice and stay with it. Like a muscle that needs to be exercised our talents and our gifts need to be exercised if we are ever to be truly great and therefore, accomplished.

"Most of the important things in life have been accomplished by people who have kept on trying when there seemed to be no hope at all." Dale Carnegie

For many of us I think the word "accomplished" can be intimidating as if only a Ballerina is an "accomplished" dancer or a Grammy Award winning artist is considered to be an "accomplished" musician/singer.

I want to believe that if we are living true, true to ourselves and our hearts and in keeping with what God wants for us in this lifetime, then indeed we have accomplished much.

Christians believe; "God has a plan for your life and if God's word is believed and obeyed God's will can be fully accomplished in one's life."

Whether or not you "believe" in a higher power, a God source, I think most of us would agree that we know in our hearts and our souls when we are living true to ourselves and therefore are feeling and living an accomplished life.

Each one of us defines "accomplished" as it relates to us and our journey in this lifetime. My own personal best definition of an "accomplished" life models this Henri Nouwen quote;

"Did I offer peace today? Did I bring a smile to someone's face? Did I say words of healing? Did I let go of anger and resentment? Did I forgive? Did I love? These are the real questions. I must trust that the little bits of love that I sow now will be many fruits, here in this world and the life to come."

How do you define "accomplished?"

Adjust and Adapt

We must learn to adjust and to adapt as life is ever changing. To stay stuck in yesterday's news is like living from behind. Most people hate change. It is like it throws their equilibrium out of tune. I have always embraced change. I love new things and I love to learn. We are all evolving.

History is great but that is exactly what it is, history, the past. Every aspect in our lives depends on how we adjust and adapt to change. Life changes when we leave home, when we get married, take on a new career job, purchase a home and have children. It changes when we embrace new relationships and when we let go of old ones.

We adjust to that new baby or new work place environment. We have to figure it out and to learn again. Many people will suffer a sort of "norms crisis" with their new environment. That new baby cries and disrupts our previous peaceful past. We work with new people that we instantly gel with and others that we may barely tolerate. But we learn from all of them.

I've always been the "change charger" in our family and my husband the "slow and steady one." Together we make a great couple as a result. A guy that has worked for the same organization for 34 years and lived in the same house for 21 years is not a guy who easily embraces change.

When our kids started leaving home, I had the hardest time. The number one job that meant the most to me was in being a mother. I soon learned to take my career and my writing more seriously. These things are what makes me, me. Being a mother was only a part of me not my total being.

Adjusting and adapting to letting my kids go wasn't easy but now that I have I love my freedom. Less responsibility after decades of being responsible for so many others feels great. Life is easier with less people to please.

I never thought I would be so happy with less people in our home and I am. I think you get to an age where all you really crave is peace. It is so easy to fill our lives up with everyone else's drama and issues but often at what cost? Perhaps the cost is in denying ourselves and our own needs and wants.

My husband is newly retired and I don't think I have seen him smile so much! At the end of his career he had reached the highest level that he had wanted for himself, as a General Superintendent. At that level the demands were great and time was a commodity that he often didn't have. You could physically see what that job was taking out of him. Meetings and meeting and always on 24 hour call back for the past 6-years, every waking moment checking his communication devices. He was needed and worked hard to fill the needs.

But the truth is that if we drop dead today, life goes on, not one of us is irreplaceable. So he gave it is all then one day he declared, "I am done, I am not going back. It hasn't been fun for a long time." Today we have raised our kids and worked our careers. With two pensions between us, no mortgage and adult children we are free from decades of responsibilities and it feels so new and so good too.

Together we are adjusting to living with less by choice and in spending our time together and doing the things that we love to do. What a blessing! Who knew that during all those grinding it out years that this day would arrive and we would still be young enough to enjoy it.

What is next in retirement? Sleep, sun and some fun! It is time for travel and some classes at our local college, things like Chinese cooking, meditation and ball room dance. All those year we grabbed at responsibility and embraced it and yet today for the first time we are both being very selective about what and who we want to be responsible for, having kids, a home, a career is all about being responsible. We have been there and done that.

We are embracing our future and looking forward to making all the necessary adjustments and adapting to the newness of what comes next.

Adjusting and adapting, that is both the beauty and the secret of life. Adjust and adapt … it makes everything and all of life's many changes just so much easier.

Adopting a Child and Becoming "Mom"

In 1992 I met my husband when I was asked to babysit his infant babies so that he could attend the funeral of his 29 year old wife. After delivering twins she died. He literally had all three of his family, his twins and his wife on life support when she passed away.

Everyone in my office knew my daughter and witnessed just how close we were, she was a pre-teen at the time at just 11 years old. I always loved children and worked as a camp counselor for more than 5 summers at two different camps. I was also an older sister to three young siblings. My first "job" was babysitting and when I became CPR trained and a "Candy Striper" at our local hospital, my list of babysitting opportunities grew.

Taking on and "adopting" twins who had a mother pass away absolutely touched my heart. My own daughter had her father die when she was 2. My thoughts were, "Life is tough enough without at least having a mother."

Kids rule! As they did in our house and I remember the early years with my husband Brian when he would state that, "I am not even on the totem pole; I am the guy at the bottom who holds it up." He felt that most all my attention went to my daughter and the infant twins who were just 87 days old when I began caring for them.

In being pre-mature they had numerous extra sight and hearing tests and often were below scale on most tests performed by their pediatrician. There were concerns over their developmental delays and when school started so did their many educational challenges. We brought in tutors and often they were in support classes. In third grade the teachers recommended retention.

I recall the concerns about their ability to attach since they went for weeks without being held and surviving in an incubator, their birth mother never held them, fed them or changed their diaper. There are no photos that exist of her holding them or being with them. There was never any bonding time because she passed away so soon.

The female twin was unresponsive for almost a year to any hugs or loving touches. It was on her first birthday where you could hug her and she would finally hug you back. For months with all the tubes and the pricks of being in the hospital and on life support, the early "touches" they experienced had pain associated with it.

Raising my own daughter was easy for the many years she lived at home as she excelled in school and I seldom was called with any concerns or behavior problems. With the twins I was called almost every other day, one child had emotional concerns and one had educational concerns. It was a lot to manage and their father really didn't know what to do.

I found myself giving way and yielding to his decisions since he was their biological parent. Sometimes his decisions conflicted with what I would have done if it was my biological child.

We raised our kids understanding they had "parents in heaven." Raising children is work; it is a ton of work. Trying to make a difference in another person's life is a meaningful and selfless commitment.

As with any child you never know what you are getting until they arrive and you never find out how you have done until they are grown up and raised.

Recently I asked a friend who wants a baby, "Why don't you consider adoption?" Her response was swift; "*I am not going to invest 18 years into a child so that they can turn around and at 18 say; "you are not my mother!"*

It happens often, kids are raised up by parents and then seek out their "real mom" or their "birth mom" and often disrespect the mom that actually was there for them. They minimize what "mom" did and they make her out to be much less than what she truly was so that they can justify their own actions.

Taking in another woman's child and loving that child like they are your very own isn't an act of an unloving person; it is an act of selfless giving and an open and loving heart.

When the twins were growing up, there was no other mother, she died. I was the mother, period. I always knew they would want to know about their birth mother and even though I never met her it was me who would try and share what I knew about her and ask their father to contribute to the dialogue too.

One day while in high school our daughter rushed in and said, "Mom guess what, when you were driving behind the school bus, my friend asked, "is that your "stepmother" and I told her, "no that is my "only" mother, the only one I have ever known." I was stunned but appreciated it.

Recently I have been reading case studies on adoptive kids that have an attachment issue and have all kinds of personality and adjustments issues. As parents we think we can overcome the many voids some children will have. But there is much discussion about "attachment disorder" from doctors who have studied the adoptive child. We know how important "bonding" is when a baby is born, what happens when a baby is born and never has the chance to attach to "mom" and when attachment doesn't come for days, weeks and months?

Most teenagers go through a rebellious phase and often that is directed at "mom" an adopted child has an extra weapon in her arsenal the one that says, "You are not my mother!"

At the end of the growing up years, parents look back at all the memories and all the experiences they shared with their children. All the places they went to and all the family dinners shared, all the events and all the many experiences at home. Parents know that they gave it their all and they only wanted the very best for their children and to raise happy well-adjusted kids that go on and do well as adults.

It doesn't matter if it is a biological child or adopted child, the efforts are the same and there is a tremendous amount of love and care that goes into raising children, all children.

All I Ever Needed

All I ever needed I always had deep within me. Funny how when you stop searching and stop looking outward you come to know that all you ever needed you already had within yourself.

"There is something so pure, true, alive and wondrously unpredictable about a person who is feeling her inner voice. She is fully present in a way that people rarely are. And she is stepping out of the convention of who she should be to be who she is." Helene G. Brenner, Ph. D.

When we are young we are constantly looking for affirmation from outside sources and from all others. As we mature we understand that affirming ourselves is our greatest gift and the gift that is most aligned with God.

This past year so many things literally came from heaven above, like missing pieces that just arrived and they arrived when needed. I have always believed in God and in His messengers; Angels. But unlike any other year this year everything I ever needed arrived when I needed it the most. This taught me to trust in the universe, in myself and in a deeper sense to trust in God above.

A few years ago my mother passed away and to say that we had any real significant relationship in decades would be a complete untruth. Our relationship was a huge void for me. Yet this year many things happened and people re-emerged that knew us, my mother and me from another time. A time when I was just becoming a teen more than 40 years ago and things happened this year that can only be described as 'gifts from God."

Without going into the details, I met people many people that embraced me and during this time something significant and profound happened that literally was more than 31 years due. It should have arrived over 31 years ago and only found its way to me this year, more than 30 years later.

It would affirm for me that someone or several someone's from Heaven above were looking out for me. My core knew that I already had it all. Throughout my life, I have been scared to death to die. Today I am no longer fearful, I don't want to die at least not yet but I know that when I do I have made my peace and could go to God at any time knowing that whatever came my way, I did my best. I may not have gotten it all right, all of the time, but I always tried my hardest. What else and what more could anyone ask of me?

Real character isn't about how we handle the easy stuff, it is about how we handle the difficult challenges that we all face. When we are tested by adversity our character or lack of character shows itself.

"Daughter, you took a risk trusting me, and now you're healed and whole. Live well, live blessed!" Luke, the Message

'I am leaving you with a gift --- peace of mind and heart. And the peace I give is a gift the world cannot give. So don't be troubled or afraid." JOHN 14:27

Something magical happens when we let go in love and when we are in touch with our core, our hearts and our souls sing when they are aligned together. When we stop the anxiety that comes from searching outside of ourselves and stand in the moment and at peace with what lives within, we come to understand that all we ever needed, we already had ...

Alone at Heaven's Door

We enter this world alone and we leave it alone. From the rearview mirror what have we done with our life, what will be said when we arrive alone at heaven's door. Most people have amazing relationships with their families, their parents, children, co-workers and friends. Our neighbors live along side of us but the truth is that when we exit this life, we shall be alone at heaven's door.

As I age it becomes more and more important to side step the people that want to drag you into their war and their fight. We have to know ourselves and love ourselves. Loving ourselves isn't just what we do for ourselves but what we do for the entire world. People that have self-love are not interested in hurting anyone. They have an inner peace, are content and happy.

It is really hard to watch the mother of the Boston bombings; she is in such denial over her two sons. For her to accept that they killed innocent people she has to own being the parent of two murderers. You can see how shaken up and hurt and angry she is, it is easier for her to believe it is a set up. Her love for her sons and her denial is her coping mechanism. No one can convince her otherwise, she keeps saying that her sons were "loving sons" but clearly their actions were not of love.

Parents tend to see the best in their kids, they look at them with love and acceptance and often through "rose colored" glasses, but kids grow up to be adults and somebody somewhere has adult kids that are capable of murder, destruction and hatred. If not there would be no acts of violence in this world.

We bleed out for our children when they do and say things that are based on hatred rather than love, often parents become the target of that hatred. It can be easy to take it personally and get hooked into their cauldron of hatred. This is the biggest test of all, to know yourself well enough and side step anyone else's desire to pull you into a place of rage, anger, hate and destruction.

When we arrive at the "pearly gates of heaven" and when we leave this life, it won't be about what other people did or didn't do to us. **It will be about what we did or didn't do**. It can be so challenging being the object of someone else's hatred but we must remember who we were before their hate and who we are after their hate.

Americans are hated by other countries just for how we live? We don't ask others to live like us; we accept that each life comes with the freedom to choose how to live. I am struck by how some people can carry hate in their hearts for decades. How some can hate people they don't even know and never even met.

It doesn't matter what "they" do, it matters what we do! As human beings we can be angered and want to take revenge, "an eye for an eye" but what does that really accomplish? When we kill people who have killed people to show that killing is wrong, then we too become killers.

At the end of my life all I want is to know that I tried, that I did my best and that I operated from a loving heart. We all make our share of missteps in life. If we can fix it, fix it and if we can't fix it, we need to leave it and let it go.

We arrive alone at heaven's gate, we will be humbled in death and we need to remember that as we move along from day to day here in this life.

The question we should ask ourselves is, what we need, need to do within ourselves to maintain a loving and peace-filled heart. And not just when it is easy and going our way, but all of the time ... because there will come a day when we alone will be standing at heaven's door.

Always a Country Girl at Heart

"I spent 20 years trying to get out of this place, I was looking for something I couldn't replace, I was running away from the only thing I've ever known" Bon Jovi

"Where I ran off because I got mad, and it came to blows with my old man" Montgomery Gentry

There have been many songs and stories about the growing up process and leaving home. Many times it is a struggle to break free from parents and strike out into adult hood.

I was that kid that couldn't wait to leave it all behind, I had bigger and better plans for my life. I grew up most of the time on a 33 acre farm in New Ringgold, Pennsylvania just outside of Tamaqua. And half of my growing up years was also spent in Allentown, Pennsylvania. The contrast from New Ringgold to

Allentown was huge. Allentown was a city and back then seems like such a big city to this girl while growing up. City life was busier and seemed to offer so many more opportunities than life on the farm.

The farm afforded all the things you would think of like open spaces, barns, fruit trees and a quieter simple life. My mother cooked, baked, sewed and kept house. When she transitioned to life in Allentown, she became a successful high powered career woman. As a young girl I witnessed both ways of life.

Allentown seemed cool and the farm was something that I thought I could easily do without and leave behind. However as I have aged it truly was the values I learned while growing up on that farm that sustained me. I learned about faith in God, taking care of the land and farm animals, taking pride in country and in living a pretty basic life. I may not have appreciated antiques back then like I can today or a homemade skirt or scratch baking and cooking as much as I do now.

I was a teenager in the 70's and my father's love of country music and my mother's love of big band and ball room dance music were easily replaced by rock and roll. They just weren't cool or at least I didn't think so.

Funny how you grow up and then can see how great those things were and yet at a certain age all you want to do are distance yourself from it. Today I can see where so much of what I am attracted to and where so much of my belief system reflects back to those years on the farm.

When I travel with my husband and he drives his car I always feel like I am back in high school since he listens to classic rock and roll all the time. For me, I have retreated back to my roots and listen to country music most of the time. I love the fact that country music tells a story and so often is about real life lessons. You can go to a live show and take grandparents to grandchildren because you know that they aren't going to say or do anything that is offensive like curse.

The things that I fought so hard to get away from in my journey to becoming my own individual self are the same things I have returned to with an even greater admiration. Things like homemade pies, hand sewn clothing and hand knitted sweaters and scarves. I love older homes, open spaces, antiques and the moral code and values that I grew up with. Things like the golden rule, respecting our elders, pride in country, family and home and a stronger belief in the Lord our God.

"It's a four letter word a place you go to heal your hurt, it's an altar, it's a shelter. One place you're always welcome, a pink flamingo, double wide. One bedroom in a high rise a mansion on a hill. Where the memories always will keep you company whenever you are alone after all my running, I'm finally coming home. The world tried to break me; I found a road to take me home. There ain't nothing but a blue sky now, after all

my running, I'm finally coming home." Coming Home *from* Country Strong Gwyneth Paltrow

Just like from the story of the **Prodigal Son**, eventually we all return home. For me, I was always a country girl at heart no matter where I traveled that sense of home has always stayed with me and remains a huge part of whom I became and who I was yet to become.

"Home" doesn't have to be a place or a people; but rather something that we carry deep inside of ourselves that never really leaves us.

Amazing and Awesome Young People Doing Amazing and Awesome Things!

There are so many good and amazing young people doing really amazing things with their lives. They are focused, driven, spiritual good people doing the work and getting the job done. They have set goals for themselves and do and did whatever it takes to achieve them.

The news hits us with all that is wrong with our world and when kids do the bizarre and negative hurtful things with their lives. The good kids the ordinary kids that are slowly grinding it out and working toward their dreams and their own professed finish line need to be recognized and applauded.

Right off the bat, three really great young people that I know are doing amazing and awesome things with their lives. It wasn't easy for them nor was it hard for me to think about them; they had their share of conflict and up and down choices and up and down days, but they never give in or give up.

This weekend my former neighbor/mother's helper/friend stayed with us at the beach. I have known her since she was just 8 years old; today she is 29 years old and a Montessori school teacher with a Bachelor's degree. She volunteers at the local Pet Rescue and is independent of her parents. Alicia is an amazing young person and certainly a daughter to be proud of, and that doesn't mean that she hasn't suffered from her own growing pains and some rub with her parents when she was younger. She had her issues. Today she says, *"I know they were right, I really appreciate them today and all that they have done for me."* As a teenager she couldn't see it, today she readily does.

Tim is my "tech guru extraordinaire" that created my website and already had his own company while still in high school. We e-mail and we text and we meet up for lunch. He is a third year University of Maryland student and very active in his fraternity. He is an all-around awesome kid that is sure to have an amazing future. He has faith in God and is an academic. He has many friends and is so likeable. You couldn't hope for a better son, truly one to be proud of, he knows who he is and strives to do his best at all times.

Maria just travelled across country to San Francisco, she recently graduated from college got her first car and went to Mexico, Las Vegas and now is calling San Fran home. She is working for a startup company and I have no doubt she will be successful. She sets goals and achieves them.

What do these young people have in common? They all have faith in God; secured their education, work towards giving back to the community via several causes and non-profit work. They set goals for themselves and then work the path that leads to attaining them.

There are amazing young people all around us, young adults that work really hard are well educated and give back tirelessly to causes that mean something to them. All three of the young people I write about here come from Maryland and I couldn't be prouder to know them, support them and call them my friends.

Opening yourself up to young people, young adults that are doing great things in big and small ways is the surest and best way to stay young and relevant yourself.

Here is to the next generation of young people that are doing such great and awesome things with their lives and where so many others are sure to benefit from them!

Carry on and stay the course guys … I am so proud to know you!

An Easter Blessing

And He will raise you up on Eagle's Wings Psalm 91:4

The Lord has risen

May you find peace and an abundance of love and light

In the spirit of the season

With bright pink tulips

Cherry blossoms abound

Vibrant yellow forsythia

New rich green grass

Lit with bright and shiny endless blue skies

There are miracles in every moment

A fullness and newness in the air

Hope lives eternal

May you know the richness and exuberance of every single day

The belief that every moment in every life truly matters

And that life is so much bigger than any single soul

Because I live, you also shall live John 14:19

And The Summer Became the Fall

"And the summer became the fall I was not ready for the winter" from the song Nightbird by Stevie Nicks. I am never *really* ready for winter, I mean yes I have the coats, the hats, the boots, the gloves and scarves but mentally I am a summer and a sunshine girl.

I've come to appreciate the fall more and more each year, its harvest time. I like the cooler temps in the evening and "sweater weather."

Right now although we are still in August, some schools have gone back from summer break and I can see a few leaves that have already fallen from our trees. Recently I heard the weather man say that it is now becoming dark just before 8:00 in the evening.

I love pumpkins and making more "comfort foods" and taking advantage of the harvest. Apples and apple pie making always makes me happy. It won't be long before all the leaves have fallen and the days get shorter and darkness comes earlier, and we witness the fields plowed and in rest mode.

"And when I call, will you walk gently thru my shadow"

"And the winter is really here now and the blankets that I love, sometimes I am surrounded by too much love" Quotes from Nightbird written by Stevie Nicks.

Winter always feels like that like, the shadow of night after the summer filled with light. Let us pray that this fall and winter season is filled with an abundance of both blankets and love for all. Tis the season to remember everyone with love and warmth and light …

And Then We Die …

But have we truly lived? We all know that death is a definite, no one escapes it! If I live to be 100, I will only have known and experienced 100 summers and 100 Christmas holidays. It doesn't seem like that is a whole lot so I have tried my best to live as full of a life as I can live.

When I was widowed at just 23 years old, I learned how quickly and unexpectedly life can be taken away. Through the years I have encountered people who when they learn this fact say, "oh I am sorry." But for me it was a huge gift. It drove home for me how precious life is and that I wanted to get the full experience out of every single day and every single experience. I learned NOT to take anything for granted, our time here is not a given and it is limited.

I learned to appreciate the here and the now. My husband was also left at just 32 years old, when his wife Stacey unexpectedly died. Together we are mature beyond our years and often associate with people that are much older than us. Our peer group never really got it. Why would they? When I was 23 and declared a "widow" my peers were immersed in living while I was trying to comprehend death.

This "gift" has strengthened my faith in God, my understanding of life and of death. Initially when it first happened I couldn't understand it. Then one of my older work associates stated, "Find a tree and visit that tree. Visit it in the spring and the summer and then again in the fall and the winter. That is life and that is death." I learned this almost 30 years ago and it has been the view of life that I have come to understand. We are living and then we die just like that tree I visited in every season and every stage of its life.

When my first husband Randy died I had the following poem, Comes the Dawn, read at his funeral in 1983. I still live by it today. He was the one who shared it with me and it wasn't that long before his passing that he shared it. Although his death was accidental and unexpected, I have often thought to have shared this with me, he might have known he was coming close to the end of his life and it was his way of saying good-bye.

Comes the Dawn

After a while you learn the subtle difference
Between holding a hand and chaining a soul
And you learn that love doesn't mean leaning
And company doesn't mean security
And you begin to understand that kisses aren't contracts
And presents aren't promises

And you begin to accept your defeats
With your head held high and your eyes wide open
With the grace of a man, not the grief of a child
You learn to build your roads
On today, because tomorrows ground
Is uncertain for plans
And futures have a way of going down in mid-flight
After a while you learn that even sunshine
Burns if you get too much
So you plant your own garden and decorate
Your own soul, instead of waiting
For someone else to bring you flowers
And you learn that you really can endure
That you really are strong
And you really do have worth
And you learn and learn ... and you learn
With every good-bye you learn

(Author Unknown)

Through the years, people have told me, **"Your life is so interesting!"** Some of it is by design and some of it is purely by life circumstances. However, I can and do appreciate it all. I do my best to squeeze every moment of life out of this life, this life that God has given to me.

As much as we know that death is coming nothing really prepares us for it, or for the loss of the people that we eventually lose to death. My mother was famous for saying, **"We live in hope and we die in despair."** I don't know how I will die but I do know that I do live in hope. I hope and I pray for love, for health, for understanding, for compassion amongst other things and I hope and I pray that when my time ends here on earth I will know that I have lived fully and with few if any regrets.

And as much as I know that I want to live, and to live for as long as I can, and with as much zest and exuberance as I can, I also know "and then we die."

So let us all live and live fully and with no regrets!

Angry Kids

Where I don't want to define all kids by the angry actions of some kids I still have to ask and to wonder why so many young people are so angry and driven to violence and destruction? A few years ago we had a teenaged boy take a gun and kill his parents and his brothers. This young man came from a good family and neighborhood and a family that provided numerous opportunities for him and his brothers. Years later I can't help but still feel the sadness and shock at such a senseless act of violence and hatred.

Not long after I read about another teenaged boy who committed suicide when his father took his gaming system away from him. Yesterday in my own backyard neighborhood a teenaged boy brought a shotgun to school and opened fire in the high school cafeteria. We say it was "lucky" and "could have been far worse" when just one student was hit and hurt. That young boy, that victim of a senseless gunshot is in critical condition and fighting for his life.

I can't stop asking myself, "Why?" "Why are so many young people so angry and acting out with guns and violence?" "Where did they learn that this was an appropriate response?"

We seem to be a society with fewer and fewer boundaries and with a lesser code of values. I've heard it said that "anger is fear turned inside" what are these kids so afraid of? Not so many years ago we had kids in an artsy area dying their hair cotton candy pink and light blue. Then after coloring their hair they had it teased out large like a clown's crown of hair, their entire look screamed and said "Look at me!" And most people did in fact look at them. These same kids with this dramatic look would respond in anger with, "what the f--- are you looking at?" It just didn't add up?

There are always signs that something isn't adding up when these young people communicate in violent ways. I have worked with many kids through the years, first as a camp counselor when I was just a teen myself then as a young mother before moving on to a special needs school and then a youth retreat house. I have witnessed drug and alcohol addictions and teenagers who used their sexuality to gain attention. But over the past few years it seems we have more and more kids who have access to guns and who aren't afraid to use them and turn them on to others. So many kids are quietly crying out for love and attention and some kind of help. Gone unheard that quiet cry seems to be getting louder.

As a parent my question is, "what aren't we giving them? What are we missing? What could/should we be doing differently?" As a teenager I had my share of anger and frustrations but it never caused me to want to get a gun and to use it. If anything my anger and frustration often drove me to want to do more and to be better, to be a better person. I wrote it out and cried it out and danced it out and sang it out.

Today many young people seem to lack the concept of what comes next? What comes after that time of rage and the acting out? There seems to be a disconnect between feelings of the moment and what the next day, next week next month and next year, would and could be for them. Is it a lack of hope? Is it an inability for forward thinking? Is it about an inability to move past the pain?

I've hear the connection of having been bullied to now these young people righting those wrongs by acting out in violence against others. Or the blanket statements of "mental illness" all these kids must be mentally ill to respond in such violent ways. Then comes the response, and so often that includes things like metal detectors and more police guards at schools.

Yesterday shooting at Perry Hall High school brought the news to us and in that news I learned that this school has close to 2,500 students. How much attention can any one single student receive in such a large school? I am not blaming the school but I am questioning if such a large population of young people, can ever receive all that may be necessary to support each and every student in attendance.

We can focus on how this kid got and used a firearm and we can focus on his mental health but the bigger question is why are so many young people so angry that they feel like this is an appropriate response? Getting guns and using them and pointing them at innocent people that literally have nothing to do with their anger and frustrations.

I don't have the answers but my fear is that until we get to the real root of the problem and teach our kids appropriate responses to their anger and frustration we will sadly see more of this behavior in our society.

We must learn to lead and to respond with love. The only way to combat anger is with more love and embracing all young people and helping them to find creative and productive ways to express their anger and frustrations. So much great art is born of pain. Where metal detectors and police guards may be one response a healthier response may be to find a constructive way to deal with life's disappointments, rejection, anger and frustrations.

Anxiety – Do Not Go There!

To avoid anxiety just don't go "there!" "There" to the doctor or to the dentist to that job interview or to take that exam. Avoid the stressor that is causing the anxiety and problem solved! Right, just don't go "there."

It isn't that simple though is it? We need to see the doctor, the dentist and how will we ever secure that new job unless we are willing to interview for it? That exam that we dread just may be the ticket to an elevated position on the job.

Then there is the good anxiety, the moments before we get on that airplane to our tropical destination or getting ready to attend that much anticipated concert. Our excitement is high, we are anxious and we are excited.

The trick seems to be how we manage our anxiety. The things we dread or are nervous about seem more difficult. We may not want to do them but have to go "there" to get ahead or to get well.

A few things that have helped me, take deep breaths, take a long walk; imagine the experience with the desired positive outcome. I remind myself how accomplished I will feel once I have gone "there" and completed whatever it was that was causing my anxiety in the first place.

Yesterday morning was an anxious one as my husband left for a huge state exam; he has been in class for a full year in preparation. Passing this state exam means a lot to him. He prepared well and was about as ready as anyone could be. I was thrilled mid-day when I heard from him. The test was over, he feels good about it and the results will arrive within six weeks. No more anxiety, well no more over this particular exam.

On this same morning I was headed out to my dentist to have some work done and yes I was anxious. Then I had a huge presentation concerning a new book project. My husband and I were equally as anxious but for different reasons and it all went really well. Brian made it through his anxiety and I made it through mine.

Anxiety doesn't have to be a bad thing, it can be what helps us to prepare, and it also reminds us to be ready and to be alert. Our anxiety can reveal many things. It tells us that we are alive and feeling and present, we are aware that what is to come is anticipated, maybe dreaded but sometimes necessary.

So here is to handling whatever makes you anxious and knowing that much can be accomplished when we manage it, and when we get to the other side of our anxiety. Often this means we have completed something that is of value. We wouldn't be anxious if it didn't matter to us.

Appreciating Our Parents

Our parents are everything to us when we are kids. They are our first "teachers" and our first significant relationships. They are our first family. Many kids grow up and have a deep love and respect for their parents. They appreciate them. They get along and they are family.

And many adult children leave home and never fully appreciate their parents. Maybe some never really "get it" until they are parents themselves. I've often thought of those that criticize their own mother and father, how about holding off on that critique or criticism until you, yourself have invested 18, 20, 25 or more plus years in the life of a child.

Parenting can be so rewarding but it also can be a thankless and never ending relationship. A relationship where you may know the highest levels of pride along with the most stunning disappointments. There are never any guarantees.

Parents often take it on the chin, they become a target for their children when life throws these adult children a curve and when things don't go their way. Kids get into trouble and need mom and dad to help them out.

When we hurt people, any people, including family members and yes that means "mom" and "dad" too, we have to be grown up enough to own what we have done and ask for forgiveness. When we grow up we own our actions instead of blaming others. At some point in our lives, we take responsibility for who we are and everything that we have done.

We don't get to disrespect our parents, lie to them and lie about them and then sit back and wonder why they don't rush in and offer us a hand when we are struggling. Relationships just don't work that way.

In my support group of estranged parents I hear all kinds of stories. Some kids don't just grow up and leave home but want to burn the house down upon their exit. Often the stories shared are beyond what any parent ever imagined with they were raising little "Johnnie" who knew that all that love they had for their sons and daughters could one day be turned into such heart break.

Family fights that result in parents and grandparents that will never see their children or their grandchildren again. Kids that decide to punish mom and dad by their estrangement and then taking the grandchildren with them.

I wasn't surprised when my mother "disowned" me, not really. I came to her and told her that her husband was a child abuser. She had two choices 1) believe me and leave him or 2) discredit me so that she could stay married to him. She chose the latter. It wasn't about me. Her desire to stay with him superseded all else.

My life was NOT easier without my mother in my life. It just wasn't! I don't know any child, young or old whose life is easier without mom and dad. At what age does our life get easier without the love and support of our parents?

I always wanted my parents to be proud of me. I never wanted to hurt them or to disappoint them and in many ways I know that I exceeded their expectations. Maybe it wasn't initially when I first left home but soon after. I remember my mother as an Administrator working at University of Maryland hospital. She wanted to play "matchmaker" and fix me up with a doctor. I don't think she would have done that if she didn't have a high opinion of me. And when I was a Realtor and just 26 years old I saved $8,000 to purchase my first home. I needed $5,000 more to close the deal and she loaned it to me. I paid her back early in just 10 months of the 1-year that I had promised.

Keeping that relationship respect worthy was important to me. Yet I know that I also caused them grief when at just 19 years of age I proclaimed, "I am getting married!" and married a man that was 15 years older. It wasn't their choice but they stood by me. And less than 5 years later they would "stand by me" as I put him to rest and buried him.

I always appreciated my parents and I never did anything to outwardly hurt them. My mother was so hard working I never wanted to burden her so I took care of myself. My parents divorced and my dad went on to create a whole new family adding three more children to the five that he already had with my mom. He didn't have much to give me but every time I visited him I left with money for gas and food. Often he gave me fruits and vegetables that he grew in his own garden. I appreciated it all.

In his death, he would leave me with two of his paintings. They are cherished possessions. Just like the two slate top antique coffee tables that I own, they were gifts decades ago from my mother. I have a Fannie Farmer Cook Book that she gave to me in 1979 as a wedding anniversary gift for my first year of my marriage. These items wouldn't really hold any value to most people but they do for me. They are gifts from my parents, parents who have died and I never stopped appreciating them and all the things they gave to me and tried to do to love and support me.

We mourn when they die, we grieve our loss. But what did we do when we had them in our lives? Did we appreciate them? And did we appreciate them ... enough?

Many of my friends have lost their parents as they have passed away. They grieve the loss and feel the void. Others still have their parents and they continue to love them and support them. As we get older we have a greater sense on just how precious life is and how all our days here are numbered.

Parents aren't perfect and neither are their children. My father was many things and many things that he did were hurtful to our family, and yet I never hated him, I tried to understand him.

I never hated my mother either, I didn't like the choice she made in staying married to a man, her second husband who was known to me as a child abuser. Her choice left me no choice and it wasn't ideal.

Soon I will be celebrating my 55th birthday. I have been a parent since I was 21 years of age. That means that for 34 years I have been "mom" and in that time I did many things right, from breastfeeding to graduation from a highly respected private prep school to an Eagle Scout, our kids had numerous opportunities and many accomplishments. They were well supported. And when I fell short or was less than perfect, I still had peace in my heart knowing that most everything was done from my heart.

One day our parents will die and we will be left knowing that we either loved them and appreciated them and can feel good about that or we will be sorrowful for all the days, weeks, month and years when we chose not to embrace them.

Arrested Development

Arrested development has been defined as ***"an abnormal state which development has stopped prematurely."*** To me that is exactly what estrangement does, it is an abnormal premature ending to both the development of the relationship and the stopping prematurely of the relationship.

My relationship with my mother ended abruptly when she was in her early 50's the age where I am at in my life now. I would never know her in her sixties and her seventies until when she died. We lost decades of interacting and history that was never to be. I have health questions and as I face my own "change of life" it would have been nice to have that family perspective and family history. Obviously I know my birth date but not the time of my birth. There are pieces missing from the puzzle. There are pieces that only a mother would know and would have within her to share.

My kids would miss out on their grandmother and in knowing and seeing my family and our roots and history. My daughter estranged at just shy of her 18th birthday, she will have huge voids in her life as well. Voids that just may contribute to a state of "arrested development."

We often replace that which has been lost to us; I have "other mothers" and "other daughters" that have filled many of the voids. Those relationships are highly valued loving relationships. However, nothing can truly take the place of the woman who gave you your life or who you gave life.

Today I read a piece about "Things That Will Disappear in Our Lifetime" the list included; the post office, the check, the newspaper, the book, the land line telephone, music, television and even privacy. We all grew up with these things. But is family on its way out too?

Many of us will face our futures without our adult children, kids that we raised that decided we weren't important or worthy. My estrangement support groups continue to grow in numbers. Parents are sharing their stories and many are no longer embarrassed by the estrangement of their adult children.

Many parents have been forced to live without ever having an adult relationship with their children. The most common things you hear is that the kid's state 1) abuse 2) control 3) no control 4) stalking and 5) disagreements over issues. The adult children feel justified in dismissing mom and dad from their life. Often taking the next generation with them, and leaving the next generation without ever knowing their grandparents and therefore their family history and their roots.

I've heard stories where parents call to tell their adult children that they" love" them and days later receive a legal "no contact" order in the mail. There are adult children that regularly use the law to distance themselves from the very people who gave them life and raised them, their own parents. It is surprisingly common in estrangement. Family courts where children literally want a "divorce" from mom and dad. Kids accuse mom and dad of all sorts of things to justify their choice of estrangement. Some are founded and many are deemed unfounded.

What is the real cost though to "abnormal premature ending" of family relationships, namely parental?

How does that adult child continue with normal maturation and life experience when they have chosen a form of "arrested development?" How well adjusted can you possibly be when you don't have peace, love or any relationship with the people that raised you, cared for you and parented you?

I really believe that to hate your mother, is to hate yourself because that is where you came from. Anyone that has the power to disregard their past will disregard most anything in life. If you don't value your own mother, what will and do you value?

As a daughter who felt I had no choice due to sexual abuse in the family to sever ties with my mother, I was acutely aware of the cost. I knew the voids I had and I did my best to fill them with healthy relationships. Some voids would never become filled. What I did have though was a husband that always loved me. And a desire to forgive and move past it, learn from it and continue on without adding any more hurts.

I have often said, "I had to do so much more that most people just to feel normal." That was my response when people told me "you are so accomplished" or "your life is so interesting." I knew the holes I had and all the wounds that I suffered. I did my best to heal and to minimize any "arrested development."

Many parents have lost a big piece of themselves when their children have made the choice to exit their life. Some talk about the loss of a "will to live."

But what about those adult children, what have they lost? All their reasons and the rationale, their stories and excuses aren't going to make up for the abnormal premature loss of parents. Somewhere "arrested development" is sure to show itself.

What will they use to fill their voids? Will they make healthy choices? Or will they medicate their feelings away? Could these same adult children hold up to the yardstick they have chosen to use to measure their own parents?

It is in many ways a throw- away society with disposable everything, sadly many have chosen to devalue and throw mom and dad away too. It will be interesting to see what history does with these adult children and how their own relationships with their children will fare for them when they themselves have set the example.

How many of them will have children that will follow this parent and model those same behaviors. How many will suffer from some sort of "arrested development?" Only time and history will tell …

"As Is"

I have come to believe that the most Godly love is a love that loves "as is" when we accept people for who and for what they truly are and can love them "as is" we are as close to God's love as we can ever be in this life.

After I recently read a post by Robert Downey Jr I had this sense that he saw his mother quite clearly and exactly as she was, imperfections and all and he loved her. Isn't that what we all aspire toward? To be loved for who and what we are and as were are in any given moment in our life. Perhaps sometimes we are easier to love.

In my lifetime I have experienced quite a bit of "conditional love" and most of it waned when I failed to meet others expectations of me. If I was true to myself and if I spoke my truth, I was, at least in my family deemed "unlovable."

My father always loved me and he loved me "as is" I loved him that way too. We saw each other with warts and all and we chose love.

With my Catholic upbringing and my Italian roots from my mother's side, I would learn about "conditional love." It started in Catholic school where I was taught that even if all my work was correct that only God was perfect and not me so a 100% was never attainable. This taught me to push harder but it also taught me that I was never going to be good enough, no matter what I achieved, it would be deemed as less than perfect.

The harsh criticisms from my mother's family affirmed my feelings of inadequacy too. If you did something they didn't approve of it was like the classic mob mentality, **"you are dead to me."** I am at an age where I can laugh at it now and also where it has been 100% affirmed for me. My mother would die and I would be excluded from her obituary. **"You are dead to me"** was very real for my family and in my family. This action said nothing about me and spoke volumes about those that chose to do it. Now they are married to a life of filled with hate and a desire to prove that they are "right" and "good" and of course that would make me the intended receiver …?

You see this in the Amish community where people are "shunned" from all family members and from the community when their actions/behaviors are deemed unacceptable. The response is not one we would expect from a God loving people.

The God that I know is an all-loving God and he loves us all as he created us all and created us "as is."

From my family I would learn to be critical mostly with myself and with those closest to me. Nothing was ever good enough, nothing was ever perfect. It worked for a while as it made me a high achiever. I aspired to be "excellent" in all that I did.

It would take until my early thirties before I would learn that real love doesn't impose conditions and it doesn't deem any other human "unlovable" it accepts people, all people "as is" I was that kid in school that never had a specific group. I easily moved within all circles, always finding something good in each group that I was a part of, it didn't mean though that I was blind to each group and their strengths and their weaknesses.

"When we judge people, we have no time to love them."
Mother Teresa

Often the people that sit in judgment are the most insecure people, they typically don't love themselves and it shows itself by how unloving they are toward others. Love begins from within and it ends from within, period.

"When you point one finger, there are three more pointing back at you." The next time you hear or you witness unkind words and actions coming from someone, anyone, look a little closer, you can almost guarantee they are striking out because of their own inner insecurity. When we feel good and we feel loved, there is no need or any desire to try and diminish anyone else.

Love is always the answer! It is the answer to all the brokenness in this world. When we feel the need to hurt and to harm others; that is exactly when we should be looking inside of ourselves and asking ourselves, what exactly is going on here?

When we become the "black sheep" or the "scape goat" it is coming from outside of ourselves and comes with someone else's agenda. Every single day I work with people that are hurting and grieving. They are experiencing loss, often by death or by estrangement. I give them my time and I take their phone calls, e-mails, letters and text messages, I try and offer comfort, understanding and unconditional love, I don't judge them.

There has been no greater gift in my lifetime than to experience my own loss and grief and to turn it around and use it for a greater good and to become; 1) more loving 2) more compassionate 3) more forgiving 4) more understanding and 5) peace filled.

We can never change what other people do and what they say, but what we can do is change how we respond. The greatest challenge in our lifetime may very well be responding with love and with acceptance and learn to love all people "as is" and as God himself made them to be.

Asking Her Father

It's nice to see that some traditions have staying power and still ring true for so many young couples wanting to marry. Yesterday I was at my nail salon getting my nails done when I began talking with the young lady next to me. Later that afternoon she was going ring shopping with her soon to be fiancé'. She shared the story of what it was like when her boyfriend "asked her father" for her hand in marriage.

They had been dating for several years and the parents openly accepted him. But ... dad wasn't so quick to say "yes" but replied with "I will let you know after I discuss it with her mother." It wasn't long before the much anticipated answer was "yes." She talked about respect, the respect her boyfriend had for her and for her father and mother. She knew that this would translate to the best possible start to their married life.

Later that day I attended a wedding myself and this young couple also began with tradition in "asking her father" for his daughters hand in marriage. As I sat through the church service and later the reception you could see all the friends and family support for this newly married couple. They definitely have all the markings for making it and staying together and I have to believe it begins with respect.

"Over the years I have counseled many young couples and the couples that begin the marriage process with "asking her father" are by far the ones that manage to stay together." Father John

As a wedding officiant myself I see it too. When a man loves a woman and respects her and her family of origin enough to "ask her father" it sets the stage for a healthy and happy beginning. This single act lets the family know that this is a good start to a life that is beginning with inclusion and with love and with respect.

In a world that is ever changing it is so refreshing to see that some traditions survive the test of time. On the way home from the wedding yesterday I couldn't help but ask my husband about it. What would you think if someday you were in the position where a young man came to you for the sole purpose of "asking her father" and his response was without thought "it's still the right thing to do!"

Be a Blessing!

Tis the season of giving, who and what can we be a blessing to at this most wonderful time of the year? There is always someone that can benefit and be lifted up by our actions. Our giving spirit is what we do for ourselves. The benefits to others that receive our gifts are an additional benefit to them and to us.

Most years we donate food and clothing to local nonprofits that are serving the neediest populations. This year we decided to shop at our local dollar store for toothbrushes, toothpaste, deodorant and shampoo for 25 people. The cost is nominal compared to the amount of people that will use these products.

If cash is an issue volunteers at your local hospital, for a few hours a week our time can relieve the pressure of the working staff. You will be appreciated!

There is a lot of heartache over the holidays with families that are estranged or ill or even deceased. Traditions are lost with those that have left and or moved on and many families feel the void. This can be a time of grief or a time to create new traditions.

Years ago when a family member moved on we chose to create new traditions, this often included traveling. We went to Nashville, Tennessee and to Key West Florida. Going new places and creating new memories took much of the sting out of our loss. It was fun and made it easy to move on.

"You can't spend your life in the graveyard of guilt dealing with corpses of the past. If you continue to work with the dry bones of dead issues, you too will begin to decay. No amount of work will resuscitate a corpse. Sign the death certificate and bury the past." ~ Pope Francis

Pope Francis has it so right; I have been so guilty of hanging onto the past and grieving for that which was not mine. What a huge waste of time, talent and life. Life is for the living, live it!

We can be a blessing to so many people to many others who need us, love us and appreciate us. Go where the love is and thrive, tis the season.

Be a blessing ... Merry Christmas!

Be the Friend That You Would Want To Have

Be the friend that you would want to have, treat others the way that you would want to be treated. Just like the golden rule. It sounds pretty simple and yet so many friendships are challenged by jealousy and doing things to another that you wouldn't want done to you.

Luke 6:31 and as you wish that others would do to you, do so to them.

Over the past few years I have been looking closely at my friendships but also my friends and how they relate to their friends. A few conversations have come out of this idea and overall the number one deal breaker was a friend that was either jealous and/or not supportive.

What makes a good and true friend?

1) A good friend is honest and when something doesn't seem quite right they let you know.
2) A good friend is fun and interesting and you look forward to being together.
3) A good friend supports you with your dreams, goals and ambitions.
4) A good friend is someone that you can trust who won't steal your boyfriend or husband or your children.
5) A good friend shows that they care about you.
6) A good friend sees you at your best and at your worst and supports you either way.

Love one another with brotherly affection. Out do one another in showing honor. Romans 12:10

What are the deal breakers with a friend?

1) Being dishonest and talking negativity behind your back.
2) Someone who always requires more attention and care than what they contribute. Not just on occasion but most often
3) A Debbie-downer, no matter what you want to accomplish they just can't see it or are openly non supportive.
4) Someone who can't be trusted, they steal your boyfriend or husband or your children.
5) Their actions tear you down and show that they don't care about you.
6) They are only present if they can gain by being with you.

"But your back turned and the knife fell and you swear that payback is gonna be hell. Now you just can't trust anybody cuz a friend was just a snake in the grass, can't you see you can't see tomorrow as long as you are looking back. Got your feet wet, got your heart broke, didn't pan out like you hoped" As Long As Your looking Back by Gary Allan

Years ago I invited a friend over for dinner and the first question was, "Who else is going to be there?" That immediately struck me as odd; shouldn't just being with me and my husband have been enough? This person turned out to be a social climber and not a friend at all.

I watched another friend who was openly proud that they had more access to her friend's husbands' business and business accounts. If there was trouble in paradise this friend was in it for the husband and not for her girlfriend. It seemed odd to me? It was weird the displaced loyalty or lack of loyalty and the open acknowledgement? All I could think was I wonder what the wife, your so called friend would say and think and feel if she heard that?

Another friend shared with me how their friend told them that they weren't good enough to remain friends. Even if true, why would you say that to someone? Clearly this wasn't a friendship at all.

When you have a friend who is happy and successful in their own right, they have no interest in being jealous or trying to tear you down. Friends that are accomplished want to be with others who are accomplished.

A good friend is that friend you can call when you get in a jam and they will drop what they are doing to come and help you. A good friend is invested in you r success both personally and professionally, your success makes them even happier to know you.

A good friend makes the effort, the effort to see you and be with you and be a part of your life and your milestone accomplishments.

A friend is not someone who tries to come between you and any of your relationships. They don't tear at you to try and make themselves look good. They aren't jealous of who you are and of what you have.

Having friends isn't the same as having a husband or life partner, yes my husband is my friend he might even say he is my best friend but he doesn't take the place of my girlfriends. Girlfriends lift you up; when you beam they are beaming too. When you are happy they are happy for you and when you are sad, they lend an ear and offer support.

A friend may see you do something they don't agree with or like or even approve of but they don't divide you from the ones you love over it. They don't try to gain at your expense. That's not a friend but rather someone who wants what you have and is jealous and self-serving.

In the end we learn forgiveness or as Jesus would say in **Matthew 6:14-15 For if you forgive others their trespasses, your heavenly Father will also forgive you, but if you do not forgive others their trespasses, neither will your Father forgive your trespasses.**

Be the friend that you would want to have and if you can't, excuse yourself and say goodbye.

In order to have a friend, you must first be a friend …

Be My Valentine Spread Some Love

"Where there is love there is life." Mahatma Gandhi

In our house we celebrate Valentine's Day, it is a day for love and about love. We gift tiny presents. It could be balloons, flowers, candy hearts, hearts, special dinners, special desserts, cards and just about anything that comes in the color of red and takes the shape of a heart. Red hearts are hot, red hearts are love.

There has never been one year in our 21 year history where we haven't celebrated Valentine's Day and spread the love. Our kids and our friends often receive little gifts too. I probably make out the most since my husband is very tuned into celebrating love and celebrating each and every Valentine's Day that we have been together.

Most often I receive the traditional flowers and chocolates, usually a funny card and a serious one too; often we celebrate dinner at our favorite restaurant. For me though, the real gift, the biggest gift is the effort my husband makes. He goes off on his own, reads and reads those cards until he finds the one that best represents what he feels. And honestly it is the one time during the entire year that he makes that dinner reservation all by himself. I love the effort, the thought and it is all in the details. He is deliberate and he is thoughtful and he is on a mission to show me how much I mean to him.

Valentine's Day isn't just for lovers or for couples, it is for everyone. It is a day to spread the love.

It can be a time when singles feel more alone and there is a way around that, like in the movie Valentine's Day where the singles party together. Spend time with family and with friends have a Cherry coke or a Berry martini. Eat one good piece of chocolate. Get your hair cut or nails done. Pamper yourself, love yourself. Buy red and pink flowers for yourself or for another.

Be the loving person to someone else that you would want to be on the receiving end of.

Give the dogs a special treat, leave tiny gifts like candy hearts or those cheesy elementary school Valentine's for the next guy who takes that seat on the bus or the train. Write it to "You Who I Don't Know" and sign it "A Believer in Love." Leave a single flower; it doesn't have to be a rose for a co-worker who doesn't have anyone special in their life. Make cupcakes decorated for Valentine's Day; bring them to the office and share them with everyone.

Just think how great it would be if we all took this day to make it a day to show more love all the way around. We can share little kindnesses like taking that extra minute to talk to the mailman and letting him know you appreciate the work that he does or that gal at the coffee counter by appreciating her smile.

Last year I received my Certificate of Ordination so that I could legally marry couples, I want to be part of their beginning when everything is good and new and full of love and promise. A small part of their love story. Celebrating love within ourselves and with others is probably the greatest gift of all. If you don't have a significant other, have many others that are friends that you can share some love with on this Valentine's Day. Be a part of the positive, loving energy force and bring love with you wherever you go and toward whomever you meet along the way. Dedicate this Valentine's Day 2013 to love and lots of little loving acts of kindness. Make the effort, do it for yourself, be the giver, the lover and watch what comes back to you. Love naturally meets up with more love.

"A loving heart is the beginning of all knowledge." Thomas Carlyle

Valentine's doesn't have to be just for couples, take grandma or grandpa to lunch and celebrate, buy the office assistant a candy bar, bring love and joy where you go and watch it grow. We spend enough time dwelling on loss, anger and hurt, what if we spent more time fostering love and kindness.

My wish for this Valentine's Day is that we will all celebrate our hearts, our love, and our life and do so by lots of little acts of love and kindness. It doesn't have to be expensive, it doesn't have to be big, and all it has to do is come from the heart.

Where there is love, all things are possible ... Be my Valentine and spread some love ... Happy Valentine's Day!

Beach Love

My soul knows no peace like the sounds of the surf slapping up against the sand. Since I was a teenager I have enjoyed a love affair with the ocean. I love it in the summer, I love it in the winter, I love it in the fall and I love it in the spring. There is never a season where I don't appreciate the God given beauty of the beach and the magic of the ocean. I will travel to most any location for the sun, the sand and the surf.

In 1990 I sold my home in Baltimore and I moved to the beach in Ft. Lauderdale where I lived for a year. My family was decimated by claims of abuse in the family and then a long term relationship abruptly ended. I needed to heal and I knew I couldn't survive a winter in Baltimore. Winter always represented the death season to me so off I went to the sunshine state. It was a bittersweet year.

I would never have moved to the beach without the heartaches that entered my life. In that year, I wrote and I prayed and I sat on the beach. I found peace and I found strength there. Friends couldn't console me the way the ocean could and did. A year later I would emerge stronger than ever. I was new again.

In the late 1990's I married on the beach, a small intimate wedding with my husband and our three children and our witness couple and their child. It was and remains a God blessed union. Our honeymoon was a cruise on a ship where we took in the Caribbean and fell in love with the islands, St Thomas and St John. The water colors of turquoise, blues and greens are just stunningly beautiful.

My husband and I built a tiny little house in Lewes, Delaware near Rehoboth beach that we frequent numerous times each year. Once a year we make our way to Florida, it doesn't matter where as long as a beach, an ocean is included. Key West is always a favorite destination.

I can just sit and I can just pray for hours on the beach. I do my best soul searching and my best writing and praying there. My soul is calm at the foot of the water, a calm that I seldom know in my busy life. I can be alone at the beach and yet I never feel alone there. The presence of God is so great for me while at the ocean. Even if you are a nonbeliever, who or what created our amazing oceans and all their true and natural beauty? The year I lived in Ft. Lauderdale I remember hearing visitors from Europe say, "this can't be real it is just so beautiful!"

The ocean always feels like home to me. Unlike people, it never lets me down and is always right there for me, whenever I need it. From the time I was a young adult I dreamt of owning a house that was right at the foot of the ocean and had a long stairwell that took you right to the sandy beach. I dream of writing a bestselling novel there and enjoying my husband and our dogs and fine wine and healthy foods. In my dream it is a beach like Rehoboth or Bethany beach where you have all the four seasons. And in my dream we honker down and live a low profile life six months of the year and then spent the remaining six months travelling to promote my book. Just when we are exhausted from our travels we return for another six months of seclusion. It is a dream that have never died and when we win the lottery that is where you will find us.

I don't need the people or the concessions at the beach, although I do enjoy them in the summer season. I have been on the boardwalk in Rehoboth beach during frigid winter weather when you would have to look really hard to find any other people. And just as I have enjoyed that solitude and aloneness I easily appreciate the high demand and the high traffic of all those fighting for their space on the sandy beaches during the summer season.

Our country is so blessed that you can travel at any time of the year to a tropical weather location. After a really hard winter up north, I seldom make it through February or March before the ocean calls my name and once again I head to one of those tropical locations. There are very few places and a few people that will I fly or drive over 1,000 miles to visit but the Ft. Lauderdale beaches and the Keys always and at any time, I'm there.

Just like in the movie *Beaches*, if I knew I was dying and had a limited number of days left here on earth, that is where I would spend my time. You would find me breathing in the air, taking in the sounds and watching the wonders of the water at the beach. And just like Hillary states in this movie, **"I don't even remember what I was mad about and I don't care. Whatever it was that you did, I forgive you."**

Like gasoline in the car, my tank is full, revived and ready as I have filled my soul with peace and with love since I just returned from an extended beach stay. I am already planning my next visit it won't be more than a few weeks until I return. I can't say that I have to do anything when I am there, it is just in the "being" in that environment of more water than the eye can capture against a never ending skyline.

Just like in life the beach affords infinite possibilities, and for me an abundance of love, hope and peace.

I find the presence of God there, and I find it over and over again. I have beach love …

Become a Fan!

Be a fan! Support your favorite baseball team, football team, musical group, theater, the arts, an author; just about anyone that is doing work that you can appreciate is worthy of your support. Get behind someone or something that makes you feel good about supporting them and also lifts you and them up.

My husband is one of the best fans! He loves the Baltimore Orioles and in his words, *"a true fan is one who supports you whether you are winning or losing."* I just love that! Let's face it, it is really easy to get behind and stay behind a "winning" team. But a true fan is the one who stay with you during the high times and the not so high times.

Anyone who knows me well knows that I am a huge fan of Country Music Artist, Gary Allan. This summer we will attend yet another one of his fan club parties in Nashville Tennessee. I can honestly say that I am a "true fan." Gary has his share of success but it has been quite a few years since his last #1 hit.

Just recently the single **Every Storm** from the **Set You Free** album became another number 1 hit song for Gary Allan. There is no question that his band and he are all enjoying a recent high. I can't wait to attend the fan club party and celebrate their most recent success.

But you don't have to be a baseball player or a musician to have "fans." A fan is a supporter, someone who appreciates what you do and follows you.

We can all be a fan and we can all have fans. Lift someone else up and be a blessing in someone else's life. Promote the good works of others, become a connector and bring people together. If you like an artist's works, their painting, tell them and support them. Meet writers and authors at book festivals and connect one on one with people that are aligned with you and what you like and can appreciate.

And if you are fortunate enough to have a few fans, let them know that you appreciate them too. We weren't put here on this earth to hurt and destroy each other, we were put here to love and to appreciate one another.

Take what you like and leave the rest behind. Not everything is meant for everyone. But when you do come across something or someone that speaks to you, let them know. Be their fan, become a supporter and enjoy knowing that you are a part of something that is more and bigger than yourself.

Been There Done That

As we age we begin to acknowledge all the many experiences that we had whether they were personal or professional. The older we are the longer the list. One of the challenges in aging is to stay relevant and young in spirit. We can choose to keep our inner child alive and well or we can deny it.

That inner child that says, "I can do that!" And has a curiosity for all that is new and yet to be experienced. But there is also value in the aging person that can reflect upon "I have been there and I have done that!"

This week two friends had new book come out, for one she has written several books although this new book has a new genre and a new publisher and the other had his very first book hit the market. I am proud of them and pleased with what I have read. A younger Bernadette may have been envious and even jealous but the truth is that I am neither. I have been there and I have done that. Now I am able to be genuinely supportive and appreciative of their works.

Life brings change in its own time and its only way, the only thing that we can truly count on is that life will change. Nothing lasts forever and nothing stays the same.

Few things in life hold the same appeal as they did in the beginning, we either transition with the changes or we opt out. Anyone in a long term marriage understand that there is an ebb and a flow. What makes a marriage last is that agreement that the two parties share. In essence that agreement if it endures the test of time says; I am here for you, I am here for you today and for tomorrow and when you are attractive and when you are unattractive. When you are glowing I will be there to bask in that glory and when you are down and out I will offer you a safe haven. In essence couples that are in it for the long run understand that.

Not every day is going to go your way. We mature as we age and we come to understand that as we grow and change and so do all those that surround us.

In my lifetime I have had an easy time with "hello" and struggled with my "goodbyes" and I have been working on that. I have learned to trust what you know and to let all the rest go. This has saved me much grief and heartache. When it comes to hanging on; I have been there and done that. And in retrospect it is not healthy.

What is important is what is ahead, what is yesterday has already been done, we have been there and we have done yesterday. The quest is for all that is yet to come and all that is ahead of us.

"May the God of hope fill you with all joy and peace in believing, so that you may abound in hope by the power of the Holy Spirit" **Romans 15:13**

Behind Bernadette

A few years ago I had a book titled, *Behind Bernadette* and it was literally about to roll of the presses when I received a nasty letter from an attorney. Not only did I receive a letter but so did my then employer. It was from a family member who joined with other family members so that my story would never be told. They wrote letters to numerous people, most of whom they never knew or even met.

My childhood was in a family of abusers from alcohol abuse, verbal abuse, physical abuse and even sexual abuse. Where they were right and got me? I didn't have the right to identify the abuse victim. And without being able to do that I couldn't explain the family estrangement.

It was the first time that I wrote a whole story book with a beginning a middle and an ending. It was long and laborious and I was feeling so accomplished when it was finally written. I cried through many of the pages and relived parts of my past that I had not thought of in decades. It was very cathartic and healing. It was intended to help others. I was encouraged by many sources and had hundreds of pre-sales requests.

When my lawyer read it he said, "I couldn't put it down, this is the kind of thing that Oprah gets behind." I had another friend who read it and wanted me to speak to Junior League and another that wanted me to present to Alcoholics Anonymous.

I don't know that I would ever have had the strength or the courage to write it if my sisters had not decided to omit me from my mother's obituary. Decades earlier I had walked away from them. Much of our family history was rooted in lies, cover ups and abuse. In the end once again it was confirmed for me as to why I walked away. I had to save myself.

What I learned from their success in killing my book was priceless. I learned that I was right. I learned that they were more committed to attacking me than they were to uncovering the truth and family secrets and had no interest in the health and wellness that comes from owing your past and your truth.

They gave me a huge gift by their actions, I was finally able to let go of any hope of reconciliation and in time I was also able to forgive them. My life is so much more than any single book or body of work. If not for their actions I would not have had such clarity on so many things that were once open wounds. At the end I had clarity and I had peace. Everything happens for a reason ...

Believe

Believe! It is that time of year again, with Thanksgiving just behind us as we look forward in anticipation for the Christmas holidays. We look ahead in welcoming in the New Year. I can't help but reflect upon the word "believe" for me it is right up there with "faith" and with "joy."

This year, I will pray on "believe" and I am making the choice to see the good in life, and in people and in the world. I am making the choice to see the good and to believe in the goodness of all people even the ones that show me otherwise.

Earlier this month a coward crossed my path, he knows who he is and I know who he is too. He is a person who doesn't have the courage to sign his name and face me head on. I could choose to respond with anger but I choose to respond with God in my heart. I won't allow this coward to bring any of his toxins into my life or into my heart. He didn't do his job, literally, and when he was called out publicly, he responded in a cowardly way. After his cowardly actions, he decided to "unfriend" me on Facebook.

What he did, does not reflect upon me at all, but speaks volumes about who he is and his complete lack of character and integrity.

When you take a stand and stand up for what you think and what you believe inevitably you will make someone unhappy along the way. The problem with this guy, honestly, if the same thing he did to me, was done to him, he'd go home crying to his mommy. There is no doubt about it.

Last year I attended a Marianne Williamson lecture, she writes about and speaks about love and I can't imagine her ever being a target. Yet during her lecture, she spoke about the cowardly actions of someone who didn't like her views and her political position. They went on a campaign to try and harm her reputation.

What strikes me with my situation and with her story is and was, if you don't like someone's position, their comments or ideas, don't listen and don't read them! And if you must react and respond why not take it directly to the source?

I believe that most people are really good people and good people try and effect change by going to the source. Any person, who hides his identity, isn't taken seriously and is seen for the truth of what motives them. Their motivation is purely to hurt. If they wanted to help or express an opposing view they would have had the courage to own their own statements.

As a writer who often writes about real life experiences, and real life situations and real life opinions there is no doubt in my mind that not every reader is going to have the same beliefs that I have. I share mine. I am willing to listen and to hear others. My husband loves me dearly, and yet even he doesn't agree with me 100% of the time. My views are mine, and my beliefs are mine.

This holiday season my word is "believe" and I plan to "believe" in the goodness of all people, in the grace of God and in the divinity of the human spirit. I "believe" that 2013 is going to be an amazing year for me personally and professionally. The number "13" has always been a really lucky number for me!

You've got to have faith, and joy and you have to believe. Believe.

Best Parenting Advice I Ever Heard

When it comes to advice about parenting, everyone is an expert or so they think. I once had a dear friend tell me *"advice is free and maybe that is what it is worth, nothing!"*

In retrospect there are probably two lines that I have heard in my more than 30 years of parenting. The first came to me from movie producer James Robinson when I was just a young waitress in my early twenties. He had seven children of his own and they all seemed to be doing really well.

He said, **"Kids, when they deserve your love the least is when they need your love the most."** Through the years I have reflected upon his statement.

However just recently I read a line that really stuck with me. I wish I had this stream of consciousness much sooner. The line was; **"Don't handicap your children's lives by making their life too easy for them."** After reading that I had an immediate moment and thought about how often both my husband and I have been guilty of this one.

Our intentions were good and we thought we were helping but it wasn't helping but definitely enabling them to do less for themselves and for them not to take responsibility for their choices and their own decisions. Simply put we gave them much too much and did them an injustice by making life far too easy for them. We couldn't see it at that time. Today we clearly do.

For us our parenting years are far behind us but to anyone who is still in the parenting trenches I believe both lines seem to be 100 % true.

1) Kids, when they deserve your love the least is when they need your love the most.
2) Don't handicap your children's lives by making their life too easy for them.

Prayer for Grown Children – Marian Prayer Book

Lord, as Mary's Son, you experienced the love between parent and child, a love that begins as one of total dependency and matures into a love of equals. A parent ought to feel a job finished at that point, but it doesn't work that way, at least not for me. I continue to worry about my grown children, and their lives, jobs, and families. If I could I would probably try to protect them from all problems, much as I tried when they were small. Fortunately for them and me, I have no such power.

I know that they must make mistakes in order to develop to maturity. I know their lives will include problems, and in fumbling for solutions thy will discover themselves and their values. I pray, therefore, not that you protect them from all evil, but that you give them strength to conquer the evil they meet. I pray for myself, too.

Let me learn as Mary learned that day you remained behind in the temple, and gently reminded her that you were about Your Father's business. Help me to know when to be silent and when to speak, when to help and when to refuse. Develop in me the discretion and tact I need to be a good parent for my grown children. Amen.

Bigger Than Your Brokenness

We are so much bigger than any one life event. There isn't a person alive that hasn't experienced some form of "brokenness." The longer we live the more of life that we experience. Events that are painful in life can be a catalyst for change and they can be what inspire us to do something good and even great.

A very close friend has grieved the loss of her mother for decades. She is a wonderful and truly accomplished teacher, a daughter to be proud of, for sure. She has memories of her mother, like most of us some are great and others are not. Another friend never knew her mother as she died when she was just an infant. Now in her 60's she still grieves that loss.

Then there are mothers who have children that decided that mom was not good and not worthy and have estranged. They suffer from their own brokenness.

Each one of us comes into this world with our own strengths and weaknesses and with our own gifts and talents. We are all so unique. Some people are just wired to love and they are so good at both giving love and receiving love. Other people are natural born haters. They can easily find fault, are critical and can make a case and justify their lack of love. We are all so much bigger than holding on to hatred we are all so much bigger than our brokenness.

When I study people that are quick to judge and view the world through anger and hatred, I see where their brokenness continues on. We can change that if we want to but it takes strength and fortitude and a deep desire to move past our "list of wrongs" to a new "list of rights." We are bigger than our brokenness but only if we want it for ourselves.

As we study conflicts and anger and hatred, there is no better place to look than at some of the most poverty stricken violent neighborhoods in Baltimore City. Recently we all got a bird's eye view of a culture that wishes to destroy and abuse and break down rather than to build and to succeed. It is a culture that is rooted and often moves from generation to generation. It has become clear that throwing money at the problem is not the answer. It is deeper than all that.

Our belief system teaches us who we are and it teaches us what we are worth we all have that inside. People that value themselves, feel valued and value others are not people that destroy other people or property. Baltimore City has a segment of people and a large portion of their population that believes their brokenness is bigger than themselves. Unless or until they can believe that their life is worth more and can be better and move past their brokenness, there really won't be any significant change for the better.

Our birth rite and our genetic make-up have a lot to do with how we are wired. Are we wired to view our life with hope and with a desire to do more and do better or are we wired to respond to life and life events with anger and with hate?

So much of our make-up stems from our first years when we were formed, the years when our parents were our greatest influence. Did we have good role models? Were we loved and cared for? Were our needs met? Or did our parent's brokenness define them? Did they overcome it or did they create more of it?

Our mothers are key influencers in our life. Did they teach us well? Like most mothers my mother had her gifts and her talents and her strengths and weaknesses. Professionally she was admired and respected by many. She was an intelligent and strong woman. She also was combative at times and a classic "enabler" through most of her adult life.

My detachment from her started early. I had one therapist tell me I detached as early as 18 months. What I do believe is that she had issues with me and I had issues with her. If she wasn't my mother she would never have been in my life. I really didn't relate well to the kind of person that she was. My longing was for a mother that could give me more attention and more love and support. That wasn't the role that she played. I didn't communicate that very well and the siblings that could were easier for her to manage and to relate.

What I did learn was that I was so much more than my brokenness and that as an adult is was my job and my responsibility to fix me. It wasn't her job at all. Part of my wellness and healing was about my ability to forgive her and let it go. A loving heart doesn't coexist with a heart that has anger and hate. I was committed to love. I didn't want hurt or hatred to define me or my life.

Often we want to place blame. As a teenager I thought like a teenager. I blamed my mother for my parent's divorce when clearly it was my father that had stepped out of their marriage. Even knowing that I still chose to blame her. Then one day you grow up and you view things as a mature adult.

Some people will take the good and leave the rest behind and others will hold on to all that isn't good. For whatever reasons it must serve them well or they wouldn't be doing it.

What I know for sure is that our "brokenness" only defines us if we allow it and if we want it. We can all be so much more than our brokenness ...

Happy Mother's Day weekend to all the mother's out there! Most of us want the very best for our children and most of us did the best that we could with what we had at the time ... and for that we should all be celebrated!

Bitter or Better It Is Our Choice

Earlier today I caught up with an old friend, she is like a sister to me. She is that friend that makes me happy, she calls me out when I am wrong, supports me at my best and at my worse. She gets me and in many ways we understand each other, in many ways we are alike. In her company I am lifted up and we always learn from one another.

Today she said something to me and about me. She said. *"After everything you have been through and I could name the list, you continue to amaze me because you could be bitter and you aren't, you have one of the biggest hearts I have ever witnessed. I know a lot of people and most would be bitter but not you and your heart."*

She is right I could be bitter! She knows me well as we have been friends for 18 years now. The list is long on what I have experienced in my lifetime. Some of it is really very hateful, hurtful and unattractive. But my heart doesn't work that way. I have always viewed every single experience as something I could learn from. What was this or that supposed to teach me and by viewing everything as a learning opportunity I grew my heart bigger and I became better and not bitter.

We don't get to control what happens in our lives or what other people do but we do get to control how we choose to respond to it. I may not always be happy with the outcomes of the things that have hurt me. But I always responded with a heart and with a conscience and in a way that I could live with, this allowed me to be better and not bitter.

When we rise above it, when we are faced with adversity and heartache, our own character is tested. Real character isn't about how we handle the easy stuff in life, it is about how we handle the challenges and often it is about how we act when no one else is looking.

On reflection one of the things in my life that I am most proud of is how I handled my first husband's death and his funeral. He was previously married and divorced with two children. When he died his kids were young and still in elementary school.

When I was asked who I wanted to be in the first car with me my response was swift and heartfelt. I had his children and their mother with me. To me, it was the right thing to do. When I met him he was already divorced, his ex-wife and his children never did anything to hurt me. My view was that having them with me and close to their father was the right thing to do and it was one that I could easily live with.

The single line that has helped me the most in my life is from the book, *The Four Agreements* and I have written about it often, the quote is; **"nothing other people do is because of you, it is because of themselves."** Not only has this made sense to me but it has virtually saved me and released me from the hate and the lack of love from others. Their actions are their choices, when someone chooses to behave in a certain way that is all about them.

The people that set out to hurt other people are lacking peace and love and there is usually a good reason for that and normally it comes from what they have done and their own actions. They are living in a way that requires them to justify their behaviors. If they can make someone else look bad they can justify what they have done. This may work in the short run, but in the long run, they have to live with themselves. We may be able to fool others, but we know who we are and what we are made of, we know better than anyone else.

I have never viewed myself as a "victim" but rather as a "survivor" and this allowed me to "survive" and even thrive in the face of adversity. I have also learned that just because I have a heart and a conscience that I shouldn't necessarily expect the same from others. Some people just don't have it.

We could all be "bitter" over something if that is what we decide but we also can choose to be "better" and being "better" just feels so good and right and contributes to making us better! Given the choice I choose better over bitter every single time...

Birthday! It's My Birthday!

Another year has passed us by, where does the time go? In a few days I will celebrate yet another birthday! I am reflecting back to my childhood birthdays, young adult birthdays, milestone birthdays like "sweet 16", "18", "21", "25" and then "30", "40" and "50." They all meant something; there was a new phase to anticipate, a new era, and a different time.

My "50th" was my last big birthday and I had several cakes, parties and huge gifts! Literally a dear friend personalized a huge purple chair for me! It included significant people in my life, my dogs, my animals, my books, religion, ethnic background and more. Clearly it was a well thought out gift. I remember at least three birthday cakes that year.

Then there are other years you just want to fly under the radar. I clearly remember my 25th birthday and working really hard as a waitress, taking classes and I was already widowed and had a 4 year old daughter back then. I was sad and my mother knew it. I left her house after picking up my daughter who she was babysitting and headed to a local Chinese food restaurant. Just after we ordered our food, my mother showed up. She wanted to try and cheer me up, she knew that I wasn't happy with where I was in my life and she didn't want me to be alone.

When I look back I seldom remember the gifts I received, unless of course that huge purple personalized chair but what I recall are the memories and the people who loved me, celebrated with me and were there for me.

This year we are headed to Ft. Lauderdale, Florida to celebrate my birthday, my husband's recent birthday and our wedding anniversary all wrapped into one celebration. It won't be about the gifts, although my husband insists, but rather about creating new memories and celebrating good times with the people that love you and that you love right back.

Together we have aged and we have a greater sense of time and purpose; we know how we want to live out our remaining years. What reflect on what have we done with our lives and what do we still hope to accomplish. I have attracted so many wonderful Libra sisters through the years, female friends who share a birthday close to my own birthday.

My celebrations are like this phase in my life right now; they are quieter, more thought out and deliberate. There is an inner joy and smile that celebrates my life more internally and from a quiet peaceful place. There is much more grace in how I go about living.

And more than anything I am happy to be here, to be alive and to be making contributions to this world. Only God knows how many more birthdays I have left here on earth, but for now, it's my birthday! It's my birthday!

Boots, Books and ...

Every time the Bravo show *Watch What's Happening Live* host Andy Cohen talks about the three things he is currently obsessed with and then rattles this off, I think about what I am currently most obsessed with. Most of us are collectors, there are things that we like and admire and collect. For some people it is sports memorabilia and for others it might be art or music. I have a small salt and pepper shaker assortment that I like collecting. In the past I have collected Barbie dolls and dishes in a variety of china patterns.

I have a record collection of vinyl records that I have held on to through the years, I am told they are making a "comeback" but for me they were never out. I have fond memories of many occasions at our beach house with my husband and us just playing our vinyl albums together. We have the original *Beatles* records on Apple Records and a huge collection of *The Who* along with dozens and dozens of other artists. We like the music but they also represent our teen years when we saved our money and ran out and purchased vinyl records. He tells his stories and I tell mine and we are reminded as to why we are together and just how much that we have in common. We grew up during the same time and enjoyed being teenagers in the 70's.

Today the three things that I am obsessed with are my boots and my books and an Apple iPad application that allows me to make short clips of video film. I am having fun with the film!

The boots are amazing and I want to wear them every single day, they were a Christmas gift from my husband and something I would never have afforded for myself. I tease him that when I die please bury me with these boots on because I love them so much and quite frankly I don't want anyone else getting them. Is that bad?

Then there are my books, I collect them and I hoard them and I am kind of selfish about them too. Mostly because I like the pages to be clean and crisp. I can remember borrowing a book from the library and opening a page and finding somebody's left over "yuck" on the page and that about did it for me. Now I purchase what I want to read and I do it for two reasons; 1) to enjoy the book over and over again and 2) so that I can support the writer. As a writer myself, supporting other writers is really important to me.

So what three things are you currently obsessed with? What do they mean to you and what do you have that you love so much that you really would not enjoy sharing it?

Right now I am on a quest for Easter related salt and pepper shakers; I haven't really seen any that speak to me. I saw ones at Cracker Barrel restaurant recently but they were really small and plain. I want ones that make you smile when you look at them and yes I do share them with our guests …

My books make me happy, my boots make me happy (and keep my feet really warm and they look great) and my salt and pepper collection is both useful and decorative. Now who is next to being featured in my next home spun Apple FxGuru video?

Have fun and surround yourself with the things that you love and that make you smile and help to create memories ...

Breaking Trust

I don't think there is anything harder to overcome in any relationship than when trust has been broken. To be given someone's trust is one of the greatest gift one person can bestow upon another. To have our trust violated is one of the worst feelings. Many relationships don't and won't survive a trust that has been broken.

Babies are born with a natural ability to trust and it is the parent's job not to violate that trust. When a babies needs are met they learn attachment and to trust. The hardest lesson for an innocent person is to have trusted and then have that trust violated.

Teenagers often test the boundaries of trust in the family with their parents. Parents want to know their kids are safe and where they are and what they are doing. When a teenager lies about where they are going and who they are with, when they conceal their test grades and report cards when they choose to lie and deceive their parents, the bonds of trust are broken.

In a marriage trust can be broken when one person breaks the agreements that have been set forth in the marriage. In a work relationship trust may be broken when a supervisor cannot trust that the people they are tasked with leading are not being honest and doing the work expected of them.

There are all kinds of ways we can break trust and all relationships suffer when trust has been broken. When we can't believe someone whether a friend or a family member or a co-worker and others we must decide if the relationship is worth continuing because without trust there is no basis for the relationship to grow.

To have any kind of intimacy with another human being, we must first feel safe and know that we can trust them. Trust them to be honest, trust them not to hurt us, trust that we can share our most personal and intimate thoughts and they won't use them to their advantage and to hurt us.

Look at any relationship that has ended badly, you can almost guarantee that it broke apart because of a broken trust. When we trust another we give them the power to hurt us.

Micah 7:5-6 *"Put no trust in a neighbor; have no confidence in a friend; guard the doors of your mouth from her who lies in your arms; for the son treats the father with contempt, the daughter rises up against her mother, the daughter-in-law against her mother-in-law; a man's enemies are the men of his own house."*

My husband has often accused me of being "too trusting" and he is probably correct, I am the one that usually trusts the most and the easiest and gets hurt the most. He is trusting of very few people and only opens up to a handful of people. He is very cautious with who he trusts. He is what I call "city smart" he knows to protect himself and rarely opens up to people. I know that I know him best and I know that he trusts me. I do my best to preserve the trust we have between us. I value him and he values me. We trust each other.

I first learned to distrust in my neonatal family. I learned it from my mother and from my sisters. I learned that they couldn't be trusted and that was hard to accept and to understand but it turned out to be a truth that showed itself over and over again until I finally removed myself.

As a mother who has raised children I tried my best to instill the value of trust in our kids. Often as teenagers they tested that trust as many young people do. Then when trust was broken it had to be rebuilt or the relationship was left to suffer and deteriorate.

The only people that can really hurt you deeply are the ones that you have trusted the most. A few years ago a longtime friendship of 30 years ended abruptly. The facts are not disputed. This "friend" encouraged our then teen daughter to "lie" to us, (her parents) and to be "mysterious" with us and to set up accounts that we would not know about.

When confronted first by my husband, my friend of 30 years said, "Let me tell you about Bernadette" and tried to bad mouth me to my husband. He was smart enough to remove himself; he didn't want to hear it. When I confronted her, the response was, "You know Brian isn't the person I would have chosen for you." At this point my husband and I had been together for 20 years.

My therapist said, "She doesn't sound like a good friend" another friend said, "She has always been jealous of you and wanted what you have." Clearly something was off, I trusted her and it turned out that I should not have.

We learn that trust is fragile and that it can be broken and it can be restored but takes work to do that. What should my former friend have done when our 18 year old was acting out as most teenagers do at that age? She should have acted like a friend and a supporter of our family.

She should have told the teenager, "Kids your age have issues with their parents all the time, go home and work it out." Instead she encouraged our child to deceive us. This former friend helped to break up a family and this kid is left to suffer the consequences. And no matter what she says now, in self-preservation mode, we were supposedly "friends" for three decades so how bad of a person could I have been?

When you are close to someone you know exactly how to hurt them. You know where they are the most vulnerable. If you can fix it, fix it. If you can't fix it, you have to let it go. Sometimes trust is so broken that nothing you can do will restore the trust.

When I have hurt someone or broken trust and we all have at some time in our lives, I have done my best to make amends and make it right. Making amends isn't what we do for the other person it is what we do for ourselves. We make amends to help fix the brokenness that we ourselves have created. When we are genuinely sorry for the broken trust we have a desire to stop the hurt in another and try and restore what we ourselves broke.

It certainly is harder to trust someone again after they have shown us that our trust meant so little to them. One of the things I hear over and over in my support group for parents of estranged adult children is that they love their kids and probably always will but, "How can we ever trust them again?"

Without trust there can be no real relationship and broken trust is really hard to come back from ...

"The fundamental glue that holds any relationship together is trust." Brian Tracy

Broken People

Several years ago I was talking to a Catholic Priest and I was telling him about a little girl that I knew. I told him about her childhood trauma first at just two years of age and later when she was seven years old. After hearing about the losses and trauma she had endured by such a young age he said, *"Do the math, she is broken."* It sounded so clinical and yet it made sense to me. I hated seeing that as an adult she was still struggling and making one bad decision after another. She has a history of playing the victim and of blaming others and hasn't spent much time on her own healing. The problem is that she isn't a little girl anymore and now an adult she has impacted so many people's lives in destructive and hurtful ways do to her own brokenness. I've heard it said, **"Hurt people, hurt people."**

Not long ago I was standing just outside an elevator when three women exited the elevator. The one in the middle was being held up by the two ladies on either side of her. It didn't take but a moment to recognize that she was high and under the influence of drugs. Her front teeth were missing and her clothes were dirty, she was coming to social services for food, clothes and care. When I watched her I thought it is a beautiful warm sunny September day just after noon and without a cloud in the sky and this woman was in an altered state. She was missing out on the natural beauty of this day. I couldn't help but wonder, what happened to her?

What pain is she masking that is showing itself in her drug use? This woman was someone's daughter, sister, mother, aunt, cousin, friend, and how has her drug use impacted not just her life but the lives of the people in her family and within her friends.

A social worker was telling me that it had been reported that at any given time 1 in 6 people in America is suffering from some form of mental illness. Most people will know their share of pain and heartache and will suffer at some point in their life. But what makes a person struggle through and another turn to drugs and alcohol to medicate their pain away? How is it that some people can take their trauma and do something good with it, by sharing and helping others, and some never get past their own brokenness?

What makes a person remain a victim and another person in a similar situation become a survivor? At the end of the day, a broken person impacts all our lives by the actions that they take. They don't live in a vacuum and their actions have a ripple effect in our entire community.

I don't have the answers, all I can do is pray and thank God that when I was faced with my own trauma, hurts and losses I had enough inner strength and faith in God to push through it to the other side. No matter what we are facing, no matter how difficult, it doesn't last.

There is a new song out by **Country Music Artist Gary Allan** that is called, *"Every Storm"* and goes *"Every storm runs out of rain, just like every dark night turns into day."* For people that are suffering and struggling, I pray for them to know less dark nights and many more sunny days!

Bullies

"You just can't give people permission to wreck your life."
President Bill Clinton

This statement was made to Lisa Ling when the topic of bullies was discussed. Like so many young people, when Bill Clinton was a child he was bullied and often made fun of because of his weight. Look at how far he made it in his life? But the sad reality is many other kids don't make it and often turn to suicide to end their pain associated with being the target of unkindness and bullies.

The book, Bullies, Tyrants and Other Impossible People by Ron Shapiro addresses this subject in the business arena. There are people in our society that were bullies as kids and grow up and continue to bully their way through their adult lives and into corporate America.

Some people truly enjoy hurting others and bullying other people. Most people believe it stems from their own jealousy and insecurity. It is their way of pushing someone else down to promote themselves. When you think about that how sick is that? In order to feel good about yourself, you have to make someone else look and feel bad?

I've known my share of bullies and a few of them are in my family. They have even gone so far as to call their action and derogatory statements "love" there is nothing loving about saying unkind things about anyone and trying to push someone else down to either protect yourself from the truth or try and justify your own bad behavior.

Caleb Was Lost On the Beach

It was hot and it was so crowded on the beach that day. The weather was sunny and hot around 90 degrees and the water temps were nice at around 73 degrees. The beach was packed on this Thursday and so many people were in the water.

As I sat in my chair I noticed a little boy pass me. He was shaking both his arms and he was muttering, ***"oh no not again, oh no not again!"*** Initially I didn't know what he was talking about so I followed him with my eyes. It didn't take that much longer for me to understand that he was lost.

He was wearing blue swim trunks and he was lean and really tan skinned. He had gone about 20 feet to my right when he was moving right and then left and then right again. Clearly he was distressed. A woman stood up from her beach blanket and started talking to him. You could see he was hesitant to speak with a stranger. I watched as she convinced him to go to the lifeguard stand with her.

I decided to walk over there myself. I had witnessed where he came up from the water and my assumption was that his family had to be closer to where I was sitting than over there by this lifeguard. The female lifeguard was calm and invited him to sit up on her chair. It was there that he seemed less agitated and to calm down.

As he tried to say his name not one of us could understand him and then he spelled it, "C-A-L-E-B." When asked his age he said, "I am 8 years old." He sat for a few minutes. All in all it seemed to be about 7 to 10 minutes had passed from the moment when I first noticed him.

All I could think was "where are this kids parents?" and "don't they notice their child is missing?" Then Caleb stood straight up in the lifeguard chair and I saw him wave his arms. He bends down to jump off when a man came and took him by the hand. The other lady and I walked back to our own place on the beach. I kept Caleb in my eyesight though. The first guy was calm and didn't seem to mind that Caleb was missing but once he got to the left of my beach chair another man gave him a good scolding and clearly he wasn't happy with him. He stood there and looked so hurt and so sad. He looked so small.

Minutes later I watched as Caleb now had both arms wrapped tightly around a woman and she was holding him just as tight in return. It must have been "mom" I thought. Then I watched him cry and cry. He cried those kind of sobbing body moving tears. His tears brought me to my own tears. Thank God Caleb was returned to his family and nothing bad had happened to him, I thought to myself.

Just after witnessing Caleb's reunion I started to think about those high anxiety times I had known with my own children.

There was a time when one of then went crabbing and didn't return on time. I remember walking to the crab docks and finding them and first came that relief then anger for the anxiety that I had gone through. Then another child said they were going to the community pool and when I went to check up on them, the lifeguards said, "They haven't been here all day."

My children are all raised now and we no longer have to worry about an 8 year old walking off or away from us at the beach. But every parent knows that feeling that moment when we can't locate our child and the fear and the panic set in on us.

After watching Caleb reunite with his mother I had a nice long cry, I cried for him, his parents, their reunion and all those other kids that never find their way back home. Caleb was lucky he may have been lost on the beach that day but ultimately he did find his way back home to the very people who loved him like only family really can love him. So many other kids get lost and never make it back home.

When I thought about it, all the right people came to his aid, no one had a dark or evil thought, I thought what if he was taken by someone who was evil and had their own motives. Caleb wasn't my child but in that moment in time he was every mother's child and every single mother's worst fear. Thank God he was found and thank God he was returned safely back to his own family.

Carpe Diem Seize the Day

A close friend said she learned this from me, Carpe Diem to seize the day! And I learned it from my first husband Randy Moyer who died when I was just 23 years old. It was in his dying that I was taught to live and to live fully. People and places will come and they will go from our lives, what we have is our life and in my living the desire to live my life to the fullest and best use.

What we know for certain is that not one of us will escape death, we have a limited amount of days here on earth, and the question is how do we want to spend those days?

"Waiting for the fish to bite or waiting for wind to fly a kite. Or waiting around for a Friday night or waiting perhaps for their Uncle Jake or a pot to boil or a better break or a string of pearls or a pair of pants or a wig with curls or another chance. Everyone is just waiting." Dr. Seuss

I've never been good at waiting, I always wanted it now so I could move on to doing the next thing, whatever the next thing is and was for me. I tested out as a "project" person and not a "maintenance" person. Some people can just grind it out day after day, my thrill and my skills were about the heavy lifting.

What could I do with what I had to move on to the next stage of growth and development. How could I keep challenging myself and continue to move forward. Waiting always seemed like death to me. Inaction is what I could and would do when I could no longer live and in my death.

Yesterday I celebrated my birthday, one of the best ones ever, the real take away though was my birth, my life and what do I want to do with what time I have left to live. Seize the day!

I accepted a new challenge in the workplace, a tab bit out of my element in location however the mission to support the most vulnerable of our society drives me forward. In my ability to use my writing skills, and to tell a compelling story in just a few weeks I wrote a grant. It won't be the biggest grant request I have ever written, however it is one that will fill a need. Taking the day and a cause and our own skill set and using them to do well is what carpe diem means to me. It means use this time and this day to make a difference, however big, however small, make a difference in this day and in the world.

There are things in life I never thought would happen and they did and other things I never knew could happen and they happened too. Good things and bad things. I've learned to live life as though I was preparing a meal, what ingredients do I have and how can I best combine them to make something wonderful.

In Randy's death and for my husband Brian, in his wife Stacey's death, we both learned how to live fully. We celebrate everything!

In the fall, it could be as simple as celebrating the abundance of apples by making apple pies. During the holidays like birthdays and Christmas it could be travelling to places that we love, like Nashville and Key West. We can watch a movie, read a book and have a conversation and be fully engaged and seize the day! It doesn't have to be grand or be expensive, it is about taking what we have and what we know and making the most of it.

"The important thing is not how many years in your life but how much life in your years." Edward J. Stieglitz

Caveat Emptor, Let the Buyer Beware

We seem to be living in a time where there is no margin for error. Failure used to be the pathway to success; if you failed at least you were trying. Today we leave little or no room for error. We want guarantees that the purchase or the acquisition will be a good one and that it will be a success.

But the reality is that we never know what we have purchased or what we have gotten ourselves into until we are on the inside.

Years ago, when you purchased a home, it was "caveat emptor" let the buyer beware but today we want to hold the seller responsible for what they knew or what they should have known. I imagine when I purchase a honeydew melon or a cantaloupe that it will be good once I cut inside it. However, I am also aware that I won't really know what is inside that melon until I actually do cut it open.

Buying a home can be risky business; you really don't know what goes on in a house until you live in it. Even new home construction does not guarantee that the house will be problem free. You can purchase all the certificates and inspections money will buy and even that does not guarantee or keep you risk free.

Several years ago I purchased a new home and part of the inspection was a standard termite inspection. Inspection was completed and clean, came out with no problems. Imagine my upset when just before moving into this home, I had the carpeting taken up only to reveal that the hardwood floors had been eaten away by termites. There were 4-rows of hardwood flooring that were gone. Termite damage!

When I called the inspection company, their response, "we only guarantee accessible areas." The whole house had hardwood floors and 80% of it was carpeted. Therefore 80% was not "accessible." What value or guarantee did that termite inspection certificate really hold?

Relationships can be the same way, you never really know what you are getting until you peel back the layers and can see inside. Recently I was chatting with two young girls who are just 20 years old. They went to school together from elementary school and forward, they vacationed together. Their families were close. They were really good girlfriends. Then they had a falling out when a third friend entered their circle. Later and for a short time all three girls lived together. During that time, it was discovered that the third friend was the catalyst between the first two friends and their many years of feuds.

It took getting them all together, in a living together environment, before they could uncover the root of the problem. Once discovered they sent the third girlfriend on her way. It turned out she was pitting both sides against one another for her own gain. She had no boundaries and betrayed one of the friends before it all came out into the open.

Sometimes we think we have purchased one thing or acquired a new relationship only to uncover it wasn't what we thought it would be. Let the buyer beware or "caveat emptor" is principle in commerce: without a warranty the buyer takes the risk.

Every day we make purchases or we go places and it is a leap of faith, we truth that what we have purchased or where we are scheduled to go will be a good thing. We do our best to pick that perfect melon. We want one that is ripe but not overly ripe. We want to know that it will taste good. The truth is we have no guarantee that it will be what we are looking for until we can open it up.

The same can be said for raising our children, we invest heavily in them, and we hope and pray for the best results. But the bottom line is there is no guarantee, same for our friends and our spouses. We do our best to uncover what we are getting, is this good, is this right and we do our due diligence. In the end there is no real way to know.

So let the buyer beware, "caveat emptor" and uncover what you can, learn all that you can and in the end you have to lean on a certain amount of faith. Because no matter what knowledge you obtain, whatever you uncover, or don't, it's called life, and life doesn't come with a guarantee.

Centered In the Silence of Our Hearts

Being centered and listening to the silence of our hearts can be challenging when we are living a full life. There is chaos and noise and chatter all around us. This voice and that voice chiming In and often it is truly difficult to remain centered with so much outside of ourselves going on.

"Somewhere we know that without silence words lose their meaning, that without listening speaking no longer heals, that without distance closeness cannot cure." Henri Nouwen

I think it is more important than ever to "retreat" and take time for silence. Listen to that inner voice that knows what is best. It is easy to get caught up in causes and in other people stuff and the drama we see everywhere around us.

Prayer, meditation, alone time, quiet time all can aid us and take us back to our center our core being. Just as Jesus retreated to the desert for 40 days before beginning his public ministry, we often need to retreat to regain our own focus. Retreating can help after a hardship or in times of question to allow us to find our center again.

From No Greater Love by Mother Teresa

Silence of our eyes
Silence of our ears
Silence of our mouths
Silence of our minds
… in the silence of the heart
God will speak

"We need to find God, and he cannot be found in noise and restlessness. God is the friend of silence. See how nature – trees, flowers, grass-grows in silence; see the stars, the moon and the sun, how they move in silence … We need silence to be able to touch souls." Mother Teresa

What do you need to do so that you may hear the silence of your own heart? What aids you in becoming centered?

Children of a Greater God

Over the past several years I have spent numerous hours around kids with special needs, kids with emotional and educational challenges. One of the things that stood out after observing so many of them is how happy they appear to be in person. Some of the most loving and huggable adults and children are with special needs like autism. At a distance they may seem to be in a world of their own and yet they are content in that world. Few of them are interested in maliciously hurting anyone.

Many artists and painters have been diagnosed with a disability, so often attention deficit disorders are with some of the brightest and most artistic people. So much great music and art is born of pain. Often it is a result of suffering that shows itself in lyrics and paintings that resonate with people.

Raising children is one of the most selfless acts anyone of us will go through, as a parent you have to be willing to put your children ahead of yourself. Kids have immediate needs and can and will pull at our heartstrings like no one else. I had a teacher once who made the analogy that raising children is like planting a garden. Each plant needs water, light and proper nutrition.

Some plants are sturdy and stable and can withstand the elements some are seasonal, an annual and others perennials. Perennials come back year after year, sometimes with less vigor and other years with a greater presence. Gardens need to be weeded and guided too. Some seeds take and grow like crazy and other seeds never take root at all.

I have witnessed kids that have difficulty with verbal communication and still they can read and write masterfully. There are kids that have come into this world missing a limb or with poor vision or hearing and yet overcome these obstacles and are quite successful in life. Then there are kids that are born healthy and whole but life has beaten them up and they crash and burn. Some take their pain and turn it around and make good of it. I truly believe that God made these children with greatness in mind. They are supposed to do something good with their disability or challenging life circumstances.

Last week I met "Ann" she is an adult social worker who works with rape victims and sexual assault victims. Ann wasn't raped but she is the product of a rape.

Of course my first few questions were, "What was your relationship like with your mother? Did she love you? Did she hate you?" Ann responded with, "I was so loved by my mother" she further stated, "It was my own stuff, my own feelings that I had to reconcile." When working with a rape victim Ann often becomes a target for their anger. They tell her, "You don't know what it is like to be raped" her response is to tell them, "I am a product of rape." In time, Ann gets their attention and their respect.

Ann knows she could just as easily have been an abortion but her mother wanted her and loved her. Ann was the one who made poor choices when she was just a teenager; she pressed all boundaries and acted out in numerous ways. Her mother never wanted to tell her but Ann was insistent on learning about her biological father. She wasn't prepared for all that she uncovered. At one point Ann knew she was at a crossroads, was she going to play the victim or was she going to turn it around and use it to help other victims.

Today, as a seasoned social worker Ann knows how devastating it can be to be a victim of sexual assault, she is compassionate but she is tough on the survivors that she counsels. One person can see devastation and other people see opportunities for greatness. There is a reason why things happen the way that they do.

So many times we look at someone with a disability or with educational and emotional challenges and we look away or thank God it's not us. When you sit and listen and talk with kids and with people that seem to have less, perhaps when we look close enough we can see God in action. Many of these children truly can be seen through the lenses of Children of a Greater God. They have so much to offer and when we learn to remove "dis" and appreciate "ability" we can help to facilitate their God given greatness.

Christmas Past

Our Christmas past, we all have them, the childhood ones and the young adult ones and then the adult Christmas past too. Some Christmas holidays stand out more than others. I will never forget the year I lived at my grandparent's hotel when I was just seven years old, because my mother went back to nursing school to finish and secure her degree.

My parents came bearing gifts, and that year it was so special. I got the Barbie doll I wanted and her pink convertible car. Yes! I was a Barbie doll girl and proud of it! That's not all Barbie and I have in common, we were both born in 1959.

Most of the Christmas holidays that I recall as a child have fond memories like the year my mother bought us all bicycles. Five daughters received five bicycles! And we were thrilled to have them. When I was a young teen we lived walking distance from our church. Christmas was celebrated by attending midnight Mass and then coming home to a feast of Italian pasta and the seven fishes. We always had ribbon candy and Italian nougat candies in the house.

I also remember one of the first Christmas holidays after my dad first left home. He had a new girlfriend and it showed. He was never one for shopping and I received many gifts that year including my first "shoulder bag" a purse that I had asked for, my mother was miserable and dad seemed to have found some new joy in his life.

Most parents remember the first Christmas after being a new mom and dad and I have clear recall of that as well. I also remember 1992 when Brian and I first came together merging two families to become one. My gift that year still hangs proudly in our living room; it is cast paper art of a "Mother and Child." We were deliriously happy to have found one another and to have united as one family.

Then the "red turtleneck" year when all five of us dressed in red turtlenecks in front of our Christmas tree for the family photo used to adorn our Christmas cards that year. We also all shared in a hefty case of the flu and the tree never got fully decorated nor did the refrigerator full of food get eaten. We survived though and we survived all together as one family.

When our oldest daughter left home it was time to forge new traditions and staying home didn't feel quite the same without her. So we went to Delaware and created a new beach house Christmas and years later we would travel. First to overnights at the Hershey Hotel and then days through the holidays at The Gaylord Opryland Hotel in Nashville and also Key West Florida Christmas holidays.

During all those years we had two big careers and often worked right up to the holiday and then off we went. The four of us, two parents and their twin children enjoying numerous holidays at holiday destinations where we took in amazing decorations, theater, Christmas concerts and wonderful holiday meals together. We were together and very much a loving family of four.

I can't say that I had that many "bad" Christmas holidays; there were a few though, like the year my 5-year relationship with Michael ended and he bought me a file cabinet as a Christmas gift? Yep the romance was gone and he was trying to support me as I entered my Real Estate career. I was beyond hurt and not ready to let go.

Or that first Christmas after I came back from Florida to Maryland, I had gone away for a year to make sense of so much pain and upset in my life and in my family. My long term relationship with Michael ended just after I found out there was a sex abuser who married into our family. He had damaged our family beyond repair and I was both bitter and angry.

That year I grew stronger and came back home to begin again. It was a Christmas when I was waiting for my commission checks and had no money for Christmas shopping. I roasted a chicken for my daughter and myself, went to Mass exchange the few gifts I had for her and then couldn't wait to fall asleep so that I could wake up and have Christmas behind us. My family was so gone from us, and the pain was excruciating. I couldn't do anything to fix it either. I knew what they chose to deny.

When you have a sad Christmas it certainly makes you appreciate all the good and exciting ones all the more. But when we strip it down Christmas is about love and peace. Those heartbreaking Christmas pasts were void of both love and peace.

Today we have so much love and peace in our home. We are so thankful for what we have and what we share together. Peace is something that lives inside of us and not predicated upon what anyone else says or does.

Sometimes we remember the gifts we received and the places where we celebrated, but I think for most of us we remember who we were with that helped to celebrate and make it so special. Our Christmas pasts are memories that we can cherish always.

No one knows what lies ahead for us, what this Christmas will look like compared to our next Christmas. Or what a difference one year can and will bring. We have no way of knowing who we will have lost and we will have gained in just a year from now. I suspect that is why we need to stand in the moment and take it all in, this Christmas is here and upon us and it won't take long before it is also a memory and nothing more than yet another Christmas past.

Merry Christmas! Enjoy every blessed moment for it all passes far too quickly …

Comfort and Care

Women are notorious for being the caregivers and nurturers, as a group we typically think about everyone else before ourselves. We give to our partners, our children, our friendships and our homes. We love loving and caring and to give.

There is nothing wrong with being the giver; I have often said, "Giving is for the giver."

But how do we care for and comfort ourselves? What do we do to soothe ourselves and our own self-care? What are you doing for yourself?

Some of my favorites include;

Long hot bubble baths

One piece of really good chocolate

A mani-pedi with hot stone massage

Walking on the beach

Cuddling up with a great book or a good movie

Fresh cut flowers in one of my favorite crystal vases

Sitting in the sun

Beach walks or bike ride

My favorite music as loud as I want to listen to it

Writing, re-writing, writing and re-writing

Really fresh fruits and berries

Quiet time for prayers, meditation and reflection

Playtime with my handsome husband

One of one time with a good friend over a meal or a cocktail

Time with my two little pooches

Gardening

Taking time for myself and caring for myself always makes me a better wife and mother, a better friend and a more successful career woman. Time for just myself makes me happy!

Invest in yourself and everyone around you benefits too ...

Confession Good for the Soul and the Heart and Maybe a Few Laughs Too

After my mother died in April of 2011 I received an e-mail from a former Priest friend of our family and of my mother. They too had become estranged through the years. He found me on the internet, looking for me and thinking that perhaps, I may have died. When he read my mother's obituary he was confused knowing quite well that she had five daughters and not just the four that were named in her obituary.

We have been communicating for almost two years now and a few days ago, we finally caught up in person. He has wanted to see me, I felt like I had done the work and was as over it as I could be. I had enough counseling, support, friends, clergy and love around me. And the universal conclusion was it wasn't about me. It was decades of lies, cover ups and scapegoating. The lies, the biggest fact, that my family would go so far and try and rewrite history by denying that my mother ever even gave birth to me.

On the ride to meet with him I decided I was going to ask for a full-fledged, "confession" sans church and any walls between us. I was certain he wanted to minister me and I was going to let him.

He obliged me and when I finished confessing my sins, he asked, **"Is that all you got?"** We laughed and I thought about it and replied, **"Yeah that's pretty much it."** After receiving my penance I smirked and he looked at me with a question on his face, I said, **"That's what I pray every single day, Is that all YOU got?"** And together we both laughed out loud.

What I couldn't have known ahead of time was how much he had aged and that he was in youth and family ministry where sexual abuse had occurred. The demise of his relationship with my mother was very similar to mine. He was aware of another victim. When he tried to communicate this to my mother, she lashed back at him, by accusing him of being a drunk a womanizer and projecting onto her husband what Catholic Priests have a documented history of doing to young boys. He had no choice but to walk away from her.

His story was much more like mine than I could ever have imagined. If you came to my mother, came bearing the truth, any bad news and challenged my mother, you would pay dearly.

We didn't spend our time together by bashing my mother and his former friend though, but rather trying to understand how someone so bright could and would stand blindly by her husband who was accused of sexually abusing children.

Sometimes you forget things then something triggers a memory. When I was just a little kids either late elementary school or perhaps middle school we invited one of my friends from our neighborhood to join us on family vacation to the Jersey shore. Diane had lost her mother to cancer and she came along with us to the beach. My mother had invited a male friend of hers to join us. It was during this trip that my mother's adult male friend tried to sexually abuse my girlfriend. My mother had to go home and report him and tell my friend's father about the sexually abuse attempt.

I can't help but wonder what it was about my mother that she was repeatedly attracted to these kinds of men, was she herself sexually abused as a child?

It's amazing what lengths people will go to cover up for a child molester and how they point outward instead of looking at their own role in the cover up. What it must have been like for my mother to know on some level the truth about her own husband and her position in refusing to acknowledge the abuse and in turn to support the victims.

By the time Father and I were able to meet up I was over it. They are dead and with God now, perhaps they have confessed their own sins. I can't worry about that or any remaining family members that choose to live in denial.

I know how blessed I am, I know that years ago I would have given just about anything to have an ally like Father, someone who knew what I knew and who tried like I did and who was just as hurt as I was.

Before we parted company we prayed together, we prayed for all those affected by sexual abuse, we prayed for the families of both the abused children and those adults that sexually abuse. Our last prayer was for my mother, who had so many wonderful gifts and talents. I couldn't square the negative things she has said and done to hurt me, her own daughter and to discredit me, but I could try and understand how someone who always had to be right, would have such a hard time accepting that they were so very wrong.

Crazy for Coconuts!

Always loved coconut in candy and cookies and coconut cake but now we have the health benefits of coconut in coconut water and coconut oil.

Coconut oil benefits hair care, skin care, stress relief, cholesterol level maintenance, weight loss and helps to regulate our metabolism. It has been said to provide relief from kidney problems, heart diseases, high blood pressure and cancer and more.

Coconut water has more potassium than four bananas and it super hydrating. It is often a base for all kinds of smoothies and energy drinks.

I recently found a coconut product that I just love and it not only works great on my hair but is much less expensive than the argon oil products that I was using. Can't say enough good things about Organix Hydrating Coconut oil spray. It is weightless and makes my hair look healthier and feel healthier. I am crazy for coconuts!

Creative Hands, Handmade With Love

I have always had a deep appreciation for most anything made by hand; I believe I can feel the gift of love through those creations. It could be homemade pasta noodles, or special tea cookies or a knitted scarf or afghan.

In 1978 Mamie Moyer, my first husbands grandmother gave me a gift that she handmade. It is the most beautiful ivory colored afghan. She loved me from the very beginning and told her grandson, *"This is a good woman, take good care of her!"* That afghan was given to me in Allentown Pennsylvania 35 years ago and I have as much love and value it today as I did back then.

That cherished ivory afghan moved from Allentown, PA to Beaumont, TX to Timonium, MD, to Carney, MD to Ft. Lauderdale, FL, Sparks, MD and for the past 21 years Lutherville, MD. Where I went, it went! She also gave me a handwritten recipe for her famous sour cream pound cake. I cherish the recipe just like her handwriting on that recipe card.

My grandmother Ida Totani gave me several knit and crochet pieces that I have treasured through the years. It was September of 1980 just one month before my daughter was born that my grandmother gave me the most beautiful hand knit white Christening gown and coat with a matching cap and booties for my baby shower. Not that long ago I had it preserved and framed. It was beautiful 32 years ago and means even more to me today.

Mamie Moyer lived until her late 90's and my Grandmother Totani until the age of 101, their handmade gifts of love will live on long after they did and God willing long after my own passing. They are items to be treasured. I have several knit afghans and crochet pieces from my grandmother too. These gifts were made from her creative hands and the love still bleeds through the yarns. There is nothing they could have ever purchased for me that came from a store that would have been as treasured.

For Christmas this year my friend Joy gave me a beautiful knit scarf that she created with her own hands, I can feel the love. And over the summer my friend Jon gifted me a handmade rosary, there is something so special about the creative hand that can make things, gifts that feel like love and are so valued and cherished.

Recently my husband and I enjoyed homemade Pappardelle noodles; this was the best plate of spaghetti we have ever eaten. In being Italian, we know our pasta and this pasta was homemade and made with pride and much love.

I love handmade soaps and handmade candles. There is nothing like homemade from scratch cookies, cakes and baked goods. There is something so special that comes from the creative process and the handwork of an artisan from the cheese maker to the jewelry maker and beyond.

Creating something and using our hands to create and to build pleases God and gives us a sincere sense of accomplishment. Celebrate your own creative gifts and support the creations of those that create with their heart and soul and in items where you can just feel the love. Appreciating creative hands; and all things made with love …

Dads and Daughter's

It has been said that the dad is the first love for many girls and how they relate to their father often reflects on how they relate to all the men in their life. I always got along with my dad and I can't remember a single fight with him. I can also say that I have a great marriage and many wonderful men in my life that are my friends. So from where I sit that statement concerning girls and their dads and how it shows itself in how they relate to all the men in their life is 100 percent true.

I loved my dad and I love men! I think it is because they are typically "drama free" and don't play games. They cut off that which doesn't work for them and often don't look back after making their decisions. When I was a Realtor I was told by a colleague, "you do business like a man." To me that was a compliment since I didn't play games and looked at the goal and what the best approach was in getting there.

My dad and I were really close when I was a little kid. Initially I was the son that he never had and I was his namesake. I was a tagalong and often sat at bars alongside of him. We both dressed in jeans and jean jackets and I loved driving with him in his Jeep. He was a tough guy and a manly man. He was a two term Korean War veteran. He loved women and women loved him. When I was just thirteen years old, I worked in the same hospital that he did, when I went to lunch I would see him sitting at a table filled with women. I would chuckle, I had to laugh. He was always surrounded by women and would have seven girls before he finally had a son.

When I started driving I often went to visit him and his second wife. As a teenager, I found refuge in his home, my mother and my sisters and I never really got along. For years dad opened his doors to me. He was the first male to ever tell me that I was "beautiful" and although he never criticized my dating choices I do recall one time when I was dating someone that I introduced him to, and he asked me, "Have you been wearing your glasses?" That was the most I ever got as far as criticism and I heard him loud and clear.

My father gave me away when I married and carted me away from the cemetery when I had to bury my first husband. I never doubted his love for me. I saw what he did with his own life and I grew to understand his demons and his own personal struggles and battles. He was "old school."

I was happy that my father had a chance to know my second husband before he died; I know that he was happy with my choice and both my husband and my father seemed to like one another. Dad was many things he was a carpenter by trade, an artist, an engineer, a husband and a father to 8 children. He had five daughters with my mother before they divorced.

He did many things honorably and his demon was alcohol which he eventually beat. At the end of his life he died at home and with his dignity and never wanting to be a burden to anyone. He made peace with all the people that mattered to him. I will always be thankful for our last few visits and the two precious pieces of his artwork that hand in my home.

My father being there for me as a young girl translated into me finding a great husband who would also be there for me as a grown woman. I don't know that most men fully understand the importance of the father-daughter relationship and how it transfers into all other male-female relationships for the daughter.

This Father's Day I am reflecting on the love that I shared with my father and all the many influences that he was in my life. By far the biggest one was that he was there and never turned away from me, he never denied me his love. And today I have a husband that is there and never turns away from me, or denies me his love. I don't think it is a coincidence but rather a reflection on the dad and daughter bond that I was afforded as a child, thanks to you dad!

Dance Dance Dance

"I danced in the morning when the world begun
And I danced in the moon and the stars and the sun
And I came down from heaven and I danced on the earth

At Bethlehem I had my birth

Dance, then, wherever you may be;
I am the Lord of the Dance, said he
And I'll lead you all wherever you may be
And I'll lead you all in the dance said he

I danced for the scribe and the Pharisee,
But they would not dance and the would not follow me
I danced for the fishermen, for James and John;
They came to me and the dance went on

I danced on the Sabbath when I cured the lame,
The holy people said it was a shame;
They whipped and they stripped and they held me high;
And they left me there on a cross to die.

I danced on a Friday and the sky turned black;
It's hard to dance with the devil on your back;
They buried my body and they thought I'd be gone,
But I am the dance and I still go on.

They cut me down and I leapt up high,
I am the life that'll never, never die;
I'll live in you if you live in me;
I am the Lord of the Dance, said he."
Lyrics by Sydney Carter (1963)

"Dance like no one is watching.
Love like you'll never be hurt.
Sing like no one is listening.
Live like it's heaven on earth." William Purkey

When was the last time, you just turned up the music and danced, danced like no one was watching?

Be the dance and just go on, just dance, dance, dance ...

Dear Estranged Adult Sons and Daughters,

This open letter is for you. For almost 17 years now my child has been estranged from me. At one point she was the absolute love of my life. I would have died for her, period. I wanted more for her than what I ever wanted for myself. When she was growing up many friends shared with me that they wished they had the kind of relationship we shared. I really believed we were close, very close. I never dreamt that one day she would walk away and never turn back. Nor did I ever comprehend her hatred and deep desire to hurt me. More than 15 years into the estrangement and she still tries to hurt me.

When children are little they are easy and often their love for us comes easily. When they grow up they begin to judge us. I can say that I have letters in my child's own handwriting that told me how much she loved me. I can say that she attended numerous proms and the one time I could not go to the dress shop with her, she shared this dialogue with me; "Mom all my friends were bringing me dresses, lots of dresses and none of them were right for me. Then I asked myself "what would my mom do?" and "I knew that you would look for an ivory colored gown and as soon as I realized that, I immediately found the perfect gown in ivory."

I share this because it was unsolicited when she shared this with me. My sense was that although I had to work and couldn't make the appointment she had at the dress shop with her girlfriends, I was in essence there with her!

For more than 23 years I was estranged from my own mother. What did my mother do to me that I felt this was an appropriate thing to do? It was confided in me that my mother's husband was a sexual abuser. I believed the child that shared this and I never wanted my children around him after this information was made known to me. My mother didn't want to hear it or to believe it. It was easier for her to make me out to be a bad person rather than face the truth about the man that she married and stayed married to until he died. She loved him above all else. I was eliminated from the family. And I made it easy for her to do this by walking away.

Regardless of how justified I thought I was in removing myself and my children, this was not an ideal situation. I was angry and I was hurt and I was disappointed in my mother. This lasted for many years until I came to peace and acceptance. We never reconciled before she died. My sisters would decide to delete my existence from her obituary. Today I have more peace than ever before, I know that she knows the truth now.

Regardless of the details of my story I am here to tell you that there are no winners in estrangement. As justified as you may believe that you are in estranging from your parents, it is not healthy. It is not normal. It is not an act of love. If anything it is an act of intolerance.

The saddest thing for you is that if you have children, no matter their ages and or how close you may be at this time, by virtue of the fact that you have chosen this, you have now modeled behavior for your own children. They are very likely to dismiss you from their lives the same way they have witnessed you do it to your mother and/or father. Believe it. Case studies support this.

What you are in essence modeling for your own children is that 1) parents aren't important and can be easily erased from your life 2) disrespect 3) silent treatment 4) judgment 5) lack of tolerance and lack of forgiveness. What you are losing is your roots, your family history and heritage. If you are a biological child you miss out on your family health history. Your children are missing out on knowing their family and their grandparents. Lost years can never be made up.

I believe that most all parents love their children. Maybe it isn't perfect but they aren't perfect and neither are you. No one is perfect.

If you are estranged because of what you have done you should try and make amends before they die. As bad as it may be, most mothers and fathers are loving toward their children. If you do the work and fix what you broke they will probably at least try and forgive you. And if for some reason they can't at least you will know that you tried.

Like many of you I have other relationships that I created through the years, I have "other mothers" and "other children" that I have loved and have loved me too. They have helped me to heal and to fill many of the voids. But the reality is that no one can take the place of our birth parents. That history cannot be re-written. And our children come from us. They are a part of our being and our souls and our hearts are forever connected.

Do you need to be "right?" or do you need "peace?" Loving ourselves allows us to love others, loving our parents is an extension of self-love because whether you like it or not, that is where you come from.

No one said that you have to see them every day, no one said you have to speak with them every day but having peace with your parents is what you do for yourself. Remember one day your child will grow up and they too will judge you. Could you measure up to the same yardstick you have chosen to use to measure mom and dad? Would you want your grown adult child treating you the same way that you have chosen to treat your parents?

It's not over until we take our last breathe. Making peace with your parents is making peace with yourself. Forgiveness is the gift that you give to yourself!

Make 2015 the year of love and of forgiveness and watch how much better your life becomes when you aren't holding onto anger or ill will toward others.

Peace and love,

Bernadette A. Moyer

Bernadette on Facebook at www.facebook.com/bernadetteamoyer

Or e-mail and connect at bmoyer37@aol.com

Dear Parents of Estranged Adult Children,

This open letter is in response to the many e-mails that I receive asking for my help and my insight into estrangement. Most often the person writing to me has read my P.E.A.C.E. Parents of Estranged Adult Children Everywhere located on my website Bernadette A. Moyer at www.bernadetteamoyer.com

Just this week I received two heartfelt e-mails from parents in pain that are dealing with the aftermath from their adult children and their estrangement. Most often the estrangement includes taking the grandbabies and grandchildren with them.

Where I am not an expert I have experienced estrangement on both sides. My mother didn't speak to me for 23 years. My crime I conveyed a message I received from a child who stated that my mother's husband was sexually abusing them. I believed the child, my mother and all family members did not.

As a teenager my child would walk out of my life. Our estrangement is now 15 years in the making. She would write her college essay about me calling me many wonderful things, a month later when I said "no" I went from "awesome" and "amazing" to an "abuser." I have numerous letters in her own handwriting stating how wonderful a mother I once was to her.

You can't make this stuff up …

What I say to all that contact me, first and foremost I am so sorry. There is no greater pain than to have a child that you raised and loved and adored turn on you and/or walk out of your life for good. I immediately encourage them to try everything humanly possible to work it out. I sincerely believe that it is not in the best interest of the adult child nor the parent to be estranged. I don't believe that it is normal or natural for either side.

Only after every attempt has been made to have a mutually respectful relationship do you stop and save yourself. Many times the number one complaint shared with me is that parents are accused of "stalking" these adult children. I immediately have to laugh for two reasons 1) my child still accuses me of this even though I have not seen or heard from her in 15 years and 2) a normal loving parents loves their child and wonders about them and how they are doing.

I did everything humanly possible to reach out to my child. There was and is nothing on the face of this earth that will "fix" what issues she has with me. I have come to believe that she believes her own "story" which is a far cry from what happened and how I lived it and remember it.

As a teenager children do not have fully formed brains. It is a fact and yet at 18 they are legally allowed to make adult decisions. Where most teenagers go through a period of hating their parents, it is the immature ones that stay stuck in that hatred. Obviously for whatever reasons it serves them well. The must be getting something out of it or they wouldn't do it. It might be for people to feel sorry for them or to help them and often is about manipulating people to do things for them.

Once you have accepted that there is no other way, you must save yourself! There is life after the grief, after the heartache and after the disappointment. It isn't easy and it doesn't happen overnight. It took more than a decade for me to declare "enough!"

I am so much better off without the drama and being the target of hatred. Finally after more than I can share here the bonds once held are no longer in existence. It is now me the parent that is finished. I have written my obituary and I have made my final requests for my death very well-known and documented.

When it is over it is over! If you can repair or restore your relationship with your adult child, you should put all efforts into doing so and if it can't be repaired or restored you have to let go of it.

Letting go with love and giving her back to God who gave her to me in the first place, is my final act of love. Once again I gave her what she wanted and she won. But in the final analysis I finally learned to save myself and to create a full rewarding life without her. There is life after children. There have been numerous recent studies that show having kids is not all that it is anticipated to be and often does NOT create a more meaningful, rewarding or peaceful life.

You can find me on Facebook at
www.Facebook.com/bernadetteamoyer

The number one take away is that you are not alone! Many others are experiencing the same loss and heartache. Find a support group, or a support person, it helps.

God's Peace and Prayers,

Bernadette

Death in the Family

It seems like a death in the family is when the family nuts become even nuttier. Its official my husband and I are without parents as they are all deceased now. His father John was the last to go. His mother died first and then my father and my mother before his dad recently passed too.

My first experience with death was at 23 years of age when my first husband died. I was so humbled and my heart was huge, I included everyone. In my vulnerability my heart grew. I have come to believe that I am either really naive or just big hearted, perhaps a bit of both. I had this idea that death should make you find your heart and that there is no greater time to be in sync with our hearts than when we have lost someone to death.

For a fleeting moment I thought that when my mother passed it would be a time for all her children to come together. She had five daughters and I had been estranged for more than two decades.

When she died I thought maybe the sisters would come together but that was really short lived when her obituary was published naming her four daughters and I was excluded. That doesn't happen by accident. And not so long after her passing they would come together and write nasty letters to my employer(s) and others. They weren't involved with me for several decades, but they felt they had a right to try and hurt me. What they did was affirm for me as to why they weren't in my life.

When my dad died he made sure he had peace and called all his children together. My husband was holding his mother's hand when she departed this life. It was during this time that his father asked him to handle his affairs when his time came.

Unfortunately he didn't have a will since he never owned a car or a home or other property. One of his sisters would decide that she should handle their father's affairs and so rather than fight her; he reluctantly agreed and handed over all important papers including the life insurance. What his father wanted handled peacefully his sister made a court case over, and my husband let go of her fight.

Now that his father has passed all other family members are fighting within themselves and trying to bring my husband along with them.

The truly sad part is that this is not what his father wanted, he wanted his affairs handled. He had already secured a plot and had paid for the opening and the closing so that he could be put to rest with his beloved wife of over 55 years. He had insurance and it should have been a smooth and easy transition.

When people die, we should find our hearts but so often family members will lead with their egos and use the death for their final act of hate, anger and jealousy over their other siblings and their family members.

I have witnessed aggressive hate filled responses within families when a parent dies. I have witnessed it in my family and in other families. It seems like death in the family can bring out the best in people or the absolute worst in them.

I have also witnessed families that respected their parent's wishes, allowed the adult child they named to handle their affairs and their departure from this life with dignity and with unity so that all the family could grieve and grieve in peace.

How we welcome life and how we say good-bye to those that mattered to us, says much about us but it also says a lot about how we loved. Did we show them that we respected or disrespected their final wishes? Did we come together in love and show respect?

The good news for my husband is that he is a man of faith and a God believing man, he knows that John is reunited with Marie in heaven and knowing this affords him all the peace he will ever need. He was a great son to his father and his father was always so proud of him and his many accomplishments.

His father would also be pleased that rather than fight with his family he chose to walk away, take the high road and be better than all that.

Death in the family stirs up much in the family, sadly not all of it is good, but in the final analysis we have to live with our actions and our own decisions and make our own peace ...

Denied

Just before my father died he shared with me that one of his daughters, my sister sent him an announcement to her wedding. Although he was not invited to attend his daughter's wedding. A friend is distraught because she is estranged from her daughter. That same daughter is about to give birth.

Oprah interviewed Drew Barrymore just after she gave birth to her daughter. An infant daughter that Oprah met and was shown on national television, this grandbaby had yet to meet her grandmother.

I know what it feels like to be denied. My daughter's son would be five months old before I learned of his birth. It was just months after our estrangement began. I knew then that if she could go through an entire pregnancy and birth her first child and never reach out to me, she never would. At that time I was devastated.

My friend is a loving mother and grandmother that wants nothing more than to be a part of her daughter and grandbabies life. She is completely crushed. Her heart is bleeding out and her daughter seems to care less.

Drew made comments about how her relationship will be different with her daughter. Oprah who has never had children of her own agreed that by Drew raising her daughter differently would make all the difference in the outcome. Her relationship with her daughter. Yet studies show that daughters who are estranged from their mothers and model that behavior will have a higher likelihood of another generation of estrangement.

My father had aged and was pretty easy going at the end of his life, yet when he shared with me that he wasn't invited to his own daughter's wedding, I could feel his hurt and disappointment.

These are big decisions to withhold parents from weddings and births. These decisions can't be undone. My friend is so broken-hearted and her grief is undeniable. My heart was so big after I gave birth to my daughter. I was filled with love and with joy. There was not one person I had any mal feelings toward at that time. Somehow having a baby just filled me up with unlimited love.

Parents do the best they can while raising their children. There isn't a single parent that I know that wouldn't be there for their child, if that child really wanted and needed them. I know some parents exist like that, but not the peer parents that I have associated with.

Did you ever think of her?

I received an e-mail from a reader asking me if I ever thought about my mother during our estrangement. What a great question! I told her the short answer was "yes" and that I would subsequently blog my answer in greater detail.

In the beginning of my estrangement from my mother I thought of her every single day. And like a child I couldn't believe that she didn't come for me and try and make it better. I held out hope for many, many years. And like much of the grief process I went through the many stages until I came to acceptance.

I was so hurt and angry in the very beginning. Partly because I had nowhere to go. I didn't do anything wrong, nothing. My mother's husband was accused of child sexual abuse and I believed the child that made the accusations. I still believe it happened. Once it became known to me I wasn't going to allow any of my children in his company. There was no big fight only one time that I told her and her husband. He sat there neither admitting it or denying it and that would be the last time that my mother ever came to see me in my home. I didn't know it at that time, but I would be erased from her life.

When days, weeks and months passed and it silently became clear to me that I was now being excluded from all holidays and communications I was blisteringly angry. In my walking away he got away with it and he was held in high esteem by my family.

My sisters all sided with my mother and with him. I was now a complete outcast.

Because I was a mother myself I was certain that one day she would come around and seek me out. One day she would find her heart for me. But that never happened. Through the years I tried a few times. Not a word from her. Nothing. Not ever.

After anger comes acceptance and I had gotten on with my life, I met a man, adopted his pre-mature infant twins and together with my then pre-teen daughter we created our own family. It was healing. We married and he loved me and loves me.

Did I think of her? I thought of her often. I thought of her when I met my husband and I knew she would have liked him. He was Italian Catholic and so was she. I thought of her when my daughter was Confirmed and graduated from the eighth grade. I thought of her when I changed careers and was successful. I thought of her on my birthday, on her birthday and on mother's day. I thought of her at Christmas and at Thanksgiving and at Easter.

I thought of her when I made homemade spaghetti and meatballs. I thought of her often. I cried many times. I prayed and I prayed.

When her husband died I thought okay maybe now that he is gone she will finally find her heart for me. I again wrote her and once again no response. Not a word.

Her death was sudden and I know exactly where I was and what I was wearing when I received the news of her passing. I can't say I grieved the loss because I had already grieved losing her. What I grieved was the hope that we would ever come together again in this lifetime.

I only saw her once during our 23 year estrangement it was around the ninth year of our estrangement. Her sister was getting married at the same church I attended as a child and where I was confirmed. She was holding the church doors open when I arrived with my husband. I looked her straight into her face and she looked down at the floor as I walked past her. She knew.

I don't cry for her at all anymore. I have much peace in her passing. I believe in God and I believe in Angels and I believe that my mother knows the truth about her husband now. I also believe that she knows that I never once tried to hurt her.

So to the writer who asked "the question" "did I ever think of my mother?" Absolutely yes, yes and yes. Today I have moved far past the disappointment and the hurt and the anger. Of course I could wonder how it might have been different but the truth is I don't go there. I know that for whatever reason(s) it wasn't meant to be for us. This is my life and this is my story.

A story that has never changed ... a story that I have lived and shared and helped many others who are also walking through estrangement. It is not easy and it is not ideal but for me it was a part of my life and I survived it. Today I am happier than I have ever been and much more at peace too.

Do Something Good with It

"Thank you for your story. I read your P.E.A.C.E. (Parents of Estranged Adult Children Everywhere) article. I was hurting today and after reading your website I feel better. I have been estranged from my 27 year old son. I have grief in a similar way that I had when I lost babies to premature birth. I want to reclaim my life back and surround it with joy, love, and memories. I don't want to wait anymore. Thanks for being here." A new reader 9.23.13

I have often said that so much great art and music is born of pain. I am more and more convinced that when we experience pain and trauma we are supposed to do something good with it. Turn it around.

There was a time when I could never have talked about my pain associated with estrangement it was so personal, so painful and I was completely hurt and humiliated. Then one day I not only talked about it but I wrote about it. Purging my pain through the pen has always been so cathartic for me. It has definitely helped me in the healing process.

Just about every few days I hear from someone about their pain with estrangement often they want to share their story and their total disbelief. I didn't write so people would "thank" me but that has been one of the many blessings.

So much healing takes place when we share our pain, pain shared is pain divided. We tend to put so much of our happiness on other people. Then if/when they leave our life or act in ways we can't comprehend we are unhappy. We can't control what others do and say but we can control what we do and say.

There is an opportunity to take every negative thing in life and to turn it around. There is good in everything if we are willing to look for it or willing to make it happen. Pain can be a great motivator and we can use it for the good!

"True happiness resides within you. Most people are searching for happiness outside of themselves. That's a fundamental mistake. Happiness is something that you are, and it comes from the way that you think." Dr. Wayne W. Dyer

Our happiness is a choice, our choice. When sad things, bad things happen in life we are tasked with turning a negative situation into a positive one. It can be done.

What can you do with your hurts and heartaches that will turn them into something good and positive? If you think you can, you can!

Like the reader who wrote to me stated above, *"I don't want to wait anymore"* what are *you* waiting for? Life is for the living, live it! Do something good with "it." Whatever "it" is ...

Does the Potential for Evil Exist in Every Person

You can't help but be struck by the evil acts of people like the Boston bombers and now this Ohio man Ariel Castro, where three young girls were held captive for ten years. They were tortured and raped. Forced to live like an animal and caged. The person responsible now claims to have been sexually abused as a child. A rationale person would think that if you were molested and raped as a child, the last thing you would do it to bestow the same evil acts upon others.

Studies show that kids that are abused often grow up and become abusers. Sexual abuse is often a learned behavior. Many times this is just one reason why a sexually abused child denies help and does not seek out counseling. The reality for these three victims that are now young women is that they were forced to live with and to learn evil behaviors for an entire decade.

How is it that some people can go through victimization and trauma and turn it around and help others, while some become just like their abuser? Does evil exist in all people or is it learned behavior?

A few years ago I was with a group of teenaged girls who enlightened me on "mean girls" there was a movie and a series about just that "mean girls." Most of these girls came from privilege and from wealth and high education and yet when they didn't get their way they became "mean girls." They had no boundaries and would do anything to hurt someone else that may have been a threat to them. They sabotaged others success, lied about them and did anything and everything possible to get even and to get back at someone.

Most often it was teachers or parents or a rival that was a target of mean girl's behaviors. They were often motivated by jealousy or poor self-esteem. They may have become friendly with their group of friends or boyfriends. There was no low that these self-professed "mean girls" wouldn't go to in an effort to hurt another person. It was calculated and just plain hateful, vindictive and evil. Is this potentially in every single person?

If you know that your behavior is wrong, is based on lies and driven by your need to hurt someone else or your own self-preservation, and you continue is that the definition of an evil person? Clearly there is a lot of evil in our world. We have people in our society that hurt other people for their own gain.

According to a "course in miracles" every response we have is either out of love or fear. The people that are threatened by our religion or our way of life and act out on those feelings are most probably coming from fear.

Yesterday Dr. Kermit Gosnell was found guilty of murdering infants through the process of abortion, however these babies were almost full term. The prosecutor asked in closing arguments, "Are you human?" These babies were born still moving, whimpering and breathing when he snipped their spines to kill them. This is a Doctor and a man that is supposed to preserve human life.

What causes someone to be so evil and to hurt and kill the defenseless? Where is their heart and soul? This isn't about the right to abort; this is about babies killed that could easily survive. Where is the empathy for another human life?

From the "mean girls" to the bombers, abductors and baby killers, where are their hearts and souls and their inner sense of what is right and wrong, where is their conscience? How do these people live with themselves? What causes this kind of evil in people? Students, a school bus driver a doctor, they seem to come from all walks of life.

What will the "excuse" be for Dr. Gosnell as he enters the penalty phase? He was abused as a child? When will the blame of the past stop being a defense for the actions of the now and the future? A criminal mind, a sick mind, something is seriously lacking in our society when we have so little value for human life.

I don't have the answers, but I do know that the only way to seeking solutions is to first acknowledge that there is a problem.

If Perception is Reality, Does the Truth Matter?

If perception is reality, does the truth even matter? You can take two people who witness the very same things and yet report on it in completely different ways. How does this happen? Do we believe what we see and what we know? Or do we believe what we want to believe?

If you were unaware of the recent riots in Baltimore City I could take you to several neighborhoods in Baltimore city where you would walk away with a high opinion of Baltimore. I could take you to Oriole Park at Camden Yards for a baseball game and you could take in a state of the art professional baseball park that is loaded with all kinds of amenities. You would see that Baltimore has a lot to offer or to Harbor East with beautiful water views and numerous boats on the water. We could share a wonderful meal in Little Italy or many of the other famed restaurants in Baltimore. I could show you inside John Hopkins hospital that is truly a caring and innovated hospital and respected worldwide or tout the many accomplishments of Loyola, Notre Dame and John Hopkins Universities. The Baltimore Basilica is stunningly beautiful too. All are located in Baltimore City.

But if the only thing you witnessed about Baltimore was where the recent riots occurred and the knowledge that Baltimore City just had one month with more than 40 homicides, would you ever believe that this was a good place to visit or to live or to eat?

The same can be said for our relationships where we see the best in others of the very worst in them. Do we see people for who they are or do we see them for who we want them to be? Do we judge them on one view or a total picture? I work with many parents who are bewildered by the things their adult child have said about them, their truth doesn't match up with what the parents say and believe to be the truth. Does the truth matter? If we say something long enough does it become our truth rather than what actually transpired? If we perceive it to be true, does that make it so?

It's been said that in a court of law often the side that wins has the better debater and the truth takes a back seat. There is a term called "convenient truth" where what is expressed is just that "convenient."

I've worked in public relations for many years, always highlighting the accomplishments while downplaying the weaknesses. In these situations you could do the reverse and have a very different outcome and yet both presentations would/could be based in truth.

Our own perceptions can be our own truths. The prism that we view life from is based on our reality and our own unique life experiences. "Black lives matter" is a slogan that has popped up in Baltimore and I personally would never have isolated "black" my perception and my reality would be more aligned with "all lives matter." Because in my reality I never experienced being "black." We think we know and yet one of the wisest statements I ever heard was "you don't know just how much you don't know."

Does the truth matter? If we perceive it does that make it true? If perception is reality, does the truth matter?

Don't Sweat the Small Stuff

When I was just a teenager in 1977 at just 17 years old my father used to tell me *"don't sweat the small stuff."* Often I found refuse at his house after my parent's second divorce. Yep! In their craziness they married twice and divorced each other twice. My mother and I were like oil and water, we just didn't mix. I couldn't or wouldn't play the game that she had with all my sisters the one that would have required me to have an "adjusted" reality to view things their way.

We were told *"not to air our dirty laundry in public"* and living with my father who was a raging alcoholic required us to live in shame. We never brought friends home because we never knew what personality of his was likely to show itself. Would It be Dr. Jekyll or Mr. Hyde?

I was sensitive probably considered "overly sensitive" I saw it all and took it in. My parents fought like cats and dogs, dad turned to alcohol and other women, my mother sharpened her tongue and her professional skills at being a nurse in the critical units of a well-respected hospital. What skills she lacked in her personal life, she surely made up for in her professional one.

With all the family craziness and by today's standards it would have been viewed as an "abusive" environment for raising children, no doubt. We were raised on fear and loads of Catholic and Italian guilt. We knew not to get into trouble and did our best to make our parents proud. Looking back I don't think it even ever occurred to them, to make us proud that they were our parents. It was a different time.

My parents both claimed to have grown up in "poverty" yet their parents stayed married their whole lives until "death do us part." My mother was afforded many opportunities growing up as she was in the marching band, played the clarinet and the piano. Her parents owned a hotel and bar business and they never knew hungry.

The biggest void in my father's life was when he was growing up his baby brother died at age 7; this caused his mother to grieve him for her entire life. I suspect dad learned to get attention by being the "bad boy" with a young history of drinking and womanizing. He was always popular with the ladies.

We grew up in a time when **"children were seen and not heard"** and a common response to childhood tears was; **"You want something to cry about? I'll give you something to cry about!"** And yet we never ever felt abused by our parents. We respected them just because they were our parents.

I wasn't the daughter that painted her bedroom black or the one that got busted with a naked boy in their room and totaled the family car. Nor was I the ones that demanded attention by their high grades or their failing ones. I was the one that took it all in and most often kept to their selves.

Growing up with grandparents that were immigrants and survived the "great depression" I learned early on around recycling and being a good steward with all that was given to me. When Vietnam was the war that we were engaged in, I wore my P.O.W. bracelet proudly and as a young pregnant wife in my early twenties I religiously watched the Iran hostage crisis and we all endured "gas rationing" with odds and even days when you could have the privilege to purchase gas. At that I could fill the gas tank of my 1971 Ford Pinto with just $5.40. Cigarettes and yes I used to smoke were a mere 60 cents a pack.

As a fully grown woman now in my 50's I look back and never blamed my parent's for my shortcomings, I never had a sense that whether I was successful or not that somehow it was their fault. Rather I grew up knowing that if I wanted something I could work for it and achieve it and this included my own happiness.

My story is real, considered "interesting" by some and others may view it as sad or dysfunctional or abusive and yet I never ever felt that way. I saw it for what it was and looked at everything as a learning opportunity, what was I supposed to learn.

I knew my parents were people with their r own issues and flaws, I never expected them to be perfect. They had their own wars, their own inner demons and their own life challenges that they were facing.

The greatest gift my parents bestowed upon me was their faith. They were both Catholics and we grew up being Catholic. I was baptized and later confirmed. Where I may not always believe in the Catholic Church; I have always believed in God.

I am proud of my beginnings and of being "sensitive" I was always tuned in, I know that my parents have transcended this life and are now positioned in the next life with a life that affords them all the peace that they may have been lacking here on earth.

Every single person here on earth can declare themselves a "victim" of some sort or a "survivor." How we view ourselves and our lives is our own choice. We can find a reason, a reason to be a lover of life or a hater of life.

We can find reasons to love our family and our parents or not, what we can't do is go back and recreate our history. Our history is ours and it is not changeable. What it is; is a tool that we can use to gauge our future. What do we want to retain and what do we want to discard.

My father wanted me to develop a "tougher skin" he wanted me to let go of my anxiety and by not "sweating the small stuff" he wanted me to appreciate the bigger picture, where at 17 I was unable to achieve that, today I not only don't "sweat the small stuff" but I have the life skills to understand that it isn't a perfect world nor does it have to be perfect. I take my sensitivity any day but I now know how to manage it.

We age and we come to understand that all our power was always there within us, it wasn't with our parents or our siblings or our families nor with our children or our friends, all that we ever needed we already had and it was always there, there inside of ourselves.

I appreciate everything ... because good or bad, it is all a gift, it is all the gifts of life and of living ...

Edging God Out – EGO

What happens when we lead with our ego? When we edge God out of our decisions and of our lives?

There are people who always think they are right; they anoint themselves the judge and the jury often doing so to fit their own agenda. I don't know of anything that is more self-serving than acting out in self-preservation. When the need to be right rules over the need for love and peace.

For decades I have witnessed these behaviors in my family, being right and self-preservation was their guiding light. There was little if any humility. They could never be wrong, look at the alternative, give and opposing voice or a viewpoint any consideration. I always knew that I hit a truth when the response was extreme anger and destruction. The ego had to rule.

Yet most often ego really is all about edging God out and ruling as though you have the supreme seat, the only view and self-preservation is the motivating force.

I think about those same family conflicts and if they were handled with some humility, a desire for peace and for understanding and how those outcomes could have been so much healthier and God like. It is definitely in the gene pool in my family, where there is no room for compassion, understanding and for therefore for God.

There were many things that I could tolerate, many times when I looked away of looked the other way. What I couldn't do and what I won't do is pretend that there wasn't a child molester who married into our family. I couldn't do it. I knew I could never have Thanksgiving or any other family holiday and share a turkey dinner with a known child abuser sitting at the same table.

My decision wasn't about ego nor was it about a need to be right, it was about knowing the difference between what is right and what is wrong. And in my absence and in removing myself and my family from harm's way and never deliberately setting out to hurt any others I would still become the scapegoat and the target of rage.

One of the greatest gifts I ever gave to myself, an adult daughter of alcoholic and enabling over eater mother was when I gave up living in shame. The healthiest things I ever did was always striving and making the choice to uncover it! Whatever "it" is or was but letting go of ego, letting God's light shine upon me and whatever situation I found myself in, understanding that self-preservation is only fooling yourself. The bottom line is most people already know the truth.

There is so much healing and wellness in removing the shame, letting go of ego, bringing in the light and facing our life with God.

The ones who hide, lie, scheme and scam, re-write history all in the name of being right and in keeping their egos in check have truly only accomplished one thing, they have edged God out.

Today I pray that those who are living in shame, in the dark and in denial face the light of God our Father for all the peace and love they so richly need for healing and deserve to have to live fully and richly. Amen.

Empowered by Volunteering

There is something so empowering about using our time and our gifts and talents to volunteer. When my oldest daughter was a student at Maryvale Preparatory School I started volunteering as part of the mothers club. Each Christmas holiday I would anticipate their annual Christmas Bazaar and I couldn't wait to kick off the holidays with this event. For days I would bake cookies and cakes to sell at the bake table and then I would volunteer to work at the bake table and sell them at the Bazaar. It was just so much fun and a great way to start my own Christmas holiday and get into the spirit of giving!

Later, I was employed by another school, a nonprofit where I worked in a development team. It was there that I helped to recruit volunteers, train them and work with them. I recruited board members, special event committee members and interns. All good experiences and some of the college interns were just exceptional. The volunteers that I worked with and recruited came from all professional backgrounds. Some were in the private sector and some in the public sector. Each volunteer brought their own gifts and talents to the table and they were happy to share them.

Having been on the side of the volunteer and then helping to manage volunteers, I always had an appreciation for them. They were empowered by their ability to share what they knew and what they could contribute and as an organization we were empowered by their support.

This past year I was afforded numerous volunteer opportunities and just loved them all. I made a new girlfriend by volunteering to help write her life story. Vicki has an inspirational story of survivorship and I was thrilled to be asked to assist her. Little did I know what a gift she would become in my life. Another friend needed help at his restaurant so I went in and worked with Nick and baked a few things for him to sell. He wanted to pay me; I was thrilled to help and enjoyed a free meal and that was paycheck enough for me. I knew he appreciated my efforts.

My friend Suzanne asked my husband and me to work her booth at the Saint Gabriel Italian Festival this past July, so that she could attend a family function. We worked really hard, were crazy busy and had a great time doing it. This Sunday we are headed to "Pray and Play" where we will volunteer and help to raise money for post-abortion support. I am not sure what I will be doing but I am happy to help my friend Joy with such a worthy cause.

I served as a volunteer board member for a nonprofit that specializes in the arts. It was there that I met many artists like painters, musicians and writers. Being around such talent only enhanced my life and my desire to expand my own artistic expression. I went there to help them raise funds, and little did I know just how much they would lift me up and add to my life.

More than twenty years ago I volunteered to adopt and raise infant twins, after their birth mother died. I raised a son and a daughter as though they were my own biological children. During the discernment period I wrote my list of pros and cons, why I should and why I shouldn't get involved. All I could think about was what I had to offer. It never occurred to me what this huge decision to volunteer and become their mother would add to my life.

Over the years as I ran special events, I have witnessed all kinds of volunteer efforts. We had volunteers from Community College donate hours of massages for a women's slumber party and numerous local authors donate their books and speaking talents just to name a few. It was always a thrill to match up a need with a volunteer who could help to provide that desired service.

For many years I have been approached by up and coming writers, often asking me how they can get started on writing a book or could I read their work and render an opinion. I am both flattered and humbled to help them. My mantra is always the same, **"just write"** and **"write from the heart." "Oh and don't worry, you can always find a good editor!"**

Earlier today I was approached by a 14-year old girl who happened to pick up a copy of my **Halfway Home** book. I donated it years ago to Catholic Charities in Baltimore. She read my book; some parts made her cry and touched her. She communicated to me that she has her own story to share. She often writes poetry and wants to be a professional writer. I am thrilled to assist and to mentor any young new writer. Her desire to write and her reaching out to me is so empowering. We all have gifts and talents and we all have something to offer.

Volunteer work can be so meaningful and helps to add purpose to our life. When we can offer up our gifts and talents from baking a cake to manual labor like painting and spring cleaning for a nonprofit it adds value to our own life as well as to those on the receiving end of our volunteer efforts. Giving is for the giver and volunteer work is always empowering.

I encourage everyone to find a cause that you can support and one that just may need your gifts and talents and volunteer them. You will be so happy and feel so uplifted and empowered by doing so.

Everyone Has "A Story"

Everyone has a story! We all do! They say, **"Writers are observers of life."** Every few months if not every month I hear from someone that thinks they want to write and they have a "story." They have a story to share. Usually it is about something they experienced and learned from and wish to share with other people.

I think we all crave a "connection" the ability to connect to others and find common ground and share. We are all more alike than not. That is probably why I have a hard time when people do things to others that they wouldn't want done to themselves. But that is another story.

When I am approached my answer is always the same, "just write! Jump in and start!" For most of us our "story" is already written we just need to get it down and share it. Often times the hardest part is the jumping off point and just getting started. Most often I find after starting is just flows and takes on a life of its own. It is for me, a truly organic process.

I also ask the same question, **"Who is your target market audience?" If** you are writing for yourself that is a diary or a journal. If you are planning to write your story and you wish to share it with an audience, who is that audience? What group of people will read your written work? What do you wish to accomplish by writing and then sharing?

Most everyone can relate to someone else and their experiences. We are not alone. There isn't something that has happened that someone else hasn't already experienced but the difference might be how we handled it and what we learned from it. Can we now inspire another person with our writings and our story, our life experience?

I have also heard it said that you need to have a certain amount of life experiences that most often come with age, until you really have something to write about and that is worthy of sharing. I always encouraged my kids to write. Many times they would ask me, "But what should I write about?" I always had a list that I could just rattle off things like 1) what is feels like to be a twin 2) what it feels like to know that your birth mother died and you never got to know her? 3) What you had to do to become an Eagle Scout 4) baking your first cake 5) first dates and the list goes on and on.

We all have "a story" and we all have something we can share. Stephen King wrote a book years ago titled, **On Writing** that I found helpful. I also used to read books about marketing your story and your book. There is no greater high for a writer than to be read, to be understood and to have that reader connect. I have often said, "That is my paycheck" when someone reads me, gets me and can connect to me from something I have written and shared.

There is a lot of healing for many people in writing, I, myself included and everyone has their own form. I think of it as an art form, the way we express ourselves and how and what we share. Just like an artist with a painting. That art makes you feel something and it is an expression from the artist. Writing to me, is that same experience. It should make you feel something.

So here is to all the writers out there that have a story to share, my advice, just write! Jump in and just get started, you never know where it will lead until you write it! Write!

Expect a Miracle

What if all the energy spent on worry and fear was replaced with putting energy into miracles? Like many people I have a vision board, this is where I create a visual and place it on my board. It can be pictures of trips I want to take, people I want to meet and experiences I wish to have among other things.

We have to imagine it before it can come to fruition. Everything we do starts with a thought, every action we take begins with our thoughts. Every dream we have is our thoughts in action. It can be so easy to get caught up in the negative thoughts and things in our society. But what does that do to our own thought process?

I read this earlier today and just can't agree more; "a society divided by political correctness." No matter whom I talk with today, young or old, male or female, gay or straight of color or whatnot, the conclusion is the same. We are living in a divisive time. Our country is as divided and as angry as we have ever been. The question is why? More and more groups are being accepted and yet we are not together. Something is off ...

A few days ago I was reading comments on a site and one person said, "It makes me uncomfortable." This was in reference to religious comments and beliefs and in my opinion fairly main stream. However it did cause me to pause and think about that.

Have we become less and less tolerant as a society? Even if we didn't smoke cigarettes, we used to tolerate those that did. Today we show outrage. Religious expression was your choice to express it or not, today that expression may make someone else "uncomfortable."

Pot smoking used to be somewhat underground and had a kind of derogatory attachment to it. Today in some places it is sold in stores. Same sex couples are getting married and in television ads. Yet with all this progress and acceptance, we seem to be even more divided?

We want to believe our advancements are more progressive and smarter and healthier and yet we don't seem to be any happier.

So getting back to "miracles" what will it take to get us to a place of less division, more acceptance and real love? Who doesn't want to be happier and embraced and less angry? Who doesn't want to be loved?

The miracle that I am praying on and meditating on is for less conflict and more love. Love is the answer. I was watching Oprah with the Wayans family. There are ten children in that family and they all have a lot of talent. Many are actors and comedians; most notable success is *In Living Color.* Yet during this family interview it was uncovered that they don't hold grudges or fight. There are no estrangements and when they disagree they always end it with "I love you."

They grew up in poverty. The single common thread was "family first" regardless of what business opportunity. Many times business opportunities arose that could have divided them but all family members at all times agreed, family first and that love was the only appropriate response even after a heated disagreement. I think we can all learn from this family and take a page out of their book. Imagine your miracles and put that out into the universe and let us see what happens ...

Expect a miracle, leave all judgments for God, because who are we to judge. And what if we begin and end everything we do and we say with love. I love you.

Yes, I am imagining a miracle! I am expecting a miracle!

Families That Vacation Together - A Day at Rehoboth Beach

It has been said that "writers are observers of life" and this writer certainly believes that to be true! During a recent trip to the beach I enjoyed doing what I enjoy most; people watching. There were several families near us as we sat on the sand and took in the sun and the sights.

The family that most caught my attention sat directly in front of us. It was a multi-generational family with grandparents and their adult children along with their children. They all seemed to get along and to enjoy each other's company. I enjoyed watching them interact.

What struck me was the respect and the love that was communicated to the elder "mom" and "dad' and just how loving they were toward one another. A grown son with his girlfriend (no visible wedding rings) asking "Mom do you need another towel? Here take mine." He then walked toward her and helped to make her more comfortable.

Then there were the adult children with their young kids and the cousins were all playing and building sand castles. The unmarried aunts and uncles were playing with them and running into the surf together. Again more love more support and all about getting along, surely memories were being made.

I witnessed a young mother discreetly breast feeding her baby and with dad watching over them. Later a little girl that came out of the water and had some difficulty finding her parents in the large crowded beach. A woman immediately reacted and offered to help her, soon she was reunited with her family.

There is a lot that goes on at the beach. I am tuned in and take it all in including my husband who zones out listening to his iPod, eyes closed and in another world up until the heat gets to him and he has to cool off in the water.

When I sit there and look around at all the people, I wonder where they are from and what they do for a living, I read their t-shirts the ones that read "Penn State" and "Key West" along with so many other messages.

I remember when our kids were little and all that sunscreen and the hats that we wanted them to wear to avoid a sunburn. We have so many memories of all the kids and their beach adventures. One of my favorite memories was when the twins were just toddlers and wore matching boy and girl bathing suits that were from Disney and 1001 Dalmatians themed. They were just so cute with the puppy spots and in black and white with red. They loved the water and we loved sharing it with them.

The beach is like camping without the tents, watching people settle into their little piece of real estate for the day and eating food that they brought or that they purchased from the boardwalk. It's just fun to watch.

It is so easy to pass the day away at the beach and I always feel like, "my soul knows no calm like the sounds of the surf slapping up against the sand" I am renewed by my time spent there.

I hope all families get to have that experience of sharing recreational time together enjoying mom, dad, grandpa and grandma, cousins and aunts and uncles all enjoying life and one another and creating memories. It really doesn't get any better than that!

Fasnacht (doughnut) Day

Sometimes it is spelled "faschnacht" it is the English name for a fried donut and observed on Shrove Tuesday, the day before the Lenten season begins. Having grown up in the Northeast of Pennsylvania I was aware of and often celebrated Fasnacht day with a donut. Well, actually, probably, maybe more than just one!

In parts of Maryland the treats are called Kinklings and sold in bakeries on Shrove Tuesday. The word Fasnacht is German meaning Fast (verb to fasten, fast) and Nacht meaning night, eve, and the eve of Lent.

Shrove Tuesday is also known as Fat Tuesday, this is said to have come about in preparation of fasting during Lent and giving up rich and fat foods such as eggs, milk, meat and rich buttery dishes. Families were encouraged to eat up the rich foods in their pantries. In England they call Shrove Tuesday, Pancake Day.

Ash Wednesday is the beginning of the most Holy Christian holidays following Strove Tuesday and a time when many choose fasting and repentance for the 40 days leading up to Easter Sunday.

As a kid, I just knew it to be "donut day" as an adult I love the little bit of history that came about during this period just before Lent and just how it was celebrated. You don't have to be a Christian to enjoy pancakes or donuts; sometimes it is fun just to say the word "Fasnacht" and to understand what it means.

In case anyone is looking for me, I'll be picking mine up at Brown's Market in Loganville, PA, they are the best! This should hold me over and through the Lenten season this year, when I plan to indulge far less. I can already anticipate the experience in getting my bag, they offer plain, glazed and powdered and they are larger than most donuts, they are fried and you can taste it but they aren't greasy and they are just so soft and fresh.

The smell at Brown's is intoxicating and that first bit is well worth the trip. There is a separate stand at the market just for donuts on Fasnacht day and many have called ahead with their order. It is just fun to be a part of it and to celebrate Fat Tuesday. Who doesn't love a really good donut?

So on the next Fat Tuesday, support your local bakery and enjoy a fresh donut.

Happy Facnacht Day!

Finding Joy in Each Day

This WASN'T the day I was expecting to have; I had a laundry list of things to accomplish today. This is Holy Week and we are headed to several places in a few different states before we settle down and relax to enjoy Easter Sunday. My new stainless steel kitchen appliances were due to be delivered and installed and they were cancelled due to "weather."

So it appears that Mother Nature had others plans and of course I heard all the warnings and weather reports but in my mind spring is here. Snow should have ended for this year. But not so! Over the weekend I was tempted to transition to lighter clothing and I guess it's a good thing that I didn't.

Then I took a good hard look around outside and it was just stunningly beautiful. The trees look like they have been iced with pure white snow and crystal clear reflective ice. It is just beautiful outside!

So I decided to just enjoy it and find joy in doing things here at home. I spent extra time with my two furry friends, sipped my coffee a tad bit longer and decided to make food. Sunday's leftover turkey is today's turkey corn chowder soup and I tried a new flourless chocolate cake recipe with crushed cherry vanilla icing. Baked homemade bread is now baking as I listen to Adele playing on the CD player and looking out into this winter wonderland.

It is a joy filled peace filled lovely day and I guess Mother Nature decided we needed a weather holiday. I am reminded that we can find joy everywhere around us, that we just have to be receptive to it.

My Easter destination weather is anticipated at close to 60 degrees, but for now I am taking in the last of what I suspect may be winter snow for 2013 and I am finding much joy in doing so ...

Find joy wherever and in whatever you are experiencing ... because after all it is a great day to be alive!

Food Is Love

I am a foodie, always have been and always will be! Whatever job I have held always had a kitchen even if that kitchen wasn't its mainstay. Food is love and it nurtures and nourishes us all. That hot cup of tea on a cold morning or that warm beef stew with freshly baked bread doesn't just warm our tummy but it warms our hearts and our souls too.

Whenever I am feeling like I am not productive enough I so often make food. I like creating it cooking it baking it smelling it looking at it and ultimately sharing it.

There is nothing like a roasted chicken or turkey slowly cooking in the oven or watching the garlic cheddar cheese biscuits rise in the oven. Simple pleasures like the scent of pure vanilla or a freshly peeled orange or chocolate cake made from scratch. The smells and the vision before the eating is all part of that "love" experience.

I could make a meal out of a Bloody Mary by hanging a chunk of salami and a piece of Swiss cheese on the salted rim or a rim adorned with Old Bay seasoning and a few steamed shrimp on the side, add a slice of lemon and lime and a few olives and who needs anything more for lunch or dinner?

Along with my love of food comes the love of trying new things and even though I thoroughly enjoy the cooking experience, there is nothing like having someone else cook for you. Good food brings people together and it warms them from the inside out.

Yesterday it was a beef roast with potatoes, carrots and onions and homemade pizzelle cookies today a vanilla custard pie and tomorrow homemade pasta and meatballs from scratch. Food that is made with love is made to transfer that love. Food is a universal language that brings us all to the table. That sense of community that we crave right along with the foods that we crave help to satisfy our most basic needs.

Feeling happy, make food and feel even happier, feeling sad and make food and feel good. Sharing food is sharing one of our most basic needs. When our sense of smell and our sense of sight are married to our hunger for food we fill that basic need and we feel embraced by love.

Enjoy shopping for food, enjoy creating and making food, and then ultimately enjoy sharing food and feel the love! Happy Sunday and now go make some food … and don't forget to share it too.

For the Love of God

I have never believed that just because I was born and raised Catholic that my faith was "right" and all other faiths were "wrong." I have met some of the most God fearing, spiritual believing, faith filled people and they are not Catholic. Some may have started out in the Catholic faith but couldn't remain because in their words, "I didn't feel embraced." I am blessed to have numerous Jewish friends and friends who practice their faith in many religious groups and I have friends that are non-believers too.

Where is God's love in any church that doesn't embrace a person looking for grace and God's love in their spiritual quest?

Some people aren't embraced by their church because they are divorced and remarried, had an abortion or are openly gay among other reasons. There are numerous reasons why some people don't feel connected to "Church" yet have a profound relationship with God.

Imagine being gay and sitting in Mass in your Catholic church pew and being told there is a petition we want you to sign opposing "civil union" and knowing that you love God, love your Church but that your Church doesn't approve of you and your lifestyle? Imagine people a teacher in a Catholic school system and knowing that your gay lifestyle would cost you your job if it was discovered by the Church you love and have worked in for decades?

What about the children born to parents who were married and years later receive a church "annulment" stating that in the eyes of the Church your parent's marriage has been declared null and void? Did that act of "annulment" bastardize the children born out of that marriage?

What about the guy working in youth ministry for the Catholic Church and yet he is living in fear of losing his job because he isn't married and is living in "sin" with his girlfriend? Or the Priest or Catholic school teacher that won't risk "termination" by attending a friend's marriage a "civil union?" Is this God's way or people who think they are God creating the "rules" for all of their followers?

When I married and went to my Catholic Priest we talked about "normal sexual relations" he said, "It is perfectly normal to have sex with your husband" and everyone knows the Catholic Church encourages pro-creation. But that guy, that Priest took a vow of celibacy? Isn't he "normal" too?

Recently I read on Facebook a comment stating "Everyone knows The Catholic Church is no longer relevant" I was stunned to read this and then the writer attributed it to the Priest and sexual abuse history.

Last year I worked for a Catholic Priest and in his first few months with the diocese, I heard him make derogatory comments about politician Sara Palin, and about a beloved Priest he lived with and also about the Priest that preceded him. This guy was high ranking? There was no love in this guy nor was their God in his statements. Yet he holds a respected position for the diocese and he didn't even try to hide his disdain?

Half joking and half serious I can say, "The easiest way to lose your faith is to go work for them." Or like a Priest said to me, "The people in the pews will never witness what you did and if they did, there wouldn't be anyone sitting in those pews."

As a teenager I went to my friend Ellen's Bat Mitzvah where they were told that in being "Jewish" they had the "supreme" faith. Even back then I took offense to this statement; did they say they were better than persons of other faiths? Does every faith believe they are the superior faith, the chosen ones? What kind of God would declare that one faith was supreme over others?

In a conversation with a Catholic Priest I asked, "Is there any person alive that is living their life 100% by the Catholic teachings?" His immediate response, "no" and yet so many are critical and show little or no love for those who live and think differently from them.

Many talk about the "haters" in our society today, and how divided we are as a country and as a people. One would think that this is the time to embrace people and not to further the division. What would Jesus do? Where is the love of God? Where is our acceptance and tolerance for others?

What I Know for Sure

What I know for sure is that God is love and that God wants us to love everyone and to come together in love and in respect. Each one of us is a child of God and we are all to be celebrated for our own uniqueness. When we declare that we are better than others or that our way is the only way we are coming from fear and ignorance and not from God and God's love.

For the love of God, I pray for tolerance and for acceptance for all people. Love is an open heart and not a closed heart of judgment.

For the Love of Pie

Who doesn't like pie? Sweet banana cream pie, classic apple pie, peace crumb pie and savory chicken pot pie just to name a few. I am known for my mile high apple pie and classic pumpkin pie. Recently after a trip to the Finger Lakes in upstate New York where they are known for their grapes and wineries I had to try the local grape pie. It was made from concord grapes with a crumb topping and pretty good! Of course my husband was like I'm not trying "grape jelly pie." His loss!

When I was just a little kid we lived on a farm that was once an orchard and we had apple trees, peach trees and a cherry tree. Mom would hand us that classic old fashioned wire fold up basket to go pick our own fruits and she would make us individual pies. It may seem decadent today but life on the farm was simple and fruit trees grew fruit in abundance. Pie was just one answer to all that fruit so was canning and making homemade jelly and jams. We loved our fruit trees but Mom and her pie was always a welcome treat.

As an adult I often celebrated George Washington's birthday by baking my own cherry pies, harvest season meant many pumpkin and apple pies and in the summer I love making peach pies and blueberry pie. To me there are two important components to a truly great pie. You need a nice flaky crust and a wonderful filling. I love fresh fruit pies.

The Amish are known for their pies and for their Shoofly pie. Traditionally they come in either wet or dry bottom. Since I am the only family member that enjoys them I do buy a slice when I visit Lancaster, PA and my choice is the wet bottom version.

As a teenager I worked in a restaurant/diner where when you walked through the front door you were greeted by a revolving glass pie case. They had onsite baking and made wonderful pies. One of the most popular was a fresh strawberry pie. My husband is known for saying, "in business, do one thing and do it really well." We had this experience at Monica's pies in Naples, New York just a few days ago. That is all they do really great pies, all the fruit pies and chicken pot pie. Monica's pies are well known and she was once featured on the food network however, they no longer ship their pies. You can stop in and buy their pie or enjoy a slice at the many area eateries who serve them. I do recommend the concord grape pie if for no other reason that eat local when you visit!

Now that we are entering the summer season with so many wonderful fruits and the fall with apples I do go into pie making mode. I could see myself like Monica with a little pie shop and a sign on the door that reads, "ring bell for service" Monica appears in full apron as she is making pie until it is time to sell her assorted pies.

I left her shop inspired to try to make my first ever concord grape pie and a chicken pot pie. I also plan to make many more pies. Who doesn't like pie? There is virtually a variety for every taste. So here is to lots more pie making, pie eating and pie enjoying.

So go make a homemade pie or buy a pie and support a pie maker!

Forever Changed

In life there are many things that happen where the end result is that we are forever changed. A child is born in complete innocence and yet life takes its turns where they are no longer innocent but become seasoned to the ways of the world. Life isn't always like a Disney movie for most of us with a *Happy Ending* all of the time.

Most of us would agree that after 9/11 we as a country lost our innocence. I remember as a young woman in my early 20's flying on People's Express. We not only didn't go through security check points, we kept our shoes and clothing on and carried our own bags. We didn't even pay for our tickets until we were already inflight. Talk about trust.

When I spoke with Europeans many years after 9/11 they said, **"American gave in they lost their souls and their way of life. The terrorists won then and they continue to win today."** We did. We lost our innocence and our sense of trust. Our answer to their hate and harm was to distrust everyone including ourselves. We no longer trusted that we would be safe when we fly. I cried for many of my first flights after 9/11. I cried when I felt like a criminal that was scrutinized while going through security and I often cried when I safely landed at my destination and was reunited with my family members. Each flight experience was an acute reminder of all that transpired on 9/11.

Parents have kids and they hope and pray for the best. There isn't a parent alive that thinks their child will be incarcerated and end up in prison. A child comes to us completely dependent, helpless and innocent. Life is what happens to them both the good and the bad.

Children are sexually abused and their world view changes, they learn fear, deception and their trust are violated and broken. They can be forever changed as a result. A parent loses a child to death or to estrangement that their hearts and souls are shattered. They can be forever changed. Their innocence and their ability to trust in all things good have been compromised.

When we are young and innocent we have no way of understanding what a gift that innocence truly is and how easily it can be damaged where they become forever changed. Most of us would never move forward if we knew what was ahead for us.

The challenge to life, and even more so as we age and witness so much that is hurtful and damaging is to try and hold onto our innocence where whatever has transpired may make us forever changed that it doesn't destroy the best of us. Like my father used to say, *"It is too late to close the barn door after the horse is already gone."* Often we can't get our innocence back once it has shattered and been taken from us.

One bad apple can spoil the whole barrel but only if we allow it. We will never be the same after 9/11 but we shouldn't give in and allow our trust in the goodness of people and our innocence to be forever changed. We will experience our share of loss and heartache and disappointment in life, I guess the real challenge will be to keep our hearts and our souls and refrain from losing our hope and our childlike innocence.

So often what attracts us to little babies and to puppies and kittens is their complete innocence. They are new and have been unharmed by life. They are trusting.

Like the child that sees a challenge and earnestly declares, *"I can do that!"* We must all declare *"I can do that!"* we must not allow the damage done by others to harm our hearts and harden our souls or we become forever changed.

Here is to changes that lift us up and make us stronger and a better person and to overcoming those that potentially can shatter us, because to be forever changed by the evil and hurts of other people and their hatred is to overshadow our own goodness and allows the evil to win. We are stronger than that, a loving heart may be challenged by others and by life events, but true love, a love based in a God source never really dies.

Forget New Year's Resolutions!

Forget resolutions this year I am going with affirmations! Can anyone remember what "resolutions" they made last year?

And I bet that if you do it is because you have the same ones lined up yet again for this year. Me, I am not doing them, not again, no resolutions this year! Nope! Nada not!

Every year it is the same thing all the home shopping networks are selling gym equipment and all the weight loss places have a special "FREE this month" join us now ads. This probably after most of us packed it on during the holidays. Well I didn't overindulge this year nor did I pack it on with that I will get to it later approaches to diet and good health.

Then how long does it last before we are "off" of our plan and binge eating again? It seems like a push me pull me existence.

So this year I have decided to go with affirmations, all positive talk in an effort to meet my goals. Things like "you rock!" "You are great" "you are full" "enough" "love more" "live more" all positive talk speak to reach my target. I am deliberately NOT going to deny myself but affirm myself. Going with the positive affirmations, messages like "you can do it!"

I am jumping in and I am naming the year 2014 as my affirmation year! No resolutions, no more setting myself up or starting something I won't or don't finish. The year of positive living and affirmations already sounds so much better than "my resolutions!"

I have affirmations! I already feel light and free and like there are endless possibilities and I won't be limited or boxed in, like the sky is the limit and there are so many wonderful things I want to affirm … positive living = positive outcomes.

<u>Okay here goes …</u>

I love and accept myself unconditionally

I approve of myself and feel great about myself

I am unique and a very special person

I am free and make my own choices and decisions

I radiate love and respect

I am well loved

I deserve all that is good and I release any need for misery and suffering

My mind is full of gratitude for my lovely and wonderful life

I am never alone, the universe supports me

Today and every day the door is open for endless opportunities

Bye bye to New Year's resolutions and hello affirmations! It already feels so much better!

Forgive Yourself

 "And forgive us our trespasses as we forgive those who trespass against us" The Lord's Prayer says it all. So many of us have a hard time with forgiveness and most of it seems to stem from our inability to forgive ourselves. .

When we really look at abusive relationships, anger, addictions, pain and suffering we see that so much of it is self-inflicted. What are we trying to cover up and to medicate and when we look really closely we can ascertain that most often we blame ourselves and we can't forgive ourselves.

We are attracted to that abusive relationship when we don't feel that we deserve any better and in our not believing we deserve better is so often about our self- esteem and our inability to forgive ourselves.

"When we know better, we do better." Maya Angelou One of the greatest gifts of aging is learning more and knowing better. The words to say to yourself are, **"You did the best you could with what you had and what you knew at that time."** And then forgive yourself.

No one wants to see child abuse and child molesters prosecuted and held accountable more than I do. It is a disgrace the way many institutions have handled child sexual abuse. My own Church should take a good hard look at themselves just like Penn State was forced to do. There is no excuse for any cover up in this day and age. We now know better. The problem though that I see is we want to hold them accountable to today's standards, to what we know and believe today.

For whatever reason, victims often blame themselves; it is NEVER, ever a child's fault!

Decades ago, when much of this happened, and it wasn't ever right, the norm for handling it was to cover it up. It was covered up to protect the criminal but also as an attempt not to further humiliate and shame the victim. Until we can fully DE stigmatize sexual abuse just like any other crime, sadly it will continue. With it will come many mental health issues that have been driven into darkness rather than faced and brought into the light and wellness.

This is what I would want to hear my Church say, **"We really didn't know any better, we didn't fully understand the degree of harm and the damage the Church cover up contributed to the abuse. This was something that was never talked about. Today we know better and we are doing better".**

This was a taboo subject that was never discussed and when it finally was it was where law enforcement came down on one side and mental health care providers on another side.

Today we want to hold thirty year old abuse acts to the standards of what we know today. We are so much more evolved and better educated today and yet we still have a population of victims that have not received the care and the treatment necessary for them to forgive. Without forgiveness they are so often stuck.

Like Jesus said, **"Forgive them Father, for they know not what they do."**

Much of the poor handling of the sexual abuse cases can point back to ignorance and then, it was the lawyers and the insurance companies. Who live by the mantra, **"do not accept blame, or fault".** They know they will pay if they do.

Victims often blame themselves, and then start a never ending cycles of more abuse, low self-esteem and a lack of the ability to forgive themselves and in turn to forgive all others. Like a magnet drawing in even more abuse and a destructive never ending cycle attracting more abuse and more and more an inability to forgive.

Forgiveness is defined as the cessation of resentment, indignation, or anger as a result of a perceived or real offense, disagreement, or mistake, ceasing to demand punishment or restitution.

When we can't or won't forgive we hang onto our anger." ***Anger is like drinking poison and waiting for the other person to die."*** Carrie Fisher

The only person who dies inside is the person who holds onto anger and who is unable to forgive. Think about it? Who can't you forgive and let go of, and why? Anger keeps us connected in negative and in destructive and unhealthy ways.

"The obstacle is the path." Zen Proverb

When we are stuck we are unable to move forward, we must deal with the obstacle to do so. Holding anger is the surest way to stay stuck. Forgiveness is the best way to let go and to move ahead.

"Forgiveness is not a sign of weakness." Dalia Lama

I believe that forgiveness is a sign of strength and of character and it is what you do for yourself. It is the gift that you give to yourself so that you are free to love. The angry person and the unforgiving person seldom if ever attract love. Only love attracts love.

And so we pray, Our Father, Who art in heaven, hallowed be Thy name; Thy kingdom come. Thy will be done on earth as it is in heaven. Give us this day our daily bread. **And forgive us our trespasses as we forgive those who trespass against us.**

Forgive yourself and the go about forgiving others …. It is the greatest and the most loving act of kindness that you can gift to yourself.

Free Yourself

In order to fly we cannot be weighed down by things or by people from our past. We must be free.

Before an eagle of God can really start to fly into the heights that God has in store for us in this life, the eagle must break off any chains that are keeping him down and on the ground. For some of us these are issues from our past.

Jesus came to set the captives free and ones that are stuck may be stuck in wrong thinking that may come from past experiences. We must learn how to fully let go of our past before we can go full steam ahead with our divine destiny.

People get stuck and they get stuck in divorce, death and estrangements in relationships that have ended. I was guilty of this with a significant lost relationship and then it occurred to me, "How much more of your life, are you willing to lose to someone who cares nothing about you?" When is enough, enough?

We feel badly in the loss and we want to retreat and to give up burying ourselves, we pull the covers up and over our heads. But what does this really do for us? Does it make it better? Does it take the pain and the loss away?

We need to forge ahead in spite of our pain, forge ahead to newer and brighter futures. "**Do not be afraid or discouraged, for the Lord will personally go ahead of you. He will neither fail you, nor abandon you. DEUTERONOMY 31:8**

Free yourself from that which is holding you back, like the eagle that God intended for you to be. Free yourself and soar like only you can do!

Get Married!

I love being married! I love it that I am a wedding Officiate! And that I legally officiate marriages. Marriage is a union of two people that decide to make a life together. They support one another through the ups and downs of life.

"Marriage is a conservative principle." Ted Olsen

Many people were surprised when Super lawyers David Boies and Ted Olsen came together in support of gay marriage. These guys teamed up and took on same sex marriage as a "civil right." And they took that argument all the way to the Supreme Court.

David Boies and Ted Olsen were known as one Democratic super lawyer and one Republican super lawyer who teamed up to overturn Proposition 8, California's ban on same sex marriage. In 2000 they faced off in *Bush v. Gore* which basically decided the Presidential election.

Not that long ago Pope Francis went on record as saying, "it's not my place to judge" he stated this in regard to same sex relationships. But this blog isn't about "gay marriage" it is about "marriage." What makes a marriage important? What makes it respected or worthy? Why marry?

Mental health advocates have studied marriage and determined that married couples live longer and live happier lives if in fact it is a healthy union of two people. We all know couples that tried marriage and it didn't work for them, maybe it wasn't the right partner or maybe it was bad timing.

In a few weeks I will personally celebrate my 17th wedding anniversary. We have been a couple for the past 22 years. We had our share of trials and tribulations, we didn't always see eye to eye. Some of the most challenging years were the ones when we actively parented three children together.

The past few years have been some of the happiest as were the first few years. The first years were happy because we were so thankful to have found one-another after being young and widowed. We also had a clean slate between us. But as most couples in a long term marriage know, there can be "stuff" that comes between you.

If I had to single out one thing that I learned in my marriage was that I didn't need to be right or to win! If I needed be the "winner" then my husband would have to be the "loser" and why on earth would I ever want the man that I married and love to be a loser? I don't. I don't fight at all anymore. Nothing is worth it to me. I don't like how fighting feels so I just don't do it. When things get heated I remove myself. When things calm down I go about trying to have the necessary dialogue. It seems to work for us!

Living with a life partner will require you to adjust and adapt and to learn and grow. Being single allows you to be selfish, you can do what you want to do when you want to do it. Being married means thinking as a team, what is best for both partners not just one single person.

We've heard it all singles that want to remain single or singles that want to find their life partner. Married couples that are happy and those that are unhappy. Couples living together and others separated and divorcing. There is no "one size fits all" model for making a marriage work.

It takes a long time to get to know someone, often it takes years to fully appreciate how they are wired. The best part of having been with my husband for over two decades now is that we really know one another now. We've had the fights, the disagreements, the pulling apart and the coming together. We know that for us, our best life is together. We still appreciate each other and we still really like each other. We enjoy each other's company.

Marriage may not be for everyone, but when you find the right one, you know that getting married is natural and you just can't imagine your life any other way. It takes time, it takes trials and tribulations, a sense in your heart and your soul that this is the person I am supposed to live my life with. And once you have found the right person you know that instinctively you must **get married!**

Happy Anniversary Brian! I have more love and acceptance for you today than ever before!

Glorious Spring Season!

Oh, the glorious Spring Season! What a lovely time of year when the birds are singing, flowers are blooming and the trees are budding. Everything feels new again and there is a sense that anything and everything is possible. If we are blessed to live until we are 100 years old, we will only know 100 spring seasons. Each year they mean more and more to me. Spring is the season of hope and my faith teaches me a time of renewal. What will I plant this year? What will I paint this year? What will I write? What will I create and make new again?

Every place I look I see blessings abound, goodness and riches in the most simple yet God given beauty. We can witness it in our sky, our ground, our places, our people our wealth and abundance. It is our choice to see it, to believe it, and to achieve it. God is good comes from opening our eyes to all that is good and all that we have here in this lifetime. We know from womb to tomb that our days are numbered but what we don't know is how will we spend them? It becomes more and more important as we age to celebrate everything!

While Living

Please do not bring flowers upon my death

Bring them to me now, while living

Please do not tell me when I am gone

Tell me now, what is good and what is wrong

Please do not wait, show your love

That I will comprehend, please do not depend

On tomorrow, this way, we shall have today no rain of sorrow

Please live while living, give during time of devotion

As to no regret, I knew your love while living

Not sad, not blue, I take with me, so much of you

I take to you while living ...

In this season where are days are longer and warmer, there is hope and new life through the natural order of life, the miracles of rebirth and of renewal. This is a time for plantings and a time for growing and doing good with our life and with all that God has created for us, within us and around us. These days are blessings and we should fill them with abundance and with gratitude. Oh this glorious spring what will you do? How will you celebrate and spend *your* spring season?

God ... Love...Forgiveness...Acceptance ... not just words ...

Many years ago I had someone tell me that I should have "killed" the person who they said "molested" them. Even in my most angry days I never wanted to do that. And yes I had anger over it. But for me the truth is/was I should be a "murderer" to right the wrongs of a "molester" how was that going to change anything or undo it? How was that going to make it all better?

In my life I have been challenged and I didn't always get it right but the one thing I did have going for myself is that I was willing to look at the problem rather than deny it. Buddha says, "Everyone we meet is either a lover or a teacher." I find the essence of this to be true. I was hurt by the denial, dismissal and actions of my family. My salvation most times was to write my way through it. This always helped me to heal my own hurts.

God made me and he made me my mother's daughter, my sisters sister and my daughters mother and what he did and what he created can't be undone by any one of us. Whether they like it or I like it, it is the natural order of our creation in this mortal world. Even larger than that is the spirit world where we are all connected as brothers and sisters. I was struggling with "family stuff" that was obviously meant to hurt me. People that have not been in my life for several decades say things and do things to hurt me. They stay connected to me through their anger and their hate rather than by love.

My moment of clarity arrived at a Marianne Williamson lecture. I have followed her works, her books and her writings for over 20 years. The day before I went to see her I was feeling pretty down over the many years and layers of family stuff I had been carrying around inside of me. I always know you can remain a victim or you can turn it around and make something good from it. Like most people when hit I do have that urge to hit back but I know that is not the best response. Two broken abused sides meeting up in their anger and brokenness isn't going to right any wrongs or heal any hurts.

I didn't grow up in a vacuum I grew up with siblings who endured the same things that I did. There was trauma in our home and lots of it. I have spent much of my adult life undoing so much that I experienced as a child. We all know that as adults we are no longer afforded the blame game, whatever happened or didn't happen, at some point it is our stuff. We alone are responsible for it and for our life and how we move forward.

My sisters would write and publish my mother's obituary and they would decide to put it out there and NOT include me as her daughter. They did this under the umbrella of, "it's what our mother wanted" all of them are mothers. My question is, "What mother and what kind of mother would deny that she gave birth to her own daughter?" Don't you see how hate filled this choice is and was? Initially I took it on the way that they intended it to be, I took in the hurt, the denial and the "bastardization" but then I went and listened to "A Course in Miracles" and was reminded that a mortal human being can't put aside what God has created. I am my mother's daughter and my sister's sister regardless of that public omission in our mother's obituary.

I have always believed in God, I have always strived to operate out of love even though at times I have fallen short. Forgiveness is the gift that we give to ourselves. We let go in love so that we are free to love. When we harbor hatred and anger and we are unforgiving and unloving we are not coming from a God centered place of love but rather from an ego centered place. Do I need to be right? Or do I need peace and happiness?

Everyone knows the truth, everyone has the answers already inside but when we let our ego rule we are moving off center and operate from a lack of love. There is such a depth of beauty in real love and real forgiveness. I have learned that I must pray for the very people that I have been wronged by. That I must hold myself up and over the hurts and come to forgiveness and acceptance, I choose love, I choose forgiveness and in doing so, I choose God.

The power of words, you can use your words to heal or to hurt, to love or to hate. Love is forgiveness and acceptance and it is the only real response in a God centered soul. God … Love…Forgiveness… Acceptance they aren't just words! So here is to prayer lists that include the people that we love and the people who have harmed us and need to be loved …

Going Home

Is going "home" a place or a person or a feeling? Pennsylvania will always be "home" to me and yet I have not resided there in more than 30 years. I was born and raised there. All my childhood memories point back to Pennsylvania.

When I go there I visit places that I used to frequent, places where my parents took me as a child. Places that I went to when I became a teenager. My parents are deceased now and most of my family is dispersed throughout the country.

But going "there" brings me back to my roots and my center, my soul lives on but "home" is where I was formed. Like most of us we can't go back, not really, we may visit but life and things change. "Home" takes on new and different meanings throughout our lifetime.

The song by Miranda Lambert, "The House That Built Me" was really popular and hit a chord for many people. The lyrics read, **"I thought if I could touch this place or feel it, this brokenness inside me might start healing, out there it's like I'm someone else, I thought that maybe I could find myself."**

Often Christians will refer to going "home" as returning back to God at the end of this earthly life.

Going Home

by Colin Moffett

Going home to the glory, my flight it is waiting

Just delayed by hearts fading beat

When God finally calls, no hesitating

For I at least my Saviour will meet

Once I heard how much Jesus cared

Claimed Him as my Lord in a prayer

Cleansed and ready, my soul prepared

For Heaven's home and I am going there

"A man travels the world in search of what he needs and returns home to find it." George Moore

Many times we look to external sources for peace and love and yet often what we really need lives within us. Home is where the heart is and home is wherever we are, this past year I learned over and over again that all I ever needed I already had, it was there within me. I was always "home" wherever I was because I was at peace.

From the lyrics to Coming Home by Gwyneth Paltrow

Home

The world tried to break me

I found a road to take me

Home

There ain't nothing but a blue sky now

After all my running

I'm finally coming

Home

"May the God of hope fill you with all the joy and peace in believing, so that you may abound in hope by the power of the Holy Spirit" Romans 15:13

Gone to God ... Gone to Glory

When I go to God
St. Peter gives a wink and a nod
When I get to Glory
They already know my story

At the pearly gates of heaven
I hope this is what I will hear
You did good your heart is pure
God is ready now be rest assured

When I go to God
I will have passed through this life
When I get to Glory
God knows no more strife

St Peter leads me to God's grace
There are angels abound
Now we meet face to face
Calm cool and quiet, not a sound

Heavenly Father embraces me
Once again I am whole
The songs they are singing
Pierce my angel spirit soul

As I move forward, who do I see
To my right and to my left
All those before, that mattered most to me
God stands before us, He is our host

When I go to God
When I get to Glory
I won't have to speak a word
God knows my story

The Lord is my light and my salvation
So why should I be afraid?
The Lord is my fortress, protecting me from danger
So why should I tremble? PSALM 27:1

When I go to God
When I get to Glory

Goodbye to All That

Letting go of possessions, people and places that once held value in our lives can be so difficult to do and yet at the same time it can also be so freeing. Lately and probably over the past few years I find myself purging possessions and people that no longer give me the same pleasure and/or opportunity for growth that they once did.

For years I collected Barbie dolls and probably had about 30 highly collectable dolls in my collection. I had an original 1959 Barbie from the year she was born, Scarlett O'Hara Barbie from Gone With The Wind, 101 Dalmatians Barbie, Angel Barbie, Birthday Barbie, Christmas Barbie and Wedding Day Barbie just to name a few. Then a few years ago I started donating them just a handful at a time as a mini collection to silent auctions for nonprofits that I supported and held dear. I was so happy that they brought in much needed funds and were going to make someone else happy just as they did for me. Last week I gifted two favorites; Angel and Holiday Barbie to two precious little girls. Their joy and their glee was just so rewarding and seeing how happy those dolls made them made me equally if not even happier.

My husband caught the giving bug in his decision to support me in my professional fundraising goals while breaking up his sports memorabilia collection. One year he gave me his prized autographed Ted Williams baseball to donate. It was after Ted's death and came complete with a full set of authentication papers. That ball was used in a live auction to benefit disadvantaged children. My husband paid a mere $60 for it and it gave him joy for many years. The night of the auction that $60 signed baseball brought in $2,400! My husband was thrilled and admired by some of the most elite in that gala dining room on the evening of this black tie fundraising event. He was filled with joy and I was so proud to have him as my husband.

As I have gotten older and through the years I have received some high end gifts like authentic Burberry pieces. Last week I re-gifted a Burberry scarf to a friend that I adore. I wanted her to have something special and something that was of value but also once belonged to me. The joy for me was in the giving. I've believed for a long time that, "giving is for the giver."

There are organizations that need just about anything that can be donated to lift up someone else that doesn't have. Some organizations collect shoes for people who have none and work suits and professional attire for people who need them to secure employment and food for the hungry.

When our twins were younger they learned the gift of giving at a very young age. Often they had birthday parties and invited their entire class. Because they were twins they didn't want their guests to feel the burden of purchasing two gifts. Our twins asked that donations be made to nonprofits they named and who supported kids who had less than what they did. I can recall several years when they raised somewhere between $600 and $1,000 each year by doing this. I also remember how empowered and joyful they were by their own abilities to help by raising money, kids helping kids.

Ecclesiastes 3

A Time for Everything

1 For everything there is a season, a time for every activity under the heaven.

2 A time to be born and a time to die. A time to plant and a time to harvest.

3 A time to kill and a time to heal. A time to tear down and a time to build up.

4 A time to cry and a time to laugh. A time to grieve and a time to dance.

5 A time to scatter stones and a time to gather stones. A time to embrace and a time to turn away.

6 A time to search and a time to quit searching. A time to keep and a time to throw away.

7 A time to tear and a time to mend. A time to be quiet and a time to speak.

8 A time to love and a time to hate. A time for war and a time for peace.

I have come to believe and to understand that some people and places have a time and a place too. Sometimes you have to let go for they no longer add to your life but take in ways that leave you in an unhealthy place. I have learned for me it is best to do so with love. Given the choice I can be a forever friend and yet at times this is impossible to achieve.

My friends have often filled many roles in my life, many voids that were left by my family. In my history with them and my desire not to lose more people I have been guilty of hanging on to relationships that I had either outgrown or ones that were destructive. In my rose colored glasses approach to life, I let many things go that in retrospect should have been dealt with in an appropriate and respectful manner.

In my conscience decisions to purge possessions, people and places that no longer fit for me, I have freed myself up to entertain other people, places and yes other possessions too. I have allowed myself the opportunity to continue to grow and to learn and to make room for that which can allow me to do so. My giving away and giving way to letting go has allowed others to benefit as well.

I have always been so much better at "hello" but I am learning the necessity of saying "goodbye" with grace. It is often said that the closing of one door opens another as does the freeing and giving away those things that no longer serve us well. Letting go, giving away and giving up can be a gift.

Here is to knowing when to let go in love and how to do it with grace, and when it is time to say Goodbye to All That!

Green Green Grass

People always think the grass is greener on the other side. The truth is that green grass can grow anywhere we plant our feet if we so decide. We can make and appreciate green grass wherever we are just like we can declare the "grass is greener on the other side." Often it is no greener and quite possibly less green!

We take our "stuff" with us wherever we go. The real challenge is managing our "stuff" rather than changing the "grass." In essence if we don't make the inner changes to adjust to the ever changing world we live in, it makes no difference what the outer world looks like.

Most people avoid or dread and often don't like change. But the catalyst for growth and learning is most often directly coordinated with our ability to weather change. The only real constant in life is that there will be change. Period.

One of my least favorite lines is "but that is how we have always done it" this suggests an inability to promote and foster change and says much about a person's inability to do things differently even when what they have done, no longer works. Or the small minded mentality of "taking it back." Nothing changes if that is "how we have always done it" and if/when we proclaim to "take back." Taking back is exactly that moving to the past and behind.

It has been said that the definition of crazy is doing the same things over and over and expecting a new and different result.

The Catholic Church has an opportunity to grow again with the new Pope even non- believers find him to be a breath of fresh air. When he came out publicly and stated "who am I to judge?" It was in reference to gay relationships. For many elders this was difficult to hear. The very idea that a church they loved and supported could make such a turn around. This Pope is smart enough to know that to grow again, to be relevant in people's lives and to attract youth and young adults that readily embrace all people, that he, as the leader must be willing to change the dialogue.

Everything changes! I came up in a time when abortion, same sex relations and pot smoking was viewed as immoral and illegal. It was against the law and certainly against Catholic teachings. Where I have my own personal views on these things, the reality is all three will become legal in my lifetime. I make no judgment.

If we want a better result, a newer different result we must be willing to green the grass where we are planted and be receptive to wise change that has a proven record of results. Simply put if you want more you must do more. Being comfortable is often at the expense of being successful.

Every place we visit and every place we live offers us that "green grass" if we decide that is what we want it to be. You can be successful and you can be happy wherever you find yourself. Green grass or no grass at all, it is about the choices we make and the view that we have …

Grief Walk --- Books That Saved Me

Through the years I have tried to learn from my grief, from the losses I have experienced. While going through it, books basically saved my life. There were times when it was 3:00 in the morning and I was alone and sad, so often it was a book that I turned to that comforted me.

People often ask me what I recommend and all I can do is share what I read along the way. My grief walk began in 1983 when my husband died and I was just 23 years old. I tried to understand how someone so young and so full of life could just die and be gone.

During this time I read **On Death and Dying** by Elisabeth Kubler-Ross and **How To Survive the Loss of a Love** by Melba Colgrove, PH.D. Harold H. Bloomfield, M.D. & Peter McWilliams.

I shared **The Fall of Freddie The Leaf** by Leo Buscaglia with my young daughter, trying to help her to understand the life cycle and the death of her father.

Later when I experienced family estrangement I read the following books;

Women and The Blues, Passions That Hurt, Passions That Heal by Jennifer James

Motherless Daughters by Hope Edelman

Surviving Ophelia by Cheryl Dellasega, Ph.D. (my own contribution is on pages 209 & 210)

A Return to Love by Marianne Williamson

The Language of Letting Go Daily Meditations for Codependents by Melody Beattie

The Four Agreements by Don Miguel Ruiz

Today I read and re-read books by Joel Osteen, Joyce Meyer and Marianne Williamson. Specifically, **I Declare** by Joel Osteen and **Love Out Loud** and **The Confident Woman** by Joyce Meyer. And all of Marianne Williamson books.

My most recent reads and re-reads are **The Purpose Driven Life** by Rick Warren and **The Untethered Soul** by Michael Singer.

I am also a big fan of all works by Henri Nouwen, they include;

The Return of the Prodigal Son: A Story of Homecoming

The Inner Voice of Love: A Journey Through Anguish to Freedom

Bread for the Journey

The Way of the Heart

I love books and I love to read, I am certain that if I wasn't a reader, I would never have been a writer. Inspirational cards and music have also soothed my soul and helped me along the way in my own grief walk. Support groups with people that have and are experiencing the same type of loss is a huge help and so often was a Godsend for me. *"Pain shared is pain divided."*
Michael Pritchard

I hope that my list will help others ... today I am in a really good place; it was and remains a process. The only way that I know to get out of it, is to go through it.

Grocery Store "Bernie" My Angel

Today I got up early to beat the rush at the grocery store, it is New Year's Eve day and after being away from home for several days it was definitely time to restock the refrigerator. I made it through the Amish Market before the crowds and then on to the grocery store. I was in "get it done" mode. Barely awake as I left home I hadn't even had my coffee yet. I was out and about.

When I made my way to the line at the check-out I was feeling pretty accomplished since there was only one person ahead of me and I had secured everything I needed to cook for the evening. The checker was a guy and he was nice. Almost too nice since like I stated I had not yet had my coffee. He was talking and talking telling me how he separated my foods in their bags, where the eggs were and how he protected the glass jars I was purchasing. And I was like it's early; I am on a mission and wow you are talking up a storm!

I took each bag from him placed them in the cart and handed over my card, this time he was telling me to have a safe and Happy New Year and not just for me and for my family and it seemed like he was going on and going on ... it was much more involved than the normal quick "Happy New Year."

When I finally took the time to look at him I noticed his name tag that read "Bernie" and I said "I'm Bernadette" he immediately said "did they call you Bernie" I responded with "yes my father is Bernie and I was named after him." He smiled large and said "Bernie?" I said "well actually Bernard." His smile grew. He continued to chat with me and from the beginning he was so sincere, so caring, you would have thought they were his groceries that he was taking such good care of when placing them into the bags for me.

The thing is I could have missed the whole thing. I wasn't really present as I was so geared up to what I was doing and what I needed to do next. I smiled wide as I left there. I thought it was a sign from my dad above. It was "Bernie" alright the one that went to heaven several December's ago. For me, it was my dad Bernie who has been looking out for me in a whole new way since he departed this life.

This past year 2014 has been filled with blessings and angel signs and I have been so blessed …. Most of us are blessed but so often we aren't open and we are rushed and closed off. When we open our hearts and our souls and when we are receptive our own "Bernie" angels light our way and protect us. Soon after my joy I looked up and said "thanks dad, happy new year to you too!" and then I had a few tears that rolled down my cheeks …

Whatever is ahead I am able to face it because I know that God is with me and that my angels are always with me. I am never ever alone and that is as simple as a visit to the grocery store or any other places that I find myself.

Happiness is an Inside Job

It has taken a long time for me to understand that happiness is an inside job. It was my husband who taught me this. Overall he is very content and can take or leave most things. Brian has an inner peace and strength about himself. He is always so supportive of me. For more than 15 years, when I was running huge social fundraisers he never missed a single event. He never hung onto me for his good time either. He would circulate and was okay with being in a crowd and with people or by himself.

Through the years people have told me, "you two look good together" but what they could never have known was our back story, our family history. We are very much alike and have a deep understanding on what it is like to move past the limitations of your first family. We also had the same track record in love. Brian and I both had a spouse who died and left us with children and another significant relationship end when they cheated on us and left us for someone else. We know what it is like to be hurt by love.

My husband Brian is one of 6 children, I am one of 5. Neither one of us is close to our siblings. He is the only one who moved away. He grew up in the inner city of Baltimore, in the "hood" the projects. They were really poor as kids. None of his siblings left there, not one of them owns a house or an automobile. He pushed past his initial life circumstances. Brian got an education and continues to educate himself as he is still moving up the corporate ladder.

He is the most responsible of all his siblings. When his mother passed his father had him take over. He isn't the oldest but was appointed the guardian for his father's care. Brian learned how to live without his siblings. In childhood family photos most often Brian is on one side of the picture alone in contrast to the other 5 who are grouped together. It appears to have started when he was just a toddler.

I am one of 5 girls and like my husband I have no relationship with my siblings. We weren't exactly well off as kids either. They have not been in my life for almost 25 years now. And just like my husband they appear when they want to try and bring me down. They presume to know me but have not been in my life for decades. I don't allow myself to get caught up in their cauldron of hatred.

My husband had and has an easier time accepted that his siblings are not a part of his life. I always wanted my situation to be different; I mourn for how I would have wanted it to be not for how it truly is and was with them. Like my husband's family they don't add anything positive to my life.

It took a long time for me to learn that my happiness was my responsibility. Mine alone. I have so many friends and even more acquaintances. Every job I ever held was in a highly social setting. Many people have lifted me up. And I have been called "inspirational" by more than a few people.

No matter how many people enhance our lives, we come into this world alone and we leave it alone. Today I am probably more content and happier than I have ever been. It isn't based on other people or on things but truly comes from self-love and self-acceptance. I know my strengths and I know my weaknesses. I know who I am and I know my truth. I have an easier time discarding those relationships that are unhealthy and non- supportive.

Accepting that my happiness is my responsibility has allowed me to create an inner peace of love supported by my own strength. I don't know why it took me so long to understand that everything I ever needed was already there inside of me. Better late than never … I suppose …

What I would say to anyone who is unhappy is you need to fix that. You alone have all the tools to be happy. It is there and it is inside of you. People may try and bring you down and may try to hurt you but that is their unhappiness and not yours.

We are all responsible for the life choices we make and the way we live our life. If it isn't right for you, then it just isn't right. Change it. No one can make you happy, no one, but you.

Happiness is an inside job!

Happy Dance Happy Dance ... Where There Is Love

Where do you receive your happiness and where does your bliss come from? These past few weeks most notably the month of June have been chock full of blessings. June is traditional the month for love and marriage and I have been a part of three marriage celebrations in just four weeks. It has been an amazing month of celebrating both love and marriage.

Celebrate love in anyway and every day that you can! It is the only thing in life that really matters. Tomorrow my friend of more than 30 years is getting married for the very first time and I am truly honored to be the person who will officiate his wedding. Last night at the rehearsal dinner he said to me, "I've loved you from the moment that I met you!" Honestly I think that is one of the nicest things that anyone has ever said to me. We met in 1982 and his mother used to babysit for me. His family loved my daughter like she was their very own child.

All too often we dwell on our losses and the people that don't love us. What a huge waste of time! There is love everywhere if you are willing to see it and to receive it. Love comes from that puppy that just can't wait to see you and showers you with puppy dog kisses. It comes from the neighbor child that rides up on their bike for a chat and from the friends of your children who stop by and want to see you and tell you how "awesome" you are. Love comes from that friend that seeks you out at the last minute to do lunch just because. It is your spouse who sends you a text message saying, "thank God for you, I just love you so much!"

People that receive love are usually the ones who put love out into the universe, and in sending out love to others, it just naturally comes right back at us.

Whose life can you make better? Who and what can you do to create love? We see much in our world and so much of it is about loss, hurt and pain. What if we collectively agreed to counter balance the negative with more love please?

There is a bliss that comes from the act of loving; it is a joyful soul that knows that love can cure just about anything that ails you. There are no limits on what and how much we can love. We can exude a never ending supply of love only inhibited by our own selves.

For me my happy dance all begins with and ends with more love please. Jump in and just do it! There is nothing more attractive than a man or a woman that knows how to give and how to receive love. We were born to be loved and we were designed to be loved and we are wired to love, both to give it and to receive it.

Happy dance, happy dance, where there is love, love much and do love often! Just imagine that if no matter what we are faced with we just naturally respond out of love and lead with love?

Where there is love ...

Happy Healthy People Have No Room for Hatred

Think about it? People that are happy with themselves don't utter words of hatred. They just don't! Happy and healthy people have no room for hatred.

What would someone have to do to you where after decades you are still intent on hurting them? Or is hatred alive in a person because it has more to do with them than with any other person? Do a person's outward sign of hate reflect upon how they truly feel about themselves?

People have forgiven rapist and murderers, and looking at that it makes me reflect on how? Why? What allows them to forgive and move past it? In contrast how it is others get stuck in feuds that go on for years and are from far less than rape and murder.

When I began reading about hatred and preparing for this blog I was coming from a place of trying to understand why any person would waste so much energy on trying to hurt another person? When we all know that letting go of anger and hate allows us to be open to love and happiness. Given the choice wouldn't most people choose love and happiness? What kind of person makes the choice to hate?

Rather than try to understand any persons desire to hang on to hate, I decided to look at people that are open and loving and what traits and characteristics they had. Most often the single personality identifier was being happy with themselves and success; they were successful in their career, in their relationships that translated into being happy. Happy people don't dwell on trying to hurt other people, they don't pick fights and they don't try and make others look bad.

Love and hate don't co-exist. A loving person comes from a place of acceptance and an open heart. A hate filled person comes from a place of fear and lacks a sense of self- worth. Imagine if the "haters" invested the energy spent on hurting and hating others and instead used that energy to do something to better themselves?

Happy New Year, I pray

Happy New Year, I pray. I pray for you for your health and wealth and happiness.

I pray for peace and for love and for tolerance, tolerance for all people, not just the ones most like us.

I pray for the sick and the weak and the elderly. I pray for wellness and vitality.

I pray for understanding and for patience. I pray for the suspension of judgments.

I pray for a better world for all of God's children.

I pray that we are fed, safe, protected and understood.

I pray for the strength in families, in communities, in our country and in our world.

I pray for those who are lacking peace and love in their life that God will grant them the gift of peace and love. And that their hearts are ready and open to them.

I pray for abundance and wealth in the riches of all life and all of our life experiences.

I pray that good will always win out over evil.

I pray that we share in gratitude for all that we have, for the faith that we need and for love, to give love and to receive love.

And above all, I pray for peace within the divine of each of one of our souls on this day and all the days of our lives.

I pray. Happy New Year, May all your dreams become a reality and your prayers be answered. Amen.

Home is Where the Heart Is

It is a wonderful lazy Sunday is November just before Thanksgiving holiday and our home is warm and comfy. The house smells like homemade cinnamon and fresh blueberry muffins. There is a fire burning in the woodstove and the dogs are resting quietly.

My husband has the sports channel on blaring what I call "soap opera for men" as the announcers make their judgments and predictions on who is favored to win today's scheduled football games. For Baltimore Raven's fans this is a big game day as the Raven's play rivals Pittsburg Steelers. Locally there is much excitement in the air.

I'm cleaning house as I have the automatic oven cleaner on preparing in anticipation for Thursday's big turkey day feast, and going through clothing for donations. I am assessing what our home needs as we prepare for the cold winter season and the wonderful holidays from Thanksgiving, Christmas and the New Year. Making my "to do" list and holiday gift lists too.

This year is our 21st year celebrating the holidays in our home. There is a calmness that comes with having all adults in our home, unlike the many years with our children. There is a great sense of peace and wellness here.

Our cupboards are full, the freezer is stocked and in a few days a cord of wood is scheduled to be delivered. We have cut back our rose bushes and our sea grass plantings and secured our yard ornaments now tucked neatly in the shed.

Everywhere around is that cozy comfy sense that just seems to come with this time of the year. My husband and I feel so blessed with abundance and good health. We love our life and have peace at home and in our hearts.

As we look around with the constant discourse of our government and our societal debates, we thank God for all that we have and the people we are and continue to become. Our life is good and it is laced with gratitude. We have turned away from the "news" and media sites that seem to thrive on discourse and upset.

Like Dorothy from the Wizard of Oz, "there is no place like home!" For us, wherever we are, home is where our heart is and we hope and pray that all those who are struggling come upon this wonderful place for the first time ever or yet again.

God's Peace and Prayers on this wonderful Thanksgiving, Christmas and New Year's holiday season! May you have a wonderful home filled with love and heartfelt happiness always.

Home Sweet Home

We love to travel and just recently came home after a 10-day road trip. It was a trip we had discussed for years and was intended to be our "we are 55" celebration having just turned 55 years old. It was also a celebration of our over 22 years together as a couple.

The trip was great! It could not have gone better. The weather was outstanding and we got along so beautifully, it was perfect.

There is nothing like going away from home to help you return home even more appreciative. We love our home and have an ability to make a home wherever we find ourselves. We love sleeping in our own bed.

Home to us isn't just a place as much as it is a feeling; it is a feeling of safety and of wellness to be "home." Our dogs were the first to greet us, it was clear by the lengthy and exuberant kisses, jumps for joy and reception that they were happy we returned home.

Coming up from South Florida where the weather is tropical and we sunbathed and wore shorts and sandals, to driving back north where the trees are changing colors and the temps are cooler and require much more clothing, was a welcome change after our trip. All that was old became new again.

Our trip did what it was supposed to do it refreshed our hearts and our souls and allowed us to relax and stop, to take our time and to flow through our days without any specific agenda. We definitely vacated our normal home life routines.

Coming home safe and sound is a blessing! Our return has inspired us to go again with our home life. It feels great to be home. We anticipate the lovely changes of the season and are looking forward to our Thanksgiving! We are so blessed and so grateful just to be alive and to be home together.

Isn't life great and isn't it wonderful just to be home …

How Can I Make You Happy

Not that long ago I was visiting Nashville, Tennessee. Nashville is a favorite travel destination for both my husband and me. We try and go at least twice a year. We love country music, the downtown club scene and Opryland at Christmas. The people are kind and so friendly.

On this occasion we travelled to Franklin to shop and check out a few antique places. When I walked into a shop the owner came to greet me. Instead of the usual "hello" and "can I help you?" He said, *"How can I make you happy?"* It immediately made me smile and I thought, how nice!

What a refreshing way to greet someone, "how can I make you happy?" Do we even think that thought, let alone say it out loud? What if we did approach everyone with a mindset of "how can I make you happy?" Rather than a "What can I get from you today?" Or "What can you do for me today? "What a nice shift in our mindset.

Just thinking that thought of how I can make someone else happy, makes me smile. So often we are stuck on ourselves, our feelings, our wants, our desires. Yet most mature adults know that a life of service and of giving is much more fulfilling.

Last week I was driving through a Delaware self-serve toll that costs 50 cents, the guy ahead of me tried using the coin changer machine, it appeared it wasn't working. I could sense his anxiety. His tag read Pennsylvania tags, he looked like just my father, and I easily had the 50 cents so I drove around him and paid his toll. This guy was so appreciative. He had enough money to pay but watching him become flustered I felt compelled to help. The appreciation from this old man was well worth the 50 cents as so much more, he made my day.

There are opportunities every single day to be a giver, to be a positive life force. To make some else's day better is a gift too. Yesterday I was walking through a big box store when a father and son were coming up directly in front of me. The father gently guided his son over so that my pathway was open for me to proceed. I gave the father who seemed a bit serious a big smile of appreciation. The smile that he returned to me was priceless. Those smiles cost absolutely nothing and yet I know that it made me feel good and I have to assume that father was feeling good. His huge smile was wonderful!

Today, go out into the world, maybe not saying it to every single person we meet along the way but in thinking it, "how can I make you happy?" Little acts of giving and of kindness go a long way. Be the do-gooder and watch just how much goodness comes right back at you.

How can I make you happy?

How Do You Make Those Big Decisions and Define Success and/or Failure?

How do you make your big life altering decisions? What determines a move to a new location or a new job or a new marriage or to have children or not? Life can be filled with decisions and numerous choices some are easier than others and sometimes we just do what needs to be done.

Obviously there are consequences for our choices and in my obvious choice to be married I have just as obviously chosen not to date anyone but my own husband. In having children I made the decision to be a mother and to create a stable home and to raise them. In being a career woman I made the choice to work outside of our home. Every choice had a lifestyle that naturally went along with it.

Through the years I have heard friends and acquaintances say, "you are so lucky to have twins" or "you are so lucky to have a second home at the beach" but the truth is "luck" had very little to do with it. Deciding to raise twins was a choice they came to me on angel wings since their birth mother died. It was work and many times it was a very rewarding choice and other times a real challenge. Having a second home is wonderful but it is also a lot of work and a financial responsibility. Each life choice affords us gifts as well as responsibilities. I didn't bring children into my life or my pets into our home or create a home or marry my husband without the decision to love and to care and to accept responsibility for them.

But what about the choices I made that no longer fit for me or my life? A bad choice can be as simple as a pair of jeans that are far too tight and do nothing to flatter you. At what point do you decide to let them go?

I am a list maker that traditional pro and con list and after that exercise I generally go with my gut. I have lived my life with the notion that anything I tried and recovered from was an experience a life lesson rather than an outright mistake. Can we ever "fail" at anything if we never even try it? What and who defines "success" or "failure" for us in our own life?

Every single day people make choices and sometimes they move forward on them and other times they retreat back as to declare that is not quite right for me. Many years ago I owned my own retail gift shop, I loved it … success! It never really made much money … failure! I am better for that experience and I learned so much but in the end it was financially costly and yet I still have many fond memories of owning it.

Almost a year ago my son enlisted in the United States Navy he studied hard for the ASVAB test and eventually aced it, he entered as a "depper" in their Delayed Entry Program. As a result of his Eagle Scout status he was promoted from entry level of E-1 to E-3 up two grades. For six months he went to monthly group meetings and individual one-on-one meetings. He read the books, watched the videos and took in much knowledge. According to him it was his first "adult" decision. His father was thrilled and I was apprehensive. He is a loving gentle soul and not someone I could see as a soldier. When I asked him "what would you do in a kill or be killed situation" his response was "I guess I would do what I had to do." I got on board with his decision and supported him.

Late tonight I am going to the airport to pick him up, he is coming home. He feels like a "failure" after 5-weeks of boot camp. My view is different from his, the Navy did their job and "broke" him and he did his job and "tried his best." Turns out it wasn't what he wanted after all, it took him 2-days to make that call and tell us. He didn't want to let us down? Honestly I am nothing but thankful! I am so happy he tried it and if it was meant to be it would have been. I have gratitude that my son is coming home and it isn't in a body bag, or dismembered or suffering from trauma. He left home very determined and confident he is coming home somewhat defeated. I am his mother and I love him and I support him. I will help him to regain his confidence and dust his off, love him and encourage him to move forward with yet another life choice.

Within every "failure" there are lessons we learn that help us to "succeed" I can hardly wait to hear all his stories on what he went through and the experiences he had just as I can't wait to watch him dream yet another dream. For this mom, my son is a complete success because he tried so very hard to succeed and had a willingness to try something that was completely new to him.

In our own life my husband and I are also facing big life altering decisions. When should he retire from his job of 33 years? Should we play it safe and stay in our home of 20 years? How about that Bed & Breakfast I always wanted to own and operate? Should we do the Florida move? Build another house? Should I work for myself or accept a position with another organization? Take an early retirement? These are all big life altering decisions. We do what responsible decision makers do as we gather information, we explore our options, we make our lists of pros and cons but in the end like all decisions it is a leap of faith. We trust that our decisions will work for us and we know that if they aren't right we will make the necessary adjustments.

What we know for sure is that each decision comes with its own set of circumstances, its own risk and responsibility. In each choice to do something we will have decided NOT to do something else. Making a decision not to make a move is in itself a decision ... the decision to stay.

So ... how do you make your big decisions? And how do you define "success" and how do you define "failure" for me, the only real failure is the decision not to even try ...

How Can I Help Myself and You Get to Heaven

Assuming you believe in heaven, and I do, what if, every person we met and every relationship that we have our intention was simply "how may I help you to end up in heaven?" Imagine that. Touch the joys and troubles of your friends and neighbors. Shared life is a shared prayer.

If we lived our entire life with that single goal, to bring out the very best in every single person we meet along the way. Our lifetime would already become "heavenly" for that act of consciousness alone would change the current societal thrust from being divisive to becoming one of love and unity. Just that thought alone, my only motivation for each and every person I meet along the way is simple.

What might I do to bring out the best in everyone and help to set them up for a life and an eternity that is heaven worthy.

"Common sense is the measure of the possible; it is composed of experience and prevision; it is calculation applied to life."
Henri Frederic Amiel

How may I help you to get to heaven? What if we just started with one single person our spouse and our life partner and we approached that relationship every day with a single motivating thought and followed those thoughts with actions. What may I do to help you to live a life that sets you up for heaven?

Think how good you would feel about yourself, if you approached life with that desire and made that single declaration?

How about if that became our theme of the day and therefore our goal for this lifetime? How may I help you get into heaven? As we age we think about all that we have done and all that we learned and all that we endured. Most often we do think about what comes next. Where the body may perish the soul lives on. If we lived a heavenly life, wouldn't we be predisposed to a heavenly afterlife?

What I know for sure, whether you believe in heaven or hell, we create our reality here in this lifetime. Is it a heavenly existence or a hellish one? I have to believe that if I align myself and those closest to me to get to heaven not only have I worked toward a noble cause but I am much more likely to leave this heavenly life for the heavenly afterlife that I imagine it to be.

Here is to living a life that is heaven worthy for all those that we encounter in this life and the next. Amen.

Hurt People, Hurt People

When James was just nine years old, he witnessed his father shoot and kill his mother and then his father shot and killed himself. James witnessed it all and he has every right to his anger. He has been in and out of mental health care facilities and schools for children with emotional challenges. For days and weeks James seems to be doing well and then an anger episode that generally lands him back in a medical care facility.

Most of the professionals that treat James believe he has a 50-50 chance, he can go either way. He will either end up in prison having hurt someone or he will end up down on his knees and God will use him in a bigger and better way that he could ever have imagined for himself. James is hurt and he is bitterly angry. The loss of both of his parents by his father's act of violence has sent him into the unknown; he was an above average student and now is completely lost. This is trauma at its worst and a lot for a young boy to carry with him.

He has a professional team that supports him along with his maternal grandmother who absolutely loves and adores him. This is a true story, however, the name has been changed.

Many of us walk around with far less hurts than James, yet there is hope for James and for anyone else who has been hurt. The deciding factor, will James find it within himself to take his anger and hurt and turn it around and do something good with it? What road will he travel? Will it be bright sunny skies or more darkness and despair? In the end, only James can make the choice on what road he will travel down.

Every single one of us can claim to be "hurt" over things that happen to us in our lifetime, the question is "what are we willing to do about it?" Obviously James didn't ask for the hand that was dealt to him and yes it is so unfair, but like the bell that can't become unsung, James has to take it hurt and learn from it. He has to use it to gain a deeper understanding that hurt people, hurt people. Clearly there is no excuse for the killings by his father; James will no doubt have a lot to overcome.

For every hurt in our life we are afforded an opportunity, we can do something good because of it or we can use it to justify our own poor choices. I don't know James's father story but I can't begin to imagine why an adult would kill the mother of their child and then themselves in front of that very child.

Life can be cruel but it can also be joyous. Bad things do happen to good people. My hope for James would be that he finds an outlet to express his anger and that it eventually leads him to help others. That James can rise above his family circumstances and know that God loves him and wants so much more for him.

May God guide James along the way and hold him near as he struggles with heavy burdens and moving forward with his life and may God bless all those struggling with anger and hurts …

I Am an Adult Daughter of an Alcoholic

It wasn't a secret; it was pretty obvious to anyone who took a good hard look that my father was an alcoholic. He finally after decades of anger and abuse, after marrying my mother twice and divorcing her twice came to grips with his drinking problem. They say, "It ain't the whiskey." There was definitely a lot going on that resulted in his abuse of alcohol.

It wouldn't be until after leaving my mother for good and starting a new family of his own, my father finally stopped drinking. To his credit I believe he lived the last 30 plus years of his life clean and sober. But for me the damage was already done. I grew up in a home with a raging alcoholic who deviated between Dr. Jekyll and Mr. Hyde personalities with great ease and regularity. As a kid I was never quite sure what personality would show itself. He could be the most fun and charming man and switch to complete rage in seconds. I lived in fear and in shame. I never wanted my friends to see what I saw so I kept them out of our house and always showed up to the outside world in control and with a fake happy front. To compensate for my father and his out of control behaviors, often I was a complete control freak.

When I became an adult my father would openly talk about his years of alcohol abuse and all the damage his drinking did to our family. It was no longer a secret talked about behind his back but open and on the table. He could admit to his drinking problem which allowed him to beat it. He made different choices that allowed him to be a better husband and a better father to his second family.

I knew what I knew, yet it would take a good girlfriend to write a piece for my book titled, **From an Adult Daughter of An Alcoholic** before I could say those words, **I am an adult daughter of an alcoholic.** I knew it yet saying it out loud and to myself made it much more real for me.

I know the stats, children of alcoholics are more likely to become alcoholic themselves and I also know that I married a confirmed alcoholic when I married my first husband. You would have thought I would have known better and yet I did what was known to me and was comfortable to me.

My dad's drinking problem showed itself in his depression, in his missed days of work, in his multiple infidelities, in his run ins with the law and in his anger and his violence. The drama at home was never ending. His heaviest drinking years coincided with my birth until he left our home for good when I was just twelve years old.

I grew up with incredible shame as a kid, never allowing anyone close enough to see what I saw. I lived in high alert mode. I could hear his car coming two city blocks away and I could smell his Lucky Strike cigarettes from the entry of our home on the first floor to my third floor bedroom. His unpredictable behaviors scared me.

As a little kid I had to go to speech therapy classes because I stuttered and I hid rather than have anyone really know me. They say in Alcoholics Anonymous, "You are only as sick as your secrets." Our family had our share of secrets and it was pretty sick. No one that knows me today would believe I ever stuttered or that I have any difficulty in communicating. I have learned for me that it is healthiest to live an open and an honest life. I just feel better this way. No more hiding and no more shame.

Yet I loved my father. I eventually understood him and I forgave him. When alcohol controlled his life our life was a living hell. He drank to unwind and relax yet so many times it resulted in his rage and violence. Most of that rage and violence was directed at my mother and my sisters. The younger ones may have avoided some of it but my older sister and I witnessed severe trauma and episodes that were so violent that twice he landed in jail.

The first time, for me was the most horrific and landed him in jail for more than 40 days. We lived on a farm in Northeast Pennsylvania back then. I was just a little kid when I saw him point a gun and shoot at a car filled with people. I was in that car. He could have killed me or anyone of my sisters and or our mother. Fortunately he missed. He went to jail came out and blamed my mother. He was still in denial over his alcohol abuse and nothing really changed. My mother stayed with him. Her family knew of this and it eventually led to estrangement. She made a choice and it wasn't the welfare of her children. She was staying with her man. My mother was the classic enabler. She was a nurse and in the helping profession, she tried her best to make it all better. She thought she could change him.

The next episode would be years later, my parents would be going through their final divorce and he had already moved out and in with his girlfriend. At this time we were living in the city, in Allentown, Pennsylvania. During this episode, he was drunk came looking for a fight with my mother and in her absence took out his rage on my oldest sister. He beat her black and blue and he went to jail for the second time.

In his words, "I walked home from jail the next morning and I decided I would never drink again." And as far as I know he never did drink again. After that I could sense his sincere sorrow for the many years of abuse and trauma. In his sobriety he was humbled and had to face his past. It was not a pretty picture and he could no longer hide behind alcohol.

I know that it was hard for him to hear me recite what my first husband put me through; so much of it was similar to my father's previous behaviors. I make choices that modeled what I knew and what I witnessed as a kid. The good news is and was that once I got a clear look at what I was attracted to and how much it resembled my past from what I knew as a child, I no longer made those same poor choices.

Part of changing and trying NOT to repeat patterned family behaviors it is admitting that they exist and learning there is another healthier way. We all have choices.

My father would be having another birthday later this month, he lives in Heaven now. I miss him and think of him often. I wished I would have had more of his sober days in his company. I know that in his core he was a loving man who painted, planted a garden, grew vegetables and loved his wife and all eight of his children. I'd be willing to bet that he would have taken those drinking years back if he could have. What he left me with was his struggles, his lessons learned and his determination that good would win over evil. It took a lot of strength for him to beat alcohol and he did beat it. I loved him drunk and I loved him sober, sober was just so much easier.

I Am In Love with Hope

"We live in hope and we die in despair." Charles Dickens

"A leader is a dealer in hope." Napoleon Bonaparte

"Everything that is done in the world is done by hope." Martin Luther

"Hope sees the invisible, feels the intangible and achieves the impossible." Charles Caleb Colton

I could go on and on quoting really greats quotes that direct us toward hope, without hope and faith we die. I am a "hope" junkie! I live on it and I am in love with hope!

Without it, what would we have? We hope for a better world, we hope for better health, we hope for sunny days, we hope for bigger bank accounts, we hope for good friends, we hope for success. We hope for love and for peace and for purpose. We hope for better days.

But what is hope, is it an idea, a thought, a way of life, prayer? Is hope about having faith? I don't think a day goes by where I am not hopeful and filled with hope and faith.

There is such a great high that comes from hoping that all things go well, our city is high on hope. The hope is that our beloved Raven's will win yet another game and then win the Super Bowl too!

What would we become without hope? We live in hope and I am in love with hope. Hope for all that is good and great, hope for a better world for all of us. Hope it is a really good thing!

Hope … what you are hoping for …

I Am ...

I am strong, I am successful, I am a survivor, I am loved, I am loving, I am kind, I am giving, I am happy, I am content ...

Or what else do we tell ourselves that maybe isn't helping us at all? Things like "I am sick and tired!" tell yourself this and sooner or later you will become both "sick" and "tired." We are so often so hard on ourselves with negative comments about ourselves when it would be just as easy to recite positive affirmations.

The brain is the computer system of the body, what goes in is what comes out. Give yourself kind compliments and encouraging thoughts and do so often. Be your own best friend! You are worth the best of everything and if you don't think so, why on earth would anyone else?

Start with things like ...

1) I am happy
2) I am wonderful
3) I am loving
4) I am good
5) I am successful
6) I am worthy
7) I am beautiful
8) I am a child of God!

Desiderata

"Go placidly amid the noise and haste, and remember what peace there may be in silence.

As far as possible and without surrender be on good terms with all persons.

Speak your truth quietly and clearly; and listen to others; even the dull and ignorant; they too have their story.

Avoid loud and aggressive persons; they are vexations to the spirit.

If you compare yourself to others, you may become vain and bitter; for there will always be greater and lesser persons than yourself.

Enjoy your achievements as well as your plans. Keep interested in your own career, however humble; it is a real possession in the changing fortunes of time.

Exercise caution in your business affairs; for the world is full of trickery.

But let this not blind you to what virtue there is; many persons strive for high ideals; and everywhere life is full of heroism.

Be yourself. Especially do not feign affection. Neither be cynical about love; for in the face of aridity and disenchantment it is a perennial as the grass.

Take kindly to the counsel of the years, gracefully surrendering the things of youth.

Nurture strength of spirit to shield you in sudden misfortune. But do not distress yourself with dark imaginings.

Many fears are born of fatigue and loneliness. Beyond a wholesome discipline, be gentle with yourself.

You are a child of the universe, no less than the trees and the stars; you have a right to be here.

And whether or not it is clear to you, no doubt the universe is unfolding as it should.

Therefore be at peace with God, whatever you conceive Him to be, and whatever your labors and aspirations, in the noisy confusion of life keep peace with your soul.

With all its sham, drudgery, and broken dreams, it is still a beautiful world.

Be cheerful. Strive to be happy.

The first time I read the above I was in high school and I have often thought of it through the years and read it over and over again. I think it is still relevant and valuable food for thought.

"You are a child of the universe; you have a right to be here!" What are you telling yourself? Just remember it starts with I am

_____

I Could Make A Career Out Of "Doing" Coffee ...

They say the best deals are made on the golf course, but for me, I do well with having coffee or a lunch or dinner meeting. I could make a career out of "doing lunch" and many times I do! It is all about networking with friends, family and professional associates. What better way to get ahead in your personal life and professional career than to share a meal.

Yesterday it was lunch with a friend in banking, last week it was coffee with my college aged computer guru buddy and tomorrow's lunch is with my favorite Catholic Nun. A few weeks ago it was a casual lunch date that brought about the possibility of a new career for me. It was so unexpected but I mentioned something at lunch and in just a few hours I had received a phone call and an appointment to meet with the Executive Director for a position that seems to be right up my alley.

These opportunities aren't accidents they are meetings to share a coffee or a meal and to network. I have made some of my biggest real estate deals over drinks and dinner and I have received some of my greatest professional accomplishments that began with a simple lunch date.

Where phone calls, text messaging and e-mail has taken over for so many of us, nothing beats that old fashioned face-to face meeting that happens when we meet up for a lunch or dinner date. Relationships are so important to our overall health and taking the time to share a meal with a friend or a colleague has numerous benefits for wellness.

Just last week I met up with my old supervisor who also happens to be a Catholic Priest, he is just an all-around good person and always worth spending time with, we are good friends and like family. Our relationship is about trusting each other, supporting each other and lifting each other up.

When I have coffee with my friend Suzanne, it is an automatic guaranteed natural high. There has never been one time that when I left her company my heart wasn't joy filled. My friend Joy has that same effect on me.

I seriously could make a career out of "doing lunch" I don't know what my meeting with Sr. Cecelia will bring tomorrow but I know one thing for certain, she is one of the wisest women I know and just being in her company elevates me. She lifts me up!

Earlier tonight I had dinner with my college aged son, my heart is warmed and my soul is uplifted. Life is good! So ... let's do many more coffee dates, lunch meetings and dinners with family, friends and colleagues.

I seriously could make a career out of "doing" coffee ...

I Date My Husband and I Date Him Often

After more than twenty years together my husband and I still date each other and we do it often. Late yesterday I arrived home from a girl's weekend at the beach. When we finally got together after being apart for a long weekend we decided to head out to our state fair. We go just about every year when we are in town.

Being with my husband always brings me back to my high school years. Getting into his car and listening to his music is the same music I listened to in the late 1970's. It is classic rock and roll and each song reminds me of when I was just a teenager.

We love the fair and not for the typical things that so many young people go to the fair to do, we never go on the rides, for us it is about eating junk food that we would never normally consume and visiting the farm animals. We enjoy seeing who won the first place in pumpkin and watermelon growing among other plants. We like to visit the local politicians and see who is campaigning for the next election. We always visit the Catholic nuns too and support their rosary making and prayer cards.

Together we hold hands and we eat food and we catch up on all the things we missed while we were apart. We date and we date often. It could be a sports event, theater tickets, a concert, dinner or drinks out or catching up with family and friends. Like most people who date we prepare ourselves and try and look our best. He drives and opens the doors for me. We appreciate one another and we show it by how we treat each other.

We had the best time last night just walking around and taking in the sights and the sounds at our state fair. I am reminded of what a great date my husband is and always has been. For this couple, the secret to a long and happy marriage is to date and to date each other and to do it often …

Beach date next week and NASCAR at the end of September. My birthday date is scheduled in Lancaster, PA in October and we have our Thanksgiving holiday planned along with A Christmas Show and train tickets to New York in December. We both contribute to our "dating" schedule and we find all kinds of activities to do together. Our activities are ones where we can enjoy each other's company and continue to date.

Dating is definitely our secret to a long happy and successful marriage … so here is to dating our spouses, our partners and to dating them often!

I Found "It" on Christmas

Santa brought me a new Burberry watch this year; it is the classic Burberry pattern. I love it! I don't normally talk or write about my gifts. Unless of course the gifts are of a higher meaning and for me this story is about more than the gift of a new Burberry watch.

This year the gift of a new watch was to replace one that I lost several years ago. I turned our house and our cars and just about everything we own upside down looking for that watch. I couldn't find it anywhere. I was certain it was lost for good. It has been missing for several years now.

I wore that watch as my power "career" watch; it went to all my board meetings and every place of business with me. I wore it until the strap started to tear, probably wore it to work for as many as five years. It too had been a Christmas gift.

It seems with the band becoming frayed I decided to replace it with a more trendy Michele watch with a white band. The Michele watch was a sporty style compared to the Burberry watch but I enjoy wearing it. I keep all my packaging for my watches and jewelry. I don't have many expensive pieces but I do take good care of the few that I own.

In receiving a new watch I decided to retire the white Michele watch until the coming spring and summer. This way I can wear the brand new Burberry watch that I just received from Santa. Well guess what? Guess where the old Burberry watch turned up? Seems I put it in the Michele watch box packaging and just today on Christmas day I found it.

For me this story isn't about a lost Burberry watch though, but more about how we can look really hard for something and we just can't seem to find it. Sometimes when we do find it, we can reflect on all that it meant to us. Even after it has been replaced with a newer version, that old watch still retains some value. That old watch with its value was no longer missed nor was it being searched for to find it. I accepted that it was gone. Today several years later, it has been replaced with a newer version.

My real Christmas gift, the one I prayed for, came days or even a few weeks ago. It was the gift of peace that came from learning the truth. In learning the truth I was free and able to let it go. Just like that lost Burberry watch that I had to have and so desperately searched for, I received the gift of uncovering "it." And just like the lost watch, uncovering the truth no longer mattered to me. It had been replaced with a newer and even better version of my life.

Whatever happened or didn't happen is in the past and it is over, we never get to anything new as long as we keep seeking out that which has been lost and is already gone from us. Now today, I own two Burberry watches, an old one with a frayed and torn strap and a brand new one. But the reality is that I only have one wrist on which to wear any watch at any given time.

Looking for something or searching for someone that no longer exists or holds any value only creates emptiness and anxiety. Trusting that God knows best and we uncover what we need and what we lost when the time is right for us.

I have been so blessed in a variety of ways, crying over a lost watch or a lost cause doesn't afford us all that is ahead for us. I know that now more than I ever did before ... peace on Christmas day and always.

I Had a Waterbed

Yes there was a period of time when I had a California King Sized waterbed! And another time when I drove a 1971 Ford Pinto and once was the proud owner of a real muscle car in a 70's Mustang with a 351 Windsor engine. At one point in time these things were important to me and they meant something special.

Yet it took a television show where the hostess was chatting about her "waterbed" and I had all but forgotten that I used to sleep on one too. It was another time with another guy and at a completely different period of time in my life.

Things change. It has been said that that is about all that we can truly count on in life; change. We change. Our circumstances change. Life changes.

I've sported long hair and short hair I have had jobs and I've had careers and there is a big difference. I've witnessed friends enter my life and others depart it. All in its own good time.

In high school I had a teacher who had a classic line "regret the hardest pill to swallow" and I never forgot that and have tried my best to live my life accordingly. I don't have regrets but rather lessons learned.

There is a time and there is a place. I never tire of Ecclesiastes 3 – A Time for Everything.

A Time for Everything

There is a time for everything and a season for every activity under the heavens.

A time to be born and a time to die,

A time to plant and a time to uproot

A time to kill and a time to heal

A time to tear down and a time to build

A time to weep and a time to laugh

A time to mourn and a time to dance

A time to scatter stones and a time to gather them

A time to embrace and a time to refrain from embracing

A time to search and a time to give up

A time to keep and a time to throw away

A time to tear and a time to mend

A time to be silent and a time to speak

A time to love and a time to hate

A time for war and a time for peace

Enjoy your "waterbed" period and everything that came before it and all that comes after as we come to know that nothing last forever and really the greatest gift we can give to ourselves is to live fully in this moment in time, because that is life and all that we really have ...

I Had This Idea

I had this idea that if I did the right things, the right thing would happen for me.

- What I learned is that doing the right thing was what I do for myself and it doesn't guarantee that things will turn out like I thought.

I had this idea that living by the golden rule would guarantee that if I treated others like I want to be treated they would do the same.

- What I learned is that many people want and expect to be treated better than what they treat others, I learned many do things they would never want done to themselves.

I had this idea that I could trust all my "friends" because that was the understood definition of friendship.

- What I learned is that isn't necessarily true and that trusting myself was what was lasting and most important.

I had this idea that if my husband and I worked really hard and gave our children a stable home they would become stable.

- What I learned is their stability would have to come from within themselves.

I had this idea that if I was open and generous others in my life would also be open and generous.

- What I learned is that being open and generous is what I do for myself, others may choose to be closed off.

I had this idea that most things fall into a black or white, right or wrong kind of area.

- What I learned is that many things fall in that gray area.

I had this idea that some events in my life were good and others bad.

- What I learned was that if I turned it around even the things that appeared "bad" could become good and meaningful.

I had this idea that I had to wait for this or that to happen first before going on to the next thing.

- What I learned is that the here and the now are the best times.

I had this idea that my sense of wellness and peace was connected to something or someone else.

- What I learned was that my wellness and peace were always within me, I just needed to tap into it and be open to it.

I had this idea that if I was loveable everyone would just love me.

- What I learned is that I am loveable whether others choose to love me or not is about them.

I had this idea that my happiness was connected to someone or something else.

- What I learned is that my happiness lives inside of me and is not dependent on anyone or anything else.

I had this idea if I pushed harder, tried harder did everything right that I would always end up in a good place.

- What I learned is that I don't have to try so hard, sitting back and trusting in the universe brings about all the good naturally.

I had this idea how things should be at 20 and at 30 and at 40 and at 50.

- What I learned is that each decade defines itself in its own way and in its own time.

I had this idea that life is a beautiful thing!

- What I learned is that it life truly is a beautiful thing and even the ugly and the sad and the pain of loss and of love add a beautiful dimension, and offer their own beautiful gifts, as long as we are open and willing to receive them.

"I Hate People" She Said

"I hate people" it was the very first thing that she ever said to me. And I immediately liked her. I liked her honesty and her sensitivity. I liked her rescue dog that she had with her. We were getting together for a business meeting. I heard about her and that she liked my "style" and my "décor" but this was our first meeting and she just put it out there.

"I hate people." She said

Then I learned that she has a big job at one of my favorite Catholic Universities; Villanova. She was close to my age and had her share of dealing with people.

Her opening line caused me to reflect. What does someone mean when they say "I hate people" and what has transpired that would get them to that place to express it.

That same day we spent hours together and I liked her more and more as our time together progressed. She was a high achiever and someone that expected professionalism, she had high standards.

I will never forget her, although our business together has concluded, however I will always remember her huge smile and that big wave as she left me. She was happy and so was I.

I would be willing to be that she didn't "hate" me … nope, not at all … and I am pretty sure that she really doesn't "hate" people.

I Have a Sister!

God gives us everything that we need and when we open our eyes to it, it all becomes so clear. I am an "O'Connell girl" by birth, the second born daughter of five daughters born to Bernie and Inez O'Connell. Although you would never know that I have "sisters" because they have not been in my life for about 25 years now.

Even as little kids I was the scapegoat and the "black sheep" my father favored me and my sisters clung to our mother. When dad left home so did my ally and I soon found myself on my own. And in that space of time I developed into an independent woman.

Our estrangement was over a child molester who married into the family, they sided with him and once again I was the "scapegoat" and the "black sheep" but it never bothered me, not ever. They have nothing that I want. My integrity in doing the right thing although unpopular has easily and always sustained me.

I never felt that I was missing out or missing something because I had replaced those relationships with healthy relationships. Today I opened up a friend's weekly e-newsletter and the opening line referred to her "Soul-sister" "Bee" and that would be me! I had to chuckle and to smile while reading it. Not everyone would know that it is me, but I do.

I have a sister! I have a sister who has sisters of her own and yet still includes me. Her heart is open and loving. We are really comfortable around each other. We share a birth month and a birth year and we share our Italian and Catholic heritage. We are both writers and have a deep affection for the written word. We like our beach travels and good reads and that occasional glass of wine or mixed drink.

We are both madly in love with our husbands our homes and our children. When we are together the energy is always abundant and completely uplifting. She is the "sister" that God gave to me. And far better than any sister I could have imagined for myself.

Our relationship is easy and built on respect and love. At different times we have both been one another's "911" call when family life was taking its toll or becoming a challenge. She was there for me and I was there for her.

Recently I read her book and I thought "that could be my family" it was about the history and the heritage of Little Italy in Baltimore.

The longer I live the more that I am sure that God brings us the people that are meant to be in our lives and He removes the ones that are no longer meant to be there.

It should have been crystal clear but today I had that epiphany "I have a sister!" And oh so much more … I have peace and love and all of it without the drama.

It Isn't About You

"Nothing other people do is because of you. It is because of themselves. All people live in their own dream in their own mind; they all are in a completely different world from the one we live in. When we take something personally, we make the assumption that they know what is in our world, as we try to

impose our world on their world." The Four Agreements by Miguel Ruiz

I am that person who used to take it all so personally and gets upset when an aggressive driver gives me the finger or some other road rage act. I will say out loud to myself as I drive in my car, *"I'm sorry, I didn't even see you there."* And then I think how that person could get so mad when he doesn't even know me. If I get cut off on the road, I don't get angry but most often give the benefit of doubt. They probably didn't see me there either; they weren't doing anything to me personally.

They say "perception is reality" if that is how someone perceives it, it is real to them. It took a long time for me to be fully developed enough to know that what everyone says isn't necessarily the truth. It may be their perception but it might not be mine. I have a friend who is smart enough when he hears things to say, *"Well that isn't my experience."* He doesn't just buy into what people say but rather what he knows from his own experience. Perhaps more of us should be like him.

Over the holidays, I thought a lot about my family. I spent time thinking about my mother and I pray for her soul every day. I pray that she has peace in heaven and that God has helped her. My mother was many things, like most people with strengths and weaknesses. She was one of the smartest women I know and worked harder than most people I know. She was driven. She was a highly educated administrative nurse with numerous years in all the intensive units of a well-respected hospital as well as a long stretch as a pediatric nurse. She had a zest for life and she loved food and was a pretty good cook. Many people loved her and most people liked her too.

My mother was so accomplished professionally and yet she was also attracted to abusive men. Both of her husbands were both charming and abusive. Their abuse showed itself in different ways. Was she the classic magnet in being in a helping profession? I've heard kids say that their mothers should have left abusive relationships for the well-being of their children. Maybe I used to feel that way too and then I realized she didn't think enough of herself to leave, it wasn't about her children. It wasn't about me.

For many reasons I had issues with my mother. She would leave this earth without ever once trying to right the wrongs between us. We didn't speak for the last 23 years of her life, although I did try. She didn't want to hear what I had to say. I finally realized, it wasn't about me, her world and my world collided and she would have had to change her life to accept what I had to share with her. She made her choice and it wasn't me or my truth. It wasn't about me, it never was. Yet there was a stretch of time when I was so hurt and so angry with her. I used to think, it was about her not loving me.

When you are a feeling and connected person, you tend to take it all in and onto yourself what people spew at you. It takes a much more established person, someone who really knows their own self to understand that what we take in and onto our self is our own choice.

If you let go of that fight, they are stuck there fighting with their own self. It takes two to fight. The only way to stop; is to understand that it was never about you in the first place. Some people need to be right as the expense of another person being wrong. At a certain point you begin to understand how little value there is in being right, if you are left there, standing alone.

I Named Her

I named her, I choose her first name and her middle name, and her name came from an old Johnny Mathis song and also from a little girl that I babysat when I was just a teen. My second choice was Caitlyn Marie and Christopher Michael if we had a boy. It was my choice at just three weeks of age that she would be christened in the Catholic Church. I was there and she was there too.

After taking La Leche league classes I chose to breast feed for the first year of her life. I was there for every single doctor's visit and every single first day of school and every last day too. It was me who taught her to ride a bicycle and I was there when she passed her driver's license exam. As an infant I changed diapers and as a young woman I helped support her style. I was there and she was there too.

As a toddler our outings often included the public library and she was enrolled in every single summer reading program. She loved books and was a wiz with her ability to communicate. She was an avid reader. We read together and she always seemed to have her face in a book. I was there and she was there too.

It was me who would decide she should attend Catholic schools and it was me who decided she should be Confirmed. I was there for love and I was there for support. She achieved much as an academic, she was smart, social and attractive. I was there and she was there too.

I was there for all the Christmas programs, for piano lessons and recitals; I was there for carpool every single school day. I was there and she was there too.

I was there when she fell and when she failed, I was there to cheer her on and her biggest fan when she accomplished her goals. I was there and she was there. When her father died and she was just two years old, my love and my desire to protect her from any other harm was heightened. I was there for first dates and for proms I was there for first jobs. I was there and she was there.

I was there for birthday parties and for "sweet 16" I was there for summer pool parties with her classmates. I was there and she was there too. She always smiled when she saw me and her voice always heightened when I called her. I was there and she was there.

Summer vacations always included the beach, we both loved the water. I was there and she was there too. When she graduated with honors, I was there. When we purchased her first car I was there. I was there and she was there too.

I named her. I choose her first name and her middle name. I carried her into this world and I gave her life. I was there and she was there too. She called me "mom" for the longest time, she was the only one. Then one day it was "Bernadette" and we were done. I was there and she was there and that was all ...

I Saw an Old Woman Today and I Saw Myself

On a hot and humid July day I found myself driving in Shrewsbury Pennsylvania, I was learning more about a backyard shed that we are looking to purchase. After meeting with the Amish builders I headed off to a local market known for their orchards of apples and peaches. They have a lovely bakery and I picked up a homemade peach danish and a handful of fresh peaches.

As I turned the corner in the market, I was struck by an elderly woman and her companion a younger lady. When I looked closer I recognized the woman. Her name was Bernice and we worked together twenty years earlier when we were both Realtors selling real estate. She was much older than me back then but she had really aged. When I knew her she was a force to be reckoned with. Bernice was a strong, tall and quick witted communicator. She had a passion for life and radiated energy and happiness.

Today she was thinner slightly hunched over and needed assistance in getting around. When I whispered her name her companion perked up. It was indeed Bernice. I explained how I knew her and Bernice smiled and spoke in a much softer fainter tone than how I remembered her. Turned out her husband passed away more than ten years ago and she was currently living in an assisted living center. Her companion was her niece who often came to spend time with her and take her on some short local outings like this market.

When I looked at Bernice, I saw myself. I thought that could be me in another 25 or 30 years. As we age we get weaker, quieter and smaller. The world doesn't pay as much attention to us as perhaps they did when we are younger and more vibrant. The Bernice I knew had so much to offer, she was a doer and a real contender in the real estate business. Today it was clear that Bernice was at the final stages of her life. Most of her living had already taken place. She looked good though, she was well dressed and neat and clean and really well cared for. She wasn't as sure of herself or as confident as I remembered her to be … I saw an old woman today … and I saw myself.

I Survived An Italian Mother, A Catholic Education and Three Kids ...

I survived an Italian mother, a Catholic education and three kids; in a word I survived a boat load of guilt! My mother was famous for making us feel bad if we did wrong or made a mistake. Since my parents divorced when I was in the sixth grade, I watched my mother work double-shifts to afford her five daughters. We knew the sacrifices she made even when she wasn't reminding us of them. But I also got my drive and determination and my intelligence from my mother. She had a zest for life and energy that transcended her. My work ethic, intelligence and my determination to succeed, no doubt came from my mom.

My mother worked so hard that we couldn't help but feel guilty if our behaviors or actions caused her any undue stress. She had already taken on so much with five girls and a high powered administrative nursing career.

In Catholic school I learned that God was not just Sunday service but an everyday experience and like my mother, God had provided me with many gifts and opportunities and I best do good deeds with them. I learned the power of prayer and I learned service above self. Being Catholic meant walking with God and doing so in a manner that would please Him, I had Priests and Nuns as teachers. We were "guilted" into many behaviors and we knew not to let God, our family, our friends and our Catholic community down. God could see me everywhere and He knew everything so I best be on my best behavior at all times. I learned to feel bad and to feel guilty if I didn't do my best or if I came up short.

There is nothing like raising children to make you feel responsible and guilty for just about anything real or perceived. Mothers especially internalize their feelings about their kids. First and foremost they are responsible for bringing them into the world. A mother wants everything good and all opportunities for her children. Parents will do things and go places and humble themselves for their children like they would never even do for themselves. They put their kids first and feel responsible for their children when they struggle or have difficulties. If a child comes from us and has a disability or struggles we as parents take that on as though it is our fault and we are responsible and often feel guilty about it.

My mother and my Catholic education were both rooted in much guilt and yet it was just what they knew and what they learned and did to try and motive and govern us. The feeling was if we felt badly enough we wouldn't do it! Whatever "it" was in an Italian Catholic family there was a code for living. You knew what was "right" and what was "wrong" and you were told there are two ways to do things; "the right way and the wrong way."

We didn't want to let out mothers down or our Catholic community or our children down, so we were driven to do our best and we did everything we could to avoid the guilt if we didn't.

I've read that many women feel "relief and freedom" when their mothers pass on, the hold that they have had on them both good and bad is gone. A daughter no longer has to live in her mother's shadow. As a fully grown adult I have learned that my mother, the Catholic Church and my children are all just people. Like me not one of them is or was perfect either and I no longer feel guilty when I too am less than perfect.

I survived an Italian mother, a Catholic education and three kids, I survived a boat load of guilt but the truth is I didn't just survive, I often thrived in it all too ...

If You Think You Can, You Can!

If you think you can, you can! This first came to me from a favorite teacher when I was a young girl in school. It has stayed with me ever since. The mind is the computer system of the body, what goes in is what comes out. If we believe that we can achieve it we will.

The opposite is true as well if you tell yourself that you can't do it, you won't do it. There is nothing that we can't achieve if we work hard enough for it and believe in it. One of the greatest gifts we can give to ourselves is to believe in ourselves and our own abilities.

This mantra doesn't just work with the goals that we set for ourselves like becoming the class President or securing that job.

It also can be used when we are faced with adversity. As human beings we are survivors and have a built in desire to live, to survive and even thrive.

One of the reasons I love teachers so much and have so many in my life as good friends is because they don't see the obstacle as much as they see the possibilities. They know that with effort and the right attitude everything and anything is possible.

When we are faced with a challenge and a struggle and with adversity we must learn to use the same tools of "If you think you can, you can!" If you think you can beat cancer you will try your hardest, if you think you can get over "it" "him" or "her." You will!

It is when we tell ourselves that "we can't" is when we are doomed to fail. Kids have a natural born in desire with an "I can do that!" attitude. We should remember that as we age. If we believe in ourselves and believe that there is nothing we can't accomplish with the right mind set we become fully accomplished. Then there is no challenge that we cannot overcome. So often getting through that challenge and to the other side is when we see the gifts of overcoming that which was once an obstacle.

Change your thinking and change your world. If you think you can, you can! Say it, see it, believe it and then do it!

Jealousy and Envy

"Jealousy is defined as resentment against a rival, a person enjoying success or advantage, or against another's success or advantage itself and mental uneasiness from fear of rivalry, unfaithfulness. It is also defined as vigilance in guarding something." Dictionary.com

"Envy is defined as a feeling of discontent or covetousness with regard to another's advantages, success, possessions etc." Dictionary.com Envy is one of the seven deadly sins according to Christian views.

My own view is that jealousy or envy is an indicator that you aren't living your life the way you should be living it, because if you were there would be no need for any jealousy or envy. There is not a single person alive or dead that I have any jealousy or envy toward or about, my life isn't supposed to look like someone else's life, it is supposed to look like my own unique life. Your life is supposed to look like you, which is why it's called your life.

"The worst part of success is trying to find someone who is happy for you." Bette Midler

If you want that relationship, that house, that car, that life then create it, create your life the way that you want it to be, you have that choice.

A few decades ago, I invited a girlfriend to my mother's house for Thanksgiving, we worked together that day and although the day was almost over, she did in fact join me. On this occasion she had an opportunity to meet my family and see our family dynamic. As we were about to drive out of the driveway, she said, "Your sisters are all jealous of you." That never occurred to me until she said that. They always acted like they were better than me, often targeting me with nasty comments like, **"Bernadette Cycle 3 for the overweight dog!" or "You are just like dad, why don't you go live with him."**

Recently another friend accused one of my friends of being jealous of me. That statement doesn't make me feel good; and if true it actually makes me sad for them. I think everyone who is doing what they should be doing in their own life, has no reason for jealousy over someone else's life.

When people say to me, **"You are so lucky, you have a great husband." "You are so lucky to have twins." "You are so lucky to have a house."** Or this or that, and I think to myself, luck has nothing to do with it, but hard work and being responsible does.

Yes I have a great husband, our relationship and our marriage is work, it doesn't just happen. And it is not always easy. Raising twins was work, raising any child is a huge amount of work as is maintaining a home. Everything we have comes with work and with responsibilities.

Every once in a while I look at luxury cars, a white BMW convertible, we could afford it and I could go get one if I really wanted it. But then I think about the payments and the upkeep and I think do I really want that car? Do I need to have it? When I see them on the road I appreciate their beauty but I'm not jealous or envious of the person who owns it?

When someone else is having success, I always think to myself, good for them, now it is one more time closer to my turn. There isn't anything that anybody else has that I want that I couldn't go get or make for myself and it I can't then I accept that it isn't meant for me. That my life isn't supposed to look like that, it is supposed to look like my life not theirs.

"Welcome to the wonderful world of jealousy, he thought. For the price of admission, you get a splitting headache, a nearly irresistible urge to commit murder, and an inferiority complex. Yippee." J.R. Ward

When we create the life that we want to live, the life that we were meant to live, there is no reason for jealousy or for envy.

Job Interviews and Blind Dates

Does it seem like job interviews might just be a tad bit like a blind date? Where we don't know what we are getting until that actual face-to-face occurs and we are looking at this person, the candidate? In one setting we are looking for a professional relationship and the other for personal reasons but either way, we are looking at the potential candidates to fill a void, a slot or a position.

For many years I held interviews to fill a variety of positions from assistants to managers to directors and interns. My gut instincts were almost always right on target. In the dozens and dozens of professionals that I have engaged in employment, few times did I ever sense that I made a bad call or that I made a bad decision.

Much of the decision making came from my ability to retrieve the answers to questions like did I view the candidate as someone that I could manage and work closely with and did they carry themselves professionally. Could I trust them to do their job and what kind of trouble shooter were they? When faced with a challenge could they work their way through it and find answers? Or did it stop them in their tracks? Were they self-motivated?

It has been decades since I have dated or even been on a "blind date" but it seems like when we bring people into our circle whether it is for professional reasons or personal ones, we want to make sure that it is a good fit.

Last year a friend went out of state for a big job and a big interview when she returned we were discussing her interview. Her read was that she didn't get the job. She was 100% certain it was not going to go her way. We were actually talking about it when the call came in and she was offered the position.

What she thought and what actually happened were two completely different outcomes.

In the past few years I have interviewed for new jobs and interviewed with potential clients all the while being "on" and knowing that you are being ranked and judged. Can this person fit the bill? I have asked the key questions and been asked the key questions. "Why do you want to work here?" "What can you do for this position?" "Why should we hire you and work with you?" and the classic "Where do you see yourself in 5 years and 10 years?"

Last year I interviewed in a panel interview after making it through several screens. They did their homework as it was one of the most notable interviews I ever faced. I left there uncertain as to the outcome. Within hours I was called and accepted the job. I loved the panel that interviewed me.

About a year ago I interviewed almost across the street from where I live, I immediately knew I did not like the person nor did I want to work with them and for them. I am certain she sensed it too.

My answer when people asked me how an interview went is always the same, and it is the same when I am interviewed by potential clients, "I gave it my all and you never know what the competition is and who else they are looking at to fill the position." As a result I never take it personally if I don't get the job.

Last month I interviewed for an hour and a half with an Executive Director, I liked him, I liked the mission and the location. I had a great tour of their facility and I learned so much. It is coming up on a month and I haven't heard a single word. What I know is that he had four candidates and that I thoroughly enjoyed our time together and I learned so much more about the work that they did. It was a good interview whether I got the job or not and I would be willing to financially donate to their cause. They are doing such greats works with a mission that is both near and dear to my heart.

Today my newest job interview was cancelled due to a snow storm. This will give me a longer period of time to study their works and to imagine myself working there. What I know for certain is that I always end up right where I am supposed to be and if it is meant to be it will be.

I do think though that job interviews like first dates and blind dates have some things in common. We are looking to include or disqualify the potential candidates. We do judge people by how they look, how they carry themselves and what type of education do they have, we want to know that they can handle what they are signing up for whether it is for a job or a relationship.

Our social skills and our communication skills are tested when we interview just like they are tested when we are dating. In the final analysis, interviews and dates are very much alike when it comes down to it because we never really know what we are getting until we risk engaging that potential person.

So here is to all those that are taking risks in relationships for both securing employment and finding love and companionship. Just putting yourself out there and going through the process adds to our skill set. Each encounter offers us something new to learn. We learn about others and we learn about ourselves.

Just For Fun!

"Did you come just for fun?" She asked. I didn't know her name as we shared pleasantries while we both waited for our husbands to bring the cars around. She was from Jackson Mississippi and we had been staying in the same hotel in Biloxi Mississippi. When I told her we came from Baltimore Maryland in her very southern Mississippi accent she wanted to know if we "came just for fun." I had to chuckle because I guess we had made this trip for fun.

Her baby girl was in a stroller and lit up when I smiled at her, according to her mother she just turned one year old. I was reminded of how often babies just took to me. How I loved kids and was always enlightened and having fun while interacting with them.

As we drove off I couldn't stop thinking about her question and her glee when she asked it. In our more than twenty year history together my husband and I both had a lot of responsibility in our lives. For decades we had the two big careers that demanded our attention 24/7 along with raising our three children and managing two homes. We were always busy and we were always working. Sure we had fun but fun was the last thing on our agenda. We always had a lengthy "to do" list and that meant work.

Since his recent retirement after 35 years of employ we have slowed down quite a bit and in that slowing down we have carved out much more time for having fun!

Our trip to Biloxi was "just for fun!" We went to the pool and to the beach and we drove 45 minutes and enjoyed a day trip to New Orleans where we attended a Jazz Artists Festival. I had my cards read we ate at Café' Du Monde and we shopped. We attended a live musical concert of one of our favorite country music artists at the Hard Rock Café. We had a blast! It was a trip that we both agreed upon was a lot of fun. One of our best ever.

In retrospect we often gave up "fun" for the seriousness of the numerous responsibilities we had taken on. Now I think more and more about living our lives and doing more and more things that are "just for fun!"

So ... are you having fun? And if not what could/should you be doing differently to incorporate more fun into your life?

Here is to living a life that includes trips and experiences and events that are truly "just for fun!"

Kindness Counts

Last week I received a lovely card and inside the card was a gift card to one of my favorite coffee houses. It was completely unexpected. So who sent it and why? It was a young 29 year old professional who share the same love for development that I have enjoyed. All I did was to take his phone call and give him my thoughts and some advice. We never met in person, he works with a very dear friend of mine and she recommended me to him. It was a lovely chat and very rewarding in itself. The card and gift card was the cherry on top.

This guy is going somewhere; he is polite, energetic and knows how to cultivate relationships. His act of kindness wasn't lost on me and was so nice and truly appreciated. You could say he made my day.

During this same week we had lunch and a drink at one of our favorite pizza places up at the beach. While eating our pizza a group of bikers came in and there were seven of them. I know this because there weren't enough seats together for them to sit together. I overheard them talking about going to the bar upstairs when I said, **"We can move down, how many seats do you need?"** My husband and I moved way down so they could all sit together. Our kindness costs us nothing yet they all expressed their gratitude. When it was time to pay our check we noticed our drinks weren't on the check. When we questioned the bartender she said, **"It is on me, thanks for giving up your seats so I could have more customers to serve."** Another win-win! We never expected a free drink we just did what anyone would and should have done.

Every single day we are faced with opportunities to act out in kind ways. Neither of the two stories shared above were motivated by wanting to get something. They were just kind acts that cost nothing but make you feel good about being considerate to others.

We can easily get caught up in situations where people may not be kind or giving or we can be that "change charger" who thinks about others and who offers up acts of kind behaviors throughout the day. I have often thought that "giving is for the giver" but how nice to be recognized and appreciated for acting in ways that are kind to others …

Know Yourself Love Yourself

"To thine own self be true" Shakespeare ***"Are you living a life that is more in tune with your "authentic" self who you were***

created to be or your "fictional" self who the world has told you to be?" Dr. Phil

It is so important to know yourself. In a world that is quick to judge and where people can be fickle in both love and hate, it is more important than ever to love yourself, understand yourself and to know yourself.

When you have lived in the same home for twenty one years you have collected many things. Cleaning out a home of twenty one years is no easy task and literally can be a "trip down memory lane." In recent weeks I have come across so many things from the past. There are pictures and letters and cards and documents that represent our life in our home for over two decades. There are also the things that we brought with us and forward from our life before becoming a married couple and a family.

The history is rich with so much love and happiness and documented letters, notes and cards that prove that love existed. I came across hundreds of photographs that can tell their own story. Of course there was loss, disappointment and upset too.

There are report cards and letters of recommendation. Probably 95% of what was found was positive and upbeat and maybe 5% was upsetting. I don't think we hold onto things that upset us like we do the things that make us feel good. Yet how often do we focus on what one negative person says or does to us and wipe away all that is good.

"The better you know yourself, the better your relationship with the rest of the world." Toni Collette

The takeaway for me on this "trip down memory lane" has been that you have to know yourself. If you allow someone else, anyone else and their view of you to define you, you will become like a leaf flying in the wind. If they change their mind or their thoughts about you, you could easily find yourself in a different place at any different moment, depending upon their whim.

Where it is important to hear what other people say, it is most important to remember that much of what other people say and do is because of themselves and has very little to do with you.

If you allow others to define you, and you do not define yourself, you can't act surprised when that definition is ever changing according to another's whim and self-serving means.

"If you know the enemy and know yourself you need not fear the results of a hundred battles." Sun Tzu

Know yourself! Do not allow anyone else to define you, define yourself, only you know who you really are. People can and will turn on you if it serves them to do so. A divorce or a break up often pits one person against another, this same couple once professed undying love.

When someone that you once loved and they loved you too, turns against you, or away from you, that is about them and really has nothing to do with you. Most often people that do so do it for their own self-preservation and personal gain. Simply put, they are getting something out of it, or they wouldn't do it.

When you are firm in whom you are, others unkind words and actions won't hurt as much. Loving yourself is not arrogance or conceit, it means having a healthy regard for yourself knowing that you are a worthy human being.

To love yourself means to accept yourself as you are and to come to terms with those things that you cannot change. It means to have self-respect, a positive self-image, and unconditional self-acceptance.

Lady of the House and/or Boys Are Just Easier

I didn't ask for it but apparently I am the "lady of the house." My husband and my son have given me that unofficial title. The only thing I can say is it is so much easier with men! Even in my career I was often told while negotiating contracts, **"You do business like a man."** I took it as a compliment. Business is business and not for the emotionally challenged.

My guys are so easy and so appreciative of me and I love having them around. They are so protective of me and I always considered myself to be a strong and independent woman. I was always a cheerleader for my girls and yet it would be the men in my life that would lift me up and hold me nearest and dearest. This has even transpired with my dogs?

 I never had a male dog until the spring of 2011 and that little guy Chipper has stolen my heart. Initially my husband and son seemed to gravitate to him. I was fine with my older female Bichon named Happy. I liked him but I found his ability to pee like a water gun a tad bit disturbing. At least with Happy it was controlled this guy had incredible aim and could hit a distant and remote location.

Even with my girls I liked being female and wanted to share my elder inside knowledge. Boys were always a mystery to me; I mean I grew up with 4-sisters and a mother as the head of the household. I liked boys but had little point of reference. They liked me too. Even as a kid I preferred hanging out with the boys. In sixth grade they came looking for me to ride bikes and play kickball.

They didn't go after the other girls in the neighborhood because they wanted a competitor and I played to win. It started even younger, I thought dad was cool and often dressed in jeans and a jean jacket preferring to get around in his Jeep rather than cooking in the kitchen with my mother and my sisters.

Girls can be so emotional and with so much drama, my guys are clear headed and clear cut in their determination and decision making. They do the tough and dirty jobs too. I never have to take the trash out, clean the pool or lift heavy objects. My husband takes care of the car maintenance and I am happy to maintain our home. But where I excel most is where they are most appreciative. I cook and I bake and I cook and I bake often. They love to eat. It is a marriage made in heaven.

When my son was young just pre-teen he started opening car doors for me and taking heavy objects out of my hands. He sprang into action to help me unload my car. When I thank him his response is and was, "Always willing to help, can I do anything else for you?" How could you not find a soft spot for a kid like that?

I continue to be amazed at how you can raise multiple children in the same home in the same environment and with the same parents and they turn out so completely different. Our son appreciates us and always did and yet I honestly feel I did less for him. As a young boy I thought it was his father's job to be his role model. I had to read the book, **Raising Cain** because I truly had zero point of reference in raising a son. I don't know how I got so lucky to be surrounded by the men I have in my life but I do know that I recognize a good thing when I have it.

The homemade blueberry muffins just came out of the oven … this "lady of the house" knows how to keep them happy. And their happy is my happy. My guys are easy to please and that pleases me.

Oh and I truly believe ... **boys are just easier!**

Laugh More ... Love More ... Be Happy

I don't think we get more points when we leave this life for being unhappy and miserable. The best cure for unhappiness is things that make you happy not dwelling on those that hurt us. Laughter truly is such great medicine for all that ails us. The chemical release your brain releases neurochemicals such as endorphins gives us that high from laughter. It is a natural high. There is no greater feeling than when something strikes us as funny and we laugh out loud.

Recently I was watching Betty White's show ***Off Their Rockers,*** I haven't laughed out loud so much in such a long time. There was one short scene where a Catholic Nun is pushing a baby carriage and she happens upon two young girls sitting on a park bench. She tells them they can't take any more babies, they are filled up and so here is this baby for you to take care of. You need to do your part and help out. The nun then turns and walks away leaving the baby and baby carriage behind and with two complete strangers. She never affords them any response. Obviously what makes this so funny is that no one in their right mind would just give two complete strangers a baby, a baby they didn't ask for, and to two people this nun knows nothing about.

I hate to admit it but one of my guilty pleasures is the television show, **Family Guy,** they are without any boundaries in this comedy and say things we are taught never to say. Some of it truly is in bad taste but that's probably why I find it so humorous. My favorite is probably one of the least offensive ones titled; **Over.** You can find it on YouTube and I seriously laugh every time I view it.

According to the University of Maryland School of Medicine in Baltimore research has shown that laughter is linked to healthy function of blood vessels. It further states that laughter helps with mental stress. It can be a healthy release to laugh.

Yet when we are sad and unhappy often the last thing we feel like doing is finding things that make us feel good and make us laugh, however, it seems like this may just be what we need to do for ourselves. Happy people attract happy people just like love attracts more love. A life without laughter and a life without love is probably not a life worth living. We choose what we focus on and what we dwell on. Our world isn't perfect, our lives aren't perfect but they can be filled with more laughter and more love. It is a choice, it is our choice.

"For as he thinks in his heart, so he is." Proverbs 23:7

"We live in a society absorbed with its own feelings. Today, people are addicted to seeing themselves as victims and demanding special tolerance, favor, acceptance, or gifts. Yet a mind concerned with its own painful experiences, rejections, mistakes, or emotional hurts is one that refuses healing. Pain should teach and mature us, not box us into darkness. Hebrews 2:10 says Christ learned by the things He suffered – His pain was His teacher." From BibleTools.org

If we truly want healing, we must change the way we think. Think happy, be happy. Laugh more and love more …

Laughter and Tears

Like so many others, I am saddened to learn of the apparent suicide of actor Robin Williams. I had that same sad feeling over the untimely deaths of actors like Philip Seymour Hoffman and Heath Ledger. We hear these stories and we are shocked and think what a waste. They have so much to live for, how could they commit suicide or use drugs that ultimately resulted in a premature death. We have that same feeling when a 17 year old teen takes their life. All we can think to say is "why?" and they "have so much to live for?"

Yet everyday people both ordinary and extraordinary decide that life is no longer worth living. More than 38,000 American's died of suicide in 2010. That same year suicide was the third leading cause of death for adolescents.

Although I blog about most things, suicide has been one where for the most part I have stayed away from except in 1998 when I had a poetry book published with a poem titled "For David" that reads;

Why, you made us cry

Why, you did not have to die

You took your life

Now it is all our strife

We miss you so bad

We are so sad

Your daughter so beautiful

Your daughter so you

Why David why

What did you do?

His daughter is a grown woman now who yearns for the father that she will never know. We try and make sense of the senseless. We can't comprehend it. But the reality of life is that it is not always easy. Things happen that can and do break our spirit.

To young people contemplating suicide what I would say is that whatever angst you are feeling it will pass, the beauty of life is that everything changes. Today's sadness may well be tomorrow's treasured happiness.

"We live in hope and we die in despair" Richard Scott Harris. It seems that suicide is when hope has been replaced with despair. We may never fully understand it; it seems like a really bold move in killing oneself.

We have learned as a society to take suicide claims seriously and to support and get help anyone that is talking about suicide. I've heard it said that many of the funniest of comediennes are also some of the saddest individuals.

What we know for sure is that life isn't always easy, that asking for what you need and speaking out when you come up short might make all the difference. It has been said that "suicide" is a "mental illness" I think we can group many things into the "mental illness" bin if we so desire but the bigger question is why would anyone from a hugely successful actor to a young teen just starting out ever believe that ending life prematurely is ever better than living life fully?

Through the years I have worked with many teens and been exposed to hopelessness and helplessness of people of all ages.

We can treat for mental illness or depression but perhaps we should also use these deaths to look at how we act and how we react and how we treat our fellow brothers and sisters.

In a world that is full of darkness and fighting both externally and internally I still want to believe that love and care cure much that ails us.

Life is so fragile and we are all so vulnerable, love and acceptance over hurts, judgments and denial. If you know of anyone that is thinking about suicide please help them to help themselves. I've heard it said that if someone wants to die, to truly commit suicide there really is very little that can be done to stop them. I guess the question we all have as we face our mirror image is "what are we doing to care for ourselves? What are we feeding our hearts and our souls?"

Our "why" anyone would commit suicide may never be answered but we do live in hope. We must believe in better days and a better world and know that individually and collectively we have the power to bring in the light. When someone is weak and can't see the light perhaps it is our job to help light their way. We are our brother's keeper, we all feel the loss in actor Robin Williams deciding that his life was no longer worth living. The greater sadness knows that we don't feel that way about him and yet he felt that way about himself.

"Laughter and tears are meant to turn the wheels of the same machinery of sensibility; one is wind-power; and the other water-power." Oliver Wendall Holmes

To honor Robin Williams for all the laughter he fueled we pray that he rests in peace and that his family and friends find comfort in knowing that he leaves behind a body of work that is far greater than any single act that resulted in his death.

Imagine if we focused more and more on love and hope and helped to light the way for those living in the darkness just how great this world and could be …

Leading With Love

Sometimes it is so easy to love and to lead with love and sometimes it can be a real challenge to respond with love. There isn't a person alive that isn't going to face some kind of challenge or disappointment or meet up with someone that rubs us the wrong way. We all have "those people" in our lives. The people that test us and try us, they are the ones that do and say things that run contrary to what we think and what we believe. People that want us to feel bad, often because they don't feel good, so they push us down in order to elevate themselves. I have witnessed some of these people and have known a few of these folks myself.

When we feel attacked and someone comes at us and they come from their own place of anger, hatred and fear, it can be a real challenge to respond with love. After Osama Bin Laden was killed I read where many people were elated by his demise, some of those people were in my own family. Surely I could understand their anger and their desire for justice but what I couldn't understand was anyone taking glee in the murder of another human being.

I have seen that same kind of glee when people are happy to have hurt someone else, and when they know that their actions caused that hurt and they almost seem proud of themselves for being part of that hurt and hatred. This response doesn't come from a loving place but rather a fear based place.

Every one of us has the power inside of ourselves to lift up others or to tear at others, we can build people up or we can help to destroy them. Leading with love is the only God like response, and this is true for the easy to love and just as true for the ones that we find most challenging to love.

Leading with love isn't always easy but it is what we do for ourselves so that we have peace and joy in our own hearts and in our lives. When you take glee in hurting others, when you feel that you have the right to hurt someone else you are not coming from love but from fear. When we look closely at the people that speak ill of others and the ones who try and hurt other people you can see where it is a true and direct reflection on how they feel about themselves. A person who has learned to love themselves and to accept themselves has no interest in anger, hatred or fear.

The anniversary of 9/11 is upon us as it was eleven years ago when our country was shocked by the senseless murderous acts of a group of people that literally were trained and made a decision to murder. I have often thought about the death penalty. People that murder can be tried and found guilty of murder and their penalty can be death. It reminds me of the 60's when the anti-war tag line was, **"why do we kill people who kill people to show that killing people is wrong."** When we allow someone else's rage and anger and hatred to enter our hearts and our minds, we become more like them.

Hard as it is, I prefer to lead with love, and I do my best to lead with love and to respond with love. There is no doubt it can be a very real challenge, but it is also a very real choice. When I can't respond with love, I remove myself from that person or that place or that situation. Anger can be justified but it never serves us well when anger is used to hurt others. Our outrage and our anger should tell us some things about ourselves and perhaps be the driving force to turn it around and to do something good with our anger. Leading with love is always the best response and where hatred breeds more hatred, love breeds more love. Do we want more love in our lives, or do we want more hate, anger and fear.

Love is the only real response, so here is to leading with love and doing it over and over again. How many places can you go today, and how many people you will meet today, where you can lead with love, more love breeds more love?

Leaving Yesterday

There is nothing like a move to make you question what moves with you and what stays behind. All of a sudden you critique everything. The question becomes ***"does this fit and belong in the next life?"***

When you have lived in the same home for over 20 years it is amazing how much you can accumulate. When you raised three children there, had two adults with two big careers there and many friends there as well as several dogs that all lived there, so many things entered our home. The same things that we brought through our front doors now must exit those doors.

While in this process you begin to understand how much "stuff" you have that literally has little or no value or that its time and its place has come and gone. How it weighs you down and takes up space and energy.

In 1992 when my husband and I moved in together we brought with us much baggage, literally. He had his foot locker filled with his previous marriage and her subsequent death. I had my foot locker filled with my previous marriage and his subsequent death. They were filled with photos, memorabilia, legal documents such as death certificates and more. His past life was stored in his locker and my past life was stored in mine.

For this move they won't be making the move. Together we have declared, *"We are leaving yesterday behind."* During my spiritual training I have often heard the phrase *"We must die first so that we may live."* Or as some would say, *"In order to live we must be willing to die."*

I remember the scene from the movie **Under the Tuscan Sun** when Diane Lane's character has her last walk through in the house that she once shared with her husband. The movers are there for her to take what furniture and things that she wants. From room to room she goes around pointing at items for them to move and then instantly decides, "No not that." In the end she takes nothing and dismisses the movers. She walks out with a blue vase.

She is leaving all that stuff behind her. The house and that life are literally yesterday. She has freed herself up so that she can experience a new life.

The other part of this experience for us is the message that we want less in our lives. Our big consumption years are over. We just want less. It is easy to see where our time and our energy went during our big career days. We indulged our children and ourselves.

There are toys, games, dolls, books, clothing, baby this and baby that and a piano and rooms of furniture that once were so valued and now have no place in our life. We must first rid ourselves of much stuff and our past life. In every way, we are leaving yesterday.

To get to the next place you have to let go of the last place. During the cleaning out, clearing out process we have read and reread notes, cards and gifts that came from family members and friends. Most didn't make the cut. They were appreciated for the last time.

At first the plan was to "store" some things then we came to the united conclusion, why do that when we really don't need or want that stuff anymore.

When I listen to Pope Francis speak about greed and I instantly reflect on the "fat 1980'S" when everything was bigger and better or so we thought. Then I think about this generation and how much they dispose of. It isn't that their cell phone doesn't work and they need a new one but rather that their cell phone isn't the latest and greatest and therefore needs to be replaced.

There is a whole paradigm shift that takes place when you decide that less is more and that there really is very little that you need. These same points can be applied to our relationships. I am finally free. I no longer have a place in my heart for people that take and take and devalue me.

Like the possessions and the house and the past that I have once enjoyed, what will remain in my life will be the people and the things that I cherish and that cherish me. We are making a choice to keep and to include people and few things that contribute to the future in happy and healthy ways.

We are happy alone and together as a married couple and we are content. Our decision to move has been for more than three years in the making. We knew that we wanted to wait until our children graduated and then came retirement. We were finally free to leave so much that we once loved so dearly.

As you age you think more about how much time you have left and how you want to spend it. You understand that your days are limited and the only way to open doors for new experiences is to shed the past experiences.

Our past life dies so that we may live … and in doing so we are leaving yesterday as we boldly face today and tomorrow.

Let it Go, Let it Go, Let it Go …

Bishop TD Jakes words of advice "Let it go" and Disney's Frozen was about "let it go." How often do we hang on to things that people did and said to us? And we would be so much better served if we just "let it go?"

"When people walk away from you let them walk. Your destiny is never tied to anyone that left. People leave you because they are not joined to you. And if they are not joined to you, you can't make them stay. Let them go. And it doesn't mean that they are a bad person it just means that their part in the story is over. And you've got to know when people's part in your story is over so you don't keep trying to raise the dead. You've got to know when it is dead." Bishop TD Jakes

Not everything or everyone is meant to be in our lives forever. How often do we hang on to that which no longer serves us? Let it go!

How much mental illness or our suffering points back to an inability to let go? Forgiveness is the ability to let it go, it is what we do for ourselves when we forgive.

"If you let go a little, you will have a little peace. If you let go a lot, you will have a lot of peace." Ajahn Chah

Anger keeps us connected in negative ways, letting it go allows us to move forward with love and with grace. Brain scientists suggest that nearly 20% of us suffer "complicated grief" when we long for someone that we lost and we romanticize the memories of the relationship. Often when people die we make them God-like, all of a sudden they become perfect. We don't speak ill of the dead. Even if they were far from "angelic" they become angels to us. It is healthy for us to forget and forgive the bad stuff, it allows us to let go.

The secret is to know when it is time to let go. Hanging on to hurts or to anger or to any loss is often at the expense of wellness and growth. When we are stuck we are unable to move forward.

Remember the movie *Up,* it is a Disney film that came out in 2009 and told the story of a widower who couldn't let go. He couldn't let go of the past and the house that he previously shared with his wife. Basically he couldn't "fly" and lift off without letting go. Once the main character could let go of the objects that weighed him down, he literally was able to fly and move on and ahead.

There was no much angst in my family and so much hurt and loss. For years I kept it alive by carrying it in my head and in my heart. After my mother died I was initially indignant as to how her lack of any desire for any reconciliation and how it affected me. But the truth is she was dead and gone from me for decades before her actual passing. It was an open wound until the finality of her death.

Recently I visited her grave which is littered with messages from her other children. Their grief and loss is so new to them. I am finally free and at peace. When we can finally "let it go" we have a full and open heart that has a greater ability to love and is peaceful. I know because that is where I live now. It is a choice. I find it easier to let many more things go. So little is really worth hanging on to and what this has done for me is it allows me to be present in the moment and to live in the moment and literally one day at a time. My anxiety is far less and my joy is far greater.

The real gift is not in the holding on but rather in our ability to let it go ...

Living With Goodbye

Let's face it some goodbyes are just easier than others, some break ups are clean and respectable and some aren't. Long after the break up, you alone have to live with your goodbye.

My father knew the importance of a proper goodbye when he knew that he was dying, he made sure he met with all of his children. It was important for him to have peace in all those relationships. Our last visits were really special. He carved out time for just me, to be alone with me. I always knew that my father loved me; our last few times together will always remain precious to me. It was his parting gift to me, the gift of peace and of love.

In 1990 I went through a nasty break up of a five year relationship with a guy who cheated on me; he did so in a very public way. I was both hurt and humiliated. On the heels of this break up and abuse in my family I packed up and moved over 1,000 miles away to Florida. As I was working through my grief, my ex showed up in Florida, we reconciled for a short amount of time. This time we ended it peacefully.

Our goodbye initially wasn't good, in the end we both knew it was over and we also knew the importance of a healthy goodbye. We ended our relationship with peace and with dignity and out of respect, respect for our history of love for one another. This allowed us both to move on with grace and dignity and most of all with peace in our hearts.

We have no way of knowing when it will be our last time, the last time we see someone or are with them. The way we handle our goodbyes says a lot about us. It harkens back to respect, peace and love.

I have often thought about how fortunate I am that I never had to go through a divorce, so many seem nasty and vengeful. How is it that two people who once loved each other enough to marry and many times have children together and then go out of their way to try and harm that same person? Or family fights that end up in court, family members that once loved each other and then later can't even talk to each other. They only communicate through their lawyer.

So who wins? It is still an ex from your past, part of your life history and still your family member.

The older I get the more important it is that my goodbyes are as healthy as my hello's. Some relationships have to end. People move on or move away, some no longer are held in high esteem and their time has come and gone.

But how we say goodbye is how we will be remembered, were we respectful and kind or were we vengeful and unkind. I choose peace and love. I have said goodbye to friendships that were no longer healthy and supportive, however when I did, it was just as important to end them with peace and with dignity. Not just for me but for them too.

I remember a few really healthy goodbyes, one was in my third grade when our family was moving, and my class had a going away party for me. They gifted me with an autographed signed animal where every single classmate signed it with not just their signature but well wishes.

Many years later when leaving my job, my supervisor and several people from my department took me to a really nice restaurant for lunch and gave me a few gifts. It was nice and left the door open for continued healthy professional exchanges through the years. Both sides could feel good about their time together and with their dignified goodbye.

There is always a healthy and a respectful way to end our relationships. However, many times we are not afforded this choice. In any relationship you only control what you do and not what the other party does. When someone tries to blow you up when a relationship is ending, try and take a step back. What is really going on? Normally you can see where it points back to their self-preservation. If I can make you look bad, then I can justify my own poor behavior.

Not everyone is meant to stay in our lives forever, some people just fade away, some people leave deliberately and choose to do so with peace and love, and some only know how to end it with anger and blame.

"All blame is a waste of time. No matter how much fault you find with another, and regardless of how much you blame him, it will not change you. The only thing blame does is keep the focus off you when you are looking for external reasons to explain your unhappiness or frustration. You may succeed in making another feel guilty about something by blaming him, but you won't succeed in changing whatever it is about you that is making you unhappy." Wayne W. Dyer

You can learn a lot about yourself and about others when it is time to say goodbye, and long after the goodbye, you have to live with it. Living with your goodbye whether in peace or in anger is what will set you up for your next relationships. You will carry it with you, it becomes a part of you, so try and make it something that you can live with, something that you can feel good about. We will all experience endings, and we will all learn about living with goodbye.

Love is a Living Thing

Love is a living thing, but in being so love can and does die too. We were driving away and my heart was broken. I could see her in the rear view mirror, holding court with her friends, smoking a cigarette and wearing the little Ann Taylor dress and Coach Purse I had purchased for her. She was just shy of her 18th birthday. Little did I know that our relationship had ended.

Someone who was a friend at that time said, **"The heart that you had for her is gone and maybe one day you will be able to grow a new one."** I couldn't believe he said that! I couldn't imagine that ever being true. She was my daughter and my job was to love her and to love her forever.

Throughout the years my husband would say, **"One day she will be gone longer than you had her."** It is getting really close to that time now. When we haven't seen someone in 17 years it becomes virtually impossible to keep the love alive. Regardless who that person is because love is a living thing and it needs certain elements to stay alive.

There was a time when I fought so desperately to keep the love alive. She was used to people leaving her through death and through choice and I was going to love her beyond all that. I was going to be there even if she wasn't. In retrospect she killed my love for her. She made sure that it died. No one could really come back from the things that she did and the things that she said. No one could come back with a loving heart.

Another friend and colleague would tell me, **"You must save yourself."** It was more than a decade of estrangement at that time. Yet again it seemed so odd to me. He had a daughter and he loved her. He beamed when he spoke of her and all her many accomplishments and yet I was supposed to forgo my child and "save myself."

The last battle did me in with her. She may as well have thrown gasoline on me and lit a match. It was when it became crystal clear to me the depth and the degree of her hatred toward me. I still can't imagine not seeing someone, anyone for 15 years and still carrying such hatred in your heart. I mean for your own sake and wellness, let it go. But that last time was what it took for me to see her so clearly and to lose any remaining love I may have had or any hope of ever repairing our relationship.

Today I feel good again, really good and I am at peace. I have no love left for her and where it doesn't make me sad, I question how any mother would and could feel that way toward their child. Yet I do. I can say it out loud I can say it to God and I can share it with my family, I have nothing left for her, nothing.

I wish her all the best, I wish her the biggest and the brightest life and yet I want nothing to do with her, not now and not ever. It is the most loving act of all, pure total surrender. No one is more surprised than me. How did this happen? Well it didn't happen overnight it took years and years. I grieved for a full ten plus years, I shed more tears than I could have ever imagined. I was so hurt and so blind-sided, I never saw it coming. I was shocked.

When that very first year went by I asked a friend to try and find out how she was doing and what was going on with her. I couldn't imagine that not one time in that first year did she ever miss me or reach out for me. It would be another devastating blow to learn that in that first year she was pregnant and had her son. I didn't even know. I would learn that she had a child when he was already 5-months old. Yet another act that would disclose for me how cut off she was from me.

Then several more years would pass when a long-term friend of 30 years would direct me to our local court house. She for whatever reason was looking my child up there. It was there I would learn my grandson's name and his birthdate and who his father was and it was there that I would learn of who was raising him. Another deep cut and blow another hurt that I would have to work my way back from.

Today I am on the strong and healed side. I am as over it as any mother could be, every day I support parents in their grief of losing their children through estrangement. I can tell exactly where they are in the process by what they are feeling and expressing. For the most part their hearts are still open although somewhat shattered. I can tell by their rawness how new the cut off from their beloved child is and was and how they are managing their grief.

For all of them I hope and pray for a resolution before love dies. Because love can and will die if it isn't properly nurtured. I see so much clearer today. Love truly is blind. When we love our children so absolutely we often refuse to see or are too close to see or are in denial about our children. Being away from my child had allowed me to see things much more clearly.

I took on so much responsibility for her; I allowed myself to be the target and scapegoat and was so easily manipulated. I being her target wasn't helping her.

Blaming others is the surest way to fall short on our own lives. When we blame others we fail to accept responsibility. Pointing our fingers out and making others look bad takes the focus off us.

Or does it? Maybe in the short run but sooner or later who we are and what we are will surface. We can only hide so long. We can only blame so long before we have to accept responsibility for our lives and for all of our decisions.

You know it is over when the love is gone and so are the anger and the sadness and the hurt and disappointment. What you are left with is peace and with understanding and a desire to help all those others who are suffering like you were. Nothing lasts forever, nothing.

Love is a living thing, and love can and will die when we don't cherish it and nurture it and appreciate it.

Love is Everything

Love is everything and maybe just maybe in life, love is the only thing that really matters. I have been blessed and I know it and I am thankful to God for all the love I have in my life. In order to receive love we must first love and accept ourselves.

There are many kinds of love like the parent-child love or friend to friend love or the life partner and marriage love. We say we "love" this movie or that food or this and that place. It has been said that the word "love" is the most overused work in our vocabulary. But can you ever overdue "love" and loving?

"For where your treasure is, there your heart will be also."
Mathew 6:21

I have "treasured" many people and many things, I have loved them! And I have been "treasured" by many and been loved by them.

Love can be so hard to define. There is that chemical brain thing that happens when we experience "love at first sight" and there is that lasting and mature love that happens with a long term committed love relationship.

Each couple defines their own "love" relationship just each friend and family defines what constitutes a loving relationship. Real love is without ego. When we fully love and when we give love without expectations we operate out of a God source. The purest form of love is often what a parent has for a child. They give and they give without expectation.

Love is to be cherished and respected. It would be hard to continue to love someone who didn't respect us or cherish us. The best love is the reciprocated love that grows and grows over time and goes back and forth just like a really good tennis match where each serve was met with another serve and the game of "love" continues. The most challenging kind of love is a one-sided love.

As Christians are called upon to love all people as God our Father has loved us. **John 15:17 "This is my command: Love each other."**

Love can be a challenge at times. To respond with love when we are attacked or have been hurt is the highest form of love and the greatest God like response. **"Most people have a harder time letting themselves love than finding someone to love them."** Bill Russell

One of my favorite bible quotes is from Corinthians 13:4 (below) as I believe it is what most of us strive for in our loving relationships. **"Love is patient, love is kind. It does not envy, it does not boast, it is not proud. It is not rude, it is not self-seeking, it is not easily angered, it keeps no record of wrongs. Love does not delight in evil but rejoices with the truth. It always protects, always trusts, always hopes, and always perseveres. Love never fails. "**

Love is everything and when you are loved and can give love and receive love, you have everything! The greatest gift is love and the only thing we will be remembered for is how much love we gave and how much love we received.

Love is everything and most probably the only thing in life that really matters.

Making Amends

"The first to apologize is the bravest. The first to forgive is the strongest. The first to forget is the happiest." Nishan Panwar

For most people saying I am sorry and trying to make it right, making amends can be really difficult. Often it is our ego that stands in the way of our ownership of hurting people and then owning it and trying to do what is right to correct our wrongs. We are afraid to put ourselves out there and expose our vulnerability.

When someone has hurt us, part of that hurt often points back to the inability for the one who has hurt to own what they did and to be sorry for what they have done and to make the corrective measures necessary to rebuild the relationship.

What does making amends look like? We know how we feel when we have been hurt but do we know what we want from the person who we believe has harmed us to do and to try and make it right?

You can't be in any long term relationship without experiencing some kind of hurt from your partner. Often it isn't the hurt as much as it is what they do or don't do after the hurt has taken place that determines the success of the relationship. Forgiveness is a natural part of any long standing relationship.

My husband and I have done many things to hurt one another through the years, most often unintentionally and there have also been hurts that were deliberate. The difference for us is that our love is greater than any hurt that we can and have bestowed upon one another. Part of our marriage success is how we handle our hurt feelings and what we do to make it right between us.

It is really hard to stay angry with someone when they are genuinely sorry for what they have done. Many years ago I unknowingly drove my husband's brand new black Explorer through a highway painting site. Little did I know that his new vehicle was speckled with tiny white paint drops. I was mortified and I was so sorry. All I wanted to do was to fix it and make it right. He never even got angry with me. I think it was because I felt so badly about what I had done. I accepted responsibility, there is no doubt it was my fault.

Imagine if instead of owning it, I responded with, "What, what are you talking about? I didn't do THAT!" or better yet if I had no response at all as if it didn't even matter to me. How would he have felt about me and the brand new white paints spots on his brand new vehicle if I acted like it was nothing and no big deal?

I think this is why many relationships break apart, because something happens where there is a hurt and the lack of ownership creates the anger. It is bad enough to hurt someone that we love but then when we act as though it is no big deal is like adding insult to the injury.

My husband and I are really good at wanting to fix any pain we may have knowingly or unknowingly put upon each other. At times we have both had to make amends. Sometimes it takes some time to move past our hurt but it becomes easier when we truly love someone and when that person is really sorry for hurting us.

As a Christian woman, my faith teaches me that I must forgive those who hurt me just as Jesus has forgiven me. I have turned the other cheek more times than what I care to admit to doing. I learned a long time ago that it isn't about what other people have done to me that matters the most to me but what I have done in response that stays with me.

Some people want to drag you into their fight and their anger; they want you to fight back so you can look bad. At times it can be tricky to side step the fight but when we do we have retained control of ourselves and can live without regret.

There is a richness that can occur in a relationship when we have done the work, owned our part and made amends. This allows us and the injured party to decide whether the relationship was worth fighting for and working through or if it was time to say good bye with our dignity and that of the other party.

As I age I have become really good at forgiveness, let's just say that I have had a lot of practice at it. Forgiveness is what you do for yourself, it frees you up to love whole heartedly and it allows us our own inner peace. I have forgiven everyone; everything and I do this for myself. It doesn't mean I am a fool that will allow anyone and everyone that closeness where they can hurt me again. It means I have accepted my role, their role and done my best to make peace, make amends and fix what I could fix.

Every relationship that I chose to end I ended with peace and I have been really fortunate that the ones that I worked through have been some of the greatest lessons learned. There is not a single ex-boyfriend that I have had that I couldn't call who wouldn't be happy to hear from me. No matter what the cause of the break up I always made sure to seek peace and understand where we could both walk away with our heads held high.

When we aren't afforded the opportunity to work through our pain and to try and make it right because the other party died or left us or simply won't allow it, we must find a way to make it right for ourselves. Otherwise we carry these hurts and we play them out over and over again.

My mother never tried to fix our strained relationship and when she died I was left with this open wound. I had to find my own way to fix it so I could come to peace. I did the work. I went to my mentor a Catholic nun that I respect and I cried it out and talked it out. I went to my mother's family and talked it out. I visited my mother's gravesite and I prayed for her soul. I created a rose garden at both of our homes. The rose bushes I enjoy are a beautiful reminder of my relationship with my mother. "Non che la rosa sense la spina" translation "there is no rose without thorns."

In my life, I was called upon to forgive a sexual abuser who left a trail of abuse, deep wounds and heartaches in his path and in our family. I had to forgive him for the abuse that he bestowed upon a child that I loved. Without forgiving him I was stuck. I was stuck in anger and in bitterness and in hatred. A loving heart and a loving person can't exist with hatred. It just doesn't work that way. Forgiving him, isn't something that I did for him, it was what I had to do so I could move forward in my own life. This guy never accepted responsibility and numerous people covered up for him, his lack of ownership and their cover ups made it much more difficult to move past it and to heal.

"You don't need to wait to hear the apology to forgive. It may never come. Let forgiveness be a gift that is not dependent on

someone else's behavior, but on your generous heart." Ash Sweeney

The crime and all its fall out was horrific, the denial and the cover up were the insults to the injured parties. Professional studies have shown that where there is an admission of guilt there is a higher degree of recovery; sadly the opposite is true as well. In the denial and the subsequent denials, the victims have a much more difficult time on their road to wellness.

The people that will work with you through hurting you whether the hurts are real and/or perceived hurts are the same ones that truly love you and care about you. And the people that never own what they have done and have no interest in making it right aren't the people that love you.

Love and forgiveness go hand in hand, families that are together know this, they know they have their "stuff" and their "issues" and their "hurts" but they also know that love is greater and they work through their stuff wanting to get back to a place of love and understanding.

Families that are more committed to being "right" and making others look bad have their own selfish agenda and have put their own egos and self-preservation above the family. A loving family owns what they do and tries to make amends. A family that breaks apart often lacks love, understanding, compassion and the skill set necessary for fixing and making amends. It becomes easier for them just to dismiss it and continue their brokenness in all other family relationships.

Italians are known for their egos and their inability to ever be wrong or to show a softer side. I used to hold my Italian side of the family up in the highest esteem but history has shown me over and over again the depths of ego over heart. It would be my father the Irishman that would show his heart and take his ego out of his desire to love and make amends with all his children that also made him the easier parent to love and to forgive.

When my father was dying he made sure he made amends with all his children, I know in my heart that he left this life with peace in his heart. Just as I believe that my mother who never tried to fix things, could never put her ego aside or her need to be right, left this life with much unresolved baggage. Sad as it is, it was true.

Making amends, fixing what we contributed to breaking isn't about "them" it is about "us." There is nothing as pure as a love that is sorry for hurting others, does all the work necessary to make it right and carries on with love and peace and forgiveness.

Here is to making amends where you can and letting it go in love. And making peace with all that you can't fix, because at the end of this life, it all points back to you and your own heart

... and if you want to be forgiven you must first learn to forgive. You must learn to forgive yourself and to forgive all others.

A heart that forgives is a heart that is whole and can and does love whole-heartedly ...

Memorial Day beyond Hotdogs and Burgers, Our Great Men and Women Who Serve

Today for most of us Memorial Day is the start of summer with the opening of community pools, picnics and outdoor gatherings. We celebrate it by grilling our hotdogs, hamburgers, chicken and barbecue on the grill. Many take advantage of the Memorial Day weekend sales at the mall, car dealerships, big box stores and grocery stores. For many American's it is a three day weekend. Beach communities see it as the beginning of the summer season.

Memorial Day started as a holiday to remember the Civil War. It was a time in our history when our country that was at war with itself. It has been said to have been the bloodiest and most deadly war on United States soil.

We have expanded our definition of Memorial Day to include all military service men and women. Many of us reflect and think about all those who served and returned home, those who were injured in service and those who lost their life defending our country.

My husband Brian and I both have fathers who served during the Korean War. His father John and my father Bernie never met but they both returned from service honored with a purple heart. My dad was injured and medicated for the rest of his life as a result of a head injury he received while in Korea.

As a teenager I wore a P.O.W. bracelet, Prisoner of War and it was during this time that the Vietnam War was going on. In my early twenties I married Randy Moyer who was a two-term Vietnam veteran. Randy was in the Navy and honorably discharged after 6 years of service with a purple heart. He was blown off a ship and as a result he became an epileptic. In order for him to be fully functioning he had to be medicated every single day of his life. There was never a night's sleep where he wasn't shaking in our bed. He suffered from post-traumatic syndrome.

I will never forget when I was 8 months pregnant with our daughter the seizure he endured while driving to work. He totaled our car and almost killed the driver in the oncoming lane. His driver's license was taken away and eventually he lost his job as an auto mechanic. He needed a license to work. His neurologist said to me, me who was just one month away from delivering our first child, **"I don't want to tell you that your husband can't hold your baby but I think you should know that if he had a seizure while holding her, he could kill her."** It was my sister who came to get me in the middle of the night when I went into labor. My husband, a real macho kind of guy was not allowed to drive a vehicle.

When he died in 1983 he was just 37 years old and his autopsy read, "Drowning as a consequence of seizure." He was taking a shower, preparing to go to work and had a seizure in the shower. After he died I was left as a single mother to raise our then 2-year old daughter.

Many benefits were afforded me as a surviving widow. The VA accepted 100% responsibility for his untimely death. I was given financial support and could have used my benefits to go to school and for medical care and even to purchase a home. I never accepted any of the benefits except for the financial support. All money received was used for the best private education money could buy for our daughter. I wanted it to be used for something that would live on long after his death. The only stipulation on this support was I could receive financial aid until the day that I died. I decided to accept support until our daughter was of legal age. I remarried and it ended. I was always so thankful that Randy's service was honored by the very government that he gave his life to serve.

A flag was given to me on February 25, 1983 after the 21-gun salute and his burial. I visit his gravesite at least once every single year. On Memorial Day I celebrate like everyone else with my share of hotdogs and hamburgers but I also remember my first husband Randall H. Moyer who gave up his life to service in the United States Navy during Vietnam. He served for his country that he loved.

Many of us have friends and family members who serve in our military; it is about service above self. Let's all remember to remember them this Memorial Day and every day in between.

Miss Frushon

Every once in a while a really great young person comes along. It might not be that they are doing one thing great, but rather on how they approach life and all the great little things that they do that add to a better life. A better life for all those around them including themselves.

We give so much credit and attention to all the negative news stories, the story about Michael Brown, the stories about Ray Rice amongst others. We hear about young people that are doing drugs, having run-ins with the law and even suing their parents over entitlement issues. Yet there are numerous young people that are making positive contributions to society and so often we fail to give them their proper recognition.

I met Miss Frushon in January of this year when she responded to a social media job post I had created looking for interns. At that time I was working as the Executive Director for a nonprofit community theater and they never had an intern program before my arrival. We would be setting out on unchartered territory.

Her e-mail response was very well written and she had a past positive experience with the community theater so it was natural that I would bring her in to interview with me. When she arrived she was wearing an infinity scarf and was professionally dressed. She was just so cute! But what really impressed me was her communication skills and the way that she carried herself. Nothing about her said, "I am only 20 years old" I immediately liked her and as we reviewed the job description she seemed both qualified and eager to get involved.

I set out a schedule for her, gave her projects with deadlines and even added her to the committee efforts for both a brand new fundraising event and also to an existing gala fundraiser. I sent her on her way with work. She was in school full-time, working a part-time retail job and still willing to work 15-20 hours a week with me as an unpaid intern. She worked with me for FREE!

Much of the work I assigned her would fall into graphic design work and helping to create print ready marketing materials with a "wow" factor. I wanted collaterals that would set us apart from the ordinary. Not only did she deliver but she also brought with her two of her close girlfriends and they too made great additions to our team.

Watching her interact with her closest friend Courtney and with her peers was a wonderful and welcome sight. They are supportive of one another in really healthy ways. I've known women that are two and three times their age that still don't understand the concept of "friendship" and how important women lifting up other women really is and how women often tear at one another in competition rather than in loving and supportive ways. To her mother and her family and to her teachers I say, "Great job! This is one great kid!"

In my position as the Executive Director, it could have been intimidating but Miss Frushon was always confident. There were days we communicated by e-mail and text messages, she was busy and so was I. She also had a family that she loved and a long term relationship with her boyfriend. I can't say that she is an "old soul" I never had that sense because she really has a young spirit but she is a very responsible and mature soul.

Some days as it was getting into the early evening hours and I was still working in my office since most days I put in were 10 and 12 hours and she would just show up. Just hearing her come in off the elevator and seeing her smiling face turn the corner to my office often made my day. She just showed up to engage, to review projects to keep me updated on her progress. I never had to go searching for her. We clicked and we clicked well.

One day on the job there was tension with another co-worker a seasoned one and I couldn't understand the conflict since their work on that particular project had no overlap. When I contacted Miss Frushon to inquire she couldn't understand it either. Without my requesting it, she just showed up to share and as it turned out the other co-worker was already in my office. It was face-to-face when it would become crystal clear that the person created the drama for her own gain, tried to diminish Miss Frushon and her work and was completely uncovered for the deceptive actions that she had been getting away with for a really long time. What struck me was how well Miss Frushon handled it when she could have chosen to be angered by basically being lied about and deceptive actions to make her look bad in the workplace.

When I decided to move on to other opportunities, not only did Miss Frushon stay at the theater but was immediately promoted to become a Director of Programming. Again she is a full-time college student, paying her own University priced tuition, working a demanding job as a Director and has healthy relationships with her family, friends and a stable relationship with her boyfriend! She is really hard-working knows how to get things done and consistently exceeds expectations.

What stands out for me is her grace, her class and her poise and her ability to take what life hands her and come back even better and stronger for the experience. And she is humble and kind and comes from truly humble beginnings, she has a hunger for success and a drive and determination. She never lost her little girl attitude, the one we all had and the one that says, "I can do that!"

Miss Frushon, I will be watching you and applauding your successes all along the way and I am so proud to know you and to call you my friend! You go girl!

More Fun Times ... Please

We just enjoyed the best holiday season ever! Well I certainly did! We had so many fun times. We set out for fun and we found it everywhere. We had fun in our home and in our neighborhood we had fun on our day trips and on our holiday vacation. We had fun with our friends and with our family. It started out as a mindset and then moved beyond to our actions. We were determined to have a fun filled holiday season and we achieved it.

It was a conscience choice and a decision that we made and the more fun we had the more fun times we found! During our road trip and during our hotel stay I vowed to wear my white fur lined snow flake tiara every place we went and I did. People were always smiling at me and commenting to me "how happy I looked" and I was happy!

After a while I would forget that I was wearing it and my thoughts were "the people here are so nice and so happy and they are all smiling!" But the truth is/was they were smiling because when they saw the snowflake tiara you couldn't help but smile.

The take way for me was that we put into motion how we will be viewed and how we will be received. We do this by our own actions and how we present ourselves to the world. Whoever waited on us during our recent trip to Nashville when I wore that tiara out and whether we purchased gas or were eating out or just walking around received us with joy and with smiles and with their own happiness.

My snowflake tiara brought me so much joy but it also set the stage for others to smile and to laugh and to communicate with me. We had so many fun times! Now all I can think is more fun times ... please ... and where will I find my next tiara, for the next season or holiday?

Motherless Daughter

The mother is the one person who is supposed to love you no matter what. But what happens to us, our mother's daughter when we lose the love, support and companionship of our mother? My mother didn't speak to me for the last 23 years of her life. Our ending would come full circle with trauma just like our beginning. I was told that my mother almost bled to death when I was born and that they sent me home with my father and kept my mother in the hospital.

At the age of seven, I lived with my grandparents at their hotel so that my mother could finish school and receive her nursing degree as a registered nurse. During that year when I was in the second grade I got the mumps. When she finally came to the hotel she wouldn't risk seeing me since the mumps were contagious. She didn't want to get sick and miss school. I remember looking out the second floor hotel window as requested. My mother was in her uniform with her white starched nursing cap, white dress, white hose and white shoes. She was learning to take care of sick people and here I was her sick daughter and all she could offer me was a curbside wave. Seven year olds don't understand this kind of a decision; they just want the love and care of their mother.

Years later after I left for college but returned home for a weekend, I stayed out all night long. Upon my return my mother said, "I want you to leave now." She was kicking me out. Just before I married as a nineteen year old, she would deny that she ever told me that I had to leave. My first husband was abusive and when I went home my mother listened to me tell her about all the abuse that I endured. She never offered me a safe haven and so I went back to him. A few years later my marriage ended when I left him and he died. My mother and I became close for a brief period of time. We shared weekly lunches. During one of those lunches, I said, "Mom, I want to tell you something and I don't think you will like it but I want you to hear it from me." Her response was, "Well don't tell me."

There was a time when I told my mother I was sorry for any trouble I may have caused her. Her response to me was, "You were easy you never asked for anything." Then I had this light bulb moment, I watched my mother work double-shifts to raise her five daughters, I watched my sisters constantly going after her for what they wanted. I was so afraid to ask for anything because it might be the one that sent her over the edge. So early on, I learned to take care of myself.

When I was just 300 miles into the 1,000 mile road trip I was on, I received a phone message from my cousin. She said, "Please call me back right away, it's not good just call as soon as you get this message." I retrieved this message at a gas station when my husband was inside paying for our gas. I immediately called her back. I could tell by her voice it had to be my grandmother or my mother. My grandmother recently turned 101 years old, so I thought it was probably her. But it wasn't … it was my mother, she died. It was unexpected but she was gone. By the time my husband returned to the car, I was crying. How could she? How could she go home to meet her maker, to see God our Father without any reconciliation with me, her second born daughter? She never once tried to make peace with me, not one time in 23 years and now she was gone. Less than an hour later I received a written message from my dad's widow, "I think you should know that your mother passed away early this morning." My dad's widow would inform me just after my cousin. Not one of my four sisters ever called me, but it would be my cousin and later the women who replaced our mother, my father's second wife who thought "you should know" that my mother was dead.

When I was twenty-eight years old I had to tell my mother that her husband was doing the unthinkable, he was abusing a child. My mother and I never had a fight, there were never words between us about what I learned and ultimately communicated to her. That last Christmas after telling her I would receive my last gift that she would ever give to me. It was a large bottle of Frangelico liquor and a $50 bill. It was the coldest and most impersonal gift she ever gave to me. I was certain the liquor was a re-gift and the $50 a last minute gesture. As the years passed it would silently become clear to me that our relationship was over. Holidays came, birthdays, family affairs, special events and I was excluded. I would learn at different periods of time throughout the years that she came to town and when she did, she never once called me or tried to see me.

"Holding anger is a poison. It eats you from inside. We think that hating is a weapon that attacks the person who harmed us. But hatred is a curved blade. And the harm we do, we do to ourselves." The Five People You Meet in Heaven by Mitch Albom.

For many years I had anger toward my mother until I came to acceptance. Early on I did the grief work. I had to process the loss so that I could get over it. I went to one therapist who said, "You need to live your life as though your mother is dead." I tried this I told a few friends that she died. She had in a sense, and yet she was very much alive even though for me, it was a death. It was the death of my mother and our mother-daughter relationship.

"I wanted a perfect ending. Now I have learned, the hard way, that some poems don't rhyme, and some stories don't have a clear beginning, middle, and end. Life is about not knowing, having to change, taking the moment and making the best of it, without knowing what's going to happen next. Delicious Ambiguity." Gilda Radner

Through the years I filled the void that she left with "other mothers" older women who became my friends, my mentors and supporters. I had many girlfriends who shared their mothers and their friendship. These relationships helped me to fill the hole left by my own mother. **"Ultimately, the abandoned daughter is never completely abandoned unless she, too, leaves herself behind." Cause and Effort from Motherless Daughters, The Legacy of Loss by Hope Edelman.**

Through my girlfriends I witnessed other mother-daughter relationships. Friends who are close to their mothers, have the normal holidays together, shopping and lunch dates and many who are now caring for their aging mothers as they assist them with their health needs. And I have girlfriends who have strained but intact relationships with their mothers. Some who have lost their mother due to untimely deaths and it is never easy. It has been said that the mother-daughter relationship is the most complex and complicated of all relationships, can offer the greatest of rewards and the most difficult of challenges.

My Family Has Always Inspired Me

My family has always inspired me, and it isn't what you think either. Inspiration comes in many forms and in many ways. Sometimes we are inspired by the negative hurtful things people do and say to us as well as the loving and kind things they do and say.

As a child we lived in poverty for a while, my father wasn't working and my mother was estranged from her family. It was during this time that we received canned peanut butter and other "rations" from the government. My father had served two terms in Korea until he was honorably discharged with a purple heart. Coming home he didn't work for maybe a year or more. I remember having saltine crackers with sugar sprinkled on top and with milk as our cereal. My parents weren't doing well and they were too proud to go home for any help.

This was during my formative years and I learned the benefit of working vs. unemployment. I knew what being hungry felt like. It was during my early years that I watched my father and mother in their battles often physical and my fathers repeated in your face extra marital affairs. I learned what I didn't want in my life and I learned it by watching what I witnessed as a child.

After leaving home I married young to escape it, the problem was I married a man that was just like my father. My father was; an alcoholic, an epileptic, a womanizer, angry, violent, hit women, (my mother) honorable discharged from the Army with a purple heart and divorced with children. My first husband Randy was an alcoholic, an epileptic, a womanizer, angry, violent, hit women; (me) honorably discharged from the Navy with a purple heart and divorced with children.

How on earth did this happen? Children learn what they live; I couldn't have picked more of a carbon copy of my father and what I knew and learned as a child, if I was on a mission to do so.

When I finally left Randy for good, his parting shot was literally a punch right in the middle of my face. It was over between us, and the learned behavior patterns from my first family were over too. I was inspired by what I witnessed as a kid and my early adult years. I knew what I didn't want for myself or for my daughter. I learned about alcohol abuse, abuse and what damage guns in the home can do. I learned it as a little kid and I learned it from my first family.

Living in poverty caused me to feel shame and anxious, it also drove me to want more and better for myself.

In 2009 the first edition of my book, *Halfway Home the First 50 Years* was published. It wasn't until it was completely done, ready for sale that I realized of all the stories I wrote about, in over 30 essays, there was not one single story about any one of my four sisters. I wrote about volunteer work at 13, my friends, my parents and more and nothing, not a single word about them. I didn't even think of it, it never even occurred to me. They had been out of my life for decades and I pretty much was operating from *"If you can't say anything nice, don't say anything at all."*

I am the second oldest of five girls, I could have written about the sister that was the first to ever introduce me to pot, smoking marijuana or the one who stole my wedding ring so that when my husband died I couldn't wear it to his funeral. She did eventually return it to me. Today I could write about the "letter writer" the one who has the audacity to write nasty letters about me to the people who I quoted on my book and my previous employer. Even though she hasn't seen me or been in my life for decades. To hear them, I don't deserve to breathe air and I didn't deserve to be acknowledged in our mother's obituary as her daughter and their sister.

Why? After a less than supportive childhood and family dynamic, and I was a favorite of my father who left home when I was just 12, and I was not close to my mother. Then I took a stand against a child molester who just so happened to be her second husband. For this, I would receive the Scarlett letter. It was the last straw in a family riddled in abuse.

What they do for me? After the initial shock and anger, they motivate me to be better than them, and better than that. I have to do so much more than the average person just to feel normal. I have always been highly motivated and enjoyed a wealth of success in spite of my family and maybe even in part because of them.

The moral of the story is you can let other people define you, you can let past experiences define you, or you can define yourself. You can create your life the way that you envision it to be. Seeing my mother and my father and their relationship taught me to be anxious, living with an alcoholic will do that. Seeing the infidelity and the anger and abuse caused me to know that I couldn't tolerate it in my adult life. I may not have had the choice as a kid, but as an adult I had the choice. I didn't have to continue that patterned behavior, this time, it would be my choice.

My husband today of over 20 years is stable, loving supportive and healthy. Brian is a regular guy who comes home at a regular time and has no interest in other woman or in ever abusing me. My first family inspired me to want more and to want better for myself and even today they continue to inspire me. I only wish it could be from being positive, supportive and loving.

Either way, I guess inspiration is inspiration. When someone is doing things to defame you and hurt you, saying negative things about you, you get to choose how you will respond. Someone else's definition of you is just that, their definition and it only becomes you if you allow it to become you.

I imagine that we take the lessons, both good and bad, use them to motivate ourselves. Some people will lift you up and see the good in you; most often these are the same people that see the good in themselves. The ones who try and project nasty and negative things on others that too comes from within themselves.

By the time I met Brian, I was pretty beaten up by life, feeling really old and worn. He would rescue me. And just like the line from the movie; *Pretty Woman,* "I rescued him right back." I always knew that God brought him to me; and me to him. I was finally ready to receive genuine love.

The first gift he ever gave to me was a tiny gold crucifix and other early gifts were white flowing dresses from The White House clothing boutique for woman. He saw me so virginal, so good and so pure. When someone believes in you and sees your goodness that can be so inspiring and uplifting. Given the choice, this is how I would like to be inspired. Not by the hateful hurtful things, things, I had to work so hard at overcoming. Like the devil, their stuff projected onto me that I had to fight back to overcome it.

My family has always inspired me … the first one to push past it, try even harder and the second one to acknowledge and appreciate what love can and will do for you and your well-being, and for your health and success in life. One of the greatest gifts Brian ever gave to me was his patience with me, how often I heard him say, **"You are not alone."** With my first family I always felt so alone, so unsupported and with Brian, I wasn't alone, we have each other and we have God.

My Father Taught Me about Real Love

My father was a two-term Korean War Veteran honorably discharged with a purple heart. The injury that gained him a purple heart would leave him with a seizure disorder. Dad was one of five children born into an Irish Catholic family. His parents lost their 7 year old son Jimmy, just weeks after making his first Holy Communion. My grandmother was never right after this loss, there was never one time that I can recall when she wasn't talking about Jimmy or crying over his untimely death.

My father had another brother Michael, "the good son" his sister Katherine died in her thirties from alcohol consumption/ poisoning, Ann was the loud mouth in the family. Dad assumed the role of the "bad boy."

In the small town where he was born and raised he acquired quite a reputation as a ladies man. He was handsome and fun, and women loved him. I loved my father dearly, I always did and still, I saw him for who he was and not some idealized view of him. He was a carpenter by trade and learned to be an engineer. He built a few homes and loved to work with his hands. His soul was that of an artist, he was a painter but the realities of fathering eight children tied him to a 9 to 5 job.

My father was also an alcoholic with the classic Dr. Jekyll and Mr. Hyde personalities caused by his drinking. For most of my parents' marriage my father was unfaithful. He had multiple women in his life and fathered a child with another woman while still living in our home and married to my mother.

Dad was often violent when he drank and many times his violence was directed at my mother and us kids. There were two outstanding episodes of his rage and both landed him in jail. One included a gun and another domestic violence against one of his children. Thankfully the second episode was so horrific that after being released he never drank again. He would live out the last thirty-five years of his life sober.

In spite of all my fathers' shortcomings I loved him and I forgave him. He was and has been the easiest person in my life, to date to forgive. The only rationale I can give is two-fold. First I understood him and second, more importantly, he was sorry. He always tried to right his wrongs, even up until his death in 2009.

My father's mother was so grief stricken over the loss of her son Jimmy that she really wasn't there for my father and his brother and sisters when they were growing up. He went to Korea to fight for this country when he was just a boy at the age of 18.

During his time in the service he learned to recreate by drinking and keeping company with women. That's what he did back then. Women and booze would define him for the first part of his adult life. I don't make excuses for the things he did as they were wrong. Even he admitted to that.

His second marriage turned out to be a much healthier and a better match for him. With the births of his last two children he was off alcohol, he was happy, and present in ways he couldn't be while drinking. He was finally high on life.

Dad was there for me when I graduated from school in 1977 and again on December 2, 1978, when I married. On February 25, 1983 it was my father who picked me up from the gravesite after my husband's casket was lowered into the ground.

As an adult, when I visited my father there was never a single time no matter what age I was that he didn't try to hand me gas money or fruits and vegetables from his own garden. I have two prized paintings of his that he gave to me and they hang proudly in my home.

Even in his death he taught me about love and dignity. When he could no longer care for himself he died at home never wanting to be a burden to his family, his friends or to the system. My father taught me about real love, the kind where you give and expect nothing in return. In my father's ability to accept me and to love me "as is" I also found it easy to love and accept him as he was.

No matter what the consequences of his life choices my father accepted his role and took responsibility for the choices he made. Never once did he play the "blame game" or hide behind phrases like, "I had a bad childhood." He never pointed a finger at another person. Dad owned who he was and he didn't pretend to be someone or something that he wasn't.

I loved my father dearly, I knew him and I knew his heart. Isn't that what real love is? Seeing someone as they are and loving them in full awareness and acknowledgement of who they truly are, taking the good with the bad?

For me, his second born daughter, his female namesake, my father taught me there can be no love without forgiveness. And that we must first love and forgive ourselves before we can begin to love and forgive any others.

Missing you Dad …

My World Is a Beautiful World

My world is a beautiful world! And yes it is by design. I surround myself by people and with things that I love. Life is too short to settle for less. Toxic people and toxic things have no place in my world. Life is tough and we control so little of it but what we do control are our thoughts and our inner circle at home.

Recently with our decision to downsize many things no longer have a place in our home; they just didn't make the cut. They no longer work for us and no longer fit. Space is an issue and what remains is what we cherish and love and brings us happiness. Not only did we get rid things we no longer need or use but things that remind us of people that we no longer have any affection for. Just like in Feng Shui, everything brings with it an energy field and the only energy we want surrounding us is positive, uplifting and good energy.

Welcome to "Bernadette's world" where everything is beautiful! Our home and our world view. Our new locale takes us to a much more relaxed place and newly retired we have a much more relaxed attitude. In just weeks it is remarkable just how good my husband looks as a result of less stress. He smiles all the time now!

The ocean is a short drive for us and we go there at all times of the day and night. Just being near the water is so uplifting and seems to heal just about anything and everything that ails us.

This is my story. Each one of us has the power of mind over matter and the ability to create our life the way that we want it to be. We are filled with energy, do we want to use that energy to create something good or for something not so good. It is our choice. It is the choice that we make every single day.

We must value ourselves first and foremost. By creating a healthy mind and a healthy living space we have created the beginning stages of self-love. Then too what matters most. ***"No matter what I say, what I believe, and what I do, I'm bankrupt without love."*** CORINTHIANS 13:38

"Love means living the way God commanded us to live. As you have heard from the beginning, the command is this: Live a life of love." JOHN 1:6

Live a life of love! It starts with you and it ends with you. We are incapable of giving genuine love or receiving genuine love unless or until we can self-love. There is nothing selfish about self-love it is only then that we have a full cup and the ability to share with others. Don't go around "bankrupt" fill your cup and fill it often. Do the things that make you feel good, do the things that are healthy and keep you whole.

We are all creatures with a mind, a body and a soul. We need to nourish them all, we are a whole people. All parts of our being must be fueled for us to live at our best. To be happy and content allows us to love fully. My world is a beautiful world, is yours? If not, what might you do to make it beautiful?

Navigating Through My Estrangement

It used to be considered a "silent epidemic" when estrangement took place in the family. For the most part parents were just so hurt and humiliated that they often hid it or made excuses as to where their adult children ended up.

Today more and more parents have bonded together as a result of their adult children estranging from the family. Parents no longer feel the need to hide it and are actively seeking healing and coping skills and trying to come to peace and understanding.

Through the years I have written several articles about estrangement, the most popular ones are titled P.E.A.C. E. Parents of Estranged Adult Children Everywhere, Dear Parents of Estranged Adult Children and most recently Dear Estranged Adult Children. All can be found on my website at www.bernadetteamoyer.com and you may keep up with me on Facebook at www.Facebook.com/bernadetteamoyer.

This article is about sharing the many stages that go with an estrangement form an adult child. There are numerous stages and many resemble the same stages that we experience with death and the grieving process. The greatest challenge for many parents is that unlike a death, the adult child has made the choice to estrange themselves.

Let me share my experiences the last 17 years and also what I have learned and witnessed from the hundreds and hundreds of others that have communicated with me.

Stage 1 - The Battle Begins - Shock

The estrangement begins and sometimes it is a declaration of "I hate you" and "I want nothing to do with you." And statements like "Don't ever contact me again." Other times it is the silent treatment with no communication at all. Messages are left, letters are written and calls are made and they all go unanswered.

At this time most parents are shocked. They can't believe that little "Johnny" could react this way toward them. The parents begin to question themselves, their children and all the years they shared together. The overriding question "How did this happen, how did we end up here?"

Most mothers will express their grief through tears. They are so hurt. There is no deeper cut for any mother than to have the child that you loved and raised decide to reject you. All she wants is her "baby" back. Mothers and fathers begin to look at one another almost a silent look of "What did YOU do?" Although they are looking to place blame is not communicated as such and at least not initially.

Fathers often react differently. They feel the loss but almost immediately decide to go into "survival" mode. They will look at it from every angle and decide that, "If that is the way it is, it may well be a blessing." My own husband immediately wanted to close ranks. He accepted it for what it was and made my health and well-being his priority. I don't know that I could have ever survived without him and his love. It also caused him to look more closely at his own children and their actions. Things he may have chosen not to see in the past he acknowledged that he could no longer deny.

Stage 2 - Uncovering Some Ugly Truths

Few parents want to believe that their children are "liars" or "sneaky" or "sloppy" or have manipulated them. Few parents are willing to see their children through less than loving eyes until they are absolutely faced with the harsh truths.

Mothers just want the kids back; they want their family restored at all costs. Men see the danger in opening the door back up to what has already been disclosed to them.

Stage 3 - Denial This Can't Be Happening ... Not to me!

My grief was intense when my child left home in 1998. I couldn't imagine living my life without her. I had already suffered the loss of my first husband who died and family that I was estranged from as a result of sexual abuse. I couldn't imagine losing my daughter too. But I did. I ended up in therapy twice a week and for the first time ever I began taking antidepressant medication. She had been my reason for living and without her I felt I had no true purpose in life. Wrong, wrong and wrong but that was how I thought.

Each anniversary and each holiday and all birthdays were storms of tears and anger. How could she? How could I have meant so little to her when she meant so much to me?

Stage 4 - A Different Kind of Life

Everything changed. I changed. We moved our holidays to travel destinations and started making new traditions. Slowly but surely I began the letting go process. Her things were given to her and anything that crept up years later was given away or donated. Pictures of her began to be removed from public displays and all her photos, cards, letters and any pertinent papers were filed. She was being removed from my life bit by bit.

I would be fine years 4 and 5 and then have a complete breakdown in year 6. In the beginning I lost a lot of weight and I felt so deflated. I beat myself up pretty badly. I still had hope, I still thought she would grow up and find her heart.

Stage 5 - Coming to Acceptance

It is over! It really is over! After 10 years in I stopped crying and I came to acceptance. This was my new normal, I was living my life without her and she was living her life without me. My husband and twins filled my life along with a career that I loved.

We had many friends and beach vacations. We had peace. Life was good again.

Stage 6 - Here We Go Again!

She was in legal trouble and would strike out at me again. We had already been estranged for 13 years. I couldn't believe she could still carry such deep seated hatred in her heart. How can you hate someone, anyone so much when you haven't even seen them or talked to them in well over a decade? This would also be my biggest eye opener. It was also when my heart changed for good. Now I was done. The things that she did and the things that she said were such outrageous lies but what was most telling was the degree that she could and would go to and still want to hurt me. It changed everything for me. I could finally wholeheartedly let her go. We were strangers. The daughter that I knew and the daughter that I loved and adored was long gone. I always saw her through rose-colored glasses but not anymore.

Stage 7 - I Am Whole Again!

There is no scenario on the face of this earth where I would ever welcome her back into my heart and into my life. I gave her back to God. When I could finally do this I was free. My life was mine again. I was back to enjoying everything. It was like the dark clouds lifted and peace came over me. My mother had died and my family would show themselves yet again. I could finally conclude that I was better off without them. That I had a really nice life and it wasn't going to include them. I am softer more loving and more open but I am also so much wiser. I trusted when I should have questioned. I walked away when I should have confronted.

Today I share what I learned and I do my best to try and comfort others who are going through estrangement. I share my story I share my path so others will know that 1) you aren't alone and 2) you can and you will survive too!

Bernadette on Facebook at www.facebook.com/bernadetteamoyer

New York City and Christmas

It's the most wonderful time of the year! We just returned from the city, and what better place to begin celebrating Christmas than in New York City. When I was just a young girl my mother took me to New York City about a handful of times. My first trip there, I was probably just 12 years old. Now 40 years later I remember those trips so vividly. It was then and there that I saw my first Broadway play; it was called *Irene* with famous actress Debbie Reynolds who had the lead role. Then on another trip we saw the world famous Rockettes at Radio City Music Hall. My mother and I also went to see *The Best Little Whore House in Texas* and the film debut of Disney's *Pete's Dragon* on the big screen at Radio City. There were times we waited in long lines and in freezing cold temps to see those shows but it was always well worth it.

We would celebrate these trips with a big meal either lunch or dinner at Mama Leones or some other bustling city restaurant. Sometimes we went to Chinatown. Often we went as part of a bus trip and there was an occasion where we drove into the city while parking at the Port Authority. Coming to New York is where I would witness such diversity from my small town Pennsylvania upbringing. I remember seeing religious groups and poverty; we walked past a man that was lying on the street. One of his shoes was kicked off and no one stopped nor did they seem surprised that he was just lying there on that sidewalk. In being so young, I couldn't stop staring, but I soon learned that in New York City, you best keep walking as it is move or be moved. My desire to catch a look wasn't going to interrupt the masses of people that bustled through these busy streets.

I was so young and so wide-eyed but who could forget the skating in Rockefeller Center and the huge decorated Christmas tree. Back then I was such a small town girl, going to the city was both exciting and scary. People moved so fast and it seemed like everyone was selling something. Often we went at Christmas and I remember loving those trips. My mother would take us, one daughter at a time and it was our special time alone with her. She loved chestnuts and always purchased them from the street vendors.

Yesterday I went to New York City with my husband Brian; we have gone to the city many times before, often with friends and other times with family. But this trip was just for us. My husband works so hard and I try my best to plan activities and events to help him decompress from his hectic and demanding work schedule.

We took the train right into Penn Station and started our trip by going to the Empire State building. Later we ventured into Rockefeller Center to ice skate and enjoy a hot coffee. We shopped Macy's and took in their window decorations before heading out to lunch at Becco an Italian restaurant located in the theater district. Becco has become a favorite restaurant for us, Lidia Bastianich is one of the owners and the authentic homemade Italian pasta dishes are some of the best I have ever eaten. Besides the pasta they have homemade apple strudel that is to die for it is that good.

After a two hour lunch and sipping limoncello, we continued on with our Christmas shopping and taking in all the sights and sounds of New York City. We ate a handful of chestnuts from a street vendor, this I did in memory of my mother who is no longer with us.

Walking the streets in New York City is both exhausting and exhilarating but definitely a high point of these trips. Most of these trips we do take in the theater, most notably the Christmas Spectacular at Radio City Music Hall. This show is amazing with the parade of Wooden Soldiers, dancing Santa's and the world famous living Nativity. The Nativity is complete with live animals like goats, sheep camels and reindeer and worth the cost of admission just to view the Living Nativity alone.

But on this trip is was more about taking in the street sights and sounds of Christmas through their decorations, food and shopping, like all New York City trips it was wonderful. Christmas music was playing everywhere and as always there was such high energy and excitement in the air.

We enjoyed our easy and relaxing train ride home together, I am happy and content, and Brian couldn't have been more appreciative for all my efforts in planning this particular trip. He left his work home on this day along with his Blackberry. We return home refreshed and ready to go again. Thank goodness for Brian because in his absence that Blackberry now contains 74 new e-mails, 4 new text messages and 3 missed calls all work related and from just one missed day on the job.

New York City and Christmas just naturally go together, and for us these trips have become part of our annual holiday traditions. It's the most wonderful time of the year, and trips like this one to New York City help us add to that wonder!

No Money, No Ministry

It doesn't matter how good your ministry is, if you are out of money, you are out of business. For more than 15 years I have worked for and with nonprofits. I started as a special events manager then moved onto development director and chief operating officer. During these years I also served as a board member. My gifts and talents came from a business background that easily transitioned into fundraising. I had numerous business contacts that just happened to be really generous too.

Business people don't make excuses for making money, they know how hard they work for it and in my experience most if not all are very giving. Most not-for-profits are run by someone in the social services vocation from social workers that go on to achieve their doctorate to those in ministry. Many of these professions do not lend themselves to the workings of running a business. But the reality for any director tasked with running an organization is that virtually you are running a business. Like it or not, money will determine what you can and can't accomplish in your social and ministry driven services.

During my work, I have been approached numerous times by colleagues looking to 1) obtain not for profit status for their cause 2) assist with special event creating, planning, running and fund raising success and 3) grant writing.

Where I have not been part of a team that secured a new not for profit status, most often this goes into the hands of an attorney, I do have some knowledge in what it takes to create a mission statement, a strategic plan and run the day to day operations. The larger part of my experience has been in successful fund raising such as; special events and grant writing.

Through the years I have stumbled on more than one organization that experienced "theft" from those in positions of trust. Some were prosecuted and others, well let's just say the new administration knew the price of this kind of public relations, so little or nothing was done to these folks. The next generation, the new administration worked hard to dig the organization out of what could have been a complete collapse.

Many in ministry have disdain for money; it is as if it is dirty or wrong to be financially successful. Some of these people truly believe that all they have to do is pray and the cash will just arrive. I am not knocking the power of prayer, but, I have never witnessed loaves from bread that just fell from out of the sky. The people on the receiving end; may not have a full understanding of what it takes to secure funding for their projects, but the reality is that no money translates into no project.

For most we vote with our dollars. If an organization is doing good works we want to support them. However, if they provide services we personally may not approve of, like abortion, we don't support them. Most everyone has a favorite charity. One that does the kind of work that makes them feel good about donating. Whether it is cancer, research, education, kids, feeding the poor, most American's want to help and to donate and to try and make a positive impact in our society and for the lives of others who may be less fortunate.

We trust that the "stewards" who are charged with making sure our donation is well spent, and funding what we requested it to fund, is doing just that.

But what happens when an organization accepts a donation and doesn't do with those funds what they said they would do? Recently I met with a foundation that funds grant requests and specifically for capital improvement projects. They shared with me that on occasion they had to ask for their money back. They funded a specific project and it never happened, the trustees all agreed that the money given was solely targeted for this specific project. In the absence of performing the specific project, they demanded the money to be refunded and it was.

A colleague shared with me that several years ago; he donated several thousands of dollars for a capital improvement project. Now four years later that project not only isn't completed but hasn't even begun. On the advice of his attorney, he has sent a demand for refund letter and filed a complaint with the attorney general. This guy feels duped and disrespected by an organization that he once believed very strongly in and wanted to support their mission. This kind of thing happens, and it happens often.

We are headed toward Christmas and into the biggest giving season of the year. As a donor, I have learned to be specific about where and what I want my donations to fund. I do the research on what percentage goes to program and what percentage goes to operations. And as a fund raising professional, I know the value in perception, public relations and the necessity of following through with my donors. I know first-hand the importance of "restricted" funds versus "unrestricted" funds.

Having spent many years with my development colleagues, I can honestly say that the majority are excellent stewards of the donations they receive. But I have also come across more than a few that have disrespected the donors and the donations.

There are numerous great causes doing really great works, but as a donor you need to exercise due diligence. Be sure to 1) Do your homework and investigate 2) be certain that you know exactly what and who you are funding 3) be sure your donations are applied to where you intended them to go. 4) make certain the causes that you support are doing the kind of work that is in keeping with your own belief system.

Sadly there is fraud and misuse of funds, it happens. If you believe that a not for profit organization is improperly accepting donations and not applying them to the proper accounts you can notify the IRS, the Attorney General and the Better Business Bureau. File a complaint but before you do give the Executive

Director or the Chief Executive Officer an opportunity to answer your complaint.

Giving is always a good thing. There are many wonderful causes to support, and the ones that aren't worthy, well let's just say that without money, they are out of business. No money, no ministry and your dollars, your vote!

"No One Reads Books Anymore" Ah Say What?

A few years ago I suggested an author event to an executive director of a local nonprofit I was associated with when he promptly replied, *"no one reads books anymore!"* All of a sudden I felt really old. He was young in his thirties and I was just a few years into my fifties, since he had the trump position, I just faded away.

I was crushed! I love books! I have hosted numerous author events through the years, bringing in between 6 and 8 authors generally with a wide range of subject matter to attract many people and often as a cultivating event for a cause that I was supporting and trying to bring to a new audience.

Not only am I a writer but a published author with a few titles under my belt. Many of my friends are published authors too. I buy books from many authors that I personally know to read them and show my support. I buy books on the best sellers list, I buy inspirational books, I buy decorating books, I buy cook books, I love my books all of them.

But it was more than all that for me. I love books, the cover, the paper, the typeset the feel and the smell. That personal tactile experience of holding it in my hands I enjoy it. I have purchased books just because they are pretty and eye appealing. I currently have at least half a dozen "active" journals that I am writing in and several everyday inspirational books. I save pretty full color glossy magazines like the special ones that come out at Christmas. I am truly a sucker for all kinds of magazines and I love our local newspaper that comes out twice a week and is magazine style. It is a resort area and this paper is a must read for everything you need to know from the recent new worthy happenings to the best restaurants to the latest commerce coming to town.

I know I know ... we can get all our news online and e books and everything you ever needed to know can be looked up on the internet so why a book? Am I supposed to give in and believe that the traditional hard and soft cover books soon will be something of the past?

I sure hope not! My favorite childhood book was **Charlotte's Web,** I still love that book! I spend many many days and nights reading Dr. Seuss books to all three of my children. I was holding them and a book while rocking in a rocking chair. That was our bonding time! Yes we sang songs and listened to baby Beluga too but reading to them and then having them learn to read and reading back to me was one of the greatest parent-child accomplishments. My kids went to the library; it was an outing for us, and something we did as a family. Nary a summer went by that they weren't enrolled in the summer reading program at our local library.

Are books out of fashion and going away due to electronic books? I can't imagine it! And I certainly hope not and yet I have witnessed book stores that are closing and others that have become more like a gift shop to stay competitive.

I don't know what the future holds for books but I can't subscribe to "no one reads books anymore."

The internet and e books are great but they are also a linear detached reading experience. To this reader and writer I want that personal cuddle up with a good book, turn the paper pages, and feel the paper and handle the cover experience.

One of my favorite experiences at the end of the day includes; my bed, my blankets, my two dogs and a mound of assorted books and magazines. My book collection equals my bliss!

Long live the traditional hard and soft cover books ...

No Rain No Rainbow

It's raining! And it looks like the rain will keep coming for several more hours if not a full day or so of unrelenting rain. My flowers and plants look great! The lawn is green and we haven't had to do a thing. Mother Nature has provided rain, cooler temps and just the right amount of sunshine. Today we are just one full week into the month of June.

In the past few years we have had scorching hot sunny days by now, we seem to have enjoyed earlier and longer summer temps.

Some people are enjoying the rain; I know that I have as I slept with the French doors open and could hear the gentle tapping of the rain throughout most of the night. There is a cool breeze with clean and fresh air.

Others are having some anxiety since they have outside plans that will be impacted by the rain. I bet the beach population for this weekend is less than anticipated in the absence of sunshine. There are numerous events like graduations, fairs, festivals, concerts, yard sales and weddings that will go with plan B or cancel all together.

Today I will officiate an outdoor wedding by water's edge and at a lighthouse location, there will be no cancellation. Tents and umbrellas will be used to shield the rain. I can't help but reflect on my own wedding when immediately after our wedding vows, the rain stopped and the sun started to shine. Minutes later there was a double rainbow and all we could think was "no rain, no rainbow."

I love sunshine but I also love the rain. There is that sense of calm that you can hear and a desire to slow down that overcomes us. Take your time, it is raining!

In life we all have our sunny days and we all experience the rainy ones too. To know "up" we must know "down" to know "happy" we must know "sad." The weather reminds me of life and that we are not in charge. We don't get to pick what days will be sunny or rainy what days will be happy or sad and there is probably a good reason.

How many of us might want all sunny days? Or all beach weather? Or weather that suits our outside events? But we know that it doesn't work that way. We need the rain to cleanse the earth and to help the plants grow and to add to our water table and water sources. We would literally burn up without the rain.

Our tears and sadness are often just like the rain as they cleanse us from our hurts and heartaches. We need to cry so that we may cleanse and become new again. Every life has its own share of rain. We should learn to embrace our rainy days just like our sunny ones.

I have often thought that death must be just like life, like giving birth. A mother who goes through childbirth knows that her body takes over and that she is literally out of control. That child comes through the mother and arrives when it is ready. I imagine death to be the same; that it just takes over us and we are out of our control. That is all happens in its own natural time.

Today's rain isn't going to dampen the wedding I am officiating later today; the couple getting married is in love and ready to begin their life together as a married couple. This is their day, whether it rains or the sun is shining. The weather today will serve to remind me and others that we are not in charge and that there is a natural life force that determines things like weather and what happens in our life.

We learn that fighting the natural elements in life is unnecessary and that we should embrace them all. I love the rain and I love when the rain is over, because just like in life, after the rain, the sun returns and often shines even brighter!

Not an Ordinary Guy

I don't think that I am easily impressed, partly because I have high standards and mostly because I expect so much from myself. It takes a lot to impress me! Yet today while at the grocery store my husband and life partner of 23 years did just that!

What did he do, you ask? As I purchased a sugar free tea and stated I needed to walk to the coffee counter for a packet of sugar substitute, he opened up his wallet and pulled out a single pack of the kind of sugar substitute that I use. And what makes this so impressive? It is not something that he personally uses. He had it in there just for me.

Then we joked about how much he loves me and how many things that he does for me. All the little ways that he shows his love and this is exactly what attracted me to him in the first place.

We met the day that he buried his wife, she was only 29 years old and they had just had twins, a son and a daughter. I was asked by the mother-in-law who was my friend and a colleague as we were both Realtors in the same office. They needed a babysitter so the entire family could attend the viewings and the funeral. It was Easter Sunday of 1992. I had heard so much about them and the twins that they were expecting and then I heard about all her many health issues as a result of the pregnancy. Once the babies were delivered 8-weeks prematurely she soon went into a comma and never awakened before her death.

What struck me about Brian when I met him was that he looked like an ordinary guy. He loved sports was an avid music fan and had a regular job as a Civil Servant with the City of Baltimore. But once I had the opportunity to get to know him I found out that he was NOT an ordinary guy, not at all. He has character and drive and determination. He does the right thing.

His wife died and he was faced with being a single parent to pre-mature twins, a son and a daughter and he never once thought about NOT raising them himself. Even if that meant he would go it alone. Easily he could have hidden behind his grief and passed them off to his mother or to her mother and yet it never even occurred to him to do that. That impressed me.

He was always there for them, when they had developmental delays and health challenges and when they struggled and when they succeeded, he was there. Just as he has been there for me for 23 years now.

It truly is the little things that I love about him, he is a tough guy with pride but will show me his most tender and loving side. He cares about me and he loves me like no one else ever has, when my family did the things that they did to try and hurt me and bring me down, he was fighting mad. And wanted to engage and fight them. I'll never forget how upset he was when I was excluded from my mother's obituary, he said, "If your dad was still alive, they wouldn't have been able to get away with that. They have no class." I was stunned because he rarely speaks ill of the people in our lives until or unless he has something serious and strong to communicate.

His love has healed so many of my hurts. His support and his unwavering hold of my heart still warms my heart so. I love watching him do the many tasks around our home and interacting with our adult son and our two precious pooches.

My husband doesn't wear his heart on his sleeve but by his actions he shows what a caring person that he is and that although he may appear to be "ordinary" there is nothing ordinary about the depth of his love, caring and commitment.

O'Connell Girl ... Happy St. Pat's Day!

When I was growing up along with my four sisters we were often referred to as ***"The O'Connell Girls."*** Growing up with an Irish father and an Italian mother was our natural heritage. Both sides were very proud of their roots. The Italian side of our family was bigger and louder and more readily available to us when we grew up. Back then and to them being Italian meant everything! Unlike our society today where cultures are so easily blended my grandfather would have preferred that his daughter, my mother not just marry an Italian but an Italian Catholic. Oh how the world has changed.

It wasn't until after my father left home and began his new family that I witnessed his pride in being Irish. I had gone to visit him, I was teenaged and I was happily shocked how well decorated his home was for St. Patrick's Day. There were shamrocks and green decorations all throughout his home. If I never knew it before I knew then just how proud and happy he was to be Irish!

With a name like O'Connell I wasn't going to fool anyone or be able to deny my heritage even if I had wanted to deny it, clearly we were an Irish Catholic family. I was always proud of my heritage, I often said, ***"I am Irish and Italian and I have the temper to prove it."*** Today I might modify "temper" with the word "passion." Both Irish and Italians are known for their passion, their spirit and their pride. I certainly have mine.

St. Patrick was the patron Saint of Ireland, although it is said that he came from Britain. He had several messages he believed came from God and ultimately he became an ordained priest. It was through his own struggles and adversity that he came to be a religious man.

Prayer of St. Patrick

May the Strength of God pilot us
May the Power of God preserve us
May the Wisdom of God instruct us
May the Hand of God protect us
May the Way of God direct us
May the Shield of God defend us

May the Host of God guard us
Against the snares of the evil ones
Against temptations of the world

May Christ be with us
May Christ be before us
May Christ be in us
Christ be over all!
May Thy Salvation, Lord
Always be ours,
This day, O Lord, and evermore.
Amen.

When Irish eyes are smiling, sure tis like a morn in spring. In the lilt of Irish laughter you can hear the angels sing. When Irish hearts are happy all the world seems bright and gay, and when Irish eyes are smiling, sure, they steal your heart away."
- Chauncey Olcott and George Graff, Jr.

I've been to Chicago when they turn the river green and I shared my share of green beer and Irish whiskey but the one tradition that sticks for every single year is a pot on the stove with corned beef, potatoes and cabbage. Right now, I can smell it cooking as I write this blog.

One of the great things about St. Patrick's day celebrations are the parades and clovers and shamrocks and the luck and spirit of the Irish that goes along with it, and on this holiday we can all wear our green (the color of health) and we can all enjoy the spirit of the Irish because there is nothing better than when Irish eyes are smiling.

And one of my Irish favorite sayings is *"May you be in Heaven a half an hour before the devil knows you're dead."*

"Anyone acquainted with Ireland knows that the morning of St. Patrick's Day consists of the night of the 17th of March flavored strongly with the morning of the 18th." Author unknown

On Being a Mother

I always knew that I would get married and that I would have children and become a mother. And I knew that I would do it in that order. My belief is that the reason it takes a man and a woman to make a baby is because ideally it takes two to raise one. I never ever wanted to be a single parent. My view was that each parent a father figure and a mother figure brought their own perspective and gifts to the process of parenting children. Together they created balance.

As a teenager I worked with kids at summer camp for years as a C.I.T. (Counselor in Training) Counselor and Unit Leader, I babysat often and was the second oldest of five children. I worked in a special needs school and youth retreat house. I always did well with children and had many follow me long after the camp or school experience. I taught both swimming and archery as a camp counselor. People often commented on what a great mother I was and said things like, "I hope one day I have a close relationship with my children like you do with yours."

My kids have called me "awesome" "amazing" and the "best mother ever." I took pride in all my mothering from trying to be a good homemaker and cook to a professional career woman. I wanted my kids to see that family came first and that together we were better than when apart.

As a mother I did believe that you could have it all being a homemaker and career woman, maybe just not all at the same time.

When my daughter's father unexpectedly died I found myself as a single mother with a toddler. Not only was I going to be the nurturer but also the bread winner. I worked as a waitress in a high end restaurant for the first five years and then went into apartment rental management and real estate for the flexible hours. My goal was to be there. I arranged my work schedule around my daughter's school schedule. I was a carpool mom, a room mom a volunteer mom. Whatever it took I did to give my daughter a private school education. To receive the "parish rate" at her school I had to volunteer my time. I painted and worked the annual fundraiser. I baked and I donated.

Early on it was difficult with no money except for what I earned as a waitress. We lived in a nice neighborhood and for security reasons I took the upper level third floor apartment. When I wasn't working we spent numerous hours in the public library, our community pool and with friends and family.

Having a child takes your focus off of yourself as kids have immediate needs. Our lives revolved around her school and activity schedule. I don't need bread, milk or orange juice in my house I can live without all of them. Yet having children these were just a few of the necessary staples.

My child was the whole world to me. There was nothing I wouldn't have done for her. When her dad died I was mortified that she would never know her own father. I tried my best to make up for it. All I ever wanted was to give my child more than what I grew up with, now; early on I wasn't going to be able to do that. I had a dad, I knew him, and she never would.

After that marriage and his death I wasn't interested in any real relationships, I dated had guys in my life but for the most part kept that and them away from our home and my child. I wasn't looking for a husband or a father replacement, perhaps I should have. Friends said I was like "I am woman, hear me roar." I worked every single shift I could get and often late into the night when she was asleep.

Becoming a Realtor was professionally and personally rewarding. At just 27 years old I afforded my first home and paid for it with 6-commission checks as I assumed an existing mortgage and immediately had equity. I managed my career our home and my child.

She attended the best private schools and I wanted her to be educated both academically and spiritually. My mother was out of state and none of my sisters had children of their own. They were all in other states doing their own things. She had me and I had her. We had friends in the neighborhood and with my work. We lived well.

I was always really strong on my own and fully functioning until the impact of abuse hit. Then it was like a bridge that just tumbled down. It was like a storm that shattered our lives. The only rescue was one that I eventually created for myself and for us. It was not ideal.

For more than ten years I was a single mother. When I met my second husband and became instant mom to pre-mature infant twins, a son and a daughter along with my then 11 year old child, I welcomed the opportunity to co-parent. I could not have asked for a better partner. Not only was he the main bread winner but present in their life. We ate dinner every single night together as a family. We split the activities and I continued to have the most flexible work schedule.

We shared all the carpool activities and worked as a team to provide what was necessary. It is a tremendous amount of work and responsibility raising children. We put our hearts and our souls into being the best parents we could be.

Our children have all been so different. Our son was always so appreciative of everything that we did for him. Early on as a

Scout he spent weeks away at different camps and then every summer a ten day excursion to many states. He always missed us and returned even more appreciative than when he left home. Going away made him realize what a good thing he had at home.

The girls were always more of a challenge; any battles began during the teenage years and were always over boys, dating and sex. We wanted them to put their education and themselves first.

Kids grow up and have their own life codes and views, I enjoy hearing their perspective. The one that I most hope to hear is when they have made the commitment and carried it through to raising their own children. No one knows what it is like to be a mother until you have been one. No one knows what it takes to raise children to maturity until they themselves have done so.

For all the kids that criticize their parents, this is what I would say, when you have done the job, done the work, been there and given up your life to support another life, when you have parented for 18 or more years, then and only then do I want to hear your comments and criticism. Because until that day when you have been there and until you have that experience, you really have no real point of reference. You have no idea what it takes until you, yourself have been a mother or a father.

As we approach this Mother's Day I am celebrating my more than 32 years with kids living at home. I am remembering all the good times, the joys that they brought into my life. There is no greater purpose in life than in having a child and raising that child. To love a child and to give your heart and your soul to a child is the deepest most selfless acts in life and gives true meaning to life.

Mother's come in all shapes and sizes with a variety of gifts and talents, this mother is most proud of giving so much of herself not just for a naturally birthed child but for two non-biological children that I loved and raised as my very own children.

Having children and being a mother isn't about getting it all right all of the time, it isn't about perfection, we aren't perfect and neither are our children. It is about being there; doing the work and knowing that you gave all you had and did the very best that you could have done no matter what situation you found yourself in.

Happy Mother's Day to all mothers who have loved so deeply and who have done the work!

On Raising Twins

Be careful what you ask for because you just may get it. I always wanted more children I just wasn't sure I wanted the pregnancy that went along with having them. I remember saying to God,

"If you would just give them to me I would take care of them." Not that long after this declaration, I met my husband when his wife died leaving him alone to raise pre-mature newborn infant twins a son and a daughter.

Getting involved with Brian meant instant expanded family and me taking on the mother role for two infant babies. I will never forget our first outing was on the Avenue at Rehoboth beach in Delaware. As soon as we got out of the car people came around and started asking questions. "Did you know you were having twins?" "Is it a boy and a girl?" "When were they born?" People just automatically assumed that I was their mother.

Thank God for Brian who just appeared over my right shoulder and then he proceeded to answer, "Yes they were expected. Yes a boy and a girl and they were born on 1/23" I was really quiet and kind of stunned. He might have been expecting them but I surely wasn't.

I was asked to babysit for all the viewings and the funeral of his wife and their mother. Their birth mother never lived long enough to hold them or feed them or care for them. When I heard their story all I could think was, wow life is hard enough without at least having a mother.

Our twins would never know their mother because within hours of their birth she went into a coma and died just weeks after that. Their father was such a stand-up guy, he never once thought about NOT raising them even if that meant as a single father. He loved his children and was devoted to them.

As I assumed the mother role in the twins life after getting them at just 87 days old they just naturally became my children. I will never forget when our daughter got off the school bus while in high school and shared with me that her girlfriend asked if I was her "step mom" and my daughter said, "Mom, I told her, "no, she is *not* my step-mom, she is my mom. She is the only mother I ever knew."

We never used terms like "step-mom" "step-dad" or "step-parents" in our house.   All three of our children had lost a natural parent to death; the parents that remained just assumed the mother and father family roles.

There is no doubt that our son would never have achieved Eagle Scout without his father's devotion and dedication. He never once missed a practice or a soccer game for our daughter. I have vivid recall of him lacing up her soccer shoes and running the field coaching her on to win. It would be her team that won the Championship and no father could have been more proud.

When they were babies they had many needs in being born pre-mature with extra eye and hearing tests and numerous concerns over their development. Each child would prove to be so very different in their likes and dislikes, talents and abilities.

We read up on what it would take to raise twins and the many thoughts on the best way to approach raising them. Should we keep them together? Should they attend the same schools and the same classroom or should they be separated.

Even today more than 21 years later there are differing opinions on the best way to go with keeping them together or separating them. My husband was big on keeping them together; he always wanted them to love and care for one another. As they grew up this would become an almost impossible task.

They were just **"two completely different people"** as our son so often states. He was an honor student who struggled socially; she was social and seemed to struggle in school. He was loyal and an artist, she was fiercely competitive. They had completely different personalities, different talents and abilities.

With hind sight being 20/20 I would NOT have kept them together. If one failed they should not have both had to be held accountable. They were and are two separate individuals with different likes and dislikes, keeping them together may not have always been the best approach.

The biggest misconception in my view is that twins would be so much more work and effort than a single child. I never thought of it like that I always thought it was nice for them to have a built in play mate that was always on the same playing field and with the same age appropriateness.

Looking back I guess the only thing that I would have done different is to have separated them in school more, allowing them to grow without the other being so conscience of what their twin was up to or not. Funny how as little kids they just naturally gravitated toward "boy" toys versus "girl" toys. No one ever said the dolls were for our daughter and the trucks and trains for our son. Both were readily available in our house, both children could have played with whatever toys they chose and yet they both gravitated to the traditional "boy" toys for boys and the dolls for the girl.

Looking back it really was very rewarding raising twins and yes it was also a lot of hard work and determination. The biggest take away is that you can raise two children in the same home with the same environment and the same opportunities and the same morals and values and they can grow up and be *"two completely different people."* Neither child was all good or all bad just very different kids.

For all the parents who are raising twins I used to have a bumper sticker on my car that read, *"I used to have time and now I have twins."* One day they will grow up and move on with life and then you may not have the twins but you will have more time.

Happy twinship!

Once Treasured

How long is long enough? How long should we hang onto things? Things like funeral cards from someone who is long deceased? Or a wedding album that is thirty five years old and one of the partners has been dead for thirty years? Or holding onto our kid's artwork? Or their baby shoes or crib mobile? What is the timeframe for hanging onto various pieces of memorabilia?

So many things in life are once treasured and one day they literally become trash. I guess for each one of us that timeline is different.

Earlier this week I opened a trunk I owned since 1973. It is the classic green foot locker with black trim and brass hardware. I received it as a gift for my camping days when I was just a teenager. That trunk occupied my cabin and rested at the foot of my cot for many summers. Later it became a catch all for things that I saved through the years. It has travelled everywhere with me for over 40 years!

What I found inside probably only held any value to me and for me alone. I found all my report cards from kindergarten and forward along with my Iowa Basic Skills Test results. I found an Honorable Mention Certificate I received in the 6th grade for my science fair project.

I also found was my parent's wedding invitation complete with a RSVP card. Not really sure how I got that and my dad's business card that was used to secure construction jobs. These items were created four years before I was born. Then I came across my first husband's guest book from the funeral parlor and his many mass cards. Our candle from when we wed in 1978 and our daughters 1st Christmas card complete with her baby picture.

It was clearly a trip down memory lane. It stirred many things inside of me. I had one of Randy's work shirts. He has been deceased since 1983 and I have been with my husband Brian now since 1992.

The one thing I found that surprised me the most was our daughters crib mobile that played Mary Had A Little Lamb and it had yellow and white lambs that turned as it played. That mobile is more than 33 years old and worked as well as when it was brand new.

So ... why do we keep these things? Why do we cart them from place to place? I have lived in four different states and probably had 8 different residences and yet those items have travelled with me. On what occasion do we finally let them go?

I guess to answer that we must first ask ourselves why we kept them for so long. I think for me they represented my life. I also believe that I thought my child would want them and perhaps cherish them as much as I have for all these decades.

What struck me is literally how much baggage we cart with us. I started a new relationship with Brian in 1992 and yet I brought boxes of the past with me. Together we both had more than a foot locker that represented our previous spouses.

My husband Brian told me he cleaned out Stacey's things many years ago. So what on earth was I doing with so many "pieces of the past?"

I finally let go of most of it. I kept my report cards and photos of my baby girl. Pictures taken with my father and my mother now deceased also made the cut. I did get many laughs off the letters that I had from my two youngest sisters. Seems like both of my sisters were competing for my attention when I lived in Texas that year and at least one of them was measuring who would receive the longest letter from me. One had one with 4-pages while the other only received one with 1.5 pages and she was sure to bring it to my attention. I was amused by my youngest sister Iris when she declared at the age of 15 that our mother **"was controlling and holding her back."** Classic mother-daughter stuff, I had to laugh out loud.

But the best laugh was when she wrote to me and stated, **"Don't forget to write back, you don't want to be presumed dead!"** She was a teen and I was in my early twenties. All these years later I still had those letters from her, letters dated from 1981.

Once again I thought about keeping them. They were so cute. But the truth is that relationship ended decades ago and it was time to move those letters from "once treasured" to now trash.

There really is a price that we pay when we carry a load and carry so much weight with us. I am reminded of the Disney Pixar movie **Up,** the only way he could fly and lift off was to let go. Once he let go of the past and lightened the load, he was free to fly away.

I am definitely choosing to travel lighter these days and making choices so that I won't be held back or held down by the weight of the past. Sometimes it is just time … the past memories will always be treasured but the letting go allows new ones to be created in their place.

Our Defining Moments

We all have them. The defining moments and the defining years, they usually harken back to when we learned many valuable lessons. When we learn to drive and when we graduate and when we marry and when we have children. There are the years when we advance our careers and others when we experiences profound losses. Sometimes our defining moments come with a specific year and birthdate. I remember getting married at 19, being pregnant at the age of 20 and having a child just three days after I turned 21. I remember being widowed at the age of 23.

When I turned 25 I was completely miserable as a single mother with a 4 year old daughter. I was in an inappropriate relationship and feeling lost. My mother tried to cheer me up but the truth was I was transitioning from immature to a mature adult. I was finally taking hold of my life and responsibility for myself. That year I returned to school, changed careers and at age 26 purchased my first home. I became a Realtor and afforded not only a mortgage, but a new car and a child in private school. It wasn't easy but I was determined and driven.

At age 30 I was mourning another failed relationship that ended badly. But at age 32 I would meet my husband who would become my long term love and life partner. Together we would embark on merging our broken families as we both had a spouse die and leave us with children. It wasn't always smooth sailing but we were making it work. By age 38 I was feeling so accomplished as my child graduated from a highly regarded all girls Catholic Prep school with a fully funded academic scholarship. I was happy and I was thin and I was feeling good.

My feelings of accomplishment would be short lived because as it became time for my child to set her own course she would leave home and never look back. I grew up in my 30's and my

40's. I succeeded then and into my 50's when yet another family drama would tear at me. More angry more hate more hurtful family that would take their pound of flesh when my desire to share "my story" was about to come to the light. All was well as long as they could conceal their flaws, scapegoat me and re-write history. It was yet another learning curve for me. Once I had a much better opinion of the key players than what they ever deserved.

But all was not lost as my heart grew larger, my self-worth increased and my faith in God prevailed. What I was left with was more lessons learned and a greater sense of peace.

Time always ferrets out the truth. We can package things anyway that we like but history always emerges with the truth. As parents we have a hard time watching our adult children fail. Many times by the poor choices that they would make and yet we all made them. And we survived just like they will.

My husband says that he was also miserable at age 25 when he wasn't quite happy with the choices that he had made either. But isn't that life? It is about learning and about growing up. It was about transitioning from thinking like a child to behaving like an adult. It was about being responsible for our own lives and our own decisions.

Today at 55 we are both happier than we have ever been. Together we have much life experience between us. We know what happy is and we know what sad is and we know that everything changes and to appreciate the here and the now and all that life offers. We are alive and healthy and that is what matters most to us.

Every one of us can be mad or sad about something we can also make the decision to be happy and glad. It is through the struggle that we find enlightenment.

Sometimes when we look back at the storms that we weathered and the loss that we suffered and the pain that we endured, we can remember that each was nothing more than the catalyst for change and for growth and that it was merely time for learning another lesson.

So here is to our defining moments ... the ones that shaped us and made us who and what we are today!

Our Final Call for Grace

It is not over until we take our last breath, but one day it will end. Every single day that we are living we move one day further from our birth date to our death date. Our days here will end one day, we all recognize this fact, most are uncomfortable discussing it but it is a fact of life.

Our living says a lot about us, our death will say much too. Recently we lost two iconic comediennes in Robin Williams and Joan Rivers. Who would have ever thought that Robin Williams would decide that to die was a better choice than to live? We are all so vulnerable. Every single day we make choices from the most basic needs we determine when to sleep and how long, we decide what foods we will consume and many are to our health and others may not be as healthy. We make all kinds of choices throughout our days and our lifetime.

There is no sadder act in our society that when a young person decides that death is a choice over life. There is always something and someone to live for, life is always worth living. One bad day or a couple of bad days or even a period of bad days does not warrant an untimely death. Yet for many people life will end earlier than what we may expect.

Why a young child will ever have to fight cancer has always been a mystery to me. When I was just a kid and in middle school my mother who was a nurse was friendly with another nurse who had a young daughter battling cancer. At the age of 11 Michelle lost her battle and died from cancer. I watched that family from a distance. The two older brothers were much older and star athletes from our area. I know that this mother and this family grieved because I witnessed the love that they all had for Michelle. By the time I met her she had already lost her hair and was confined to a wheel chair. Her short life and her death left a lasting impression on me. This family continued on with their lives with much grace yet they never forgot the daughter and the sister that was lost all too soon.

During my high school years I witnessed death from three young people that I will never ever forget. One was a neighbor that I barely knew who was probably in her late teens and early twenties when she married a military man. He was killed and she became a young widow. She carried on with her life and her head was help high.

I recall two guys from high school that died pre-maturely, one named Vincent who died in a car accident after hitting a tree. He was only 17 years old, he was really popular and should have had a wonderful life ahead of him. It was not to be. And my junior year in high school one of my classmates died that November while driving to school with his twin brother. One twin died and one twin survived the car crash. Through the years I have thought of them often.

Today I am at an age where my parents are deceased and I have friends that died and some that are fighting disease to stay alive. I witness their grace as I watch them prepare for the final stages of life. When you are faced with loss, with death over life you realize how much in life truly matters and how much in life that is really meaningless and trivial.

Recently I asked my husband, "Do you think about our death and how much time we have left here?" He quickly and quietly responded with "yes." We have both known death up close and personal. We both had marriages that ended in death of a spouse. We were so young. I was just 23 years old and he was just 32 years old. My first husband and I were the parents of one child and my second husband had twins with his wife.

Our stories are similar in that it all happened so quickly, I married in 1978, had our daughter in 1980 and he died in 1983. Brian married in 1989 after a short courtship and the twins arrived in 1992. His wife and their mother died shortly thereafter.

You grow up fast when death touches your life and you have a choice on how you react and respond. You can become bitter and a victim or vulnerable and a survivor. We both choose to be survivors. We chose to honor their lives by living our best life and by living it fully. We know that one of us will become "widowed" again and we know that we will be called to face death with grace and acceptance.

I imagine death to be like life, like birthing where you have lost all control and the birthing process just takes over your body. I imagine death is the same, that when our time comes it just takes over our bodies and we die.

When I see people that go into Hospice I am always amazed at their grace, they know that death is coming and they are facing it head on, it truly seems to be the final act of grace.

I believe that most people want a life of peace and they want to die with a certain degree of peace. We talk about having "our affairs in order" meaning our wills and our final directives upon our death.

The person in my family that most impressed me with his "final act of grace" when he knew that he was preparing to die was my father. There were many things in his life that he did wrong but his death was not one of them. He made peace with his own life and all the people that mattered to him. Isn't that the final act of grace?

When I was a little kid my dad used to listen to a song called *Autumn of my Life* by Bobby Goldsboro. That term "autumn" always stayed with me. Today I am praying for friends that are losing a loved one to death and/or facing their own immortality. Death is our final teacher and our final call for grace.

For Whom the Bell Tolls

By John Donne

No man is an island

Entire of himself

Each is a piece of the continent

A part of the main

If a clod be washed away by the sea

Europe is the less

As well as if a promontory were

As well as if a manor of thine own

Or of thine friends were

Each man's death diminishes me

For I am involved in mankind

Therefore, send not to know

For whom the bell tolls

It tolls for thee.

We are born to live! We are born to get the most out of this life, one day it will end and we will be called upon to trust in our death just as we have trusted in our living. Death changes everything and it changes everyone that is touched by it. When we have peace in our own hearts, the death and loss of others and of ourselves becomes easier to accept.

Holy Mary Mother of God, pray for us sinners now and at the hour of our death, Amen.

Our Love Anniversaries

Do you have "love" anniversaries? You know from your first date day? Or first kiss day? Or when you officially became a couple day? Your wedding date?

My husband remembers them all! I try to be as good as he is with them. Of course I remember our wedding date but I admit I do have to think harder when it comes to the date that we met or when we moved beyond just being friends.

We celebrate most all of our "love" anniversary dates. We celebrate as much love as we can and it starts with the day that we met and where we met and what we were doing. We would be introduced when I was holding his baby daughter as I was babysitting so he could attend his wife's funeral. Hard for him not to forget that date. And yet we both feel so God blessed to have met one another.

Then we remember when we first went out and when we moved past just being friends. We celebrate the anniversary date from when we purchased our family home and brought two fractured families together to begin again as one.

The biggest love anniversary is our wedding date. This summer we will be legally married for 18 years, although we have officially been a couple for almost 23 years now.

It just amazes us how we got together and how much we have been through together until now. We have a history that goes on for more than two decades and we celebrate every day that we wake up together.

Our love has been all over the map with the highs and the lows that any couple that manages to change and to grow together can and will endure. We have known the highest of highs and the lowest of lows. We grew together in our thirties and our forties. We raised our children and we succeeded in our careers together. We said good bye to our parents and hello to older age. We navigated through the busiest and challenging of times and fought the good fight and surrendered to those that weren't worth the fight. We did it together and we did it with love.

One of the things that keeps us going is that we don't take each other for granted. We celebrate the every day's together and build upon our love anniversaries. Love anniversaries are important as they help us assess and gauge how we are doing. We reflect back as we look ahead.

Recently I was receiving Physical Therapy and my husband sat in the waiting room for almost two hours. When the therapist was done with me he commented on how much patience that my husband had while in his office. I said I knew that as it is his norm and I know just how lucky I am.

Love begets love and the more that we celebrate our love, the more love that we create to celebrate. It is a wonderful circle of love and of life. Remember your wonder "love" anniversaries and celebrate them all and you will never be without love.

Our Stewardship

What will you leave behind? What will your legacy be once you have departed this life? It surely won't be about "things" but rather about other people and our relationships. Did we leave this place better than how we found it?

Did we give more than we took? Did we make a positive contribution to society and to others? Did we practice love and forgiveness? What will our stewardship say about us?

We are mere stewards in this lifetime; we own nothing because if we did the U-Haul would be following the hearse to our final destination. *"For we brought nothing into the world, and we cannot take anything out of the world."* **From Luke 12:42-46**

Remember the Kansas song Dust in the Wind and the line "all we are is dust in the wind" and "nothin' lasts forever but the earth and sky."

On the date that my "Other Mother" turned 80 years old another friend lost her battle with cancer. She had just celebrated her 56th birthday. My "Other Mother" has acquired many possessions in her lifetime, the friend's departure drives home how nothing will go with her into the next life.

We take nothing with us when we leave this life we return "home" the same way that we arrived with no earthly possessions. In this lifetime we are merely the stewards of "things" and "property" and "material possessions."

Our relationships transform or transition or they die. How we took care of them will determine their fate. How do we want to be remembered? What legacy do we wish to leave behind?

Everything that we are given is one day returned. We are stewards for all living things; for our children, our animals, our family and our friends. Our employment and our career path also afford us the opportunity for stewardship too.

How we take care of the land and the people and all living things is a direct reflection on how we practiced our stewardship.

***"A society is defined not only by what it creates but by what it refuses to destroy."* John Sawhill**

Our Value Doesn't Come From Outside of Ourselves

Our value in life doesn't come from outside of ourselves; it comes from the divine within us. If we allow others to judge us and value or devalue us we will live in a constant state of flux. That relationship or job title doesn't define us. What defines us is what lives deep within our hearts and our souls.

We give our power away when we allow every single person to judge us and/or to define us. Truth is that only one person can truly define us and that person is us. My belief system tells me that God alone created us to be the unique individual that we are and that only God can define us and judge us. Others may have a different belief system that better defines them.

As living breathing humans we grow and we change and we evolve as we age and experience more in life. We become more experienced and better educated. Our age brings us wisdom and a better understanding of whom and what we are and who and what we are meant to be.

We should celebrate our uniqueness and our individuality. There is no one else quite like us and there never will be another just like us. This is the day the Lord has made just as you are the person that God alone has deemed you to be. We have free will and we make our own choices, we can allow others to define us or we can stand strong in our heart of hearts and our souls.

We are bigger than any one life event and bigger than our brokenness. Each person will have their challenges and their own issues and cross to bear. It is up to us to decide what if any of it defines us. Letting others define us is the surest way to misery and gives all of our power away.

Children are taught to seek approval, an adult who knows themselves, doesn't seek approval. A mature adult has the depth of understanding and knows their core, their own heart and soul.

When we move away from our core being, we can't be surprised when our life doesn't feel good or authentic. There is that "inner voice" that we all have that knows intuitively what is best for us. Take the time to know you and to invest in yourself and to love and appreciate yourself. When we do these things we show up with our value intact.

There will never be a shortage of people that will want to define you or place a value on you and your life. Many will try to devalue another in an attempt to raise them up. We must remain true to ourselves. Our value doesn't come from outside of ourselves; it comes from the divine within us.

Mother Teresa "Do It Anyway"

People are often unreasonable, irrational, and self-centered. Forgive them anyway.

If you are kind, people may accuse you of selfish, ulterior motives. Be kind anyway.

If you are successful, you will win some unfaithful friends and gain some genuine enemies. Succeed anyway.

If you are honest and sincere people may deceive you. Be honest and sincere anyway.

What you spend years creating, others could destroy overnight. Create anyway.

If you find serenity and happiness, some may be jealous. Be happy anyway.

The good you do today, will often be forgotten. Do good anyway.

Give the best you have, and it may never be enough. Give your best anyway.

In the final analysis, it is between you and God. It was never between you and them anyway.

Passion and Patience

"A life without passion is not living, it's merely existing." Leo Buscaglia

"Seek patience and passion in equal amounts. Patience alone will not build the temple. Passion alone will destroy its walls." Maya Angelou

Striking that perfect balance between patience and passion may be a real challenge for many of us. The life without passion is a life limited in color and yet we need to temper our passion with a certain degree of patience.

Prayer for Patience

"Let us not become weary in doing well, for at that time we will reap a harvest if we do not give up." Galatians 6:9

Our world is filled with "fast" we want it now! We want instant gratification; seldom do we see young people with patience. Like a child that has just two times on their internal clock, all they understand is "now" and "later." Many young people don't understand that many things; good things take time to develop and to evolve.

How much value do we put on anything that comes too easily for us? Opposed to the value of the things we had to work and work hard at doing or achieving?

The happiest people seem to be the ones that live a life of passion. They understand that we cannot do anything about being born or dying, but we can do so much about how we live. What makes up get out of bed in the morning? What excites us? What do we think about?

When we uncover our passion and temper it with the right amount of patience, we are on our way and on the road to happiness and fulfillment.

Here is to living a life of passion …

P.E.A.C.E - Parents of Adult Estranged Children Everywhere

What do famous actresses like Demi Moore, Meg Ryan and Jennifer Aniston have in common?

At one point in their lives they were estranged from their mother. In 2010 a survey conducted by 20th Century Fox showed that 8 out of 10 people reported that the women in their families were responsible for ongoing family feuds; 4 out of 10 reported that they were currently going through it.

A fifth of the people polled admitted that a family member died before they could make peace. Thirty percent of women have been estranged from their moms. Imagine Jennifer Aniston's mom seeing her daughter's high profile marriage to Brad Pitt and she wasn't invited to attend the wedding?

There are numerous chat rooms and blog sites most of them kept fairly under the radar where parents communicate their grief and their confusion over the loss of their adult children. Often it is learned behavior that passes from generation to generation.

Amelia's Story

When Amelia left home she was newly graduated from the Peabody School for the Arts. She was an honor student and gifted and talented concert pianist. She received a full honors scholarship to Harvard University that was academically based. In the months between graduating from Peabody and attending

Harvard she would decide to move in with her teenaged boyfriend. Shortly thereafter she became a teen unwed mother and Harvard was no longer an option.

In her lifestyle choices she would also decide to dismiss her mother from her life. A mother she once seemed to adore; wrote her college essay about and by all outward signs had a close loving mother/daughter relationship. No one was more surprised by Amelia's actions and life choices than her own mother. When her mother finally decided to go after Amelia, who was just shy of 18, Amelia retaliated with accusations of abuse. A nasty court battle ensued and the outcome was declared "unfounded" and further stated "Amelia has many mental health issues as a result of being sexually abused as a child."

Amelia was reportedly abused by a man who married into the family, when uncovered and confronted the extended family chose not to believe or to support Amelia or her mother. Family members not only didn't support by word but also by deed as they allowed the accused "child molester" unlimited access to their own babies. The declaration of sexual abuse would trigger decades of estrangement.

For many years Amelia's mother grieved the loss of her daughter and her grandchild. For more than a decade she tried many times for reconciliation and all to no avail. It took many years and heartache and finally today her mother accepts that Amelia will never be a part of her life and she is okay with this conclusion. When asked how she finally came to peace? Mother responded with, "If Amelia wasn't my daughter, I wouldn't even like her. The person she has become is not someone I would want in my life. Then I started thinking that all relationships end, some end by divorce, some by death and some by choice. Finally I am free of her and accepting of her decision. I live a very full life and it just doesn't include my daughter."

How does a mother go from giving birth, breast feeding her baby, nurturing her and providing her with the best educational opportunities, undying love and support for her daughter and then to acceptance of estrangement? Like all loss it had to be a process with the stages of grief until acceptance. In many ways it is a death. For a parent it represents a death of the future, one that their child was expected to carry forward.

Chase and Beth's Story

When Chase brought his new fiancée' Beth home to meet his mother he didn't expect the reaction he received. Chase was a successful African American male and Beth a blond blue-eyed gal, not the picture of what his mother believed was the right choice for her son. They didn't speak for over a year. Finally as a result of the up and coming wedding mother met with son and they reconciled their differences. Today more than 4-children and 2 decades later all is well in this family. The love between mother and son was greater than any differences. Beth is openly embraced and loved by all family members.

When it comes to our children we see ourselves and our future, perhaps it is easier to let go of parents as most will outlive them. Parents may represent the past and adult children may decide they want a new life apart from parental feedback, input and influence.

In my research I have communicated with many parents, mostly mothers of estranged adult children. For the most part they have real difficulty letting go of their children even when they are fully developed functioning adults. What other relationships would we hang on so desperately for? Like divorce kids also decide at times to move away from parents both literally and figuratively. Sometimes they come back and sometimes they don't.

Peggy and Her Son Dan

When Peggy's son Dan left home he was bitter and angry over his parent's decision to divorce and he began abusing drugs and alcohol. Peggy tried to get him help but because he was a legal adult her hands were tied. Initially Peggy told her neighbors and friends that Dan had gone away to college. Later she said he was living with his friends. Admitting to the truth was just so painful for Peggy. The truth was that Dan didn't want his mother in his life. The hurt she experienced was by far the most personal cut; her own flesh and blood that she absolutely adored had denied her.

Through the years Peggy would hear about Dan, he had fathered a son but Social Services stepped in and removed the boy from both parents who were unable to care for him. He was adopted by a loving family. Dan was in and out of jail for years, often drug and alcohol related charges.

More than 9 years after leaving home Dan totaled his car as a result of drinking and driving. The accident resulted in a pedestrian hit and run that eventually lead to death. Dan was charged in this death and is now serving a prison sentence. Finally free of drugs and alcohol he has embraced the one person who never stopped caring for him, his mother.

Richie and "The Will"

When Richie died and his will was read, his assets were to be divided amongst his three adult children. His daughter Janet would receive 60 percent, his youngest daughter Jane 30 percent and his son Thomas the remaining 10 percent. This fueled years of sibling upset and estrangement and confirmed Thomas's worst nightmare; he was the least favorite child. Father and son had not spoken in the last decade of Richie's life.

Marlene Dies

Marlene died leaving behind 4 daughters and a messy state of affairs, her business was failing and she owed much more than her worth at the time of her death. Her funeral was delayed for weeks because not one of her children would take any of the financial responsibility. Two of her daughters would determine they were most worthy and would try and lay claim to an inheritance that Marlene believed she had coming to her. The daughters didn't know that Marlene had mortgaged that inheritance long before her death. There was no money. The 4 sisters once close are now divided over money and possessions.

In my research the family dynamic often set in motion by a parent figure and even more often a female family member dictates estrangement. Mothers often have a difficult time seeing themselves apart from their children. But when they do take a healthy step back and away from their adult children and truly live for themselves this often allows the breathing room for a healthy adult relationship.

My Story

Estrangement would be a part of my life on both sides; my mother and me and my daughter and me. In my story it all pointed back to the same person and continues so today, although I initially blamed myself; it had to be me. As long as I remained "the bad guy" I remained the target. You could easily make the case that it was modeled behavior that carried on from generation to generation. My own mother was once estranged from her parents and her siblings although they did reconcile. My child witnessed my estrangement from my mother, perhaps it wasn't such a big leap for her to follow suit.

I can honestly say that it was not what I wanted on either end and that I beat myself up for many years over these estrangements. My mother and I never had a fight, I was told that her husband was abusing and I chose to protect the child that confided that information in me. I also chose not to hurt my mother with the accusations and I walked away. (Later an article, The Importance of An Investigation for All Parties will be published)

The last person I ever thought would leave my life was my daughter and she did. Through the years with many doctors, counselors, therapists, friends and research I would come to the universal conclusion that I was an easy target for manipulation. I allowed my desire to make up for the loss of a parent to death and accusation of abuse to make me that manipulated target. I wanted to make it all better, fix it and take the pain and loss away. I wanted to protect my children from further hurt and loss. All I really did was allow a "victim" mentality to grow and fester in my children. At that time I couldn't see it.

My mother didn't speak to me for the last 23 years she lived; I would go unmentioned in her obituary. I was the adult messenger who spoke out on a child's behalf. Having lived through it and in retrospect I did the best I could with what I knew at that time. Today I would definitely have the police and detectives get to the bottom of it. "The story" needs to be documented and preserved legally. Fortunately for me I have all the documents from teachers, social workers, detectives and other adult parents who witnessed what a child declared and also what I personally lived through. Do keep good records as this information can make all the difference in "what really happened." Abuse in all forms is often behind many family estrangements. Historically, and as the years pass, the story may change depending on who is manipulating it and why.

Today for me, it doesn't really matter what I believe but rather what I know. Did a little girl lie? Maybe she did and maybe she didn't either way my job was to protect her.

In 1998 I started my involvement in an online group where I received much comfort in the sharing of estrangement stories, clearly I wasn't alone. P.E.A.C.E. parents of estranged adult children everywhere was a place we could openly communicate our loss, our feelings and our deepest hurts in losing our adult children. I was astonished at the real life stories of estrangement but no so today. It exists but most often is not talked about because of the shame and embarrassment and the pain associated with this incredible loss.

What did I learn?

1) You are so much stronger than you think!
2) There is comfort that comes from sharing with others who are also estranged from their children. Find a group that works for you. You are not alone.
3) Forgive yourself. You did the best you could.

4) Not all relationships last, some die, some divorce and some chose to leave for their own reasons. Maybe you have decided a relationship is no longer a healthy one and end it.
5) Do not allow your children or any single person to have so much control over your life, that without them you feel your life has no value.
6) Get help! It is painful and not something you should have to go through alone.
7) Let go in love, do it for yourself and for your adult child. You gave them life; let them have their life and let them live it their way, even if that means you are not included.
8) People will acknowledge a broken arm but can't see your broken heart. Take care of you!
9) Even in the best scenario and intact families, there is life after raising children.
10) Find "other mothers" and "other daughters" who lift you up and love you for who you are. Fill the void with healthy relationships that enhance your life not ones that hurt you.
11) Give yourself time, in so many ways it is like a death and you will need to grieve your loss.
12) Accept it! Not everyone is going to like you let alone love you and some of those who don't like/love you; just may be your own biological child or family members.

13) Surround yourself with love and life! You can never have enough people who love you and support you in your life.
14) In the absence of people, I highly recommend bubble baths, fresh flowers, chocolates and beauty in all art forms. Pamper yourself.
15) Have faith whether you believe in God, Angels or any higher power, take your hurts and your troubles and hand them over to God.
16) LOVE YOURSELF! If you don't why on earth would anyone else?

In closing ...

I never ever thought I could live a happy healthy and whole life without my child. It seemed so unnatural to me. I truly couldn't imagine it. Finally through hard work and many years I hear what so many professionals tried to tell me, "You must save yourself!"

One of the best things I ever did was go to work in nonprofit for children's cause. My child's departure made me feel so devalued and that none of my hard work in parenting made a difference. After she left home and for twelve years that immediately followed, I worked as a professional fundraiser. First I worked for a special needs school for children and later a religious organization that served youth and young adults. During this time I raised more than a million dollars by writing grants, hosting special events and securing outright cash donations. In my abilities to raise funds for these groups I regained my sense of value. It was so healing for me to go on and to help so many others.

God gave me this child, and now all these years later, I have given this child back to God. When I could finally do this I found my whole heart again and my most peace-filled center, my own authentic place in life.

If you would like to comment or to share your own story and experiences please write to me at info@bernadetteamoyer.com

People Always Remember the Way You Treat Them

I've heard it said, **"People may not remember your name but they will always remember how you treated them and how you made them feel."** I believe this statement to be true.

When we are treated well by other people whether it is our family, our friends or our work associates and others, we remember that and feel good about ourselves and about being around those people. The opposite is true as well; when we treat others poorly we will be remembered for that too.

The golden rule states; "Do unto others as you would have them do unto you." (Matthew 7:12) Simply put, treat others as you would have them treat you, it seems so simple and yet many people treat others badly and wonder why they are not wanted or included in their life.

Our son called us one night when someone from his past just showed up at his job and wanted to see him and talk to him. He warned me about this person years ago and I didn't want to believe him. I thought better of her. According to him, she tormented him for years, spread rumors about him and never lifted him up. Then months later again he called to tell me she was stalking him again. He finally went to security and they told him her actions were "on the job harassment" and "stalking" they advised him to take legal action.

When he tried to get away from her she berated him with comments like, "is that how a 20 year old acts and look at your little mall job" and inferred that he was a loser and her path was better. Her behaviors were exactly how he remembered her, tearing him down and bragging about her own accomplishments. Stepping on him to try and lift her up. He says, "She made me feel bad the entire time that I knew her."

You can tell so much about a person by how they handle a break up. A friend has recently broken off her engagement and now the other party is acting out in all kinds of destructive ways. Some of it is pointed at my friend and meant to make her feel bad.

A few years ago I had another friend of almost three decades encourage our teen daughter to lie to me, and to be "mysterious" this former friend wouldn't like it if I did the same thing to her. It's astonishing how people treat others in a way that they themselves would never want to be treated. How they can't see themselves. Then too what they do and say to justify their own poor behaviors, rather than own what they did.

You can lift people up or you can tear them down but when you choose to tear them down you can't be surprised when they want nothing to do with you. We are supposed to love and/or to learn from every single relationship that we have with other people. The Buddhist belief is "every single person in our life is either a lover or a teacher."

There was a time when I worked with a teenage girl who was dating and sexually active at just 15, I couldn't believe what I witnessed, at least three times that I knew of she had a boyfriend that she was intimately involved with and simultaneously sleeping with his best friend behind his back. This same teenager showed outrage when she was betrayed? Now a fully matured adult, she has continued this same behavior.

Sometimes it is not until it is our own experience that we see what someone else may have witnessed all along. I have learned it is best to wait until people have their own experience rather than to try and warn them about what I experienced.

As mothers, we know not to drink, do drugs or smoke during pregnancy, and we can't be surprised when women do this and have babies born with disabilities. Simply put, why would any mother treat a baby in utero in such an unloving and uncaring way? Would they want the same things done to them?

There is always a loving way and a responsible way to respond in life and when in doubt a simple question of, "how would I want to be treated?" should help with the right answer.

When we lie and cheat and deceive people we know that these are actions we wouldn't want done to us. It is easy to forgive someone when they are sorry and when these ill behaviors do not continue. However when we treat people poorly when we do things to them that we would never want done to ourselves, and we continue with these poor behaviors, we can't act like we are surprised when they want nothing to do with us.

The golden rule is always applicable and one that I do my best to live by, treat others the way that you would want to be treated. It's actually pretty simple and tried and true, and when we do this people will want us in their life. People always remember how you made them feel. Make them feel good and you will be most welcome.

Perfect Parents

Our three children have "perfect parents" they never yelled at them, disciplined them or embarrassed them. They were held in the highest esteem by all three children and never did any wrong. They were the angels in heaven parents, literally. My husband and I were the earthly parents, the ones who actually raised them. We raised our children to believe that they had guardian angels looking out for them. The father who died when his daughter was just two years old and the mother of our twins who died just days after giving birth to them.

We wrote a book about the "angels in heaven" Angel Stacey to honor the mother and Daddy in Heaven to honor the memory of the father. But what we could never have known ahead of time was that some of our children would hold us up to the image of "perfect parents" angels in heaven that we surely couldn't and never wanted to compete with.

My husband nor I are "perfect parents' we did the best we could with what we knew and had at that time. We believed in our children and pushed them to succeed. We were the parents that fed them clothes them, drove them to and from school, scouts, activities. We were the ordinary and everyday parents. We encouraged them to be honest and to ask for what they wanted. We sat and listened to their dreams, their plans and ideas. We got behind the things that we could support and tried to make a case for the ones we couldn't support.

Recently I found my parents wedding day photo from 1956 when my mother was just 19 years old and my father was just 22. They look so very young and so innocent. My parents weren't perfect parents either; they were the earthly ones that raised me and my sisters. Funny though that just like our kids, my parents have passed away and now live in heaven, and just like our kids they are now "perfect parents."

Perfection is God's Business

Life isn't perfect; it wasn't designed to be perfect. Life is real. It is real life lessons in love, joy, peace, hurt, loss and grief. We are afforded a wide range of experiences in our lifetime. Who is to say which ones are good and what is bad. Every experience is intended as an experience and a lesson. The question we need to ask ourselves, are we learning? Are we getting "it" whatever "it" is?

"If you look for perfection, you'll never be content." Leo Tolstoy, Anna Karenina

Nothing in life is all good or all bad; no person is all good or all bad either. We are complicated people with a happy healthy side and sometimes we are not happy nor are we healthy and whole. No one gets through this life unscathed. We celebrate the birth of a new baby and we see 100% pure innocence. A new life that is fresh and clean and unharmed by life experiences. We see an old man and we listen to his stories of his youth and his loves and we try and imagine it. Our hearts could never have known what we could not see.

The more we age, the older we get, the more tattered we become by life and from our life experiences. As parents we love and support our children, knowing there will come a day when they are no longer our children but their own adult. **"Parents give their kids two gifts; one is roots and the other wings."** Author Unknown

As friends we love and support one another, we try and straddle that balance that line between healthy support and enabling. We want to be supportive but we want to be real and honest too. As a life partner, a husband and a wife come together to create a union, a family, both sides know that there will be an ending. A parting at some point in time even if it holds up in this lifetime, there will be an ending, *"until death do us part."*

We aren't designed or built to last forever; we aren't designed to be perfect. We are meant to be real. Happiness like grief can come and can go; being content can be sustainable. Finding contentment wherever you are, whether it is in your happiness or in your grief can be the real trick. Knowing that whatever we are experiencing, this too shall pass. Nothing lasts forever, not us nor any of our relationships or experiences. Everything has a beginning, middle and an ending. It is the life cycle.

We can't waste this lifetime worrying about what we have no control over or what will happen when we are gone. The only thing that matters is to be present in this moment in time. This is all we have, this moment, this life that is not perfect but so very real.

Chasing happiness and perfection is just that a chase, coming to a place of contentment can be lasting and sustainable. **"Contentment as defined as mentally or emotionally satisfied with things as they are, assenting to or willing to accept circumstances, peace of mind, mental or emotional satisfaction."** Dictionary.com

The Bible says about contentment, **"Godliness with contentment is great gain."** (Timothy 6:6) our physical circumstances of poverty or riches does not necessarily reflect our contentment or discontentment with God nor should it with ourselves. Being content doesn't mean we are giving way to growing and becoming more successful, it means we appreciate the process and know that we are where we are supposed to be for this moment in time.

The challenge isn't when we are standing at the top of the mountain but rather in the climbing to get there. The experience is in the climb not in the arrival. I am happy in my life right now but more than that I am content. I know that I am right where I am supposed to be, this is a stage and a phase and that it too shall pass. The good passes as does the grief. Nothing was meant to last forever. This should give us the incentive to get every little drop out of every single experience. Take it for what it is, a lesson and a moment in time, not perfect but real.

"For we brought nothing into the world, and we take nothing out of it." (Timothy 6:7) Nothing was meant to last forever, it was meant to be appreciated. We were meant to be appreciated and we should strive for contentment. *"When all the details fit in perfectly, something is probably wrong with the story."* Charles Baxter

"I am careful not to confuse excellence with perfection. Excellence, I can reach for; perfection is God's business." Michael J. Fox

Imperfectly yours, Bernadette

Proud To Be an American

We are so proud to be American! We love our country with all its blemishes, battle scars and all. We proudly display an American flag outside our home. We love our country! And why do we love America? Because our country is a country that truly has it all.

Over the past month we have travelled from Upstate New York to the Key West, Florida. We stop everywhere along the way. Our car is still our preferred method of travel. We make a point to interact with the locals.

We visit the area tourist destinations and we always make a point of checking out local grocery stores, churches, theater and restaurants. We like to go where the locals go and often take their recommendations on what we should try and where we should visit.

We have the most incredible beaches and tropical climate! We have horse farms, and wineries, grow our own grain and our own meats. We are an independent country.

People from other countries dream of coming to America, yes, they still do. We grow oranges and lemons here we have dairy farms and chicken and beef. You can grow your own garden and eat nothing but fresh fruits and vegetables.

Our country is rich, rich in natural resources. You can go from the Arctic to the Caribbean and still be in the United States of America. We have a wealth of opportunities here and some of the best Universities and world renowned hospitals like Johns Hopkins.

And yet we are complainers, constantly criticizing our leaders and our own country. We aren't a perfect people but we are generous nations. Always willing to help out when we can.

In a few days we will have the opportunity to vote in the mid-term election and every American that is eligible to vote should make sure they do so. We are a privileged people. Our system works when all of our voices are heard when the majority make a statement and we unite and align ourselves together for the greater good and common goals.

Forgotten how great our country truly is? There is nothing like a nice long road trip to remind you that in this country, in America, we are blessed and we have it all!

I am so proud to be an American ...

Randy Earns a 21-Gun Salute and a Gravesite

There is no colder place than the top of a Pennsylvania hilltop on a February day when a man is put to rest in his final destination. Randy earns a 21-gun salute on the same day that he earned a gravesite. No one saw it coming; there was nothing that led me to believe that the only man I knew as my husband and as our daughter's father would die at just 37 years old. I was so young and so ill prepared at just 23 years of age with a two year old baby girl.

I sat there in my black dress with my knees uncontrollably shaking and trying to make sense of where I was and what was happening. I know owned a new title as "widow" and in the past few days that lead up to this gravesite moment I would be pelted with questions that I literally didn't comprehend.

Questions like; Do you want a "casket spray" they asked? Who do you want in the first car with you? Do you have someone to take you to say your final goodbyes? Could you bring his suit and he will need full under garments? Can you sign this? You will have him buried in Pennsylvania won't you? How many viewings would you like? Has the military been notified? Who is handling the church service? Do you have anyone for the eulogy?

"His flight is on Eastern Airlines, we will meet the body but you need to come and identify it?" Of course I would come and identify his body. Maybe it wasn't him. Maybe this was a mistake. We had just spoken the night before on the phone. He was alive then and now he is dead.

It was the first time I ever touched a dead cold body and yes it was him. I pulled at the sheets and nothing prepared me for what I witnessed. Because he was so young and died alone and in Texas, they had automatically performed an autopsy. I was stunned by all the marks and the stitches and that coldness. He was gone. The man that I knew and had married was now deceased.

My head was swimming I couldn't eat or drink I wanted to throw up. Randy is dead. Randy died. I kept telling myself over and over again. How on earth did this happen.

I sat there at the gravesite on that cold February day as I watched every last person say their goodbyes. When I heard the shots, three rounds of seven I was aware that his "brothers" from the military were there. Each round of shots pierced my heart deeper and deeper. I could barely breathe. Then the funeral director approached me and asked, **"Do you want to stay for the lowering of the casket?"** I didn't even think when I responded with "yes!" I wasn't leaving until it was over. I knew that Randy would never have left me until the very end and I was staying there. I was staying there for him.

But when I saw that coffin lowered into the ground any composure I had was completely gone. "This is how it ends, I thought." "This is how it ends in the dirt and in the ground." My sobs escaped like a bomb that had been detonated. Those gut wrenching sobs when you can't catch your breath and your body has succumbed to the rawness of pure unfiltered grief."

Moments later I felt two men one on each side as they picked me up from under my arms and lifted me away. It was my father and his best friend Claude who came to save me. They literally carried me to the first car.

It has more than 30 years now and yet I remember it all so clearly. I go to that site at least once a year. I leave things there. I leave flowers, prayer cards, rosaries and pictures of our daughter. I know that he isn't there, not really but for me, that gravesite is his memorial place, and the only place I know where to go to pay my respects. And so I go there, I go there to that grave. Because I know that he would have gone there for me and no matter what has transpired in my life since his departure, I was his widow, when he died. RIP 2/22/83

(This blog won an award for "Best Gravesite Story" some were funny and other were sober but I was told this one brought the judges all to tears …)

Parents Give Their Kids Roots and Then Wings

"Don't worry mom, I will take it from here." These words came from my 20 year old son who just left home for the United States Navy. For 32 consecutive years, since 1980 I have been "mom" with kids living at home. The first one to go left after graduating from high school. It felt like an amputation, one day I was breast feeding her and it seemed like the next she was driving a car, working and spending her time with her boyfriend and her friends. Like anything the first time is the hardest. It would be 12 more years when the next would leave home. Last to go our son. I want to cry and I want to dance all at the same time.

Thirty-two years in anyone's life is a career. I have had many careers from waitress, realtor, store owner, author, event planner, and development director to chief operating officer and all that time, the job that meant the most to me was being a mother. It was the greatest challenge of them all. Many times I got it right and other times not so much. God knows I tried really hard. I wanted to be a mother from the time I was just married. I remember just after my first full year of marriage and finding out I was pregnant and feeling overwhelmed with fear and anticipation. The first person I told wasn't my husband, but it was my own mother. She was a registered nurse and I was scared to death.

The conversation went something like this;

Me: Mom I am pregnant and going to have a baby! **My mother:** Congratulations! That is exciting. **Me:** But I am not ready! **My mother:** But you will get ready. **Me:** No! I can't I am just not ready! **My mother:** You will get ready, why do you think it takes 9 months? You will do what you need to do and you will get ready and when the baby comes, you will be ready. You will see. **Me:** Ok, I guess ...

I did what I was supposed to do to prepare as much as I could. I went to all my doctor appointments and to classes to learn how to breast feed. My husband and I attended natural child birth classes. I gave up drinking and smoking immediately. If something was going to be wrong it wasn't going to be because I wasn't doing all the things I could to ensure a healthy birth.

My twins were adopted they came to me with their father after his wife died when they were just 87 days old. Bonding with a tiny baby is easy and I learned you can love an adopted child just like your very own flesh and blood. There is a stitched piece of art that hangs in our hallway outside of our children's' bedrooms that reads, **"Parents give their children two gifts. First they give them roots and then they give them wings."** And we did just that!

For the most part, all my adult life revolved around my children, from where we lived to how we lived. We lived in neighborhoods that included the best private schools and public blue ribbon schools. Every job I ever held outside of our home was in keeping with our kids schedules. As soon as my first child started school I left waitressing for real estate for the flexible schedule so I could be in that carpool line. I wanted to be there and to be home and present after school. I loved my jobs but I loved being a mother even more so.

Every parent who raises children knows how life altering having children is and that each child owns a piece of your heart. There is no greater act of selflessness or no greater purpose in life than in raising children. The purest form of love is when you give and give and do so without expecting anything in return.

My mother was famous for saying, "I hope when you have children, they are just like you." And when I was a teenager and giving her a hard time she would say, "When you have 18 or more years invested in raising your children then come back and critique me. But until then you have no point of reference." You can only "get it" when you have "done it" and today now that the nest has been emptied we "get it."

My husband is the most stable and "salt of the earth" kind of guy, for him he had kids at home for 20 years. Like me he knows what it feels like to have your heart literally live outside your body. He always made sure our children had what they needed and encouraged them to "finish what you start." His love runs deep although he isn't the emotional one. But watching our son enlist and swear into the Navy brought him to tears. We are such proud parents.

"Home is where your story begins" hangs over an archway in our living room and we always knew this day was coming. Our kids started here but they would leave home and begin their own life. The difference this time with our last child gone is that we too will begin again. We will make that shift as awkward as it feels right now from family to couple. With this transition we know all too well how much we have learned, have grown and have aged.

With the passing of our own parents and with the natural departure of our children, it drives home for us just how much living we have already accomplished and how our days are numbered. For our children we want the moon and the stars and the best of everything life has to offer. And for ourselves we want peace, good health and time together as we embark on yet another phase of our lives.

For 32 years, "roots" and today we celebrate their "wings!"

5 Minutes with God

Recently I read a blog about what the writer would say if they had 5 minutes alone and face-to-face with God. For several days I pondered this question. Funny thing for me, there wasn't one thing that I could think of that I would say in those 5 minutes. There wasn't one thing that I could think of to do or to say that I haven't already said to God.

Not one single thing! I talk to God every single day, sometimes I tell him I am sorry and I ask for forgiveness, sometimes I ask if I am getting it right and doing His will. Other times I tell him I'm not getting this at all, please help me to understand. Many times, I thank Him for all my blessings!

My prayers aren't that complicated either, same old tried and true, Our Father and plenty of Hail Mary's. For me it doesn't have to be so complicated. There is no question I have screwed up in my lifetime and I suspect that no one knows it better than God himself. Most of the time, I know that I am living true to God because I have been true to my own heart. A heart that I believe He gave to me. For most often I do get it right and I try hard as I can to make this gift of my life, count as much as it possibly can for the something good.

Another writer wrote about the meal they would have and all that they would do if they knew it was their last day here on earth. I didn't have that "list" either since I already have the people I love closest to me and the ones who aren't here anymore I have wished them well. I pretty much eat healthy and fresh and do the things that I enjoy. I have learned that this is it. This is my one life to be lived like it was our last day. There are no guarantees in tomorrow, so I take what I get today and try and make the best of it.

So if and when I get my 5 minutes alone with God, I'm pretty sure I know what I would say. It probably would go something like this, **"Hi it's me again. Sorry for all my screw ups, I tried** *and I'm still trying. I understand the lessons about this and that and I get it. As you know I'm still struggling with this one particular thing. Is this the time? The time that it is revealed to me, what I was supposed to learn and why it happened? And again I am sorry for the times I fell short and I truly appreciate all that you have given to me. And thank you for taking the time to see me."*

And in parting I would ask, just so I was clear *"What will you have me do now? What do you want me to do next? Thanks again for seeing me, and for never forsaking me. Thank you God!"*

Then I imagine that we would pray together, pray like we have so many times before. I have had many 5-minute sessions with God. I feel His presence in my life and I know that He sees me and loves me and it looking out for me. I know that I have been God blessed. And that doesn't mean that everything has gone my way or that my life was easy. It actually means the opposite, I have struggled, I have hurt, and I have been hurt and at times lost. Yet it was always God that took me back, God who embraced me, God who gave me the strength to carry on …

God is with me every single day, He lives in my heart. Where it might be nice to have that 5-minute face-to-face meeting with God, however, if by chance, we don't, I know that I have already had it.

Second Chances

In my neighborhood there are yard signs everywhere, it doesn't take long to realize that another election is coming soon. One of the signs is for someone that I know. I knew him before he was publicly plastered all over the news media for a D.U.I. He was/is a nice guy.

Yet now when I see his signs out there seeking re-election all I can think about is, "does he get a second chance?" This is the first election since his drinking and driving episode. For me it is more than that. When he was pulled over he said, "Do you know who I am?" Watching the videotape with his declarations of who he is? And audio of him trying to garner favor from a higher up to get off didn't sit right with me.

I don't make excuses for anyone who drinks and drives, today, we all know better. Yet most people from my generation know that we all did it when we were younger. The thing I have a hard time with is that he expected because of his elected position to receive special treatment.

A few years back we had the same kind of thing with a local athlete also accused of drinking and driving. He was underage and doing what many young people did. He was also a multi-millionaire and considered a role model. He has since received a second chance.

Our society today leaves little and often no room for error. We love to build people up and just like sport and seem to relish in tearing them down. Most people learn from their mistakes and yet we are a society that allows for few second chances. We are quick to judge and we judge harshly.

"If you have made mistakes, even serious ones, there is always another chance for you. What we call failure is not the falling down but the staying down." Mary Pickford

It will be interesting to see if my politician friend receives a second chance this election. I suspect that it may be harder since the D.U.I. I know that when I see his sign I remember it. Yet I also know that every single person alive has made their share of mistakes and where would any one of us be without second chances?

Of course one of my favored Bible quotes is from John, *"Let any one of you who is without sin be the first to throw a stone"* and Matthew *"Do not judge, or you too will be judged."*

Here is to second chances, because God knows at some point in time, we have all needed them!

Secondary Survivor

Sexual abuse has many victims, the obvious victim of the abuse and all those who suffer from the fall out. There is a tremendous amount of fall out associated with sexual abuse.

I am not a victim of sexual abuse and yet it has impacted my life in a significant way. There was a time I stood up for a child who claimed they were sexually abused. I took a stand against the person who they claimed abused them. Little did I know at that time the cost of my decision? I did not ask for sexual abuse to impact my life nor did I ever welcome it. Decades later I have learned more about this subject that I care to admit.

The term, "secondary survivors" is a term that I found in my research and attributed to all those people that surround the victim. The people who were not directly abused but whose lives were impacted by all the fall out related to the abuse.

Because the abuser had married into our family and because he had married my mother I would eventually lose my mother and my four sisters who followed our mothers lead of estrangement. When I was told of the abuse, I confronted the abuser and my mother. There was only one face to face confrontation and little did I know at that moment in time that I would be deleted from the family. They basically they killed the messenger.

The "killing" would take place in many forms from denial to abandonment to discrediting; by speaking out I became a huge target. It was easier for all involved to make me look bad rather than to take a good hard look at the person who was being accused of the abuse.

In order for my mother and my sisters to believe the truth, and to believe me, they would have had to change their life and they weren't going to do that.

Years later I had a social worker state, "It must have been really hard for you to give up your family?" without thought my answer was "What choice did I have?" The child who made these claims was not taken seriously by any other person in my family but me. In the company of the extended family they took the victim into the abusers company. They were notified of the allegations and did nothing about it. Not only didn't they protect the child who claimed abuse, but they brought their own infant babies around the person accused of sexual abuse.

From the moment this came into my life I tried to educate myself by reading up on it, talking with professionals and working in an environment where abused children were believed, helped, supported and healed.

I met with all kinds of professionals on this subject. My experience happened in the late 1980's today our society is very clear on how these matters should be handled. I met with private detectives, social workers and with child advocates. I also became friendly with several professional mental health care providers who specialize in sexual abuse cases. One child advocate made a statement that will stay with me forever. She said, **"This is not how a loving family would have handled this. They would have said, "We love you, we love this child, we want to get to the bottom of this because we don't want to lose you and this child to ever feel uncomfortable. Why are they saying this, what happened and what can we do to remain a family?"**

These statements were never made. The advocate also stated, **"What your family did is how guilty individuals react, I have seen it over and over again. What guilty individuals/child molesters do is try to turn as many people against the accuser, including the victim. It happens every single time."** She was 100 percent right.

Hopefully the sharing of my experience will help to educate. It isn't just the victim that will need help and support but all those around the victim. The ripple effect can and does destroy families. I thought it was the right thing to do, to stand up for and to protect a child. Little did I know that in doing the right thing I would be making myself a huge target?

Now more than 20 years later I can see how my actions immediately following made me an easy target. One PhD. stated, "You made it easy for them by walking away." He also gave me articles from JAMA, the Journal of American Medical Association. In those articles I read about the divide between social workers/mental health care providers and the legal professionals. The prosecutors want to prosecute these crimes and the mental health care professionals have concerns about the trauma associated with the process. What if that abused child has to relive their trauma, tell their personal painful experience and what if they aren't believed? Many mental health care professionals believe this could be even more devastating than the abuse itself.

One of the things that many parents and adult caregivers instinctively do when the child communicates abuse is to respond with a big reaction. This offer sets the tone for easy manipulation and a child that grows up and has learned not only how to get big reactions but how to manipulate people. This often furthers a continued victimization mentality.

I have learned so much and there is no perfect way to handle this, just about every day you can hear or read in the news about new cases of sexual abuse. But in reality a large majority of cases are NEVER reported. The shame, the embarrassment and the reliving of the trauma cause many victims to hold onto the abuse and to hold it inside. It doesn't go away though, it becomes part of the life of the abused acknowledged or denied.

When I made my decisions as to how to handle the knowledge of the abuse, I never dreamt of all the fall out and of the years of anger and hatred. I have people in my family that delete other people in my family just for talking to me. My crime, I spoke out on the behalf of a child victim. Today I would caution anyone taking a stand. GET a STRONG SUPPORT TEAM of PROFESSIOALS WHO ARE WELL VERSED and EXPERIENCED in CHILD SEXUAL ABUSE. You absolutely can't go it alone nor can you conceal what has happened.

By trying to protect my mother from embarrassment and a child from further humiliation all I really did was allow an accused sexual abuser off the hook. Even he deserved to have his day in court to determine the validity of the accusations. No one wins in trying to "protect" anyone from allegations of sexual abuse.

After my mother died and I was omitted from her obituary a friend of over 40 years sought me out. We were camp counselors together and my mother was the camp nurse. My friend knew my family and couldn't understand why I was not included in my mother obituary. Sadly when we reconnected we learned we had even more in common than being teen camp counselors together. Her life was also significantly impacted by sexual abuse too. And the abuse was by a family member. The difference was that in her family it was believed and the family was loving and supportive toward the victim.

Sexual abusers don't live in a vacuum, they have wives and children, and they have friends, neighbors and co-workers. No one wants to believe that their family member, friend or work associate is a child molester. No one wants to believe it, not even the survivors or the secondary survivors!

Shame and "You Are Only As Sick As Your Secrets"

"You are only as sick as your secrets" comes from the 12-step program in Alcoholics Anonymous. According to the Merriam-Webster dictionary ***shame*** is both a noun and a verb. Shame (noun) a painful emotion caused by consciousness of guilt, shortcoming or impropriety and as a condition of humiliating disgrace or disrepute. The verb shame is defined as to cause or to feel shame.

One of my friends was abused as a child; she never received the mental health care that she needed. When she was a teenager she was known as pushy and she was always getting into fights. She thought no one knew and she tried desperately to keep it a secret. Her shame over the abuse controlled her life. The shame showed itself through her acting out. All through school, her teachers called her parents to inform them of her anger episodes. In high school she started dating and one of the boys she dated said, **"What happened to you?"** She thought she had concealed the abuse but it was all over her and easy for most anyone to discern.

The abuse was so traumatic that she lied about it. She pointed her finger at someone else for a lesser crime instead of facing the horrible truth. Owning and facing her victimization at the hands of a child molester was just so painful for her. She created lies upon lies to cover up for her acting out behaviors. She went out of her way to divide groups of people so that she could continue to manipulate the truth. She lived in fear of both sides coming together and comparing her many stories. Sexually abused children are known to be skilled liars and manipulators. Their stories and lies are so often a direct result of their inability to face the truth and their trauma.

As an adult she was still living in shame and in denial. Her anger was evident to anyone that crossed her path and it limited her ability to be successful in life. She couldn't maintain a relationship, couldn't keep a job, and had numerous run INS with the law and her children were taken away from her. After all of this, she still was unable to own her past, deal with it and receive the mental health care that she needed. Instead she chose to live in shame and in denial and with an angry heart. She was convinced that no one knew and yet every single person she got close enough to eventually declared, **"What happened to her?"**

Just like the quote from alcoholics anonymous, **"you are only as sick as your secrets"** it was so obvious that she was hurting and needed treatment for the abuse she endured as a child. Many children of sexual abuse grow up with denial and in incredible shame. It is difficult for them to move past the horror and the shame and deal with all the aftermath associated with the abuse. Our society doesn't make it any easier for them either.

We label people and knowingly or unknowingly we judge them. If they were abused, they must be broken or less or damaged. Yet who gets through life without some kind of trauma or hurt or heartache? Is there anyone who hasn't at one point in their life known shame?

"At best the family teaches the finest things human beings can learn from one another generosity and love. But it is also, all too often, where we learn nasty things like hate, rage and shame." Barbara Ehrenreich

Coming from a childhood home of an alcoholic, I grew up with my share of shame. I learned to be an actor just like my girlfriend and to cope. Coping was a survival mechanism that allowed me to endure the uncertainty in our childhood home caused by having a raging alcoholic in the family. We all learned how to function in the outside world and most of us lived in shame for how it really was in our house. I stuttered, had low self-esteem, made poor choices and was unable to achieve my best in that atmosphere. I carried it with me through my early young adult years. As I received help through the years and grew in my achievements, my shame was replaced with self-love and with self-acceptance.

For me the guiding light was always my faith in God. As my faith deepened and matured I could accept that I was created by God and a true child of God. If God created me, and He created all forms of life and was with me during all my experiences, how could I give way to darkness and to shame? **I live in the light**

now. Whatever it is, that I am handed, I own it. Shame is not a place I allow myself to go. My own wellness was a result of facing my life, my experiences, good and bad and doing so head on. There is no hiding from my own reflection in the mirror. When I could face my own shame, write about it and share it, I moved from a dark cold place to a warm happy place.

We may think, we have covered up our shame but those who know us best know that something isn't right. When we lie to ourselves, we have cheated our own self from the Glory of God and all that is bright and beautiful. Shame doesn't live in the bright and beautiful world. One reason abuse continues and sexual abuse is prevalent is because it lives in shame. Abusers know that they can keep their victims silent and in the dark by the shameful acts they have placed upon them.

Our self-esteem and our self-worth is a direct reflection on how we feel about ourselves. If we have shame, we are like a magnet drawing more shame filled experience to our own selves. At some point, after the initial victimization, after the assault and after the abuse, we are only a victim if we choose to remain a victim.

As I was evolving and maturing, I had really great mentors in my professional life and really great people in my personal life that believed in me. They were willing to invest their time and talents in me. I paid them back by overcoming so much that I experienced and I made them look good by being successful in life and contributing to society. Where there is love and where there is light, there is hope and all things are possible. No living thing can grow in the darkness and in the absence of light.

For me, I had to be willing to let go of the shame and to let go of the secrets and move toward the light so I could live a happy and peace filled life. Today, I have created an environment filled with light and beauty in art, plants, colors, décor, food and all forms of life. I surround myself with people who are loving, kind and know how to love and how to lift you up. It's a beautiful, happy and healthy place to be!

Social Media Where There is No Place to Hide and Face-to-Face Isn't Required

What did we ever do before Facebook, Twitter and LinkedIn? There are numerous social and professional websites out there and most of us are connected to some of them. Our kids have only known having these communication vehicles. And yet Facebook boasts that a large segment of their user population is women aged 50 and older. That statistic would include me!

It used to be enough to have a cell phone and/or a personal computer. Now most of us are running numerous devices simultaneously. I write this as I sit with my desk top computer, pad and cell phone on my desk. This is the ready position to take on the early communications of the day.

But what did we do before all these plugged in gadgets? I believe we used to talk to each other and now more than ever we talk at each other. There is a big difference. Talking with someone has ebb and a flow and it about tennis style communication, a back and forth motion. Talking at someone is what we do with e-mail and with our "status updates." We can write and say what we want without anyone questioning us or challenging us.

I am just as guilty as the next guy of using e-mail or text messaging to communicate and many times it is easier. I can communicate what I want without having to interact and wait for a response. I have put it out there. More and more we do this as an attempt to rush through our communication needs. If I text a message I can dispense with the "hi" "how are you?" small talk and get right to the heart of my expression.

With this constant "plugged" in mode we seem to have lost a certain amount of processing time. We make instant communication without any real reflection. As someone who often comes up with a better response after an opportunity to process information this can be a detriment.

You can Google just about anyone and learn more about them. As a marketing professional we have moved away from so much that once went into print ads and now long for going viral. The more presence we have on the internet the more attention we can draw to our products and services. We boast about "going green" and not using so much paper. The paper trail has been replaced by the cyber trail.

For marketing purposes this has been a good thing as most of us do our research before we buy and the internet offers up much more than our old encyclopedia style research vehicle.

What happens when internet posts post the truth though and things that can have long lasting and damaging consequences? Or post that include untruths and slander?

Young kids have committed suicide over internet posts and we watch the demise of people like Paula Dean and others as the pile up and pile on mentality contributes to such demise. Yet we have others like many of our political leaders that seem to be more like Teflon and nothing ever sticks to them.

It has been said that books and privacy will become things of the past. We "like" and "unlike" through "unfriending" without ever having any personal interaction. We literally don't have to leave our homes to purchase most things, connect and communicate and often can work from home too.

At what cost though have we allowed cyber relationships to take the place of face-to-face communication? How will these changes show themselves in the next generation? We seem to have less and less people skills and more about "me" as our world is revolving around one way communication.

We "Skype" and "phone" interview for jobs, while never taking the time to meet people in person. Will we become even quicker to judge and take even less time to get to know others?

Many things are good that have come from the internet and social media but just like medication with its own side effects what will the "side effects" be with social media often taking the place of personal relationships?

Like most things, only time and history will tell ...

Solitude

Surrounded by life signs
Nature, nurture
Thoughts so intimately mine
In sharing space, sharing time
I, myself, my own life line

Your endless chatter
Heavens, what is the matter

Peace, I have on my own
Peace, a chance for growth and roam
Your endless needs, I pray, please recede

Sun, sand, tree, land
Child love and love of man
My solitude, my time to explore
To think thoughts, only I could adore
Flapping seagull, chopper plane, ferry boats, cars on main

I walk quietly, soft and peaceful thoughts
Chatter of little or nothing
My expansive mind, so ahead of time
Peaceful, calm, tranquil and content
My solitude, always time well spent

Sometimes All You Need to Do Is Just Sit Back and Watch

Sometimes the truly smart thing is to do nothing and just sit back and watch. There are times in life when it really is best to just let things unfold. For most of my life, I was always the first one.

I was the first one in my family and peer group to get married, to have a child and then to become a widow. I was the first one to juggle being a single mother and a full-fledged career woman. I was the first one who had a child in school and the first to afford private schooling and then take on putting my child through a prestigious preparatory school. I was the only one who adopted infant twins, a son and a daughter and raised them as my very own children. I was the one who left a highly dysfunctional family and sought out counseling. I was the first one to live most of my adult life without the love and support of my parents and siblings. I was the first one of my friends and peers to have a child graduate high school.

All of these obvious "I" statements reflect back to ownership and responsibility. These were choices that I made, I wanted to live! And I was always so anxious to get started and I was also very naïve'.

In being first I didn't have a point of reference or a role model. When widowed I looked at my own parents and realized I had already past a point in their own life experiences since neither one of them had the experience of a spouse die. I was just 23. At 26 when I became a professional Realtor and purchased my own home, my friends weren't carrying the responsibilities that I was carrying. I was not just a homeowner but a widow and a single mother raising a child.

When I was younger, I was determined and I was fearless and or I was ignorant and naïve'. I wanted more and better for myself and my daughter and I was willing to work hard to achieve it. Maybe it would have been easier or better with support, it wasn't my choice but I had little or none. Along the way, some good people took a personal and a professional interest in helping me and they did in fact do just that, help me a little along the way.

I love the phrase in the movie Moneyball when it is stated, ***"The first one through the wall, he always gets bloody. Always."*** I was first at so many things. Some of my friends are doing the private prep school thing with their own daughters right now, I accomplished the "mother" role of support in that more than 14 years ago.

I am not saying I am the best one; I was just the first one in my peer group and family. Today I am the "first one" to get to "empty nester" status too. I lived with passion in every decision ever made and every single goal set and achieved. I just believed in myself and I knew, "If you think you can, you can!"

Part of being first has also made me someone that others easily passed judgments on and had an opinion about. Those most critical never experienced what I did. My life has been impacted by death, sexual abuse, alcoholism and estrangement just to name the top 4 in severity. I am not a victim or a complainer I am a true survivor. My life is rich in lessons learned. Today I write about so many of them. My writing connects me to people struggling with many of these experiences that I have now come out the other side. Most of my writing is about what I learned and experienced along the way.

As someone who was always out their swinging the bat, trying to connect, trying to make it happen, today I am someone who is truly happy just sitting back and watching. My thoughts are you think it is easy, you think *life* is easy, let's see, what can you do?

One of the areas in my life where I have been judged the harshest was in the handling of the knowledge of child sexual abuse more than 24 years ago. To those critics I say, "What would you have done differently?" "What should I have done when a minor child confided in me that my mother's husband was sexually abusing them?" I spoke out and told anyone and everyone that would listen. No one wanted to hear it or to believe it.

Today between Penn State and the Catholic Church we all know how clear the law is on this crime of sexual abuse. Back then you couldn't get a district attorney to prosecute these crimes, without any "material evidence" I know because that was my experience.

In my life I have faced some tough situations and some really tough decisions and in the end I alone had to live with them. What strikes me all these years later is the amount of grace I have been afforded within my own self in doing so. Thanks to God who never once left me!

As I write this all three of my children are making their own decisions in life. Some of them have made huge decisions that will affect their lives for the rest of their lives. Some had incredible opportunities handed to them. And for the first time in their lives, they are learning that they alone are responsible for their choices and their own decisions. Good and bad. It is called growing up and being responsible. Just like every choice I ever made, I had to take all the responsibility that came along with them. All the accomplishments I have had in my entire life pointed back to one single thing, responsibility. I took and I take responsibility for the decisions I made and the decisions that I continue to make.

I loved the time in my life when I was "making it happen" and achieving and accomplishing so much. But today I absolutely love where I am now in the ability to just sit back and watch ... just one of the many gifts of aging and having lived so many true life experiences.

Stop Blaming Yourself

So many parents blame themselves for the way their children turn out. Earlier this week I received a long and lengthy e-mail from a parent. She is beating herself up for the lifestyle choices and the actions of her adult child. All I could think was, "if it was that easy." "If we were responsible for them." And the truth is that we control very little over what our kids do.

We are tasked with setting a good example and for setting expectations, goals and a code of conduct while we raise them. In many ways we as parents are their first teachers. But talk with any teacher and you soon find out that some kids "get it" and take to their teachings and other kids need to learn from experience and in their own timetable and in their own way.

I don't think there was ever a parent that raised kids that said, "I want my child to grow up and be a criminal." Yet many kids do grow up and become criminals. I don't think any parent raises a child and says, "I want my child to grow up and become unhappy." Yet many children grow up and become unhappy.

As parents, we need to stop blaming ourselves. Kids grow up and make their own decisions and their own choices. All blame is a waste of time and of energy. It serves no one.

If you are a parent and you are doing that you need to change your inner voice as long as you blame yourself, your child will make you their target of blame. When life doesn't go their way it won't be about what they did or didn't do but rather that they are afforded the opportunity to place blame on their parents. And many parents are willing to accept that role. I know because that used to be me.

If I had my way all my children would be deliriously happy and successful. Yet that isn't the case and it has nothing to do with me.

We can barely get our 12 and 8 pound dogs trained to do what we want, why did we ever believe we would have that control over our children? Remember when we were all guilty of statements like, "it must be the parents." Or "what kind of home did they come from." I have witnessed children that were given nothing and they did everything with their lives and others kids that were given everything and did nothing with their lives. It all comes down to choices, personal choices.

Bless instead of blame ...

As parents we can't change or even do anything differently after we have raised our children. Trust that you did the best that you could with what you had and what you knew at that time.

Stop blaming yourself ... it doesn't help anything or anyone. Forgive yourself and forgive all others ... this is the only way to move forward. Blame keeps you trapped in the past ...

Sweet Sweet Surrender

Surrender as in letting go of control and to yield to power. I am thinking about surrender is the sense of letting go and accepting that we are not in charge that there is a greater power. Our world and our existence here is bigger than just us. Not one of us decided on our birth date or our natural death date. In life there is really very little that we control. We didn't pick our parents nor did they choose us. We take what we receive and we make the most of it.

As a marketing and salesperson for the bulk of my career in both for profit and non-profit, most of my sales training taught me to go after what I want. In my personal life I have done the same. Then there comes a time when you know that you're not going to be the President or a model or any other fantasy that we may have thought was achievable at a certain age. We grow up and accept what our own unique gifts are as well as our limitations. It is nice to strive for goals, to set a goal and then go after it. Some things in life are a natural fit and meant for us and others may be a dream or a fantasy.

When we mature, we accept that we came with a game plan unlike anyone else's, our life is unique to us just as God created for us. It is not for someone else to put their plan, their agenda on us. Our surrender is to the highest and greater power in the Lord, our God.

The most wonderful thing about growing older is the sweet surrender than comes from accepting ourselves "as is" and letting go of ego. Giving way to God rather than ego, (Edging God Out) is the sweetest surrender, we no longer have to be better than them or better than that, we are good and good enough as we are, just as God created us to be.

Jesus Take The Wheel
(Lyrics by James/Lindsey/Sampson)

Jesus take the wheel
Take it from my hands
Cause I can't do this on my own
I'm letting go
So give me one more chance
Save me from this road I'm on
Jesus take the wheel

There is a natural happiness that comes from accepting ourselves and in that sweet surrender. Where we are, where we are supposed to be, what is ahead is exactly as God intended for us. *"Do not be conformed to this world, but be transformed by the renewal of your mind, that by testing you may discern what is the will of God, what is good and acceptable and perfect."* Romans 12:2

It is through the struggle that we find enlightenment. So many lessons are born of pain, but they are born to us. We are good and we are acceptable and we are perfect as only God created us to be.

"I have been driven many times upon my knees by overwhelming conviction that I had nowhere else to go. My own wisdom and that of all about me seemed insufficient for that day." Abraham Lincoln

"Something amazing happens when we surrender and just love. We melt away into another world, a realm of power already within us. The world changes when we change, the world softens when we soften. The world loves us when we choose to love the world." Marianne Williamson

There is no beauty in the fight, fighting is never attractive, but there are gifts, blessings and true beauty in the surrender. Surrender is sweet, it is humble, it is without ego and false pride, our surrender allows us to be open and receptive and ready for us to receive God's will. And God's will is so much better than anything we could have imagined for ourselves.

"You cannot fulfill God's purposes for your life while focusing on your own plans." Rick Warren, **The Purpose Driven Life**

There is nothing sweeter than our surrender ...

Ten Years of Tears

Cryin' For Nothin'
Songwriter Kevin Welch, Performer Country Music Artist Gary Allan

All of that cryin' for nothing
All of that tryin' for nothing
What has it ever got me
What has it ever taught me
I've got to keep believing
In somethin' baby
'Stead of just tryin' for nothing
Cryin' for nothin' at all

When my first husband died my mother said, "Death is easier, it is so final." She had been divorced from my father and struggled with her grief over the failure of their marriage. My husband's death was final. I had no choice but to accept he was gone for good. Maybe it was easier for me.

In 1998 I lost a child. It may just as well have been a death. I had one therapist tell me it was an "amputation." It wasn't my choice but one I have finally accepted. I spent more than ten year crying over this loss. Ten years is approximately twenty percent of my life. Against all odds I hoped, prayed and pleaded for another outcome. It was not to be.

During this time I communicated with several people through online support groups. One woman had her own website called *Pennies for Heaven*. It was a bright and inspirational site dedicated to her toddler Michael who died. Michael crawled through a doggie door at night when his parents were sleeping. The next morning they found him floating in the backyard pool. He had drowned to death. Michael's parents were young and he was their only child. I wrote his mother often and she wrote me back. We connected through our grief. Two mothers crying over the loss of a child.

I believe that site and newsletter went on for years. I read all her words. Then one day she made an announcement stating that she was writing two more issues and then shutting it down. She said she will never stop loving Michael but it was time. It was time for her to move past her tears and her grief. They were starting a new chapter in their life and having another child. I always admired how she took her grief made something positive come from it, helped others like myself and then moved forward. Maybe death is easier since it is so final. She had made a decision to move past her grief and start living a happy and whole life once again.

For me I hung onto hope, I thought in time, with age and wisdom that someday we would reconcile. Clearly that is never going to happen. What I am left with is my memories of another time and the fact that I cried for nothing. No amount of tears was ever going to change the outcome.

Grief is a process and has been a cleansing process for me. I still cry over my losses but I only allow myself a certain period of time for tears and then I let go. I won't spend ten years of tears over anyone ever again. I just can't allow myself that kind of pain and the loss of my own quality of life. They say, "The first cut is the deepest" and maybe after that much grief you learn to come back quicker.

Like country music artist Gary Allan sings from the song Cryin' For Nothin' **"cryin' for nothing' tryin' for nothin' what has it ever got me. We could not reach it and I don't know why. It took so long just to say good-bye."**

Good-bye to Ten Years of Tears ... it was a long sad rainstorm, and just like after any good long rain, when it ends, the sun shines even brighter.

Thank You! Thank You! Thank You!

"If the only prayer you ever say in your entire life is thank you, it will be enough." Meister Eckhart

Thank you for my eyes that read and for my hand that writes. Thank you for my health and my heart that loves so deeply. Thank you for my husband that I love and who loves me. Thank you for our home and our children. Thank you for my friends and my family.

Thank you for my dogs that I absolutely love and adore. Thank you for affording me the opportunity to express myself through the written word. Thank you for the warmth and the food that I eat. Thank you for the glory of this day.

Thank you for all people who read me, the audience of 2,984 people who in just 7 days read my writers Facebook page and the over 6,000 hits on my writing website. Thank you for the e-mails and the letters and the comments from the people who are touched by my writing. Thank you for the people who share their stories and their true life experiences with me.

Today, I thank you for Patrick who has done my hair for 20 years and for my friend Nick, who feeds me every time I visit him and for our more than 30 year friendship.

Thank you thank you thank you and most of all God, thank you for my life! A life that is rich, rich in love and rich in lessons learned.

Maybe prayer really doesn't have to be so complicated or so difficult. Maybe "thank you" is all you ever really need. Maybe "thank you" is enough …

Sexual Abuse

Today we all know that sexual abuse is a crime and a crime that needs to be reported. Years ago it wasn't that way and was most often buried to try and protect the victim. Protecting the victim often allowed the abuser to get away with the crimes of sexual abuse. Many times it was considered a "family matter."

The abuser is typically someone's family member, a father, an uncle, a brother, a son and no one wants to believe that their family member is capable of sexual abuse of a child. We want to think that we can tell by looking at someone if they are an abuser. But the reality is that sexual abusers are not the "boogey man" nor are they strangers. They are people that we trust or we wouldn't allow them around our children.

Most of the time they are charming and well liked, and they are also very manipulative. I had a bird's eye seat to the fall out related to sexual abuse in my own family. It would be the man that married my mother that would be accused of abuse. A child trusted me enough to confide in me and I believed them.

Initially other family members said they too believed the victim, but later they stated, **"Well if it really happened why wasn't he arrested?"** And other family that would declare with conviction, **"It never happened!"** They did not want to believe it or even hear about it. Denial was the constant. One of the saddest parts about the person who declared "it never happened" was that he/she was a well-respected long time elementary school teacher. Teachers are taught more than most professionals and they should know better. This person was blinded by their love for the abuser.

Social workers will tell you that most often the accusations will be met with disbelief in the family and then they will go into self- preservation mode. They often target the victim and the messenger rather than take a good hard look at the accused. They just don't want to believe it.

And why do they choose denial?

Because to believe it would mean that they have to change their life and they don't want to do that. Part of it is ego. We think we know when we love someone and we want to believe that we are right about them. Certainly if we love them and see their value they couldn't possibly be molesting young children?

In order for my mother to believe that her husband was guilty, she would have had to leave him, to divorce him and she didn't want to do that. Her children would find themselves on the outside looking in if they didn't go along with living her lie. I know this because that was my fate. In her denial I was to be discarded and discredited and denied. Her children later followed her lead and would do the same, right up until her death when I was omitted from her obituary. What was my crime? I couldn't along with the lies and with the denial and most of all with the hurt and the misdirected rage and anger.

Meanwhile the child and the children that were abused are not only left not to be believed but the whole thing gets turned around on them. If they can discredit the victim and any adults that support the child victim they can take the focus off of the abuser.

Once sexual abuse is reported it takes on a life of its own, there will be social workers, police, detectives and judges involved. It is a crime. The child will be put through a host of interviews and exams both physically and mentally. Are they telling the truth? Does the story stay the same or change with each telling? Are they consistent, telling the truth and are they credible?

The family and the abused child will need all kinds of support. They may become the target of rage and false accusations so that they can be discredited. No one wants to believe that "Uncle Johnny" is a child molester. Most families will fight for the family reputation over the child accuser and the victim.

Studies support that few children lie about being sexually abused and typically if the child is lying it is because parents are divorcing and the child is being used to hurt the spouse.

Some kids are easier targets than others as it has been proven that kids from single parent homes are more likely to be abuse targets. A father in the house often makes an abuser look for an easier target. Abusers like to "groom" their victims and win them over. They take their time developing trust and manipulating the child before they begin abusing them.

Think about what you would do or feel if a child accused your husband or your father or uncle or son of sexual abuse? If you were like most people you would not want to believe it. The cases that are easiest to prove are the ones where there is material evidence. Many cases are one person's word against another.

When it comes to sexual abuse, prevention is always best. When a child has endured sexual abuse their whole brain chemistry and brain functions change. They have been violated. To continue on with their daily lives and daily activities is to pretend that everything is okay when in fact it isn't. Their reality has been altered and many learn to live in a fantasy world and are very good liars. They learned to live a lie by sweeping the sexual abuse under the rug. The problem is that it doesn't go away and often plays itself out in many destructive ways.

Dr. Bradley of Lewes Beach Delaware was easily convicted because there was no denying the videotaped evidence. He was a trusted Pediatrician and abused and raped more than 100 infants and children. Penn State University where there was no material evidence, yet many credible victims. I know that Penn State took a long time from the initial complaints of abuse, until more than a decade later when it could no longer be denied.

If you are the messenger for a child victim, you will need support. You will become the target of rage and many will try and "kill the messenger" and harm and discredit you for speaking out on a child's behalf. They want to stop the message from being delivered and/or believed.

Abuse needs to be reported ASAP, it is a crime not to report it. The child victim will need support through a team of professional people that are well versed in child sexual abuse and who believe them and support them and who want to contribute to their wellness.

Suppressing sexual abuse does nothing to support or to help heal the victim. Case studies show that it actually contributes to many mental health disorders.

There are cultures that literally kill the women that are rape victims and sexual abusers were often sexually abused themselves. These are just two of the reasons that abuse victim don't speak out and get the help they need. They know that they will be looked upon in a different light.

I applaud Elizabeth Smart who turned from victim to victor and is a true survivor. She got the help, the love and the support from her family and that helped her to heal. She has a book out and speaks out on behalf of herself and other sexual abuse victims. She was able to turn it around for her good and the good of others.

Abusers count on the shame of the victim to allow them to get away with the crime of sexual abuse. A child is just that, a child. Any sexually abused child should NEVER feel shame; they are innocent and did absolutely nothing to deserve being the target of sexual abuse. We need to believe them and support them.

There is nothing to be gained by having to report that a family member is a sexual abuser, it is without a moral conscience to look away and do nothing to protect a child who communicates they have been abused. Most social workers believe that NOT believing a child and trying to discredit them and their accusations of sexual abuse can be equally as traumatic as the abuse itself.

If your family is impacted by abuse, you need to get help, for the victim and for the entire family. Always believe and support the child until or unless they are proven unbelievable. Few children are educated enough to communicate sexual abuse if it never happened.

According to the National Center for Victims of Crime; Child Sexual Abuse statistics from 2010 show that:

- 1 in 5 girls and 1 in 20 boys are a victim of child sexual abuse
- 3 out of 4 victims are abused by someone they knew well
- Children who do not live with both parents are at higher risk
- Victims often suffer with low self-esteem, suicide and mental health challenges

I can't think of anything that could be worse for a child than to have endured sexual abuse and right behind that would be to communicate the abuse and for no one to believe them.

Prevention first and care and love and support always, prayers for all the victims and their families impacted by sexual abuse.

The Aftermath of Jerry Sandusky and Child Sexual Abuse

As one of the abused mothers stated after the guilty verdict on 45 of 48 counts for Jerry Sandusky, **"There are no winners, we have all lost."** Sexual abuse statistics are 1 in 3 girls and 1 in 6 boys will be sexually abused by the age of 18. Finally after a high profile case like Penn State University and Jerry Sandusky we as a culture of people are forced to face what most of us prefer to turn away from, sexual abuse against our children. Whether we like it or not these children will be dealing with the aftermath in some form for the rest of their lives. Let the healing begin! But, it can only start when we are willing to face it, ugly as it is.

"In order for them to believe you, they would have to change their life and they aren't going to do that" A Catholic Priest on why wives and family members do not support the victims of sexual abuse.

There are many Dorothy Sandusky's out there, women who stand by their husbands in the face of mounting evidence of abuse. The siblings of their son Matt are doing exactly what most siblings do, they band together and they turn on the victim. Already the defense lawyer is saying, "Matt was a troubled kid with a history" this is what they do; they re-victimize the victims over and over again. Matt may have been a troubled kid but that was probably why he was targeted in the first place. Like those child survivors stated, **"No one is going to believe a kid."** The abusers are counting on that!

Who on earth would put themselves through this? Most often the abusers go for the weak and the vulnerable, kids that come from one parent homes with no strong father figures. It happens time after time.

The surviving victims are shame-filled and guilt laden and their stories often do change throughout their lives because they don't want it to be true either. Families are forever fractured as a result of these child molesters. With each child survivor, there are numerous "secondary survivors." Dorothy Sandusky reminds me of my own mother; my mother was standing by her man when abuse allegations surfaced. Like Dorothy she didn't want to know the truth and like Dorothy she was present in the home when the sexual abuse was said to have occurred. Extended family members that weren't even there would declare with conviction, **"It never happened."** Again these declarations were made without any willingness to question them. They didn't want to know the truth and they never even tried to get to the bottom of it.

Abusers are often very charming and skilled as they manipulate all those around them. No one, no one wants to believe their husband, their father, their step-father, their brother in-law is capable of sexually molesting a child. But what we should be asking ourselves is **"WHY, why would any child say that?"** I can't imagine what it is like to be told your husband is a child molester. I can't imagine it! But I also can't imagine that once those declarations are made, just turning a blind eye and passionately defending your husband without any willingness to try and uncover the truth.

What I do know is that if it happened in my home, I would want to get to the bottom of it. That accuser and the accused would have to come together. And just like one of the attorneys stated, "You might be able to get around 1 accuser or even 2 accusers, but how do you get around 8, 9, 10 accusers?"

Penn State did exactly what the Catholic Church has done for decades, they lawyer up, they re-victimize the victims by tearing them apart and they band together as they protect their own. They are concerned about their reputations and the financial costs. They traditionally have little or no regard for the children. Sad but true.

Anderson Cooper said it best last night on CNN, **"People turn off the TV or turn the channel when sexual abuse is the topic."** This is exactly why it continues because the survivors are 1) so shame filled and 2) no one wants to talk about it. And no one wants to believe it. Jerry Sandusky will die in prison, but what will become of his wife? What will become of his children and his friends and family members? They are also victims in this as they have lost too. What will the future hold for the children who survived? How will their childhood trauma play itself out in their adult lives? You can't un-ring this bell, you can't un-rape them.

This case will have opened the doors for so many other kids to speak out about the unspeakable. And again as the mother of one of the abused boys stated, **"There are no winners, we have all lost."**

The Black Sheep

"The black sheep is a member of the family or other group who is considered undesirable or disreputable." American Heritage Dictionary *"The most egregious form of rejection that anyone can ever experience is parental rejection."* (Hardy 2002)

"We speak figuratively of the one black sheep that is the cause of sorrow in a family; but in its reality it is regarded by the Sussex shepherd as an omen of good luck to his flock." The Folk-Lore Record 1878

Love the Same

I do not love my children the same
I love them for who they are

Each child individually named
Each child loved, just the same

I do not love my friends the same
I love them for who they are
Each friend individually named
Each friend loved, just the same

Love is love, but surely love is never the same
(Bare Breasted Heart – Bernadette Moyer 1999)

Parents may say they love their children the same, they may strive to love them the same, but everyone in every family can point out the favorite child and the least favorite. All families have their own dynamic and each family member has their own place, the role that they play in the family.

"Treatment of the black sheep is very much in line with the clinical description of scapegoating." From Bye bye Black Sheep, the causes and consequences of rejection in family relationships. Julie Fitness
Scapegoating is defined as; **"The projection of blame, hostility or suspicion onto one member of a group by other members to avoid self-confrontation."** Mosby Medical Dictionary

I have always known my role in my family, I knew that I was the black sheep and I knew that I was the scapegoat. It goes back to my very early years. From my birth to my mothers' death, she openly had issues with me. She stayed in the hospital just after I was born as I was sent home. Upon her death, I was excluded in her obituary. It was full circle. I believe now, as an adult that she taught my sisters how to treat me. She set the example.

As a little kid, I took the blame for something that I didn't do to stop the inquisition, I was punished severely however, it did end the drama. After my brutal punishment, the sister who actually did it, spoke out and owned it. By that time, the parental anger was already diffused upon me.

Oprah Winfrey – *"Years ago, I did a show specifically about the black sheep of the family. Somebody said something I never forget, they said, "The black sheep of the family is usually the person who is the most sensitive, who absorbs all of the other family members' energy."*
I could immediately relate to the above statement. As a teenager, my mother once used the word "indifference" to describe me, the truth is and was that I felt it all, took it all in, and in the end, it wasn't "indifference" at all but survival and the desire to save myself. I had to move away from them and all their scapegoating, look at myself, work on myself and ultimately save myself.

My mother and my youngest sister both celebrated a birthday yesterday, they are 30 years apart, and my mother is no longer with us. Our family is broken; the bonds weren't strong enough to survive multi-generations of abuse. The reality however is that God created this family, not my mother nor my sisters or me, and only God can break the bonds that bind us.

If being the black sheep in the family means that I am the "most sensitive" I'll take it, it could be worse, I could be one that doesn't feel anything at all, blames others rather than taking a hard look at themselves and what role they play in the group dynamic.

So here is to all those "black sheep" there seems to be one in almost every family, **"After all, the wool of the black sheep is just as warm."** Ernest Lehman

The Capacity to Love

Does everyone have the capacity to love? And how much of our capacity to give and to receive love has to do with how we feel and think about ourselves? Do we learn love? Or is it something that we are just naturally born with?

Does love beget love and hatred begets hatred? Can you love yourself if you hate the very people that gave your life, your parents? You come from your parents, so doesn't hate for your parents the same as hating yourself? To hate your child, is to hate yourself? Are we capable of loving everyone? Or do we have a type?

Is the opposite of love, hatred or indifference? What makes love grow and what makes love turn? How much of our ability to give and to receive love is predetermined or predestined? Can we change our own capacity to love?

Lots of questions I know, it seems like some people are just better at love than others. Some people naturally seem to attract love while others seem to have difficulty finding and keeping love in their life.

I am more and more convinced that the relationships we have with others is directly related to how we feel about ourselves. To love another, you must first be able to love yourself. The longest relationship we will ever have is with ourselves.

"And I think real healing --- healing that lets us hold ourselves and the injured parts of the world in our hearts, healing that teaches us how to live fully, comes from intimacy, from the ability to be with what is no matter how hard." The Dance - Oriah

"Many Christians get mixed up about what love really is. They know they should love God and others, but don't understand that loving yourself is one-third of God's equation. Instead, they mistakenly think of it as being selfish or egotistical." Love Out Loud – Joyce Meyer

I believe that all things, all things are possible with love just as I believe that without love we are disadvantaged. Loving ourselves is the first step to opening the door for others to love us too.

More Love, Lord

And this is my prayer: that my love may abound more and more in knowledge and depth of insight, so that I may be able to discern what is best and may be pure and blameless until the day of Christ." PHILIPPIANS

If you would like to respond to any of the questions above or have your own thoughts and would like to share please e-mail Bernadette at bmoyer37@aol.com

The Courage to Let Go in Love

Recently I posted a piece titled, *The Courage to Love,* and I believe that it takes courage to love. But I also believe that it takes tremendous courage to let go in love. There are people in my past that I have loved passionately and they are no longer present in my life. Some ended with a mutual respect, some ended by just quietly walking away and some tried to blow me up upon my exit. There was never one time that I tried to blow up anyone when the relationship ended, I may not have liked it but I quietly retreated to reflect, to mourn and to recover.

There is not a person living or dead that I have not forgiven for some real or perceived hurt against me. I learned a long time ago that carrying anger, resentment and hatred toward anyone for anything only hurts the person carrying it. I've heard it said that carrying hate is "like drinking poison and waiting for the other person to die."

People that have to hurt someone else upon their exit, generally do so for their own self-preservation. It doesn't look good for them to have someone else make the decision to leave them behind. Many times an exit is met with trying to justify why that person walked away. People leave us for a host of reasons. Sometimes they just need to go.

"To everything, there is a season and a time to every purpose under the heavens." Ecclesiastes 3:1 there are some people who enter our life who aren't intended to be in our life forever, for some, their time comes and then one day their time is up.

"You can be hurt by love or healed by the same." From the movie Country Strong and the song Timing is Everything. Letting go of love in a relationship whether it is a romance, a child or a friend can also take incredible courage. Some people feel safe and familiar and in that safety and familiar zone we aren't afforded the opportunity to grow as we may if we let them go.

Knowing myself, I probably wouldn't do well with a divorce. I can only imagine the pain associated with building a life with a partner and then having it end. What does it feel like to be with someone for 5, 10, 15, 20 or more years and then they are gone. Divorce happens, death happens and choice happens. It takes courage to have loved just as it takes courage to let go in love.

When we are able to trust, and to trust in a God that never leaves us, this allows us to know that we are never alone. When my husband's mother was on her death bed, taking her last breaths, he held her hand. He had sorrow that she was passing but his faith knew that she was going home to God our father.

There was peace for him in having such faith. He also displayed incredible courage sitting with her at her time of passing. He could have made the choice to walk away, instead he chose to let go in love.

As parents who have raised their children, we learned to let them go in love too. It is their life, to live as they choose to live it. It is not our place to hold them back or to decide what is right for them. Letting them go in love was the natural progression of time. We have the faith and courage to know that we will always love them but that our time together and under one roof had come and gone.

Some relationships are toxic and unhealthy and have to be terminated to save ourselves. These types are usually the messiest endings. I have heard it said that the easier a relationship was to let go, the healthier that relationship may have been. I have also read that men that remarry often fairly quickly and after the passing of their wife are not disrespecting her. But rather have a desire to connect and ultimately it reflects in a positive way on that past marriage. Simply put, if it wasn't a good experience, why would they want to do it again?

It takes courage to love just as it takes courage for us to let go in love. Both take trust and faith and knowing that where all things must come to an end, we can do so in love and in God's grace.

The Courage to Love

It takes a lot of courage to love and to try for love and acceptance. You have to be willing to try and to put yourself out there. It is easy to be selfish when you are single, but being married and having children is a decision to share and to give a part of yourself away in love. It takes great courage to embrace another human life and to live with that life and to help elevate and grow that life together as a couple and as a family.

People that are single can come and they can go but to live intimately with someone is to risk smacking up against them with all things good and all things not so good about you and about them. The decision to have children and to raise them is a decision to embrace love, to accept them as they are and to be courageous in that commitment. We don't hand pick the child that God gives us to bear nor do we know ahead of time what an adopted child will require from us as we make the choice to parent them.

I read an article about an adopted child that came from a foreign country and the parents were overwhelmed at what it would take to raise that child. They wanted to return her, to send her back. The little girl was diagnosed with both educational and emotional challenges. The adoptive parents had the financial resources to care for her but this wasn't the child they had envisioned for themselves. Emotionally they didn't think they had enough love in them to care for her and all of her special needs.

Imagine having birthed a baby and having the courage to love and then deciding this isn't the child I wanted? How does that work? How many adults are estranged from their parents today? The numbers are shockingly high. Those adult children have decided they didn't have the parents they envisioned for themselves either.

To love someone is to risk rejection since not everyone is going to love us back. I am always amused when I hear people that never had the courage to have their own children, to raise their own children yet they remark about how someone else should be raising kids. To create a family, to marry and then embrace children takes a huge leap of faith, an abundance of trust and remarkable courage. We have no way at the onset of knowing how these relationships will unfold and develop through the years. What it will cost us in time and in treasure to nurture our spouses and our children and to remain with them.

Potentially we could invest heavily in our spouses and in our children and give our very best efforts and still fail. Fail as in marriages that don't last as expected and/or children that grow up and never reach their potential. Spouses can walk out of our lives just as our children can should they decide to do so. To risk ones heart and their life and to commit that heart and that life to any other person takes a huge amount of courage, faith and trust.

In the early years, I used to joke with my husband, "I can't get married because I don't ever want to be divorced." Behind every joke there is a hint of the truth. You never know going into it if the marriage will last, will your love grow, and will you grow old together? Today more than ever we live in a disposable society, if we don't want a marriage, a child, or a parent, a relationship we walk out on them and away from them. It takes tremendous courage to stay in a relationship that can be taxing at times. Raising children who have any limitations, educational and emotional challenges isn't for the weak or faint of heart. There are days you may feel much love for your spouse and other days question that love. Same can be said for your children too.

But ... what if each person was put in our life for a reason? And what if each child was given to the people that were meant to parent and raise them? The Buddhist belief is that, "Everyone in our life is either a lover or a teacher." Every relationship is meant for love or is a person we are supposed to learn something from. The parents that want to return their adopted child might very well have received "that child" because they had the resources to love and care for her and to learn from her.

Parents abandon their children when they can't or don't have enough love or have the ability to care for them. Marriages end when the love and care ends and family members become estranged when there isn't enough love and care to hold them together. Making the commitment to marry someone means loving them on those easy happy days as well as those difficult challenging ones. Most parents will never openly discuss the struggles they face in raising their own children; they may love them unconditionally and yet at times question whether they are equipped for what that particular child may require to be happy and successful in life.

You don't pick your parents and maybe there is good reason. True love is the greatest gift any one of us will ever receive. It takes faith, courage and maybe a little luck too!

There is nothing like loving someone and having that person love you right back … so here is to finding love and the courage to love, and finding it over, and over, again.

The Courage to Say, "No, Thank you"

Did you ever have someone offer you a dessert, a nice big piece of pie or cake and you were on a diet and counting your calories? The person offering it wanted you to take their offering and you didn't want to be unkind or hurt their feelings but the truth was you didn't want it.

When I was younger I never wanted to hurt anyone's feelings and often this lead me to saying "yes" when I really wanted to respond with "no" and "no, thank you." I had men who wanted to date me and I liked them as a friend but found it difficult to say that I didn't want to date them. They may have been nice guys, but they weren't for me.

Through the years I have been offered many things like trips, dinners, events, friendships, associations and something inside told me "no" "no thanks" and I may have tried it anyway. Yet sooner or later that little inner voice that knows what is right for us, becomes louder and louder if we deny it.

Not wanting something doesn't make it bad or make it wrong, it just may make it not right for us. I have had to do so much soul searching when it came to the direction my church has taken on things like gay marriage and things I have personally witnessed them do that don't seem to be very loving nor are they very kind or Christian. Things I know would not be in keeping with What Would Jesus Do? I believe that my church has alienated so many groups of people through the years and that we are in the midst of an uprising. I don't believe they will ever have the power or the following that they once did.

It is not just church though, I witness it in politics, if you declare a side, and you have all but alienated 50% of the people in our country. Business people have learned to be "politically correct" as not to offend any potential customers. They would rather not say what they think and believe because they know it could cost them business.

We seem to be living in a time of; *"if you aren't with me you must be against me"* views on most any subject. Debate used to be healthy because you could flush out the best ideas. Having "the conversation" meant you were open to hearing all views and trying to determine the best outcome for the greater good.

Our culture has taught us to say "yes" and then go off on our own with expressing our real response "no" in a dishonest way. We fear what our heartfelt "no" "no thanks" and "that's not right" communication will bring. So we try and make it easy with a "yes" when that really isn't what we want or believe is the best answer for us.

It can take so much courage to be honest and to be truthful and kindly respond with "no, thank you" that isn't for me. And when we respond with the truth, that is when we respond with authenticity. Not everything is intended for everyone.

I still don't like saying "no" to people I still don't want to hurt anyone's feelings, but more than that I have learned that I can't be my best when I am not responding in my most authentic way. We all have to do what is right and what is best for us. In Hamlet by William Shakespeare the phrase spoken by Polonius; **"To thine own self be true"** translates to **"Do not deceive yourself."**

And saying "no" can be so healthy and so freeing and it opens the doors for us to respond with "yes" for all the right things, the ones that best defines us.

The Estranged Dad

Dads hurt too! Barely a day goes by when I don't hear from an estranged mother who is grieving over an adult child that decided to dismiss mom and dad from their life. Rarely but very rarely do I hear from the dad's. But when I do the pain shared is no different than what the women have shared. Men seem to keep it in, are more cut and dry about it and seldom do they show their grief outwardly.

When I asked my own husband "what single thing in your life has hurt you the most?'" I was surprised by his response.

This is a man who grew up in "The Projects" and who became a widower at age 32 just after his wife delivered twins prematurely. He had a younger brother that he loved commit suicide; he is a man that held his mother's hand as she died and has a father suffering from severe dementia.

His response; "our girls" and "It didn't have to be this way." He was talking about their estrangement. They chose to turn away from their family under the guise of "abuse." Both times it was over a teen boyfriend that they were determined to have.

My husband was a huge support to my daughter. One year he wrote the entire check for her Catholic prep school tuition. During high school he drove her to school every day before going to work. He was invested in her success even though she was not his biological daughter. He attended every single father-daughter dinner throughout high school and he wasn't just happy to do it but he was proud.

His twin daughter is his namesake that he took up for the entire time she lived at home. Always doing battle with anyone that came to tell him that she was failing, he didn't want to hear it or believe it. Whether it was a teacher or an employer he only wanted to hear the best about his daughter.

Many times it would be her own twin brother reporting to dad about her latest scheme and how awful she made him feel. He dismissed his only son to support his daughter. To him, she walked on water. Until … right up until he could no longer look the other way. Until she would not only estrange but declare that she was "abandoned." After all she needed to have a story to support her decisions to disrespect the house rules. And at the age of 18 she certainly had every right to live her life, her way. But we all know that when we live with our parents and in our parent's house, it is by our parents rules.

Fathers take it differently from what mothers do and looking back I would be willing to bet that my husband stayed strong so that I could be the one that fell apart.

My son describes his twin and her departure as a "low blow" and a "sucker punch" to their father. I believe she acted in haste as many teens do and at the time truly did not comprehend the magnitude of the decisions that she was making. Friends will come and friends will go, but family is forever, or it is supposed to be. He was also the one that didn't want us to go after. He stated, "She will just do it again" and "I know her better than anyone" and "we are better off without her."

This is not what any parent wants to hear. We raised our twins to have their own interests and seldom did their interests intersect. He was an Eagle Scout involved in the theater and drama; she played the flute, went to band camps and played soccer. Although we always hoped they would be close and we tried to instill in them the importance of looking out for one another. We thought it was a blessing that they had each other. Little did we know that our desire to keep them together and close was often at our son's expense and well-being.

My husband isn't the kind of guy that has regrets. He lives and he learns and he has accepted that the daughter he loved and adored didn't or doesn't hold him in the same esteem. His immediate response when she left wasn't one of hurt or of anger, his response was "I am so disappointed."

We find it amusing that you can raise kids in the same home, at the same time with the same parents and schools and everything and how one child can be so appreciative and happy and constantly reflects on all the good things he had in his childhood. He states; "I had a great childhood" and another child who was probably given even more states that they weren't happy and estrange.

From all the parents I have talked with over the 16 years since estrangement entered my life I hear many common threads. Parents that feel betrayed by their children. And their kids lied to them and lied about them. Kids that grow up and decide to estrange from their parents while making the choice to play the victim rather than to succeed in life.

The parents in my support group are the ones that are just like my husband. They are really great dads who gave it their all and never dreamt that all the efforts he put forth would be minimalized and unappreciated. My husband is a strong man, a Christian that prays every single day for the daughter that he thought he raised.

We have great memories of all our kids and all the years that we were raising them. We are so happy that we survived those years with our marriage intact and even stronger. It easily could have gone another way.

Like all the moms and dads who have done the work and raised their children; we want for our children what we have always wanted for them. We want them to be happy, to have peace and good health and a good long life filled with as much love as possible.

The Excitement of Newness

There is something so exciting about trying something new, whether it is a new restaurant, a new vacation destination, a new recipe or a new class. There is that excitement of the unknown and the ability to try a new experience without any expectations. It could be a new book or a new movie release just about anything that we are experiencing for the very first time offers us a new exciting experience without any previous point of reference. I am a junkie for trying new things! It doesn't matter if it is a new hair conditioner or a new food item. I'll try most anything at least once. Over the weekend we tried the new BLK, Black water and I have to say "never again." Not only didn't it taste good to me but I literally felt like I was drinking really dirty black water!

Tonight my husband and I tried the newest Corner Bakery in our neighborhood, it is a chain and new to our area. Like most experiences we put a toe in the water and started with just a soft drink and a dessert. The place was nice, new, neat and clean. The menu had more than one item that piqued my interest and we will return for a breakfast, lunch or dinner meal at another time.

Recently I began taking a new business class at our local college here in Maryland, Loyola has a campus close to my home and I wanted a refresher business class to add to my resume. As an adult student you just want that "A" grade and it is important to do the very best you can, at my age you take every learning opportunity more seriously. You don't have to be there, you are there because you alone made the decision to attend and you want to be there.

My husband like myself enjoys travelling to new locations, it could be a car ride or a plane flight away but we are always open minded and without a previous experience "there" we have no expectations which often makes for a guaranteed great time. We have also learned how to make everything old like new again. As frequent travelers to our resort home in Delaware we set out every single summer season to try a new restaurant. We also try parking on new to us streets, and taking in our beach place from a new and different angle. This helps to keep our trips fresh, new and allows us to discover and uncover new places.

Making time for new experiences and deliberately setting out on an unknown course allows us to broaden our horizons and makes for new learning experiences. Having a partner who enjoys trying new things as much as I do keeps our marriage fresh and alive. Where it may be easy to become a creature of habit, for me, **not** trying something new feels like a slow death and a boring life.

This week I have several "new" things lined up and I am both excited and curious and probably a tad bit nervous too! So here is to trying new things, setting out to experience a new experience and attending new places with opportunities to meet new and different people. Life is about change and growth and taking in as many new things as we can during our lifetime.

So … go somewhere new! Try a new food item! Make a new friend! Travel to a place you have never been before! Take a new class! Whatever it is … there is always excitement attached to newness!

The Golden Rule ... Always Relevant

"Treat others as you want to be treated" the golden rule still relevant and still embraced by many religious and spiritual groups. I've tried my best to live by the golden rule. If I wouldn't want something done to me, why on earth would I think it is okay to do that same thing to someone else?

I hear from kids and adults all the time, "I don't know what to do, I don't know what to do?" Well ... let's think for a moment. What would you want to be done in a similar situation?

Is it okay to lie about someone or to lie to them? Would you want this done to you?

Is it okay to cheat on someone? Would you want this done to you?

Is it okay to badmouth someone when they leave the room? Would you want this done to you?

As humans we are all flawed and we all have our own mishaps in relationships. Each one of us is less than perfect. But would you want to be lied to? Would you want a family member or a friend to be deceitful toward you?

And if we do these things, what should we do to repair them? Own it and apologize, try and fix it. Understand that you should never involve yourself in a divide that you helped to create. It's not an act of love, its most likely ego and self-preservation.

Would you want your girlfriend taking your soon to be ex-husbands side to him and being just as deceitful by taking the opposing side with you the female friend? Playing both sides, manipulating both people for their own gain are not behaviors that come from a loving and supportive person.

If we wouldn't find certain behaviors acceptable for our own selves, why would we think it is ever okay to do those same things to any other person, friend, family member or others?

People that divide people, people that divide marriages and people that divide families, do so for their own agenda. They manipulate those around them. Coming between people is never an act of love or comes from a loving place. It is manipulative, pure and simple.

Common courtesy is simply treating everyone, the way that we want to be treated. Why is that so hard for some people? Whenever "I don't know what to do" I try and think in the reverse, if I was on the other side of that situation or argument, what would I want done? When we hurt people and when we cause upset in someone else's life, we need to accept responsibility. We need to try and fix what we have done by making it right. We should always remember if we wouldn't want something done to us, we probably shouldn't be doing that same thing to someone else.

Treat others as you want to be treated … if we all did this, our world and our lives would be a healthier, happier and a better place.

The Importance of Truly Great Mentors

This piece is "prompted" by a request for submissions on mentors. I originally wrote about my mentors in an essay included in my book, *Halfway Home The First 50 Years.*

I've had a few teachers all through school that took an interest in me. There were numerous teachers that said things that resonated with me and impacted my thinking and my desire to learn and to uncover my own gifts and talents.

As an adult professional career woman, I had two significant mentors. In real estate it was my office manager Marianne. She took a real interest in my success and in me as a woman and as a mother. At that time, my mid-twenties I had never known anyone quite like her. She was a socialite and a southern belle. She had adult children and was a part of Junior League and other elite social community groups.

Marianne believed in me, she was different from my family and other teachers in my life. As a strong and successful female corporate executive she was also one of the most diplomatic people I ever encountered. The take away for me with her was that I was worth it, I was good and I was good enough. She supported me and in her support I was truly successful. Marianne was genuinely happy for me when I did well and sympathetic and supportive when I struggled. She was everything you would want in a female role model.

Because of her I was a better Realtor and a better friend and a better mother. Her support trickled down to my child as she attended "grandparents" day to support my daughter and she was there when that same child graduated from high school. She was successful and came from a place of strength. Marianne had a lot to offer and I was easily mentored by her.

The next very important person in my professional life was the President and C.E.O. of a special needs school; Dr. Ross. He was my mentor into the world of not for profit work. He taught me to think differently and he taught me that even the most broken people in our society, those with educational and emotional challenges had value. Unlike much of my Italian and Catholic upbringing he didn't judge people. He lifted them up. He never lost his childlike enthusiasm and the "I can do that" mantra for challenges. Dr. Ross took an interest in my success which ultimately supported his vision and the organizations success. He was both driven and disciplined.

Dr. Ross and Marianne both shared one common trait in their ability to lift others up, and mentor them. They had such a high opinion of you and of your value and worth that you never wanted to let them down. In that single common trait they both brought the best out of the people that they managed, supported and mentored. They are positive, upbeat and driven. They come from a place of strength, placing value and challenges on the people that they work with. They are positive people that lift up every single person around them.

I was fortunate to have had the opportunity to do more and to do better and to become more accomplished because of the mentoring support I received from both Marianne and Dr. Ross. They supported my success in two completely different worlds. One was total for profit business, real estate and the other the true social work model in not for profit work in a special needs school. Great mentors are so important and without mine I would never have known the career success that I enjoyed.

Paying it forward; as a result of the mentoring I received I have mentored many young people through the years Young adults who worked as volunteers and as interns. I did my best to lift them up and to help give them the confidence to soar with their own strengths.

The Leadership Challenge

In 2002 I was privileged to be invited and attend the book signing and release of *Leadership* by Rudolph Giuliani. It was a swanky event held at the Mayflower Hotel in Washington D.C. and promoted by the Washington Speakers Bureau. Many distinguished guests were in attendance, people like Chris

Matthew from MSNBC, Democratic strategist James Carville and "top cop" Bernard Kerik just to name a few.

As a supporter of the Washington Speakers Bureau I was allowed to bring up to three guests and we had to give our security clearance weeks in advance of attending. This event honoring Rudy and his new book was on the heels of 911 when Rudy Giuliani emerged as a true leader having endured the attacks of the World Trade Center during his time as Mayor of New York City. This book event is and remains one of the best author events I have ever attended.

The room was full and many were political rivals but all seemed to acknowledge and appreciate the leadership of this Mayor.

"For having more faith in us than we had in ourselves, for being brave when required and rude where appropriate and tender without being trite, for not sleeping and not quitting and not shrinking from the pain all around him. Rudy Giuliani, Mayor of the World, is TIME 2001 person of the year." TIME

Few people will ever know what the importance of proper leadership is and looks like until they are directly faced with adversity. This was the right man and the right time for New York City. I think most people would agree he met the leadership challenge after 9/11.

Our new Pope Francis is facing a unique time in the Catholic Church, already his leadership skills are a breath of fresh air and noteworthy. He gave up the Papal palace apartment for a more humble lifestyle and private dining quarters to eat in the cafeteria where the other clergy eat. His message isn't just in his words; he seems to speak far less than his predecessors but rather leadership that shows itself in his actions and choices.

Everyone may not agree with all his dogma but I would be willing to bet most can appreciate his leadership in his ability to walk the walk and not just talk the talk.

What is leadership?

According to Wikipedia the definition of "leadership" is defined as *"A process of social influence in which one person can enlist the aid and support of others in the accomplishment of a common task."*

The person closest to e who best defines leadership is my husband Brian. In over 15 years he has not missed a scheduled day of work nor has he taken any sick leave. Our son went all through Tiger Scouts and Boy Scouts to become an Eagle Scout because his father's leadership. Our son now has one full year of never missing a day of school or a day of work. I have to believe it has something to do with the example of his father.

"Before you are a leader, success is all about growing yourself. When you become a leader, success is about growing others."
Jack Welch

For some people leading comes naturally and for others it can be more of a challenge and even others that have no interest in leading at all.

"Leadership is not magnetic personality that can just as well be a glib tongue. It is not "making friends and influencing people" that is flattery. Leadership is lifting a person's vision to higher sights, the raising of a person's performance to a higher standard, the building of a personality beyond its normal limitations." Peter F. Drucker

Most of us are looking to our leaders, our President, our Pope, our Supreme Court and others for some kind of leadership, we want to succeed and to follow an example and the road of one who is wiser and has experience. Today more than ever with so many opposing views on so many hot button issues, leadership can be a very real challenge.

"Our chief want is someone who will inspire us to be what we know we could be." Ralph Waldo Emerson

The Longest Relationship You Will Ever Have is With Yourself

The longest relationship you will ever have is with yourself, and for me, it also includes God. The way we treat people and our honesty and dishonesty is something that only we can reconcile. So many of us are hugely invested in our parents, our children, our friends and our neighbors and where this is quite noble, the truth is that the sustainable relationship is the one we have with ourselves. Friends come and go, family comes together and drifts apart, parents age and die and children grow up and go on their way.

The biggest investment made should be where it will have staying power and last, and that is within our own self. When we look to others for our value, whether it is an employer, a parent, a child, a friend or any other we have given way to letting everyone else determine our value.

As a child who was born as raised Catholic, I learned many wonderful life lessons. I learned to live by the golden rule and to treat other people the way that I wanted to be treated. I learned the value in living for the greater good and about service above self. I watched both Priests and Nuns put everyone else above themselves. I learned to believe I was going to hell if I didn't honor the Catholic code for living. It is only recently that I have discovered that if and when you put everyone else above yourself you have basically taught people how to treat you. You have taught them that you deserve to be last.

Life is a journey and not a destination, each one of us is evolving as we age, learn and grow. Just like a flower that comes back year after year, where it may be the same type of flower it never returns looking exactly like it did in its previous bloom.

When we are young we have no way to fully comprehend how our decisions will impact us later in life. Like the teenager who decides to become a teen mom, they can never fully understand that life altering choice until they age. Parents fret over their teenagers and young adult decisions, because unlike the teenager and the young adult a mature adult has a better understand of poor choices. The choice to walk away and not take advantage of a fully funded four year college education means much more to that same adult, now grown, who does not have the advantage of a college degree that was afforded them as a teenager.

Decisions made in anger and in haste seldom stand up in the test of time. Whether our parents were great parents, mediocre parents or even terrible parents, they are the parents that God gave to us. Every single adult knows the impact of their childhood both good and bad and the importance of their roots and their home. Even in the most highly dysfunctional families, social workers and mental health care providers work to restore the health of the first family or neonatal family. They get it that the parental relationships will impact a child's life for the rest of their life.

Life is long

Most people state "life is short" or "life is so short" but it was my husband who first shared the statement, "life is long' with me. Life is long and it feels even longer when as a young person you make life altering decisions that impact your life in a negative way, for the rest of your life.

One of the fastest growing populations of people is estranged parents and adult children. This week alone I received 6 e-mails from across the country and from both men and women, fathers and mothers who are estranged from their adult children and grandchildren. The pain and heartache is insurmountable and almost every single case has set the same cycle up for the next generation. Statistically it has been proven that once this pattern of family estrangement begins, it plays itself, over and over again in future generations.

The Support Group for Parents of Estranged Adult Children, if needed you can find it on Facebook at www.facebook.com/pages/Support-Group-for-Parents-of-Estranged-Adult-Children

I have heard from parents, who had social services involve themselves and when it was deemed it was a troubled teenager, the rift between parent and child was broken beyond repair. I heard from a father who was arrested after his teen daughter claimed abuse. It didn't take long for the investigation to uncover that the teen was angry. She was angry with dad, because he took the car away from her. So she got him back by slamming herself up against the car, getting a bruise, calling police, saying dad did this and when they saw her redness and bruise, he was immediately arrested.

Now dad sees how dangerous and without boundaries, his daughter is and in his anger and hurt he doesn't want the teen back in the home. The teen daughter is limited in her ability to function without her parents support. The stage is now set for years of estrangement. The social workers once there and involved are long gone as they have moved on helping truly abused children. This family is left with the destruction and the aftermath.

Try Not to Make Mistakes that You Can't Recover From

It wasn't until one of my later career jobs that I was applauded for making any mistakes. My supervisor always saw the value in lessoned learned and in the ability to try. According to him, if you made a mistake, at least you were trying. For the effort you were applauded then came the dialogue about what went wrong and how to make it better. Everything was viewed as a learning opportunity and a chance for growth and development.

Some mistakes can't ever be repaired, nor can you ever come back from them. Murder and rape are not actions that once crossed can be repaired. Where we want to live in a world of second chances and of reform, there are actions that can be taken that you can never take back.

When you put your life in someone else's hands and when you no longer have the power over your own destiny in life you have all but ended your relationship with yourself. No one is going to know what you like, need or want in life better than you do.

Advice is great and often it is free and perhaps in being free that is what it is worth, nothing. People often have their own agenda and their own idea.

Coming from a place of strength and of self-love and acceptance and contributing to our own success and investing in our own self allows us to be fully developed mature adults. We can't get our value or devalue ourselves by what other people do or don't do.

As parents, maybe we need to do better and teach our children that the longest relationship you will ever have is the relationship you have with yourself. If you are not full-filled and you are angry, only you can do what is necessary to fix that inside of yourself.

Investing in our own self is not selfish but rather contributes to wellness and to the greater good. We all know that "hurt people, hurt people." And most often when teens and young adults are lashing out at others, at their parents and at their friends, family and community, it is because they are hurt and troubled.

I can't say it enough, the longest relationship you will ever have is the relationship that you have with yourself. Invest in you, take care of you and do what is right. A pretty good measure for me has always been that if you wouldn't want something done to you, you most probably shouldn't be doing that same thing to someone else.

The Most Beautiful Baby Girl

Most parents believe that they have the most beautiful babies, I did. I had the most beautiful baby girl. From the moment she came into this world, she was well received with open arms and a huge heart. She was wanted.

I wanted a daughter from the time I babysat as a pre-teen. My mother used to call on me to comfort and to quiet my youngest sister so that she could sleep and then go to work. I have vivid recall of my youngest sister and her tiny little fingers that wrapped themselves around my finger as I often rocked her back to sleep when she was just an infant.

My own daughter was so anticipated that I didn't touch a drop of alcohol or a cigarette the entire time I was pregnant. I attended birthing classes and La Leche league meetings to learn about breast feeding. She was full term and so very healthy.

Minutes after her birth, she picked up her head and turned it to the other side as she lay back down. She was strong and healthy at over 8 lbs. and 21 ½ inches. She took to breast feeding and she stirred something in me that I never knew before her birth. This kind of pure love when you give and you give while expecting nothing in return.

As a toddler people stopped me to tell me how cute and pretty she was, often I had to work as I was a single mother working as a waitress to support us. There were days I had to peel her off of me and listen to her shriek as I had to go. We lived in an apartment up three flights of stairs and I could hear her the entire time I walked down them and to my exit. She didn't want me to leave her.

On the rare occasion that my friend babysat her I was told of how she literally sat at the front door and waited until my return. She wanted her mommy.

I was thrilled when she began kindergarten and was one of the few children who didn't cry on their first day. When her teacher mispronounced her name, she put her hands on her hips and spelled her name correctly and then repeated it back to her. Clearly she was ready!

She was an excellent student an avid reader and well liked. She was a kid that smiled all the time and when I entered a room she lit up. If I called her on the phone, her voice always went up and heightened like she was happy it was me.

As a Catholic school student she was confirmed and attended one of the most prestigious all girls' prep schools in our state.

I watched her evolve into a beautiful young lady who attended a wealth of activities. She played the piano and had numerous piano recitals, she played softball and took art classes and went on summer vacations and to summer camp. She was a fierce debater who became President of her Mock Trials team. I watched her in our local court house; I watched her win both sides of the same argument, a court case.

I was that mother who supported and attended all fundraisers and activities from the bake sales where I personally made many of the donations to the table purchase of 10 for social events. I was there to support, donate and to help re-decorate the senior lounge and all the mandatory meetings for special event dances. She never took the bus as we drove her back and forth to school until we purchased her a car of her own.

When people saw us together they so often said, "I hope that one day my child and I will be as close as the two of you." She was confident and outspoken.

She was an artist and an intellect. She walked the runway in her high school fashion show with extreme confidence and poise. She graduated from high school with a fully funded college scholarship based on her academic success. She was stunning and social and voted by her peers as most likely to become an attorney.

My daughter was well supported and attended numerous conferences for Law and Leadership in Washington, DC and Palo Alto, California at Stanford University. I was committed to her and her success. As a teenager we purchased her first car and paid tens of thousands of dollars for her education. She was worth every investment we made in her.

My husband attended all of her father-daughter dinners throughout high school and my Real estate Supervisor attended Grandparents days. Her birthdays and school year endings were often celebrated with class parties. She had her share of pool parties and she attended numerous event dances and many high school proms.

When she graduated high school I could not have been more proud, proud because of her many achievements and proud because of all that she overcame to achieve them.

She was the most beautiful baby girl and I am blessed to have memories and hundreds of photos of her. I can't find a picture or any single image when she wasn't happy and smiling.

Then one day they grow up, leave the nest and make their own way in the world. I didn't ever have a hard time doing for her, when she went off on her own; this was when I would struggle. My heart had never known such an intense degree of love and of giving.

Our children teach us many things; there is nothing that is greater than what a parent wants for their children. For a mother, the daughter is the one female that you want to be prettier, smarter and even more successful than yourself. We so often see them as an extension of ourselves. The hardest part for many mothers isn't in the loving but rather in the letting go, yet we must.

We gave them life, we gave them life to live their life as they see fit. The greatest lesson for any parent of an adult child knows that even though they came from us, that there was a time when we breast fed them and we were literally their lifeline, they will grow up and they may never need us again.

I had the most beautiful baby girl ... and then she grew up and became her own woman.

The Mother Target

Is there anyone out there who hasn't had issues with their mother, over one thing or another, not ever? I am beginning to believe that "mom" wears the target and always has and always will. I mean without "mom" we wouldn't even have been born so surely our struggles are all "her" fault, right?

Mom didn't love us enough or she loved us too much. She was overly protective and controlling or she didn't protect us enough and neglected us. I never hated my mother, not ever. But I never really related well with her either.

So what was my beef with her? Initially it was that she just wasn't very feminine and not the mother I had envisioned for myself. She was tough as nails and often without much class. She was big and loud and boisterous. Yet I was told that these were the things that she became *after* my parent's divorce. The woman that married my father was tall and just 105 pounds;

the one who got a divorce from him was closer to 300 pounds. So what happened to her?

Later my issues were much bigger when I learned that her second husband was a child abuser. After that there was no coming back to her. She stood by him and I stood alone.

Recently I met up with one of my favorite young people. He is the same age as my twin children. We have a professional relationship but often talk about our families and issues. He loves his mother and I know that she loves him too. But … the little guy that blindly loved her is now a grown up and questions what makes her tick. He is becoming his own man and here comes the natural separation that occurs when our kids declare that they aren't just our kids anymore. But rather an adult with their own moral code, set of values and ideas on what their life should look like sans any parental interference.

Another friend loved and adored his mother, always did. He talks about her all the time, she has passed on and in his words, "not a day goes by that I don't think of her." Yet it took decades before he could confide in her that he was a gay man. He was so worried about being honest with her. When he finally told her she said, "Is it my fault? Did I make you gay?" His response, (I love) "You give yourself far too much credit. No, it has nothing to do with you."

Mothers are often so accustomed to accepting blame and responsibility for what their children do even when they aren't little children anymore. How often do we blame the parents? What kind of home did they come from? Yet sit and talk with any parents of adult children and you will soon learn how little if any control mom or dad has when their child reaches the age of maturity.

My son and I have a very different relationship than what I experienced with my girls. We are really close and accepting of one another. Yet I see that same kind of "rub" with his father that I once experienced with my daughters. So is it that mirror image thing? I watch my husband get ticked off at our son for doing the same exact things my husband, his father does. I have to laugh.

Therapists have made a fortune trying to unravel the mother-daughter relationship. They say it is the most complicated of all relationships and can offer the greatest of joy or the most painful experiences of all. I always believed that life was tough enough without at least having a mother. I don't think I would have been driven to adopt pre-mature infant twins if I thought their life would have been better without any mother at all. After their birth mother died, I assumed the role of "mom." The mother is the one person who is supposed to love you no matter what you do.

From the beginning of time mothers have worn the target on their backs. The blame game, mom did this or mom did that mom was there or mom never was there for me. It is a miracle that any mother gets it right when our expectations are so high for her. The mother is supposed to be all loving and all giving and all of the time.

How does that work though, when the target of the child's rage is so often directed at the very person who gave them life and brought them into the world? I don't believe that anyone's life is better without their mother in their life. I learned how to live without my mother. I lived without her for more than two decades before she died. I did okay but it was not at all ideal.

My husband always loved his mother and had peace with her. But that didn't mean that he was always happy with her either. In his words there were times she was "loud and embarrassed him in public." Yet he always chose love over denial. He never denied her.

When you have little children no one tells you that one day they will grow up and they just might reject you and target you with all their rage and anger. The more I talk with other parents and mothers of adult children, the more I learn just how challenging the mother-child relationship can be and is for so many.

We want "mom" to be everything, virginal, pure, perfect but cool and worldly and educated too. We want "mom" to be everything and more, we want to dismiss her too when she is not in keeping with our "vision" of what "mom" should be and mean to us. What a burden to put on anyone. When I think of it, what right did I have to expect my mother to be more "feminine" if that wasn't her, that wasn't her!

The best part about having raised our kids and knowing that they are adults now is in knowing that our job is done. They can love us or hate us, their choice. We know that we did the work. We did the best we could and there are no do-overs. I don't know if there are any women though, mothers or mothers to be that go into having children with a desire to being the target for their children just because they are the "mom."

Here is to all the "moms" out there, I know one thing for certain, we all want the very best for our children whether they are with or without us!

The Next Chapter

There is always another chapter, until we take our last breathe. There is the chapter after the winter and the spring and the summer and the fall. There is the chapter that follows the break up or the divorce, the marriage, the kids, the parents and the job. There is always another chapter as long as we are alive.

My friend lost her father yesterday, he has been ill and she has been tending to him. Loving her dad and supporting him like only a devoted daughter can do. She has spent many weekends travelling to him and staying with him. He has been a huge part of her life. Now he is gone. Those hours, days and weekends will be voids until she figures out the next chapter. What will she fill her time with?

Another friend lost her husband several years ago, they were inseparable and then he died. After her grief, she had to figure out what the next chapter would look like. Today she travels with friends and is supportive toward her children. There was a period of time when she couldn't imagine what the next chapter of her life would look like and then it arrived. Her life became full again.

So many of my peers are running from pillar to post with ailing parents and children still in the home, then there is the big career that goes along with it all and life is full. But then time gets away from us and the parents and the kids go and maybe it is retirement time. Another chapter is about to begin.

Choosing a Joyful Dance

"Don't tell me how wonderful things will be ... someday. Show me you can risk being at peace, truly okay with the way things are right now in this moment and again in the next and the next and the next ..." The Dance by Oriah

Our lives are filled with chapters and with a beginning, middle and an ending. It is up to us to use the time and the pages of our life story to matter, to matter to us and to God. We may not get what we want but we should know that we will receive what we need. God has a plan that is bigger than anything we could have ever imagined for ourselves.

"Some people think that God does not like to be troubled with our constant coming and asking. The way to trouble God is not to come at all." Dwight L. Moody

At times it takes an incredible amount of grace to move from chapter to chapter never fully knowing what lies ahead for us. Our faith allows us to take that next step into the unknown.

"Although we have only one life cycle to live, although it is only a small part of history which we will cover, to do this gracefully and carefully is our greatest vocation." Henri J.M. Nouwen

Like the novel that we can't put down and the pages we anticipate reading, our life should hold that same desire that same anticipation of what is to come. What is next, how does the next chapter read? My husband and I are about to start another big chapter in life, a chapter that includes retirement and relocation, a chapter that includes empty nester status.

We are both excited and nervous and celebratory we have arrived at another major milestone in our life. The next chapter is yet to be written but we welcome its arrival. There is always another chapter, another chapter until we take our last breathe here on earth.

This chapter could easily be called, Feeling Fabulous in Our Fifties ... who knew it would arrive so soon?

The Only Way Out of It Is Through It

This one is dedicated to all those that are grieving, whether it is from the loss of a child, a parent, a friend or a significant other. The only way out of it, is through it. Grief is something that we all experience with loss. They say the greatest lesson learned comes from the final lesson, death.

We all have people that we loved, people that are now gone from our life. They passed on or they moved on, either way there is a void that they have left behind.

For my friends who are suffering a lost child, that hole in your heart will always be there, the space that was once occupied by that child never fills up. Same can be said for those of us that have lost a parent or other loved ones. We can love other children though and love other parental figures, and other friends that help us to heal. They help to fill the void and show us that we can and will love again.

Grief is a tricky thing, while in it, we so often, can't see past it. In my early 20's I read all of Helen Kubler Ross on **Death & Dying**. I surrounded myself with books like, **How to Survive the Loss of a Love** written by a few PH.D's. I loved **Women and the Blues, Passions that Hurt, Passions that Heal**. Being widowed at 23 was a huge lesson. Losing a child years later could have destroyed me and having a mother deny me could have been the final nail in my coffin, but only, if I allowed it.

The gifts from loss were numerous, the biggest take away, celebrate the here and the now, be thankful for all the people now in your life and give thanks for all of it. Our days here are numbered. My greatest regret; comes from the times when I allowed myself to get lost in my grief. There was a period when it was at the expense of not being there for those that remained in my life. Specifically for not always being there and present for my husband Brian, who I absolutely love and adore.

I cried for more than a decade over someone. Truth is no one is worth that amount of tears or that amount of grief. Simply put, life is too short. All those lost days can never be recovered, they are lost for good. The people that stood by me, in my grief, had me, yet I was less than who I could have been and who I am. The only way out of our grief is to come through it. Some people seem to rebound faster. Every one grieves in his or her own way, space and time and at their own pace.

I am part of a support group where there is so much fresh pain. The loss is so new for them. I wish I could take all their hurts away, I wish I could say, "Get over it." But no one could have told me to just "get over it." Our losses don't go away but in time, they do become easier to manage and easier to live with. I can't take back my decade of tears but what I can do is share what I might do differently. If anything, I'd get over it sooner. When I was stuck in my grief, I wasn't able to love fully. What a loss.

Getting stuck happens yet I know that God wants us all to be happy and to love and to be loved. Death can be the greatest lesson of all. It is supposed to teach us that we shouldn't take anything or anyone for granted. Death and loss are supposed to teach us that life is for the living, live it!

I am wishing peace and much love to all who are suffering a loss, those who are grieving over a child or a parent or a friend. Once you get past the grief, it can be just like spring with a fresh new beginning complete with signs of new life.

My losses didn't teach me to love less, they taught me to love more and to love deeper and with greater respect and even more passion.

Vulnerability and Being Thirty

"**Vulnerability may be understood as the capacity to be open, to be attracted, touched, or moved by the draw of God's love as this is experienced in one's own life or in the lives of others. It is vulnerability that enables one to enter into relationships of interpersonal communication and communion with others who recognize their own weakness and need. Vulnerability requires the integrity and the strength --- indeed the power --- to risk enormous pain, to bear the burdens of the darkest hour without avoidance, denial and deception. It demands the** stamina to be open in order to be touched in one's fragility. Vulnerability implies a willingness to lose oneself, to be knocked off center by the claim of the others upon one in the hope of finding one's true self. It demands readiness to die to one's self so that one might truly live." Robert S. Rivers, CSP *from Maintenance to Mission*

By the age of thirty, I had survived growing up in my parent's home, an abusive marriage, having a child, being widowed at age 23, a second significant relationship end with betrayal. I would learn what the impact of sexual abuse allegations would have on my family. Sexual abuse allegations would destroy our family: it would be the final blow in multi-layered toxic family and sibling relationships. My childhood home was with a raging alcoholic, my father who I loved and adored "as is" and my enabling mother, who I never fully understood.

At the age of thirty, I sold my home, left a thriving real-estate career, packed up myself and my elementary school aged daughter, and began the healing and "acceptance" process by moving to the beach in Fort Lauderdale, Florida. It was bitter and it was sweet.

I Want to Know What Love Is
By Foreigner

I gotta take a little time

A little time to think things over
I better read between the lines
In case I need it when I'm older

Now this mountain I must climb
Feels like a world upon my shoulders
And through the clouds I see love shine
It keeps me warm as life grows colder

In my life there's been heartache and pain
I don't know if I can face it again
Can't stop now, I've traveled so far
To change this lonely life

I wanna know what love is
I want you to show me
I wanna feel what love is
I know you can show me

Moving to Florida for a year was a leap of faith, returning to Baltimore a year later and to begin again was yet another leap of faith. There is no question that I was completely vulnerable. I was alone as an adult with a child to raise. No husband and no family. That first Christmas was dreadful. I was broke. I started back in real estate but was yet to earn any commissions. My car was breaking down and with the move back to Baltimore, I could no longer afford private school, for that year, my daughter attended public school. I was not where I wanted to be in life.

I didn't hide my misery, looking back maybe I should have. We didn't have a tree that year and any gifts were few. I went to bed before 9:00 in the evening that Christmas night, crying and praying it would be over soon. It was and remains my absolute worst Christmas holiday. No family, few friends, no husband, no money, just me and my daughter. It wasn't a pretty picture. Having gone through that miserable holiday season, I vowed it would never happen again. Thank God it hasn't!

With that New Year, so much changed, so much goodness came to me. My commission checks started to roll in and soon I afforded getting my car fixed. I worked really hard. My child often came to work with me. She was well known in my real estate office where she was embraced and well supported. It was my real estate office manager who attended grandparents' day and her high school graduation.

That Easter in 1992 and on Good Friday, God would bring me my second husband. He arrived with infant twins, a boy and a girl, who were just eighty-seven days old. Their mother, his wife was gone. The first time I made dinner for him, he showed up with two baby baskets. The car seat carriers with his son and his daughter and they were wearing matching sailor suits. They smelled like baby magic lotion. He was handsome and freshly shaven wearing a button down yellow shirt, Levi jeans and brown leather Docksider slip on shoes. Most guys bring flowers and chocolates, he brought me infant babies. It was easy to lose my heart to all three of them.

It didn't take long for us to realize we had something really special! A Realtor friend said, *"It is a marriage made in Heaven by Heaven."* He was widowed with two children and I was widowed with one child. We had one half of a family each. When I questioned my daughter about us all coming together as a family, she said, *"Mom, I think I want it even more than you do!"*

This year we will be together twenty-one years. We are still madly in love. Our children are adults now; the oldest is thirty-two and the twins twenty-one.

When Brian and I met we were both incredibly vulnerable. We were real and we were raw. We both knew loss, hurt and heartache. Our beginning was beautiful. We never played games. In our vulnerability, we were so innocent. We immediately trusted one another with our hurts, our heartaches, our dreams, our desires and our hope for the future. We were friends first. Friends for months before any intimate relationship. We talked for hours. We spent as much time as we could together, sharing time with all of our children and between our two homes. Within six-months we became engaged to be married. Our first two years together were honeymoon perfect.

Then the bottom fell out. Any suppressed guilt Brian had just came raging out and most of it was directed toward me. They say, "You always hurt the ones who are closest to you." Another woman would have left him but I knew it wasn't about me. He needed to reconcile himself and all that transpired in just two years. For him, he was a new first time father with pre-mature infant twins, a son and a daughter. He was also left alone with a deceased wife. He was now involved and engaged to be married to a woman with an eleven year old daughter. It was a lot. He got through it. We got through it. Our passion cuts both ways, for the good and at times the not so good.

Neither one of us, all those twenty-one years ago was really solid. We both were working through the aftermath of our lives. We were just 32 years old when we met. We were so very vulnerable and yet it was that vulnerability that showcased pure hearts. We know that God had his hand on our backs, as he guided us together, and in our union to become married. There is no doubt that we are God-blessed.

"It is through the struggle, that we find enlightenment." I would be willing to bet that **"It is through vulnerability, that we find love."** The quote above from Robert S. Rivers drives that home, the importance of vulnerability for the pathway to love.

The Foreigner lyrics above remind me of the first song my husband ever dedicated to me and to us. Today, twenty-one years later, it still feels like, *"I Want to Know What Love Is"* and thanks to God, and to my husband Brian, I do! I do!

We Are All Connected

We are all connected, we are all more alike than not. In just two days I have heard from more than a dozen readers, readers that wrote to me and connected with me after reading me. They could relate. Some had an alcoholic in the family or strained relationships, some were filled with grief. Some are aspiring writers. Some made comments and thought about what I wrote. I am happy to hear from all of them, we are connected.

The take away for me is always the connections, I write for the connections I seek with all others. I share my life and my story **not** because I think I am so special but I know that my story is your story. Somewhere along the pathway of this life we will know the same experiences, some sooner than later and some to a higher or a lesser degree.

This s why we are called to God, our Father and it is because we are brothers and sisters. We are here, in this life together.

Sometimes we are happy with our brothers and sisters and sometimes we are not happy with them.

Whatever we are going through, there is someone else has already gone through it. They survived and so will you. ***"Pain shared is pain divided."*** Michael Pritchard

God wants us to love one another as our own sisters and our brothers; he wants us to forgive them as he promises to forgive us. So often the people that have the hardest time forgiving others are the same ones that can't seem to forgive themselves.

We must learn to forgive ourselves, before we can begin to forgive any others.

"Forget yesterday, it has already forgotten you. Don't sweat tomorrow, you haven't even met. Instead open your eyes and your heart to a truly precious gift, today." Steve Maraboli

My todays are so much better than so many of my yesterdays, this is my choice. We all have that choice. Do you want to dwell on the past that has come and gone, fret about tomorrow that has yet to arrive or live in the moment and appreciate all that we have right here and right now.

When we turn away from our brother or our sister is it because of them, or is it because of ourselves? So many of us can't look at what we see in someone else that is a mirror of what we don't like or want in ourselves.

God didn't just create some of us, God created all of us. The person who sits in constant judgments of others, would they themselves hold up under that same judgment?

So many great quotes come to mind, *"Be kind to the people you meet on the way up, these are the same ones you will see on the way back down."* Jimmy Durante

"Judge not, lest ye be judged." MATTHEW 7:15

My thought for today, What if everyone really was doing the best that they could for this moment in time? And if you knew that God would judge you as you have chosen to judge others, would you continue in your judgments?

We Had a Hunger for Success

My generation grew up knowing if we wanted something we had to go get a job and work for it. We didn't grow up expecting our parents to provide for us once we reached the age of maturity. Most of my friends my peer group are self-made success stories. We may have attended public or private Catholic schools but it wasn't a status symbol. If we went to Catholic school it was our parish school and not an elite choice but just what you did back then. The Catholic schools wanted you and they gave second third fourth sibling discounts. If you couldn't pay they put you on a payment plan. I am fairly certain my mother was still paying for my Catholic high school education after I graduated in 1977. And they didn't hold up my diploma either. Today if you haven't paid up by graduation, they will hold up your diploma.

My first car was a 1971 Ford Pinto that my mother paid $550. It came from my Uncle John's car lot. I got a job and paid her back and I was happy to do it. I loved working and making my own money. I loved the freedom it afforded me and the sense of accomplishment. We knew we could have whatever we wanted as long we worked hard enough for it.

But what did we do as parents? We bought our daughters first car and it wasn't $550 but it was nicely used and $8,000. It was never paid back nor did we request it to be paid back. One of our children attended a prestigious prep school and when a classmate wrecked her brand new BMW it was immediately replaced by a brand new Jeep Cherokee. The joke was the kids were driving more expensive cars than the teachers could afford that taught them. But what was the cost and what was the lesson that we were teaching our children in providing all this?

We grew up in the 60's and 70's and most of us had a healthy fear of our parents and respected all adult figures. We assumed they were older, wiser, lived longer and knew more. We didn't call it "child abuse" when we were spanked or slapped by our parents and most of us were. We called it discipline. It wasn't "verbal abuse" when our parents yelled at us. It was their fear and their concern that we weren't doing what we needed to do to be successful in life. We respected our parents and we knew they worked hard for what they were able to provide for us. We had gratitude.

So many of us grew up with a hunger to succeed and we wanted more and better and in our hunger we achieved it. We got along and accepted that sometimes hard work meant getting your hands dirty and working with and for people that you may not always have agreed with but it built character to do so.

The first Christmas after my first husband died and our daughter was just three years old I remember placing all her gifts under the Christmas tree and turning to my mother and saying, "Do I have enough gifts for her?" But what I really meant was, "How could I ever give her anything that could make up for the fact that she would never know her father." I was just 24 years old but I knew in that moment that all the "things" I was never afforded as a little girl were just that "things." Good or bad I had grown up with both of my parents.

We had our eye on the "American dream" we pursued our educations, our jobs, our relationships and bought our homes. Most of my friends afforded homes that our parents would never have dreamt of affording and some of us had second resort homes too. We loved working and going after what we wanted. We grew up believing if we worked hard enough anything and everything was possible. Our dream and our hard work brought us much success.

But ... What about Our Own Kids

Most of our kids didn't grow up with that same hunger to succeed. We may have unknowing spoiled them by never allowing them to be hungry. We provided a lifestyle that included prestigious private schools, elite neighborhoods and vacation homes. Our refrigerators we always stocked since so many of us shopped in bulk box stores. We told them their job was to get an education and we would take care of the rest. But at what expense was this for our kids?

We talk about the job market being so poor today and the price of homes and goods being off the charts. Of course some of it is relative but some of it is just crazy expensive. My Catholic high school may have cost a few thousand dollars in total. My oldest graduated in 1998 with more than 40 thousand dollars to put her through 4-years of high school. Today those same years at that same school is well over $50,000. Townhomes or we used to call then row homes or "starter homes" cost our parents in my area between $10,000 and $16,000 when they we newly built. Today those same row homes are over $250,000. How will this generation afford the "American dream?"

Some of our kids are lost, it seems like they are paralyzed in knowing or feeling overwhelmed at the notion of, "how am I going to re-create the lifestyle that my parents afforded me?" Many of them may not be able to ever achieve it. What if the richest part of your life already happened in your childhood? Where would your hunger for success come from?

Many adult kids today in 2012 are moving back home in their mid-20 and 30's because they just can't afford to be out on their own. So many of my peer friends are struggling with what we knew, learned and achieved and trying to relate it to where our adult children are in their life. Was it easier for us? Or did we just work harder? Did we steal our kids hunger by never allowing them to be hungry at all?

This very well may be the first generation that doesn't achieve more than what their parents achieved.

My husband Brian grew up in the projects in the inner city of Baltimore. By his own admission sports saved his life. He didn't give in to the drug culture or the poor pity me victim attitude. He believed he could work hard and escape poverty and he did it. It wasn't by chance or by taking a risk but rather a slow and steady wins the race approach. In 1978 he began working for Baltimore city as a laborer and today 33 years later he is upper management.

Together we afforded our children a good education either in the elite private schools or blue ribbon public schools. We both worked as a team to provide for all the extras like educational trips to Stanford University, Law and Leadership conferences, first cars, piano lessons, girl scouts, boy scouts, swimming lessons, vacations and so much more. At times we achieved these things by brown bagging it. We made the choice to decline trips to Paris France in order to be home and run our business and support our kids in summer school. We tried to show them that they were worth the effort and the expense. We invested heavily in them and we were happy to do it.

Perhaps some of these same kids thought it would always be so easy or perhaps they didn't think about it at all. It is a different time in our world today. Opportunities seem to be fewer and/or more expensive and many young people can't or won't or never had to compete for the opportunities.

Yet I can't help thinking that it doesn't have to be so hard; jump in go to work, get an education, start a business and be willing to work hard at it. Put one foot in front of the other connect one day to a week and to a month to a year and save some and spend less than what you earn. We may be the older generation and from another time but our methods were tried and true. Set a goal and go after it work hard and if you can dream it you can achieve it.

But maybe first ... you have to want to succeed and you have to be hungry for success.

We See the World As We Are

Most often we see the world as we are and we don't see this world as it is ... two people can look at and experience the same things and yet walk away with a completely different view. How does this happen? For most of us our view of life and the world has so much more to do with how we are inside rather than what is going on outside of ourselves.

"I could never do that!" Many times we see the actions of others and we declare that it isn't us and we would never do that. Our responses for many things come from how we were wired as children. If we were trained a certain way, that becomes how we react and respond, part of the growing and maturation into adulthood comes when we learn to think for ourselves and process things for ourselves.

Generally speaking, loving people respond with love and angry hurt people respond with fear and anger. Our responses come from our world view, do we see the good or the evil in people and how much of what we see has to do with the world as it is versus the world as we are?

Loving people see love. As I watched the Bible TV series, I was reminded of this; no matter what Jesus encountered he turned it into good and into a lesson to be learned. It wasn't that he didn't see the persecution and the hate and fear; it was that he didn't allow it to enter into his own heart.

When we are hurt by others, most of the time that is processed through the lenses of, "I would never do that!" and perhaps we wouldn't. But the truth is that what they have done is only a slight if we allow it to enter our heart that way. Simply put hatred only continues if we take what is spewed and own it and then put more of it into the universe. I have learned to keep myself in check by pausing and thinking through all my responses. I start with am I responding out of love or out of fear? A response of love is always a choice just like any other response. Someone else's venom and hate comes from their world view and is about them. It only enters our life and our hearts if we allow it to do so.

"The core cause of anger is a lack of self-worth. Rage is an excruciating experience of powerlessness." Gary Zukav

The day that I gave birth to my daughter was a day that my heart was filled with love, not just for her but for everyone in my family and in my world. Any hurts and grievances became past history. It was as if I was transformed out of my love for my daughter. I forgave everyone, everything. I had a similar experience the day that I buried my first husband. His death allowed me to love with such vulnerability and I forgave everyone everything. On both occasions I was my most beautiful loving self.

It shouldn't take a birth or a death for us to operate out of a pure loving heart. These were my experiences and looking back it speaks to how I process and respond, someone else may have anger in a death situation or not be as open hearted in a new birth.

When my child was born, I could never have imagined not sharing it with my entire family, and I did. Recently a friend's daughter had a new baby. She deliberately excluded her mother, the grandmother from being there. My friend is one of the most loving people and she is crushed. I know in my heart that part of her pain is because she, herself would never had done the same thing to her mother and family. This is a big decision to deny your mother access to you and your new born baby. How does this mother ever forgive such a deep hurt? Yet she must because otherwise it will be like a cancer that lives in her heart. Why would any daughter deny her biological parents this joyous occasion of a new addition to the family?

My friend is taking it all in and onto herself and yet it is her daughter who chose to shut the door on love. We respond to the world as we are and not necessarily as the world is, we do not control the actions of others. What other people do or don't do is about them and not about us.

"Choosing not to act on an angry impulse and to feel that pain that lies beneath it is a very courageous thing to do." Gary Zukav and Linda Francis

We can all make a case against anyone for anything both real and/or perceived if that is what we choose to do. But when we make that case, we need to look inside our own hearts and ask ourselves, what is really going on here? Why am I acting like this? What made me respond in this fashion? Why did I choose fear and hatred when I could just as easily have chosen love and acceptance?

Every one of us is a work in progress, but there are things that are universal and can work for everyone. If you want peace, be a peaceful person. If you want more love, give more love. Practice forgiveness so that when your time comes, you too will be forgiven.

Where we can't control what other people do and say, we can control how we respond to it. And sometimes the very best response is no response at all. Their anger and their fight lives inside of themselves.

We don't see the world as it is, we see the world as we are, anger and hate only become our reality if we allow it. Putting more love and loving "as is" allows us to be loved "as is" and brings more love to us. What you put out into the universe is what is returned to you. We must remember that when we are faced with challenging situations and people. Their stuff is their stuff and not ours; it speaks to and defines them and not us.

What would Jesus do? He would take the high road and respond with love. We must condition ourselves and learn to do the same. Love is what we do for ourselves …

We Weren't Designed To Be Perfect

We weren't designed to be perfect! It is our imperfections that make us human. We live and we learn.

The Broken Shell

We are not made to be perfect. Beauty is in the flaws. We are fragile yet strong. Life wears us down at times, polishes us at others. We break in places. We endure. It is the hole worn away in the shell that lets us see inside to its center. It's beautiful when the inside shows, when it shines.

We weren't designed to be perfect but rather to be real, to be honest and to be humble. *"Let he who is without sin cast the first stone."* John 8:7

No one is perfect. If we want to be forgiven, we must first forgive. What if every person really was doing the best that they could do? What if we celebrated our imperfections?

Often the difference is a minor adjustment in how we view things, how we see others mostly has to do with how we view ourselves. When we can learn to accept our own imperfections we are more likely to accept them in others.

We weren't designed to be perfect …

What I Learned from My Dogs

Humility - Picking up poop in public! Who else would you do that for?

Unconditional Love – Whatever kind of day I am having, they are always there to greet me with kisses and tails wagging!

Acceptance – There doesn't seem to be any difference from their acceptance of me whether I am groomed or not, happy, sad or up or down they accept me "as is."

Loyalty – Always, always so loyal … they are fiercely loyal! And oh so protective too!

Actions Count – we motivate them and teach them by our actions. And they respond in kind.

Real Communication Doesn't Require Words – When I have broken down in tears in front of my dog, she comes and licks the tears away … there are no words.

That we have the capacity and the ability to experience such depth of love and caring for living creatures and just how big our hearts can grow in loving them and caring for them.

Joy, love, laughter and all the good things in life, we love our pooches just like we loved our little children when they were young. They are our babies and like a child, they need us to care for them and to love them and feed them and shelter them.

Most of all I learned that life is better and richer with them than it could ever be without them ...

What I Learned From My Husband

What I learned from my husband is that there are good men who are loyal, kind, loving and supportive. If a man is good to his mother, he will also be good to his wife. My husband was always good to his mother. He used to drive to see her once every week and take her to the grocery store. When she was in the store shopping he waited outside for her until she was finished. He held her hand as she passed over into the next life.

My husband taught me that real love isn't flashy or showy, it is how two people treat one another when they are alone and no one else is looking. He taught me that if you don't respect yourself, no one else will. He has shown me that patience and love go hand in hand.

He didn't tell me about his character, he showed it when his first wife died leaving him alone to raise pre-mature newborn infant twins, a son and a daughter. Where most men might have fled the coop, he never once thought about leaving them even if that meant raising them as a single father.

He didn't tell me that he was a stand-up guy who believes in "staying the course" and that "slow and steady wins the race" he showed it when he went to work for the same organization for 35 years and hasn't called out sick not one time in over 15 years.

He didn't tell me that he was a good father; he showed it every single day by loving and supporting his children and my child. He didn't ever disrespect our kids even when they did things that weren't in keeping with his integrity.

He didn't tell me that I could count on him, he showed it every day when he came home from work at the same time or called to say that he had to stay late. He always showed up for me. He showed me that yes we could have a fight, but if I needed him he would be there and that his love for me is and always was unconditional.

My husband is a stead-fast guy who is loyal and giving never wanting to see anything bad in the people closest to him. He is a quiet supporter who takes it all in, and a man of few words but when he does communicate it is worth listening to.

Our son calls him "salty" because he isn't going to sweet talk anyone but tells it like it is and has really good radar about the character of other people. In 21 years there were only two people that I brought into our lives that he didn't approve of and both times he was 100% correct. He knows inwardly who to let your guard down with and who to stay away from.

My husband taught me that being a good man, a good husband and a good father is what you do for yourself because at the end of the day, the only judgments that really count are the ones between you and God.

Last year I was taken by ambulance to the hospital, I thought I was having a stroke, my doctor thought it was a heart attack, thank God it was neither, but it was at this time when I looked at the foot of my emergency room bed and watched my husband that I knew like I have always known, I married a good man. If it was the end of my life, this is the only person that I would want and trust making decisions for me. This is the guy that has loved me like no one else ever has or will. We are married together and in this life as a team.

My husband taught me many things about what it takes to be a good man, a good husband and a good father and the number one thing is that you must be true to yourself. No games, no pretense, no drama, that by doing the right things, and never intentionally hurting anyone else and by minding your own business and tending to your own life's work that peace comes as a natural by product.

I couldn't be prouder of the man I love, the husband I have and the father figure our children have grown up with …

What is Marriage?

What is marriage? For different people it can be different things. Young girls often have this fairy tale idea of a wedding and marriage with the white dress, big cake and that perfect groom. They think it will be happy-ever-after and nothing but love. Seasoned professionals who have been married for a lengthy period of time come to have a deeper understanding of marriage.

"The older I get the less time I want to spend with the part of the human race that didn't marry me." Robert Brault

"The secret to a long and happy marriage is a short memory." Lou Holtz

I do think that the ability to forgive is part of any long term relationship, we all hurt and we all get hurt, often by the very person we chose to marry. Not every day is going to go our way or be a great day but in a healthy marriage you learn to accept the good with the bad. For most people that responded to this question there was no easy or simple answer. Marriage like any relationship takes work. To live intimately with one person and to smack up against all that is good and some not so good takes commitment and courage. Love is a choice. Marriage is a choice and where it may not be for everyone, studies support that those people living in loving and committed relationship tend to live longer lives.

"We are coming up on our 26th anniversary. When I was little I dreamt of marrying a man that was perfect. Those were the dreams of a child. I could never have possibly understood how much I could trust, believe, hope in, admire and love just one person so much. My husband has comforted me in my darkest

times, made me laugh when I did not want to ... loved me unconditionally. I did find out that marriage is hard, a growing experience and can never really be defined." TS

"My concept of marriage has changed over the years. When I was a newlywed I thought of marriage as forever, until death do us part, no matter what. I didn't even conceive that there could be "deal breakers." When my marriage ended, I was able to get an annulment which helped in the healing process for me." TW

"Marriage to me means a fierce and strong bond between two spouses; one that after a while of developing decades of 'history,' neither could even think about starting over with someone else. It's a constant, it's a bond, and it is one of the most important relationships we will endure ... through thick and thin ... over mountains and valleys ... and when it outlasts all of that, it's true." SS

"To me, marriage is a companionship with another human resulting from a complete choice that we made ourselves. It is the greatest teacher of ACCEPTANCE that there is. If our marriage is fruitful, it should allow us to be our best selves so that we can grow together as partners that genuinely care about each other, all the while allowing us to be the best possible individuals we can be." DK

"You are not alone, "me" is replaced with "we" as we do and think like a team rather than as an individual. There is love and

acceptance and we are our truest and safest selves when we are together. Being there for all the good and the bad, knowing we are in it until death do us part." BS

"When my wife met someone else, she broke the bonds of our marriage. She decided she wanted him and not me. It broke my heart back then but after my divorce I learned that she really was not the right person for me. Today I am happily married and I thank God we never had children together so that it was an easy and clean break." AS

Sometimes a marriage teaches us what we don't want in a partner, some people marry many times until they get it right or run out of time. Some people are meant to be married and some aren't, to be married is to share.

My husband and I have been together for 23 years; we have known the highest of highs and known our share of grief and sorrow. The glue that keeps us together, no matter what the fight, is our knowing that we are better together than we would ever be apart.

Brian's grandparents were together for 58 years before death and his parents for 54 years before his mother died. He had really great role models in knowing what family looks like and in keeping their vows. I credit my husband for much of the success in our marriage; I never knew such a degree of love, acceptance, and commitment and of caring until we came together. He was the first person that ever taught me the value in loyalty, and true stability. He loves me for who I am not some idea of who I am. He makes me feel safe and better at everything I do. We are best friend's first and life partners second; we are in love and choose to put each other and our marriage first.

Relationships are living breathing things, often tricky to navigate but well worth the effort when we have chosen well. There is nothing that takes the place of having decades of intimate history with your spouses.

As I opened this question up I could tell that it created thought, as it did for me too. There is no easy answer, each couple defines their marriage. I have never believed that a marriage was a "failure" but rather that it may have run its own natural course. To everything there is a beginning, middle and an ending.

If a marriage didn't last "until death do us part" perhaps it was never meant to last that long, surely we learn from every relationship no matter how long. What I know for sure is that marriage is work and with the right partner worth every bit of effort.

With two decades under our belts, we don't have all the answers, but what we do have is the desire to continue to date one another, love and care for one another and to be each other's best friend. What more can we ask for?

Here is to love and marriage and to all those brave hearts that are willing to try and give it a shot! At best you will receive a life partner and at worst a learning opportunity ...

What Love Does

Love makes everything better it just does! A loving heart looks for more love and less conflict. Often I have a bird's eye seat into the "love" that couples share just before they are about to be married. You can sense right away who will have staying power and who is coming into the union full of problems and conflicts.

I have been blessed with all of the weddings that I have officiated, there was love and it was everywhere. It permeated all around them. No matter what they faced their response was love. It sounds so simple but it is so true.

They had their eyes on the bigger picture; it was all about sealing their union in marriage and much less about where they were getting married, what food and what guests would be there. The overriding sense was happy.

Even conflicts were met with love and genuine happiness. I remember being that way myself when I married my husband Brian. I knew it was right because I had peace in my heart, an open heart and zero interest in conflict. I was in my happy place and he was too. We didn't need a lot of people or a big ta does, we knew that God had blessed us and we knew that together was better than being alone or with any others.

Today I heard from one of my favorite young people, she sent me a picture of her new ring. Her guy is really special to her. She knows it is right because they have known each other throughout school. Their union and their coming together just makes her beam. I first noticed it over the summer; she just looked thinner and lighter and beamed with happiness. It is amazing when you witness that kind of transformation in another person. They don't have to speak yet their aura says so much. They are genuinely happy and in love.

Life is tough! When you find that one person that is willing to walk it with you and they make you better just for being with them, you grab them and you respect them and you appreciate them.

Young love is the best "love" because it is new and clean and carries no baggage; it is free and clear and without an agenda. Real love transforms us all, it is the coming together of two souls that connect and inherently know that life is meant to be shared and shared together.

Some people will never know love because to know what love truly is you must first be able to love and accept yourself. Love starts from within; it grows from within and builds from there. I couldn't be happier for my young friend; she is a loving, kind and giving person. Her smile lights up the room, she is accomplished in her own rite and yet paired with the right guy, and she is even happier, healthier and better. That's what love does. Love just makes everything in life sweeter and everyone in our life better …

What Really Matters This Thanksgiving

At the time of this writing I have been parenting for just over 35 years, there have been many years when I believed my parenting skills to be in line with my life's greatest accomplishments and other times when I knew first hand that I totally missed the mark.

In parenting I learned that love truly is blind, that letting go is by far the greatest challenge and seldom does it matter what we really want for our children. In the end, it comes down to their life, lived out in their way.

I have loved and lost in parenting to where my skin hurt and the hole left in my heart was at least the size of a cannonball. My children taught me the true meaning of love, where you give and you give and expect nothing in return. It is the only relationship, when it is you who brings that child into this world and you who chose to give them life. You give life to your child who may live in a way that you may never understand but you know that the gift was in the giving.

With the three children I have mothered, I learned that each child is unique and different and comes with their own likes, dislikes, talents and abilities. I learned that where environment may matter, that does not translate into same environment and same outcome for each child.

It was in parenting that I learned humility and put myself in places and spaces that I would never have gone without the hand holding of my child who led me there. I learned that children have immediate needs and the adults in my life could wait. My children taught me patience and they taught me to trust in the letting go. My kids taught me that most children will be dishonest at times and not to take it personally or believe that because your view is one of a close parent and child relationship, it will mean honesty at all times, on all issues.

If the definition of forgiveness is defined as letting go of how you thought it should be, then again it was my children who taught me how to forgive. I learned to forgive myself, before I could begin to forgive them, or any others.

As amazing as giving birth is so is the circle of life, after 34 years of parenting I have learned so much from my children and all the many enrichments they have afforded me. Our children are all legal adults now and the greatest lesson learned is that each child was God's gift to us. Then came the day when we had to trust the process and the life cycle. The time arrived when they were no longer in our care nor were they our responsibility. It was then again when we knew to return them back to God who trusted us with them so long ago and who we trust will continue to protect them and to watch over them.

What You Feed Yourself Becomes You

It has been said, *"The mind is the computer system of the body"* what goes in is what comes out. Our thoughts become our actions. What we tell ourselves is what becomes real for us. I am so strongly against that old "I am sick and tired" phrase. Say it long enough and you will soon become both "sick" and "tired."

What we feed ourselves is what we become from the inside out. Positivity is so important to living a positive life; negative thoughts bring with them their own negativity. What we think and what we believe is what we become.

What are you feeding yourself?

Are your thoughts positive and encouraging or are they negative and destructive? Yesterday I read a Facebook post where the writer used the word "dumb" to describe themselves. I know this person and they are far from dumb. I wanted to challenge them and correct them yet I didn't, because I didn't want to add any more energy or attention to their own negative description of "dumb."

Sometimes it is how we were wired as a child and we literally have to go back and re-wire our thinking. I've come across all kinds of management styles in my career from the hyper-critical to the extreme supportive. Most of us do best when we are supported and encouraged. My best manager was the one who had such a high opinion of you; she had such a high opinion that you did your best work because you never wanted to let her down. She believed in you and supported you while helping you to grow and learn, all the while promoting you.

I have witnessed what negativity in the workplace does, where there is a lack of respect and support that generally trickles down to the lowest levels. When there is a problem on the ground level, you can usually see where it points back to the very top.

Anger is most often met with anger, frustration with frustration. When something is frustrating, walk away and give yourself time to re-calibrate and then come back with a free mind and a new energy field and see how much easier things comes together.

Often what we put out and on to others is coming from within us. Walk away from anyone that is bringing you down and isn't supporting you. They are talking about themselves and putting in onto you.

If you think you can, you can! Unfortunately the opposite is true as well. Watch what you say to yourself, what goes in, is what comes out.

The Old Cherokee Story

An old Cherokee told his grandson, "My son there is a battle between two wolves inside us all.

One is Evil. It is anger, jealousy, greed, resentment, inferiority, lies and ego. The other is good.

It is joy, peace, love, hope, humility, kindness, empathy and truth."

The boy thought about it, and asked, "Grandfather, which wolf wins?"

The old man quietly replied, "The one you feed." Author unknown

What are you feeding yourself? What goes in is exactly what comes out. Positivity breeds positivity, negativity breeds more negativity.

For years I have surrounded myself with inspirational books. Currently reading several books that offer daily "food" for thoughts all positive and encouraging and I highly recommend them. They are as follows; **Dear God Hear My Prayer Today** (A Devotional Journal) Brownlow, **I Declare 31 Promises to Speak Over Your Life** by Joel Osteen, **The Confident Woman Devotional 365 Daily Inspirations** by Joyce Meyer and **Love Out Loud** by Joyce Meyer.

Music is also important, what are you listening to? Just like the importance of the food and nourishment that goes into our mouths so is the food and nourishment that we put into our minds! What are you feeding yourself?

More Love, Lord

And this is my prayer: that my love may abound more and more in knowledge and depth of insight, so that I may be able to discern what is best and may be pure and blameless until the day of Christ. (PHILLIPPIANS 1:9, 10) Feed yourself with happy and wellness thoughts, and do so often ...

When a Man Loves a Woman

When a man loves a woman, he doesn't feel like he is giving up something like other women because he has the woman that he wants. When a man loves a woman, he may fight with her, but don't you dare.

When a man loves a woman, he doesn't want to hear about what hurts her, he wants to fix it. When a man loves a woman, he knows how to treat her without ever being told.

When a man loves a woman, he shares in her victories and accomplishments and feels it when she hits a wall or a battle that she can't win. When a man loves a woman, it doesn't matter what kind of past she had, he sees her as his bright white future.

When a man loves a woman, he looks forward to coming home every day. When a man loves a woman, he looks at her when she is looking back at him and even more so when she doesn't know he is looking at her at all.

When a man loves a woman, he gives her, her space but lets her know that he is always there for her. When a man loves a woman, he is loyal; he is kind and loving.

When a man loves a woman, her happiness makes him happy. When a man loves a woman, it isn't what he says as much as it is what he does that shows her know how much she is loved.

When a man loves a woman, he wants to be alone with her but he doesn't want her just for himself, he knows that all her relationships are important to her. When a man loves a woman, her accomplishments, gifts and talents aren't a threat to him but rather enhance his own accomplishments, gifts and talents.

When a man loves a woman, she knows it from the very bottom of her heart. She has a sense of peace and feels his love. When a man loves a woman, she is a better woman for receiving his love.

When a man loves a woman, he shares all that he is and all that he has with her because he wants to do it. When a man loves a woman, he doesn't walk behind her or in front of her, he walks with her.

When a man loves a woman, he knows it deep inside his own heart. When a man loves a woman, there is no obstacle or force that will get in his way to being with her.

When a man loves a woman, he doesn't care what other people think or what they say because he knows her heart is where his heart belongs. When a man loves a woman, there is no greater love and no greater joy and he can't deny his love for her even if he wanted to. When a man loves a woman, she knows it and so does everyone else.

When a man loves a woman, he doesn't just put a ring on her finger, he has a circle around his and her hearts as one heart.

When a Woman Loves a Man

When a woman loves a man, she doesn't feel like she has given up other men because there was nothing to give up once she found the man that is right for her. When a woman loves a man, she may argue with him, but don't you dare.

When a woman loves a man, she wants to hear about what he likes and what he doesn't like. When a woman loves a man, she learns to love sports in a way she never did before, and she learns his "game" so she can share in what he enjoys.

When a woman loves a man, she doesn't feel that she has given in or given up but sees that what they decide together makes for a stronger union. When a woman loves a man, she knows that giving in isn't a weakness but rather a strength.

When a woman loves a man, she wants to feed him. When a woman loves a man, she wants to make his life easier not more difficult or complicated.

When a woman loves a man, she finds her heart like never before and she wants his happiness as much as or maybe even more than her own happiness. When a woman loves a man, she wants to create a family with him.

When a woman loves a man, she doesn't want or need to change him since he is the right man from the jump. When a woman loves a man, she thinks in terms of "we" instead of "me."

When a woman loves a man, her heart gets bigger and she is safer and therefore more open to knowing and trusting herself and knowing and trusting others. When a woman loves a man, she can be with him in the quiet of their togetherness.

When a woman loves a man, she doesn't try and make him into another girlfriend, but appreciates that he is the ying to her yang. When a woman loves a man, she celebrates what makes him a man.

When a woman loves a man, she learns that she is coupled and enjoys knowing she has a date on Saturday night. When a woman loves a man, she never stops dating him.

When a woman loves a man, she can't wait to meet up with him and catch up on all that they missed when they weren't together. When a woman loves a man, she learns to respect their differences and view them as their complimentary nuances that create their own unique couple hood.

When a woman loves a man, she knows it deep inside her own heart. When a woman loves a man, there is no obstacle or force that will get in her way to being with him.

When a woman loves a man, she doesn't care about what other people think or what they say because she knows his heart is where her heart belongs. When a woman loves a man, there is no greater love and no greater joy and she can't deny her love for him even if she wanted to.

When a woman loves a man, he knows it and so does everyone else. When a woman loves a man, she doesn't just accept his ring on her finger; she accepts his circle around his and her hearts as one heart.

What Would You Say

Earlier this week one of my readers wrote to me, she asked **"What would you say?"** She has experienced her share of grief and estrangement. She has been estranged from family members.

What would I say to the people that are no longer in my life?

For a few days I thought about it and for the most part, I have said it all and whatever I couldn't and didn't have the opportunity to express to that person, I said it to God. I gave it up to God.

I have peace, whatever situation I have found myself in, I found a way to make peace with it. It wasn't always easy but it was healthy. Letting go and giving it up is so freeing, People do what they do for themselves, if they don't want to hear you that is on them.

My first choice was and is to confront it, say what needs to be said, try and understand. Allow the other party their voice too. Agree to disagree.

There was not one thing I could have EVER said to my mother in our decades of estrangement, it didn't matter if she lived another 10, 20 or 30 years. She didn't want to know or hear that her husband was a child molester. I could never pretend otherwise just for the sake of a relationship with her. That man, her husband destroyed lives, he stole from children. He was wrong and she was wrong to support and defend him. I did what I had to do, I did what I believed was right. I removed myself and my family from a known sexual abuser. I wanted to avoid any possibility of more abuse and of other victims.

Any adult relationships I had with former friends and boyfriends I have made peace with either directly with them face-to-face or through the written word. It's not that some things aren't forgivable, all is forgiven, it just that the trust is completely broken. Trust once broken takes a lot of work to be restored and often that work isn't even attempted and therefore, those relationships can never be restored.

It is easy to forgive someone when they are genuinely sorry, harder to forgive those that can't accept their role in whatever the issues were. Yet forgiveness is what we do for ourselves. Anger keeps you connected in negative ways and it doesn't allow us to move ahead in our life.

Most often my relationships end in peace; I make the effort to achieve peace. My peace is not determined by anyone else but by me, and me alone. I do it for myself and I do it because I know that it is God's will.

It has been said that forgiveness is **_"letting go of how you thought it should be"_** I thought my mother should see things my way, she wouldn't and she couldn't. I accept it and I have forgiven her. People that hang on to their anger, need to be right, it is more important for them to have their ego at the expense of having peace. I don't have to be right, I know what I know and I let go of that which is completely outside my control.

In order for my mother to believe me, she would have had to change her life. She was never going to do that. If someone doesn't allow you to be heard, doesn't allow your voice and your position to be stated, that is about them and their self-preservation. It isn't about you.

I believe it is important for all of us to make our peace. If we can't because another party won't allow it, write it out, share it with a friend, a counselor and give it up to God.

Often it is important to be heard, but when you hit a wall, and someone doesn't want to hear you, you must go over, go under, go around but don't quit. There are other ways to be heard and other ways to come to peace.

"Keep on asking, and you will receive what you ask for. Keep on seeking and you will find. Keep on knocking and the door will be opened to you." MATTHEW 7:7

Do not allow yourself to be a prisoner of anyone who isn't evolved enough to make peace with you. If you do you have given them control over your heart and your health.

"I am leaving you with a gift – peace of mind and heart. And the peace I give is a gift the world cannot give. So don't be troubled or afraid." JOHN 14:17

When Your Holiday Season is Shaping Up to be Less Than Norman Rockwell Like

"Tis the season!" For some people and some families the Thanksgiving and Christmas holidays are wonderful and a time for cheer and for celebrations!

And for other people it may be a time of dread. Recently I read a social media post that stated "wish I could just fast forward to January" they knew they would struggle with the holidays and with their fractured family.

Sometimes the dread comes from a job loss or an illness or a death in the family. Many adults with children feel extra pressure to provide a "magical holiday" experience for young children on a very tight budget. We see images on television and in our stores of abundance and an expectation that we can and will all afford these celebrations. Truth is some people just can't do it; they can't keep up because of their finances or because of their grief.

What we need to remember is that although the holiday season is often dubbed as "the most magical time of the year" this isn't necessarily the case for every single person.

Some people actually suffer from the "holiday blues" and for them this could be the saddest time of the year. Even in families where it appears to be "Norman Rockwell" like, it isn't always perfect!

I've had absolutely great holidays and I have had a few where I just wanted to pull the covers over my head, go to sleep and wake up when it was all over. One year I had no family, no money and was starting all over in my career and at this time I had a little girl that was counting on me to make it special.

Another year just months earlier we experienced a child estrange and this could have potentially thrown us all into a holiday funk, but it didn't.

The first sad Christmas I ever had I vowed it would never happen again and that year I made food, we went to the first screening of a newly released film playing in a local historic theater? So by 9:00 in the evening we were snug in our beds. The next day I woke up refreshed and stronger for the experience. That year was the bench mark for what I never wanted to happen again.

The years of the recent estrangement we changed all traditional holiday plans and headed to Key West. According to our son it was "the best Christmas ever!" Christmas day we were sitting on Smathers beach taking in the hot sunny weather. Not at all traditional for a gal born and raised in the Northeast but still a happy holiday!

You can and you will get through the holidays and I am convinced that the sad ones are designed to make us appreciate all the happy ones. I also believe the sad ones serve as a shake-up that it just may be time to try something new and different for the holiday season.

Remember not every person out there is happy and having an easy time of it. Holidays bring about past memories with family and friends. Some for happy memories and some may drive home for us our lost loved ones.

Tips for Handling the Holidays Alone

1) Don't pressure yourself; go with your own flow!
2) Take in the FREE sites, shopping malls and heavily decorated areas may make you feel better.
3) Grab a coffee or a meal out; learn to be alone and to be okay with it.
4) Churches have all kinds of Bazaars and cookie sells, support them and take home a few treats.
5) Volunteer at a hospital, or food kitchen or pet rescue center.
6) Go to the public library and stock up on must reads and films to view.
7) Write! Write letters, cards, poetry, notes, express yourself!
8) Contribute a toy for Toys for Tots or other meaningful charity.
9) Go see a new movie, a new play or a live concert.
10) Gather with friends and family and people that love you!
11) Make new traditions and travel.

12) Don't want to be in the public? Pamper yourself.
13) Stock your refrigerator with healthy foods like fresh fruits and vegetables.
14) Take long hot bubble baths.
15) Get your music, books and movies stacked up and ready to that when the holidays arrive you have your entertainment at your fingertips.
16) Sleep! Often when we are sad and depressed we are lacking proper rest. Give yourself permission to sleep it off.
17) Paint a room or engage in a mini home improvement project.
18) Do something productive, the end result will make you feel better.
19) Make cookies, make food.
20) Can't afford to travel? There are amazing television shows and archived libraries that have travel destinations recorded for viewing, imagine yourself there!

No matter what is going on in your life and what circumstances you find yourself in this holiday season, just know that this too shall pass. Sometimes a down year is just what we need to inspire us for the next year. Not every holiday season is going to be "the most wonderful time of the year."

Count your blessings, find gratitude in what you have, focus on what you have now and not on what has been lost and you are sure to find the holidays as peaceful as they can be. And if this is the holiday season that grief prevails, remember that grief can be a gift.

You can and you will make it through the holidays ...

Grief teaches us many life lessons and tears are the shedding so that the old can be let go and the new may be embraced. After the rain, the sun always returns and so often shines even brighter!

The holidays are coming, so what is your favorite holiday movie? Or your favorite holiday music?

For me, I love the movies; *The Holiday* and *The Family Stone* and for the classic movies; *Irving Berlin's White Christmas* and *It's a Wonderful Life*. And for Christmas music I enjoy Aaron Neville's version of *Such a Night* and when Bing Crosby teamed up with David Bowie for *Peace on Earth/Little Drummer Boy*.

Remember every New Year is a chance for all that is good and wonderful, believe!

Feel free to share your story by writing me at bmoyer37@aol.com and "like" my page at www.facebook.com/bernadetteamoyer

When It Becomes Your Experience

This past year has been filled with people telling me things like "Now I get it!" or "You were right." And even "I am sorry that I doubted you." These statements came after I had an experience and shared it. My friends that came to the same conclusion needed it to become "their" experience before they could fully relate.

I could so easily have said "I told you so!" but that isn't me. Most people need to experience things for themselves and that isn't a bad thing. I remember the first time that someone responded to something that I shared with "well that hasn't been my experience." I immediately respected that statement. He wasn't going to be swayed or manipulated by what anyone said. Not long after though, what I shared soon became his experience. It was so much better that way.

"Nothing ever becomes real until it is experienced." John Keats

We can have a certain degree of compassion and empathy for what others are going through and what they are experiencing but when it becomes our own experience, we really get it.

I am always amused when I hear people complain about this person or that person or about a business, this usually catches my attention and I tend to look deeper. The person who finds fault with several businesses at the same time is usually the one with the problem. Think about it? If you are simultaneously having difficulties with three different service providers at the very same occasion could it just maybe be that it isn't all of them and that you might be a part of the problem?

My other amusing statements come from people that never ever had any children of their own but will declare with conviction things like *"kids never lie"* or *"it must be the parents."* Anyone that has raised children knows that kids do lie, sometimes it is a little white lie and sometimes it is a whopper. And by the time a child has reached their teenage years parental control is waning. Kids do things every single day that parents do not agree with and parents often have very little control.

When an organization has had 6 different "leaders" in a period of 16 months, they might want to stop pointing one finger out and contemplate the four fingers that are pointing back at themselves. Clearly with so many turnovers in a key position during such a short amount of time, they aren't doing something right. Most probably they aren't listening to the right people and/or have their own agenda. When something becomes our experience we can relate, we can understand and we really do appreciate it and we get it.

"People never learn anything by being told, they have to find out for themselves." Paulo Coelho

I think it is noble and respect worthy to suspend judgment until it becomes our experience, otherwise we could so easily become manipulated by what people share with us.

So here is to learning and understanding when it becomes our experience ...

Yesterday's Blog is Today's Trash?

"It sent chills up my spine. I love your work. Thanks." These comments received just a few hours after I posted a blog over the weekend. The comments came in a private message from someone who could relate. They had an experience similar to what I blogged about.

Writers want to be read and they live for the connections to their readers. My post was about a situation that has haunted me for decades. I went out of my way NOT to name anyone. I told a story where I questioned what happened. Did I support a victim or had I been manipulated by a liar. This has not only haunted me for decades but has been a true thorn in my side for so many years.

So when I received communication of a threat of a lawsuit if I didn't remove it, I was stunned. What I can't understand is 1) why does this person even read my blogs? And 2) wouldn't a lawsuit, a court case shine the light on this very subject? Bring even more attention to it?

Maybe I really don't get it? However, I decided to remove the blog; it wasn't one of my better ones. Normally a good blog receives 250 or more hits this one just a few and not many people "liked" it. However I do value the guy who read it, connected to it and wrote to me about it. I appreciate him.

So today' trash was yesterday's blog, oh well ... Better blogs are yet to come ... Stay tuned ...

"You Can't Handle The Truth" ... And So Many of Us Can't!

"You can't handle the truth" from the movie A Few Good Men is one of the most remembered lines of that movie. Even here the "truth" was one thing and the "reality" of the situation was another.

It has often been said, "There are three sides to every story, your side, my side and the truth." Each "side" has their own perception, their own reality, and their own "truth." Most people are invested in their "truth" as it serves them. Few are really interested in the total "truth."

Most often the reality is that we can't handle the truth. It has been documented that most addictions stem from trying to cover up our feelings and our pain. Many of us medicate our true feelings, our pain with food, drugs, sex, alcohol and other vices. We try to numb our true feelings and true experiences. We find comfort in self-medicating rather than facing our truths. Being honest and living in "truth" can be so painful for so many of us.

Why Do We Do It

When trauma strikes our body and minds, we can and will go into an automatic protection mode to save us from our trauma. Rape victims talk about disassociating from the abuse because it literally saves them from the horrific experience.

Many times facing our truth means we will have to make a change in our life. To uncover a truth often means having to step out of what is comfortable for us.

"You Are Only As Sick As Your Secrets"

Many times this is the worst thing we can do to ourselves. Living in denial and living in a constant state of untruths does not allow us to be free to love. "You are only as sick as your secrets" comes from the 12-step program; we learn that what we are trying to cover up is the root of our problem. The "cover up" shows itself by using drugs, alcohol, food and other devices to deny our truth.

Rehab, Prison, Intervention

Talking with persons in rehab and statically those serving prison terms we uncover that "pain" that wasn't handled or properly dealt with is the root cause for people in "pain" and we know that "hurt people hurt people."

The classic "intervention" is rooted in love and an attempt at getting the addict to look at the truth and how each family member had a role in that addiction. Whether it was an overt or covert role, the addict doesn't live in a vacuum. On the road for a desire to wellness the "addict" is confronted in tough love. Family members collectively decide that they are no longer willing to play their role in the life of the addict. Truths become uncovered.

This article was in process before I watched the OWN Life Class with Oprah Winfrey on 3/26/12 where the topic was "Heal the Pain" and when they polled the viewing audience, it was discovered that over 75% reported they were currently in "pain" 3 out of 4 people or ¾ of the viewers. Most people are walking around with some kind of "pain" and few know how to properly handle it.

My own experiences have taught me, "the only way out of it is through it" and as this show confirmed "feel, deal and heal." Facing our "truth" often means stripping away our addictions and our vices. Many times the "truth" is ugly and unattractive. We go out of our way so that we don't have to face it.

"You will find that the truth is often unpopular and the contest between agreeable fancy and disagreeable fact is unequal. For, in the vernacular, we Americans are suckers for good news.
Adlai Stevenson

The Truth Teller

Every family has one "the truth teller" and typically they aren't the most popular family member. I grew up in a time when "we don't air our dirty laundry" was the theme of the day. I also grew up with an alcoholic father and an enabling over-eater mother. He drank his pain away and she ate hers away. Yes the sad truth and the reality is they were both in "pain." Their pain was denied them. The price for denying their pain showed itself in their addictions.

It was easy for me to forgive my parents because I understood them. They did the best they could with what they had and what they knew for their time.

> "Truth, like milk, arrives in the dark
> But even so, wise dogs don't bark.
> Only mongrels make it hard
> For the milkman to come up the yard.
> Christopher Morley, *Dogs Don't Bark at the Milkman*

For more than 5-years I had the privilege of working in a special needs school run by mental health care providers. In this environment we were encouraged to "uncover it" if any relationship was holding "secrets" or "untruths" our leadership team was encouraged to ferret it out. The mental health care community knew the importance of "truth." These professionals knew the mental health benefit in facing the "truth" no matter how unattractive or difficult it may have been.

My later experience in working for a religious organization was the exact opposite experience. The "message" was a controlled "message" and often in direct conflict with the "truth." It was hard to square this since this church teachings were based on the importance of "confession" and telling the "truth." The reality that I experienced was a church that didn't want to hear, know or see any truth that didn't coordinate with their controlled "message." I worked with professionals that openly withheld the "truth" from their higher ups. They knew the battle of "truth to power" and that those guys couldn't "handle the truth" so often it wasn't shared with them. This created an environment that was both manipulative and unhealthy.

As a mother, I used to tell my kids, just" tell the truth" you will feel so much better when you do and you will be rewarded by living an authentic life, you can proudly walk in your own "truth." I don't know anything that can be as empowering as "feel" "deal" and "heal." There is a huge price to be paid when we decide to replace the truth with denial or with lies and dishonesty.

The Story

Everyone has a "story" and maybe the "story" is what we learn and grow from. The problem for most people, me included is that we get stuck in our story. Our story stays on long after the learning has come and gone. We keep our story alive as we continue to retell, relive and redo it. This keeps us "stuck" in the past and "stuck" in our story. Many of us are "addicted to our story." We may have given up the other vices but we replace them with "the story."

Inspirational Authentic Leaders

Lately I find myself following the teachings of Joyce Meyers, Joel Osteen and Marianne Williamson. They all come across to me as authentic "walk the walk" and "talk the talk" God centered leaders. Joyce Meyers was repeatedly raped by her own father. Yet she took her trauma and her pain and faced it and is one of the most inspirational women I have ever listened to. She is a bible believing Christian women who writes and speaks. Her newer book, *Love Out Loud 365 Devotions for Loving God, Loving Yourself and Loving Others* is one of my favorite reads and makes for an attractive gift too. She is a #1 New York Times bestselling author. *"You can suffer the pain of change or suffer remaining the way you are." "Courage is fear that has said its prayers and decided to go forward anyway."* Joyce Meyers

Joel Osteen is a minister and author and often criticized for his "mega church" my view is there is a good reason so many people follow his teachings. He is a bible believing Christian and yet when asked his view on gay relationships, his response was, "it isn't my place to look down on any person or group of people." He might live a wealthy life but he also comes across with humility. *"You must make a decision that you are going to move on. It won't happen automatically. You will have to rise up and say, "I don't care how hard this is, I don't care how disappointed I am, I am not going to let this get the best of me. I'm moving on with my life." Joel Osteen, Your Best Life Now: 7 Steps to Living at Your Full Potential*

Marianne Williamson teaches from **A Course in Miracles**, and has more than half a dozen books that made the New York Times best seller lists. She is an accomplished writer and speaker. One of my absolute favorite quotes of all time is to her credit and is as follows;

"Our deepest fear is not that we are inadequate. Our deepest fear is that we are powerful beyond message. It is our light, not our darkness that most frightens us. We ask ourselves, who am I to be brilliant, gorgeous, talented, and fabulous? Actually who are you NOT to be? You are a child of God. You're playing small does not serve the world. There is nothing enlightened about shrinking so that other people won't feel insecure around you. We are all meant to shine as children do. We were born to manifest the glory of God that is within us. It is not just in some of us; it's in everyone. And as we let our light shine, we unconsciously give other people permission to do the same. As we are liberated from our own fear, our presence automatically liberates others."

The only way out of it is through it and when we can face our "truths" and "handle the truth" then we are free from it. It no longer controls us but lifts us up to a God-centered love rooted in truth. When we truly believe we are children of God and that nothing we can do or have done will deny us God's love then we have no reason to fear the truth ...

"There is no God higher than truth" Mahatma Gandhi

You Can Find a Reason

You can find a reason to love just like you can find a reason to hate, a reason to give and a reason to take. We can all find reasons to justify our actions if that is what we decide to do. Love is a choice and so is hatred.

Imagine any relationship where you are presented with a "list" of all the things that you did wrong or were deemed unattractive to another person? A list that documents your "flaws" and "shortcomings" this "list" was presented at the culmination of the relationships. I don't know many relationships, no matter how loving that could withstand such a list. Nor do I fully comprehend why anyone would take the time to create pages upon pages of their grievances. (This actually happened to a friend where one of their family members took the time to write down all the things that they deemed wrong with them.)

Needless to say it didn't make anything better... I wonder if the list maker ever even thought about how it would be received and if they did what they expected the outcome to be? And if they were presented with a "list" how they would respond?

What I do know is that the same efforts that went into creating the" list" of flaws could have just as easily been the same energy that went into creating a list of love. The same effort that goes into hurting people can just as easily be the effort that goes into loving them.

There is a lot of talk in our society today about "anti-violence" toward women and several anti-bullying campaigns. One of the ads recently came across as though we are expected to love every single person and anything less was deemed as less than noble. As human beings we are drawn to the people that we like and we aren't going to like/love everyone.

As kids we were taught that if we didn't like someone to just stay away from them, I still think that works? Right? Not every person out there will be someone that we welcome into our lives. Sometimes the kindest thing we can do is stay away from people that are not good for us or bring out the worst in us.

We are a judgment based society, we judge people we judge them by how they look and how they speak, and we judge them by their actions and their lack of actions. We judge people by their education or their lack of education. We judge them by their religious beliefs and their political views. We all have our own yardsticks on how we decide to measure others. The problem is that our yardstick is based on our views and in an ever changing world people change, society changes and we change.

"If you judge people, you have no time to love them." **Mother Teresa**

You Don't Look Like Someone Who Has Been Through All That

What does someone who has been through "all that" look like? We meet people every day, people at the coffee counter, the grocery store, the gas station, our church and community, everywhere we go we interact with people. It doesn't take long to be here in this life to understand that everyone has a story.

Some of our stories are happy and some of our stories are sad. No one gets through this life unscathed, sooner or later we are all tested with experiences that some of us would rather never have had and yet we know that it is through those experiences that we learn and we grow. Most often it is through the struggle that we find enlightenment.

Vicki is a real person (not a fictitious character) who recently turned 40 years old, she is a wife and a mother and she is a beautiful and confident career woman too. She is loved by her husband, her parents, her daughter and her friends. She holds a master degree and currently works in a highly respected position for the United States government.

When you see Vicki you will be struck by her beauty and her smile is warm and inviting. Speaking with her you will find her to be a woman of intelligence, understanding and of compassion. But what you won't read on her face is that she is a true survivor.

At just 5 years of age, Vicki was raped by a friend of the family and at 11 she would experience yet another sexual abuse betrayal by her grandfather. Vicki survived but as a child her coping mechanism was a "multiple personality disorder" or a dissociative disorder. Alternative personalities with their own names and identities emerged to protect Vicki and to save her. As a teenager Vicki acted out in sexual and inappropriate ways. For a period of time she was institutionalize for diagnosis and treatment.

It was during this time when she worked closed with her mental health care providers and team that the multiple personality disorder was documented and confirmed. Through all this Vicki never lost the love of her parents. They struggled with their own demons and their marriage eventually fell apart. Her parents may not have always been there for support with their own drama going on but the love they had then and now for their daughter remained undeniable.

Vicki came to me through a mutual friend and asked that I help her to write her story, a book that chronicles her life path. She has moved from "victim" to "victor" but it didn't come without struggle and more than that a desire to understand and to face her trauma head on. Today she wants to share her life experience so that other victims of rape and sexual abuse can find strength and hope that they may also overcome their wounds.

In 2010 FBI statistics show that 1 in 4 girls and 1 in 7 boys will be sexually abused by the age of 18. 90% of the abuse is by a family member or someone known to the family. Almost 80% initially deny abuse or are tentative in disclosing. Of those who disclose, approximately 75% disclose accidentally. Additionally, of those who do disclose, more than 20% EVENTUALLY RECANT even though the abuse occurred.

Fabricated sexual abuse reports constitute only 1% to 4% of all cases. Of these fabricated reports 75% are from adults and 25% from children.

Consequences of child sexual abuse begin affecting children and families immediately. They also affect society in innumerable and negative ways. These effects can continue throughout the life of the survivor so the impact one society for just one survivor continues over multiple decades.

Try to imagine the impact of 39 million survivors.

You Need to Make Peace with Yourself

How often do we think and say, "If only that person would change? Or it isn't me, it is them!" We think a new relationship, a new friendship or another child will afford us what we are looking for in life. No one can give us peace, nor can they really take it from us unless we allow them to do so. Peace is within each and every one of us. It is always there, whether we choose to exercise it or not is another story.

A few summers ago I was pelted with nasty personal attacks from someone I never knew and never met. For this guy it was a game, it was about winning and he didn't care what he said and who he said it to. I have his written words where he called me numerous names. He is supposedly a professional. I will keep his letters and e-mails for the rest of my life and when I read his words I will forever be reminded of what I don't want in my life and who I will never allow myself to become, him.

Years later I actually feel sorry for him, his work keeps him connected to drug dealers, people who drive under the influence of drugs and alcohol and those accused of child pornography and abuse among other social ills. I suspect his world view may have something to do with the kind of people he frequently associates and works with.

My peace was almost shattered by this guy and his personal attacks, I never knew anyone that communicated with such slanderous statements and personal attacks like he did. My husband referred to him as a "clown" and wanted to do battle with him. I retreated; I learned a long time ago, no one wins in a fight. And then I sought out professionals that could help me to understand him and others who spend their time attacking other people rather than seeking peace and the truth. This guy was getting his information from someone that professionals had already determined in writing, "Has many mental issues." He opened my eyes to a culture of people that seem to live by, "might makes right."

I am not perfect but I can honestly say I never set out to hurt anyone; I have never looked for trouble and tried to live as peace filled a life as I can. When this guy was finished with his personal attacks on me, he then went on to question my faith in God and attack my Church. Scary that people that you don't know and don't know you, think they can pass judgment on you and question your personal relationship with God and your Church.

Today more than ever, I know who I am. Through the years, I did the work. I looked inward. It was through my managerial training, I learned that if there is a problem, first, look at yourself. What did you do? What could you have done differently? What would you do now? Like Lou Holtz often states, "WIN, What is important now."

We can't change other people, we can't change their opinions of us, founded or not, they can think what they will. But when we know who we are and what we did, what we didn't do.

When we can accept that ultimately we did the best we could with what we knew and what we had for that time in our life, then peace is not such a big leap. If we go forward and always try to do our best and come from a place of love and a place of understanding, our own inner peace is a natural.

There is no question that we will be tested. We may see things in life that seem unjust and unfair but how we react to it has more to do with us then with the injustice or unfairness of any given situation. I am reminded of a favorite prayer that hung in my childhood home; The Serenity Prayer. This prayer has been adopted by Alcoholics Anonymous and other twelve-step programs.

Serenity Prayer

God grant me the serenity

To accept the things I cannot change,

The courage to change the things I can,

And the wisdom, to know the difference.

For each one of us, I believe that no one else can give you peace, and we can never truly achieve peace with others until we first make peace with ourselves.

"You Have Helped Me So Much!"

It took fourteen years before I could write about my first husband Randy and his death. When I started writing about death and my experience I had accepted it did the counseling thing and came to terms with my grief and my guilt. Writing about it connected me to others who valued what I had to say and could relate to my experiences. They often communicated what they learned from me, so often I would receive a note, a card or an e-mail stating **"you have helped me so much!"**

In a way, it took the sting out of the pain. I was able to turn it around and help others. I did the work; I educated myself, did the soul searching and learned so much myself, before I could share my knowledge with others.

I never thought I would write about estrangement, sexual abuse, alcohol abuse but then too came a day when I had done the research. I went to therapy and I educated myself. I listened to others who walked these same paths before me. They gave me strength and courage; I knew that I wasn't alone.

Much of my personal therapy was with a really great therapist and then my writing. Taking my experiences and sharing them with others. I know the process from the beginning when you think you are the only one and feel so alone to the accepting and learning and taking that knowledge and experience and doing some good with it.

I really believe that is what we are supposed to do; we are supposed to use all our life experiences for the good, even the most painful ones. Just this week I have received almost a dozen comments like, **"you have helped me so much!"** It makes me feel good to hear that!

However, I believe that by helping ourselves first, and then, only then, are we all able to help others. If our journey includes the experience, the learning, the accepting and all the wisdom that comes with it, we become the teacher and the sisters and brothers to all those that walk just after us.

It is my greatest hope that whoever I may have helped with the sharing of my life experiences that they will come to a healthy heart too and in turn help those that come just behind them. Our experiences, the good and the bad, the happy and the sad; are gifts that are meant to be shared.

To my readers that have shared, **"you have helped me so much!" YOU have helped me so much!** You have validated my life and my experiences and so often made me feel less alone. Now that is a really great gift.

In this life, we are all connected and we are all in this together …. Peace and all good things!